The Harkness Collection

in the Library of Congress

Manuscripts concerning Mexico

A Guide

With selected transcriptions and translations by J. BENEDICT WARREN

LIBRARY OF CONGRESS   WASHINGTON   1974

Library of Congress Cataloging in Publication Data

United States. Library of Congress. Manuscript
    Division.
    The Harkness Collection in the Library of Congress.

    Bibliography: p.
    1. Mexico—History—Spanish colony, 1540–1810—
Sources. 2. Manuscripts, Mexican—Catalogs. 3. Manu-
scripts, Spanish—Catalogs. 4. United States.
Library of Congress. Manuscript Division. I. Warren,
J. Benedict. II. Title.
F1231.U54   016.972'02   73–6747
ISBN 0–8444–0093–9

For sale by the Superintendent of Documents, U.S. Government
Printing Office, Washington, D.C. 20402 Price $6.70
Stock Number 3003-0012

Preface

Considered one of the Library's most valuable and important gifts of Spanish American manuscripts and documents, the Harkness Collection was presented to the Library of Congress by the American philanthropist Edward Stephen Harkness in two installments, December 4, 1928, and October 15, 1929. These documents from the first two centuries of Spanish American history fall naturally into two groups: one relating to the early history of the Spanish in Mexico (2,939 folios), the other to their early history in Peru (1,405 folios).

The Library has published two works on the collection of Peruvian manuscripts: *The Harkness Collection in the Library of Congress, Calendar of Spanish Manuscripts Concerning Peru, 1531–1651* (Washington, 1932), and a volume containing the full texts, with translations and notes, of 48 documents relating directly to Francisco Pizarro and his brothers and to the Almagros, father and son—*The Harkness Collection in the Library of Congress. Documents from Early Peru, the Pizarros and the Almagros, 1531–1578* (Washington, 1936). The present volume, a guide to the Mexican part of the Harkness documents, completes the series of Library publications on the collection. In addition to calendar descriptions, selected documents have been transcribed, translated, edited, and presented in facsimile illustration.

Those interested in the Harkness Collection should be aware that the continuing program of the Library to photocopy manuscripts in foreign depositories has provided a substantial amount of material that complements the Mexican portion of the Harkness Collection, particularly documents concerning the Ávila-Cortés conspiracy from the Archivo General de Indias (Seville) and the Archivo General de la Nación (Mexico City).

The greater part of the Mexican group of manuscripts relates to the conquistador Hernando Cortés and his sons. Approximately two-thirds of the Cortés documents concern the proceedings before the Audiencia of Mexico and a special commission (1566–68) in 12 criminal suits against alleged participants in the so-called Ávila-Cortés conspiracy to overthrow the government of New Spain and crown the second Marqués del Valle. These 12 proceedings have been published, in part, by Manuel Orozco y Berra in his *Noticia histórica de la conjuración del Marqués del Valle, años de 1565–1568* (Mexico, 1853).

Although Orozco y Berra stated that the Ávila-Cortés documents were in the collection of José Maria Andrade in 1853, it is clear that the papers in the Harkness

Collection relating to Cortés were owned at that time by one of the heirs of the conquistador, the Duke of Terranova y Monteleone, and later by his son, Prince Antonio Pignatelli. The Prince was a patron of the Hospital de la Inmaculada Concepcíon y de Jesús Nazareno in Mexico City, and his private archive was housed there for many years. In 1926 the two royal grants now in the Harkness Collection were returned to Prince Pignatelli. According to G.R.G. Conway in his introduction to *La Noche Triste* (1942), the Cortés documents were in the archivo privado of the Marquesado del Valle in 1926.

Although the Andrade collection and the Hospital de la Inmaculada Concepción y de Jesús Nazareno were undoubtedly repositories of the Cortés documents, ownership was apparently retained by the family of the conquistador from 1568 to 1928, between the time of Don Martín Cortés, the second Marqués del Valle, and Prince Antonio Pignatelli. The Mexican portion of the Harkness Collection was assembled during 1927–28 by the noted American bookseller A.S.W. Rosenbach, who subsequently suggested to his client Mr. Harkness that he present his magnificent collection to the Library of Congress.

The Harkness Collection remains one of the most important sources of information on the first century of Spanish rule in New Spain, and it is hoped that the publication of this catalog will draw wider attention to its resources for students of the early period of Spanish American history.

I cannot conclude this prefatory statement without paying tribute to two persons intimately associated with the Harkness Collection throughout long and productive Library careers. The late Stella R. Clemence, who came to the Library in 1929, almost simultaneously with the Collection, spent 23 years in the Manuscript Division, chiefly as Hispanic manuscript specialist, during which time she compiled the publications on the Peruvian segment. Even after her retirement in 1952, she continued to assemble notes and transcriptions which have contributed to the present volume. The sustained interest and scholarly concern of the late Howard F. Cline, Director of the Hispanic Foundation at the Library of Congress from 1952 until his untimely death in 1971, helped make possible publication of this volume.

Roy P. Basler
Chief, Manuscript Division

Editor's Foreword

The Mexican portion of the Harkness Collection of manuscripts falls into three principal categories, with a smaller, fourth group of unrelated items. The earliest group of documents concerns the affairs of Don Hernando Cortés and his family and the lands in Oaxaca that formed the basis for his title of Marqués del Valle. The oldest of these manuscripts is dated 1525, when the Habsburg Emperor Charles V, who was also King Charles I of Spain, granted a special coat of arms to Don Hernando Cortés. The latest is dated 1565, when Don Martín, the second Marqués del Valle and son of Don Hernando, asked for permission to present evidence to counter a distinctly unfriendly attitude toward him that was becoming apparent in the Council of the Indies.

The second large group of documents, accounting for the largest volume of pages, concerns the purported Cortés-Ávila conspiracy, sometimes referred to as the encomenderos' revolt of 1566. These were previously published in part in Spanish, but the questionnaires that bring out most of the evidence put forth in the lawsuit against Don Martín Cortés, Marqués del Valle, are included in this guide in full transcription and translation. The calendar entry for this manuscript gives in greater detail the names of witnesses on the side of the Marqués and of the audiencia. Some of the records in this group are fragmentary, but they nevertheless shed a great deal of light on this real or suspected plan to rebel against the Spanish King.

A third group of the manuscripts includes the denunciations and judicial proceedings of the Holy Office of the Inquisition. These records date from the third quarter of the 16th century. They reveal the close church-state relationship in the Spanish Empire in America and show how ideas and behavior were controlled through such devices as the regulation and inspection of imported books and the suppression of religious nonconformity.

The remaining miscellaneous manuscripts range in date from 1557 to 1609 and include such unrelated items as a ledger of contributions to a church in Barcelona, the granting of marriage licenses, and a report of an Indian insurrection in Tlapa. In their own way, they add to the broad range of information to be found in the Harkness Mexican manuscripts.

The most visually magnificent items are in the first group of manuscripts, which includes the beautifully illuminated royal grants to Cortés and the Harkness 1531 Huejotzingo Codex. Since this codex and the lawsuit in which it was incorporated

have never been published in complete form, the Harkness Mexican document no. 2 was selected for publication in full transcription and translation, as were the two royal grants, Harkness Mexican documents no. 1 and 13. Apart from their intrinsic value as rare and authentic instruments, these manuscripts are rich in source material about the events and the social, economic, and political aspects of life in 16th-century Mexico. The symbolism of the coat of arms of a conquistador and the detailed ordinances on the treatment and conversion of the Indians furnish a wealth of information; the Indian paintings reflect the Mexican way of perceiving and record-ing events.

In view of the Spanish legalistic tradition and propensity for bureaucratic proce-dures, it is fitting that most of these manuscripts should owe their existence to lawsuits or some other form of judicial proceeding. The career and legal affairs of Hernando Cortés are similarly recorded in many other papers that are in the Archivo General de la Nación in Mexico and the Archivo General de Indias in Seville.

The Inquisition manuscripts stem from cases tried after the establishment of the Holy Office of the Inquisition in Mexico in 1571. After a suspected heretic or wrongdoer had been denounced and the officials had made an investigation, he was admonished and given a chance to confess his sins, without being told the exact nature of the accusations. He was then confronted with the charges, without their source being disclosed, and encouraged to confess so that he might be reconciled with the church. The Holy Office could pass sentence and require penance or, in extreme cases, turn the offender over to the secular arm of justice. Blasphemy, bigamy, and clerical immorality were among the most common charges.

In the civil and criminal cases, an accusation was made before an appropriate official, depending upon the political jurisdiction involved. That official would then determine whether grounds existed for a lawsuit or some other judicial proceeding. If it was decided that an accusation was valid, a prosecutor would make formal charges and the accused or his attorney would be so notified. Testimony was usually given through specially prepared questionnaires, and witnesses selected by the prosecutor and defendant would answer the questions. When an accused person had no lawyer, the judges named an attorney, and cases were subject to judicial review by a court of higher authority. Important cases that originated before the Audiencia of Mexico were sent to the Council of the Indies for review; those that were first acted upon by a municipal or provincial body went before the audiencia for review. One exception to review by a higher body occurred in the cases concerning the Cortés-Ávila conspir-acy, where the instructions to the jueces comisarios stated that they could review their own sentences upon presentation of further evidence. Many of the manuscripts do not cover the outcome of a case, and it can be assumed that lawsuits were frequently abandoned.

A brief statement of the institutional framework and the narrative of events will help to place these manuscripts in their historical setting. The Spanish were at first represented in the New World by the conquistadores, but as the need to protect royal prerogatives became evident, offices and administrative bodies were created and

filled. In New Spain or Mexico the audiencia, usually composed of a president and several judges, was the first of these arms of royal authority; it held both judicial and administrative powers within the kingdom of New Spain. The members of the first audiencia, not now considered to have been men of exemplary character, were in conflict with Hernando Cortés, who had claimed and been assigned special powers. The King appointed him Governor and Captain General of New Spain but refrained from giving him the greater powers that Cortés probably coveted. During Cortés' visit to Spain in 1528, when he set out to repair his rights and reputation, the first audiencia tried to take over his lands and powers. The second audiencia, composed of men of higher calibre, was less hostile, but Cortés still felt out of favor when he left on his expedition to Lower California in 1535. In that same year, Don Antonio de Mendoza was sent by Charles V as the first Viceroy of New Spain, a post he was to hold until 1550, when he was followed by Don Luis de Velasco.

The son of Don Hernando, Don Martín Cortés, the second Marqués del Valle, was born in New Spain, where he spent the first eight years of his life. He then went to Spain, where he later served the Spanish King in his exploits against the French. He was in his early thirties when he returned to New Spain, probably early in 1563. Relations between Cortés and the Viceroy Luis de Velasco began on a friendly basis, but soon the lordly airs and haughty pride of Don Martín and the growing partisanship of the leading families in Mexico led to a coolness between the two men. Their personal rivalry and mutual dislike reached their greatest height at the time of the arrival of the Visitador Jerónimo de Valderrama, who had been sent to New Spain to make an investigation and report back to Philip II. Don Martín chose to meet Valderrama separately, and his efforts gave the impression, probably a true one, that he wished to outdo the Viceroy in his welcome. Old animosities originating in jealousy among the original conquistadores and their descendants were strengthened, and two factions developed, that of the Viceroy and that of the Marqués del Valle.

Don Luis de Velasco died in 1565, making Valderrama and the audiencia the strongest instruments of royal authority. Valderrama had become involved with the party of the Marqués and had made the home of the Marqués his official residence. Since he had been sent out to review the work of the audiencia, this was not as unreasonable as it may seem, for his alternative had been to take quarters in the palace in which the oidores lived.

In spite of the fact that the second Marqués del Valle had received a confirmation of the grant made to his father, he was aware that his rights were being questioned in Spain, a factor that was doubtless behind the action reflected in the Harkness Mexican document no. 14, by which he sought, unsuccessfully, an opportunity to register his own point of view. The wide-spread rumor that the King was once again seeking to limit the inheritance of encomiendas (the right to tribute from Indians in a specified area) was enough to cause general uneasiness and disaffection among those who held Indians in encomienda, regardless of their personal affiliation with the Marqués del Valle or the opposing faction. There is, therefore, little cause for wonder that much muttering ensued about a distant King who seemed intent upon

disregarding the interests of the sons of the conquistadores, whose fortunes depended upon the benefits they derived as encomenderos.

It was in this context of wavering allegiances, in Spain as well as in New Spain, that informers came forth to report plans for a conspiracy to the members of the audiencia. As the detailed provisions in the royal grants indicate, the Spanish system of justice permitted that informers be paid and that the property of criminals be used to pay costs and enrich the royal exchequer. Fear, malice, or a desire to curry favor could have motivated the informers and the oidores in their accusations that treason against the King was contemplated.

The first cases were tried before the audiencia, but its exclusive power was weakened by the arrival of a new Viceroy, the Marqués de Falces, in October 1566. He was able to save some of those who were about to follow the Ávila brothers, the first conspirators to be executed. The new Viceroy was considered to be too moderate by the audiencia, and with the apparent aid of officials censoring the outgoing mail in Vera Cruz, the Viceroy's dispatches to Spain were held back. As a result, the King received reports of only the unfavorable side of the picture seen by the audiencia.

Acting upon these reports of a dire situation in New Spain, Philip II appointed and sent out a team of three jueces comisarios, who were empowered to investigate the situation and mete out justice. Only two of these justices, Licentiate Alonso Muñoz and Dr. Luis Carrillo, arrived; the third member of the group died during the transatlantic crossing. These judges were perhaps even more arbitrary than the audiencia in their dispensation of justice. Word of their actions finally reached Spain, and they were recalled by Philip II. Ironically, they sailed with the same fleet that carried some of those whom they had condemned to exile, as well as the Viceroy, Marqués del Falces. Dr. Luis Carrillo died during the crossing. The King is said to have received Muñoz sternly, whereupon the juez comisario promptly followed his partner to the grave, but the Viceroy was treated with honor and respect.

These manuscripts span 80 years, vary greatly in their length and organization, and bear the names of countless officials, witnesses, and escribanos. The records of earlier and related transactions are included in many, but the dates given in the descriptive calendar entries show the duration of each lawsuit itself, insofar as it could be determined. It was impossible to list the names of all of the people who took part or were involved in each case, although an effort has been made to list the principal witnesses in the lawsuit in which Don Martín Cortés, Marqués del Valle, was accused of treason. More detailed information, usually with a citation to specific leaf numbers, may be found in the careful notes of Stella R. Clemence and in the preliminary guide prepared by Juan Friede. Both of these auxiliary finding aids are available for consultation in the Manuscript Division.

All leaves bearing any writing with a possible discernible meaning have been counted in the collations appearing in the entries. Vestiges of earlier pagination are to be found on some of the manuscripts, but consecutive numbers have been penciled on most of the leaves by Stella R. Clemence.

This guide is very much a cooperative undertaking. The transcriptions and transla-

tions of documents no. 1, 2, 13, and a portion of 17 are the work of J. Benedict Warren, who also gave generously of his time in verifying names and dates and in standardizing and modernizing place and personal names. His advice and counsel have been of great value in all aspects of the work.

The earlier work of Juan Friede and Stella R. Clemence and the published work of Manuel Orozco y Berra have formed the basis for the calendar of manuscripts that was begun by Donald F. Wisdom and completed by Mary Ellis Kahler. Although this multiple responsibility inevitably increases the chances of discrepancies and variations in the interpretation of the manuscripts, the guide is intended to invite others to draw from these rich sources. Serious scholars will be able to examine and study the documents themselves.

MARY ELLIS KAHLER
Assistant Chief
Latin American, Portuguese, and
Spanish Division

Contents

Calendar

v el otro q̃ suçedio en el d̃o señorio q̃naue te in en in y soltibola
d̃a rreuelio basta q̃ vos le vençistes y prendistes y en la otra meytad
del d̃o medio escudo de la mano yzq̃erda ala parte de abaxo po
dais traerla cibdad de te un sitan armada sobre agua en memo
ria q̃ por fuerça de armas la ganastes y sujetastes a nro señorio y por
orla del d̃o escudo en campo amarillo siete capitanes y señores
de siete provinçias y poblaçiones q̃ estan en la laguna y en torno
della q̃ se rrebelaron con tra nos y los vençistes y prendistes en la
d̃a cibdad de tenustitan apresionados y atados con un açade
na q̃ se les venga açerrar con un candado debaxo del dicho es
cudo venga mia del un yelmo çerrado con sin timble en un escudo

atal como est de las
armas vos damos
mas conoçadas y se
mas delas armas z
ves de brios pre dece
mos y es nra merçe
q̃ las y brios hijos
tes y dellos y de ca
las ayais i tengais
mas conoçidas y
y como tales las po
dan traer e libros
y calas y ca los deca
dos bros hijos y
tes y en las otras z
y ellos quisieredes
zedes y por esta nuestra
lado sinado delescribano p̃

q̃nales d̃ias
por bias az
ualadas de
q̃ nealsitene
çores y q̃ze
di voluntad
t descendien
da bno dllos
por bias az
señaladas
dais y pue
z posteros
da bno dllos
descendien
partes q̃ ves
por bien tobie
carta por su tras
blico mandamos a

los y lustrisimos ynfantes nuestros muy caros y amados hi
jos y hermanos y a los ynfantes Duques marq̃ses condes ri
cos homes maestres delas hordenes priores comendadores y
sub comendadores alcaydes delos castillos y casas fuertes
y llanas E a los del nro conseso i oydores delas nras abdiençi
as y a todos los corregidores alisistentes y gobernadores y alcal
des y alguaziles dela nra casa y corte y chançelleria y a todos
los conçejos corregidores alcaldes y alguaziles dela nra casa
y corte y chançelleria y a todos los conçejos corregidores alcaldes
y alguaziles merinos prebostes y otras justiçias E juezes q̃na
les q̃mer ali destos nuestros Reynos y señorios como del d̃a

The coat of Arms of Hernando Cortés.

HC – M 1

EMPEROR CHARLES V. ROYAL PROVISIÓN OF COAT OF ARMS GRANTED TO DON HERNANDO CORTÉS, MADRID, MAR. 7, 1525. Countersigned by Francisco de los Cobos. 6 leaves on vellum (1 title page, 4 written, 1 blank).

> The Emperor Charles V issued a royal cedula on March 7, 1525, providing Hernando Cortés with a coat of arms as one of the privileges granted to him in gratitude for the conquest of Mexico. This original document includes a colored drawing of the coat of arms (leaf 4), describes the conquest of New Spain by Cortés, and extols the virtues and heroism of the conqueror.[1]
> This manuscript is reproduced in full transcription and translation on p. 35.

HC – M 2

DON HERNANDO CORTÉS, MARQUÉS DEL VALLE, VS. NUÑO DE GUZMÁN AND LICENTIATES JUAN ORTIZ DE MATIENZO AND DIEGO DELGADILLO. Records of a lawsuit brought by Gonzalo de Herrera and Garcia de Llerena, attorneys for Hernando Cortés, before the Audiencia of Mexico, Feb. 14, 1531—May 31, 1532. 79 leaves (1 title page with text on verso, 76 others written, 2 blank). Includes eight Indian drawings (folded) on amatl paper, which make up the Harkness 1531 Huejotzingo Codex. The drawings were numbered by a scribe but are not bound in numerical order.

> Hernando Cortés charged that, during his absence in Spain, the president and oidores of the first audiencia unjustly and improperly collected for themselves the tributes of goods and services that properly belonged to Cortés from the Indians of Huejotzingo. His attorneys brought forth as evidence copies of royal decrees which ordered that his possessions in New Spain be respected. The oidores stated that they had taken only the tributes and services that were lawfully reserved to the Spanish King and that they had acted in accordance with royal instructions, copies of which were placed before the oidores who had replaced the members of the first audiencia.
> Licentiates Matienzo and Delgadillo were also charged with harsh treatment of the Indians, and Cortés presented a questionnaire through which the testimony of the

---

[1]Juan Friede, "The Coat of Arms of Hernando Cortés," *Quarterly Journal of the Library of Congress,* v. 26 (1969) : 64–69.

Indians was given. Specific details of the tributes and services that they had given the accused in the absence of Cortés are shown on eight Indian paintings.

After hearing the evidence, the audiencia ordered Matienzo and Delgadillo to pay Cortés "three thousand and some pesos," representing income of which he had been unlawfully deprived. The sentence was appealed by the oidores, and they were ordered to send the records and present their case before the Council of the Indies, in person or through authorized attorneys, within a specified period of time. As the suit progressed, the name of Nuño de Guzmán was dropped, presumably because he left Mexico. The other defendants were under house arrest when the sentence was passed.

This document is transcribed and translated in full on p. 71–209. The Harkness 1531 Huejotzingo Codex is reproduced on p. 54. Explanatory notes by Howard F. Cline appear on p. 49.

HC – M 3

DON HERNANDO CORTÉS, MARQUÉS DEL VALLE, VS. OIDORES JUAN ORTIZ DE MATIENZO AND DIEGO DELGADILLO. Records of a lawsuit instituted by Cortés' attorneys before the Audiencia of Mexico, Apr. 4, 1531—May 28, 1532. 72 leaves (1 title page, 69 written, 2 blank).

This lawsuit was an effort to recover the pueblo of Toluca in the Valley of Matalcingo, which during Cortés' absence in Spain has been awarded to García del Pilar, an interpreter of Indian languages. García de Llerena, Pedro Gallego, and Pedro de Valladolid, who were attorneys for Cortés, claimed that the royal cedulas which ordered that Cortés' properties should be respected were not complied with and that the Oidores Matienzo and Delgadillo had deprived Cortés of the pueblo of Toluca. The defendants' attorney, Gregorio de Saldaña, maintained that (1) Cortés never had a valid title to Toluca, (2) Cortés disregarded the rights of the conquistadores to obtain land grants, and (3) Cortés should sue García del Pilar, not the oidores, for damages.

Includes a questionnaire of 12 questions presented by Cortés' attorneys and testimony of witnesses supporting the Marqués' claims; an interrogatory of six questions presented by the defendants' attorney and testimony of witnesses supporting their position; copies of the royal cedula of June 9, 1528, and the sobre cédula of September 12, 1528, which ordered that Cortés' possessions in New Spain be respected; and records concerning the imprisonment of two of Cortés' apoderados (Juan Altamirano and Diego de Ocampo) by the Oidores Matienzo and Delgadillo.

After hearing evidence, the audiencia condemned the defendants to pay 1,000 pesos to Cortés. Both parties to the suit appealed the judgment, Cortés' attorney protesting that 1,000 pesos was too small an indemnity. Appeals to the Council of the Indies were granted.

HC – M 4

JUAN CASTELLÓN, SHIPCAULKER, VS. LICENTIATES JUAN ALTAMIRANO AND GARCÍA DE LLERENA, ADMINISTRATORS OF CORTÉS' PROPERTIES IN NEW SPAIN. Records of a lawsuit instituted by Castellón before Alcalde Alonso de Contreras in Mexico, Oct. 24, 1536—Mar. 21, 1537. 31 leaves (1 title page, 29 written, 1 blank).

Castellón petitioned Alcalde Contreras to compel Altamirano and Llerena, attorneys for Hernando Cortés, to pay him in full the salary he was due for shipcaulking in

Acapulco and other services performed during the period December 8, 1535–September 1536 in connection with Cortés' South Sea (Pacific) expedition. The defendants maintained that Castellón worked only 15 days as a shipcaulker for which he had received 80 pesos and an additional 100 pesos through a friendly settlement arranged by Rodrigo de Baeza. Castellón, while in Acapulco, had been ordered by Andrés de Tapia, juez de comisión, to sail on a ship carrying supplies to Cortés. The defendants maintained that they were not obligated to pay Castellón's salary for the time employed on this trip.

Alcalde Contreras ordered Altamirano and Llerena to pay Castellón 286 pesos, and on appeal the audiencia confirmed the decision. On January 4, 1537, García de Llerena petitioned the new alcalde of Cuernavaca, Jerónimo Ruiz de la Mota, to declare the decision void. The new alcalde ruled in favor of Castellón, and appeal to the audiencia was granted.

Includes a contract signed by Castellón and Altamirano and Llerena as representatives for Cortés, dated August 19, 1535, for Castellón's services as a shipcaulker and copy of an order issued by Andrés de Tapia, juez de comisión, dated January 6, 1536, for Castellón to sail on a ship from Acapulco, carrying provisions to Cortés.

HC – M 5

ALONSO MORZILLO, VECINO OF OAXACA, VS. DON HERNANDO CORTÉS, MARQUÉS DEL VALLE, AND THE INDIANS OF ETLA. Records of a lawsuit instituted by Morzillo before Alcalde Melchor de San Miguel. Antequera [Oaxaca] May 4, 1537—Feb. 26, 1538. 79 leaves (1 title page, 77 written, 1 blank). Certified copy.

Morzillo complained that the Indians, acting on orders from Cortés' administrators Diego de Guinea and Diego Luis, were cultivating wastelands near his estancia; he assumed that this action was designed to interfere with his cattle growing and to oblige him to give up his estancia, since the Indians might claim that his cattle destroyed their crops. Morzillo petitioned the alcalde to forbid the cultivation of the lands in question. Initially, the alcalde ordered Diego Luis and the Indians to refrain from cultivating the lands.

The Indians of Etla contested the allegations of Morzillo, asserting that (1) the land was never wasteland, although it had been allowed to stay fallow, (2) the lands belonged to their ancestors, (3) they would sue for damages if Morzillo's cattle harmed their crops, and (4) their maceguales (laborers) were fleeing to the mountains because of mistreatment by Morzillo's men.

After hearing evidence and more petitions, the alcalde ruled that Morzillo must keep his cattle a crossbow's shot away from the Indians' fields. The sentence was confirmed by the alcalde after an appeal by Morzillo.

HC – M 6

DON HERNANDO CORTÉS, MARQUÉS DEL VALLE, VS. ALONSO DIAZ DE GIBRALEÓN, NOTARY. Records of a lawsuit instituted before the Audiencia of Mexico, Jan. 30—Nov. 6, 1543. 19 leaves (1 title page, 17 written, 1 blank).

Álvaro Ruiz, attorney for Cortés, petitioned the audiencia to hold Gibraleón responsible for a survey document that had been lost. The document in question had resulted from a lawsuit by Cortés before the alcalde of Mexico against Cristóbal Romero, master, concerning certain sheep and goats. (The records of this lawsuit are not in the Harkness Collection.) Romero had signed the lost surety document before the notary

Gibraleón. The records of the lawsuit, except for the surety document, had been delivered to the secretary of the audiencia, Antonio de Turcios.

After hearing evidence, the audiencia acquitted Gibraleón, and according to a notation in the records, the lawsuit was concluded at the consent of both parties.

HC–M 7

LICENTIATE CRISTÓBAL DE BENEVENTE, FISCAL, VS. DON HERNANDO CORTÉS, MARQUÉS DEL VALLE, ANDRÉS DIAZ, AND OTHERS. Records of lawsuits brought against the Marqués and his criados and mayordomos, accusing them of exacting excessive tributes and services from the Indians of Cuernavaca, Acapistla, Oaxtepec, and Yautepec before the Audiencia of Mexico, July 21[?], 1544—July 30, 1552. 328 leaves (1 title page and fragment, 318 written, 9 blank). The title page, which has been laminated, was apparently a previously used double leaf.

Licentiate Cristóbal de Benevente, fiscal, accused the Marqués del Valle, his criado Andrés Diaz, and other servants and overseers of exacting tributes and services from the pueblos in excess of those authorized by grants and assessments. Another suit, first brought on June 19, 1544, against the Marqués over 36 cargas of clothes exacted from certain estancias in Cuernavaca was joined to the other charges on January 22, 1545. The clothing was ordered withheld from Cortés and placed under the trusteeship of Licentiate Juan Altamirano until the suit was settled.

Álvaro Ruiz, presenting the case for Cortés, repeatedly pleaded for delay and in May 1545 won an overseas term or extension of time of a year and a half plus the time needed to reach a ship leaving the port of San Juan de Ulúa. This permitted him to gather information in Castile, where Cortés himself and others could reply to the charges. After over two years had passed, Licentiate Benevente again pressed his suit; Ruiz claimed that the documents had been lost at sea and never reached Castile. Finally in 1547 (the records are dated 1549 but internal evidence suggests that 1547 is the correct date) the testimony gathered in Spain by Pedro de Escobar as Cortés' representative and heard in Cuernavaca by Andrés de Cabrera as receptor was presented before the audiencia.

In answering the charges against Cortés, Ruiz claimed that when assessments had been made in 1544, the Indians of Cuernavaca had concealed certain small villages and estancias and that the Marqués and his agents had only been following general practice in collecting tributes. He further stated that the Indians whose testimony the fiscal presented were enemies of the Marqués and thus not reliable witnesses, although the fiscal maintained that they were Christians of good character.

On August 24, 1551, an agreement was reached between the Indians and Tristán de Arellano on behalf of the Marqués. Under its terms the 36 cargas of clothing held in trusteeship were to be divided between the Marqués and the Indians. Litigation over payment of a custodian's fee to Licentiate Juan Altamirano extended the proceedings until October 7, 1551. After Altamirano had presented proof that the Indians had received their share of the clothing, he was awarded his fee.

The date of the latest record was July 30, 1552, when Ruiz made a renewed appeal for the return of the 200 pesos de oro de minas that he had deposited with the crown as guarantee when he was granted an overseas term. As the records are not in chronological order, this appeal is not in the final pages of the record.

The documents include questionnaires and testimony to support or counter the charges against Cortés, legal instruments and orders required to gather evidence away

from the site of the audiencia, two copies of the original privilegio of 1529 granting the Marqués del Valle 22 Indian towns and 23,000 vassals, a copy of the assessment of tributes made on June 20, 1544, and a declaration made on October 15, 1544, of an agreement between Cortés and Don Hernando, Indian governor of the villa of Cuernavaca, concerning the return of an estancia and certain lands to the Indians.

HC – M 8

ANTONIO DE LA CADENA AND ISABEL DE OJEDA, OWNERS OF A SUGAR MILL, VS. DON HERNANDO CORTÉS AND JUAN DE CARASA, ALCALDE OF CUERNAVACA. Records of a lawsuit in the alcaldía of Cuernavaca and before the Audiencia of Mexico, Feb. 7, 1547—May 5, 1550. 57 leaves (1 title page, 54 written, 2 blank).

Juan de Torres, administrator of the sugar mill, acting on behalf of Antonio de la Cadena and his partner, Isabel de Ojeda, accused Juan de Carasa, alcalde mayor of the villa of Cuernavaca, of refusing to permit the cutting of wood needed for the sugar mill in the communal forest and of seizing 10 axes being used to cut the wood. The alcalde had alleged that destruction of the forests was forbidden by law, in spite of the fact that the Marqués del Valle had been in partnership with the owners of the mill and the cutting of lumber had been previously authorized.

The case was appealed to the audiencia, where Antonio de la Cadena demanded that Carasa be ordered to refrain from interfering with the cutting of lumber needed for the sugar mill. Álvaro Ruiz, for the Marqués, upheld Carasa's decision and appealed against the judgment of the audiencia that Carasa should be ordered to return the axes and refrain from interference with woodcutting. The audiencia confirmed its judgment in spite of the appeals of Álvaro Ruiz.

Included are a decree of the Council of the Indies of December 22, 1533, concerning a lawsuit between Don Hernando Cortés and Antonio Serrano de Cardona in which Cortés had been ordered not to interfere with Serrano de Cardona in the possession of the mill and utilization of the woods; a contract of partnership of November 7, 1546, between Antonio de la Cadena and Isabel de Ojeda, widow of Antonio Serrano de Cardona; and an arbitration award rendered in Mexico on March 11, 1539, by Licenciate Juan Altamirano and Juan de Burgos, whereby Antonio Serrano de Cardona and the Marqués agreed to settle their differences concerning lands, water rights, and other matters.

HC – M 9

DON MARTIN CORTÉS, MARQUÉS DEL VALLE, VS. LICENTIATE JUAN ALTAMIRANO. Records of a lawsuit instituted by Martín Cortés before the Audiencia of Mexico, Feb. 9—Aug. 9, 1552. 21 leaves (1 title page, 19 written, 1 blank).

Don Martín Cortés, legitimate son of Don Hernando Cortés, initiated the suit charging Altamirano, former governor of the marquesado de Oaxaca, with responsibility for the fine of 28,000 to 30,000 pesos levied against Don Hernando Cortés by Antonio Rodríguez de Quesada, juez de comisión, in 1546 for exacting excessive tributes from the Indians of Oaxaca during the period 1529(?)–1545. The Marqués' attorneys had appealed the fine and the case was still pending in the Council of the Indies.[1]

---

[1] See HC—M 14 for the conclusion of this suit.

Álvaro Ruiz, attorney for Martín Cortés, argued that Altamirano, as governor of the marquesado, had ignored the Indians' complaints and had not observed Don Hernando Cortés' orders respecting treatment of the Indians. Therefore Altamirano should be held accountable for the fine and should have prosecuted, at his own expense, the defense of the Marqués.

The defendant's attorney, Juan de Salazar, rejected the charges on the grounds that the marquesado was administered by the factor Jorge Cerón and other administrators at the time of the Indians' complaints. Further, he pointed out that Don Hernando Cortés' will provided for restitution of tributes collected illegally.

The audiencia absolved Altamirano of the charge.

HC – M 10

Don Luis Cortés and Doña Guiomar de Escobar vs. Doña Isabel de Lujan. Records of lawsuit before the Audiencia of Mexico, Oct. 9, 1556—Dec. 7, 1557. 127 leaves (2 title pages [second torn], 122 written, 3 blank).

Don Luis Cortés, in his own behalf as the husband of Doña Guiomar Vazquez de Escobar and in her name, alleged that Juan de Burgos, father of Doña Guiomar, had disregarded the rights of Doña Guiomar of succession to an encomienda in the pueblo of Cutzamala and in half of the pueblo of Teutenango. Juan de Burgos had renounced his rights to the encomienda, whereupon the encomienda had been granted to Francisco Vazquez de Coronado. After Coronado's death the encomienda had been granted to his daughter Isabel de Lujan. Don Luis Cortés claimed that as a result Bernaldino de Bocanegra, the husband of Isabel, was presently receiving an income from pueblos that had been granted to Don Hernando Cortés; he demanded that the encomienda be returned to his wife, daughter of Juan de Burgos.

The defendant, represented by Juan de Salazar, claimed that Coronado had been granted the encomienda in his own right and that Juan de Burgos had earlier renounced his rights in favor of the crown. Furthermore, Don Luis Cortés had received a large share of the estate of Juan de Burgos upon his marriage to Doña Guiomar de Lujan.

As Isabel de Lujan and Bernaldino Bocanegra were considered to be minors, many of the documents concern proof of age and the designation of persons who could act in their behalf. Other legal matters concerned the laws of inheritance of encomiendas. No final sentence by the audiencia appears in the documents, but there is an indication that the case passed to the segunda instancia, i.e., to a higher authority for review.

Among the records are the text of the grant of a coat of arms to Juan de Burgos, assignment by the King and Viceroy of the pueblo of Cutzamala and half of the pueblo of Teutenango to Francisco Vazquez de Coronado upon renunciation of title by Juan de Burgos, royal decrees covering the order and limiting of inheritance of encomiendas and the exchange or barter of Indians in encomienda, the use of Indians in gold and silver mining, assessments of the pueblos of Acámbaro and Teutenango, writs and decisions assigning the Indians of the encomienda in question to Coronado and subsequently to Bernaldino de Bocanegra as the husband of Isabel de Lujan, daughter and heiress of Francisco Vazquez de Coronado, in original and confirming decisions of the audiencia, and documents concerning the transfer and receipt of the dower property of Doña Guiomar Vazquez de Escobar to Don Luis Cortés and the obligations thereby incurred by him, including that of returning the dower in the event of dissolution of the marriage.

HC – M 11

ALVARO HERNÁNDEZ DE MADRID VS. BALTASAR GARCÍA, ALCALDE. Fragment of the record of a lawsuit instituted in the Audiencia of Mexico, Jan. 26–27, 1557. 1 leaf (torn).

Concerning house rent of 30(?) pesos of gold allegedly owed by Baltasar García. The defendant demanded that the record be returned to the secretary so his attorney could see it and that meanwhile the legal time limit be suspended. The plaintiff was so notified on January 27, 1557.

HC – M 12

LEDGER OF CONTRIBUTIONS MADE TO THE CATHEDRAL AND OTHER CHURCHES OF BARCELONA FOR RESPONSORIES BY THE ESTATES OF ELISABET BENETA SOLSINA. 1559–68. 47 leaves (15 written, 32 blank). In Catalan.

HC – M 13

KING PHILIP II. Royal cedula of confirmation to Don Martín Cortés, Marqués del Valle, of the privilegio of 23,000 vassals and 22 pueblos in New Spain, which had been granted to his father, Hernando Cortés. Toledo, Dec. 16, 1560. Countersigned: Francisco de Eraso. 16 leaves on vellum (1 title page, 15 written); 16 leaves (2 written, 14 blank).

Included in the royal cedula are a complete transcription of the original privilege granted to Hernando Cortés on July 6, 1529 (leaves 4–10), the King's detailed ordinances on the treatment and religious conversion of the Indians, an account of the lawsuit between Pedro Arellano, Count of Aguilar (guardian for Don Martín Cortés), and the fiscal Jerónimo de Ulloa, and a confirmation of the sentence ordering that the 23,000 vassals be counted and that the excess benefits be restituted to the royal exchequer by the Marqués if the number of vassals surpassed the original grant. Upon appeal of this sentence, the King conceded that the privilegio would not require the counting of the vassals but would exclude the Port of Tehuantepec. Presented in the Audiencia of Mexico, January 21, 1563, by Martín Cortés, Marqués del Valle.

This manuscript is reproduced in full transcription and translation on p. 211.

HC – M 14

DON MARTÍN CORTÉS, MARQUÉS DEL VALLE. Proceedings before the Audiencia of Mexico regarding Don Martín Cortés' request for a judicial inquiry into accusations that had been made against him. Sept. 27—Nov. 8, 1565. 10 leaves (1 title page, 9 written).

On September 27, 1565, Don Martín Cortés petitioned the audiencia for an opportunity to present evidence to refute the charges that had been made against him before the King and the Council of the Indies. He maintained in his reports that an excessive amount of the tribute collected from the Indians went to the clergy and principal Indians had incurred the resentment of the clergy; further, Viceroy Luis de Velasco had failed to order an inspection of the crown pueblos out of deference to the religious orders and had become increasingly unfriendly to the Marqués, ordering him to withdraw a page

who followed him bearing a lance, although others were permitted to display similar lances in the Viceroy's presence. Despite the provocation, the Marqués had shown proper respect for the Viceroy. He further maintained that the measurements of his seal, which the Viceroy had sent to the King because it was considered presumptuous, had been increased through a mistake of the silversmith, and the Marqués had made no use of the seal.

The Marqués stated that the Viceroy had adjusted the assessments against the Indians that had become necessary through the death of encomenderos, in a manner that resulted in the King's receiving a lesser amount of annual tribute than the encomenderos had, without comparably reducing the amount exacted from the maceguales. The resulting surplus remained in the pueblos at the disposition of the clergy and the principal Indians. When the Visitador Valderrama had come to New Spain, the Marqués himself had visited the greater part of his marquesado and had stopped the ill-treatment of Indians by their chieftains. He had treated his Indians kindly and had not asked for more tribute than was allowed by the audiencia. He wished to have witnesses from the province of Oaxaca examined, using a questionnaire which he had prepared for this purpose.

On October 11, 1565, Don Luis de Velasco, son of the late Viceroy, requested a copy of the questionnaire to answer it insofar as it concerned his father and asked that the interrogatory and evidence be examined by the audiencia. He also asked for a certified copy of the proceedings that he could present to the King. Officials of the Royal exchequer filed a petition showing that they had opposed the Marqués del Valle over the extent of his jurisdiction in the villas of Coyoacán and Atlacubaya and the crown pueblo of Matalcingo and that the Marqués was indignant because they had delivered a seal that he had ordered from the royal smeltery to Viceroy Velasco for a decision as to whether the Marqués might be permitted to use it. They also asked for copies of the questionnaire and requested that copies be sent to the King.

On October 22 the audiencia, having examined the petition and interrogatory filed by the Marqués and the objections of Don Luis de Velasco and the royal officials, declared that they must refuse to receive or admit any witnesses for questioning as petitioned by the Marqués. The Marqués could have a certified copy of the decision if he so desired. On November 8, 1565, Don Luis Velasco requested and was granted a certified copy of the decision.

HC – M 15

CRIMINAL PROCEEDINGS AGAINST ALONSO DE ÁVILA ALVARADO AND GIL GONZÁLEZ DE ÁVILA, ACCUSED OF CONSPIRACY AGAINST THE KING. Records (incomplete) of a lawsuit in the Audiencia of Mexico, July 16–23, 1566. 87 leaves (1 title page, 84 written, 2 blank).

On July 16, 1566, Jerónimo de Orozco, oidor of the audiencia, heard the testimony of Alonso de Ávila who responded to questions about his social gatherings and fiestas, his associations with prominent and discontented encomenderos and with persons involved in the recent uprisings in Peru, and an alleged plot for an uprising in which the oidores of the audiencia would be destroyed, a King elected, a nobility created, and relations established with the Pope and foreign nations. In his replies, Ávila denied any intention to conspire against the Crown. On the same day, Alcalde Manuel de Villegas went to the house of Ávila and sequestered his goods and several boxes of papers, depositing them with González Rodriguez.

The next day oidor Pedro de Villalobos took testimony from Gil González de Ávila,

using a similar questionnaire. The audiencia named Francisco de Carriazo to serve as defense lawyer; Licentiate Sedeño and the procurador Juan de Salazar were later named to assist Carriazo. Juan Caro was given power of attorney by the accused and appeared in their behalf. Pleas for extended time to prepare for hearings were refused; the impartiality of witnesses, among whom were Licentiate Cristóbal Ayala de Espinosa, Pedro de Aguilar, and Baltasar and Pedro de Quesada, was questioned, and some of the witnesses were accused of perjury. Juan Caro declared that Ávila's recent transmittal of 2,000 pesos to the crown showed that he had not intended to rebel against the King.

Terms for answering the allegations were extended only to July 23; new accusations and confirmations of prior depositions of witnesses accusing Alonso de Ávila of intending to conspire were heard from July 20 to July 23. Similar testimony against Gil González de Ávila was heard on July 18 and 19.

The final item in this partial record is a certified copy of a document in which Alonso de Ávila testified as to the good moral qualities and reliability of Licentiate Ayala de Espinosa on June 13, 1561.[1]

HC – M 16

CRIMINAL PROCEEDINGS AGAINST DON MARTÍN CORTÉS, SON OF DON HERNANDO CORTÉS AND THE INDIAN DOÑA MARINA, FOR CONSPIRACY. Records (incomplete) of a lawsuit in Mexico, July 16, 1566—Nov. 16, 1568. Part I: Records of the proceedings by Licentiates Contreras y Guevara and Céspedes de Cárdenas, fiscales, before the audiencia, July 16, 1566—Nov. 14 [?] 1567. Part II: Records of proceedings by Dr. Francisco de Sande, fiscal, before Licientiate Alonso Muñoz and Dr. Luis Carrillo, jueces comisarios, Nov. 19, 1567—Nov. 16, 1568. 204 leaves (200 written, 4 blank).

Don Martín Cortés, cavalier of the Order of Santiago, appeared before Dr. Francisco Ceynos, oidor of the audiencia, and was questioned on July 16, 1566, concerning his alleged part in the conspiracy against the King. He acknowledged his relationship to his brothers, the Marqués del Valle and Luis Cortés, and that he knew Alonso de Ávila and Alonso Chico de Molina, dean of the Cathedral, but denied any knowledge of a rebellion as he considered much of the talk that had circulated frivolous and meaningless. He asked what the accusations against him were, and the fiscal Contreras y Guevara accused him of failing to report what he had known to the audiencia. Action to sequester his property was begun, and procurador Álvaro Ruiz and Licentiates Sedeño and Carriazo were named to defend him.

After petitions for delay, Licentiate Céspedes de Cárdenas continued for the audiencia in October 1566. Witnesses who had testified in the case against the Ávila brothers confirmed previous testimony, and others were asked about Don Martín's involvement. The defense submitted questions that showed the unfriendly attitude of many of those who testified against him and emphasized their low and unreliable character. Don Martín's prior service to the King, in which he had been wounded, his poor health, and the failure of Alonso de Ávila to implicate him in his final statement were cited.

On November 28 fiscal Céspedes petitioned that Don Martín be questioned under torture, but because of his poor health he was allowed a house arrest of 30 days after

---

[1] For summaries and extracts from this document see Juan Manuel Orozco y Berra, *Noticia histórica de la conjuración del Marqués del Valle, años de 1565–1568* (Mexico, Tip. de R. Rafael, 1853), p. 3–53 (second series of page numbers).

paying a bond. His request for freedom to move within the city was denied until April, when he was permitted 100 days of freedom to administer the estate of his brother, the Marqués, who had already departed for Spain.

Late in 1567 a detailed inventory of the property of Don Martín was taken in the towns of Coyoacán, Cuernavaca, and Yautepec. In December the jueces Muñoz and Carrillo ordered that he be questioned under torture. A new questionnaire by the fiscal was meant to prove that Don Martín was part of the conspiracy; in response Ruiz presented questionnaires that showed that Don Martín was a faithful member of the Order of Santiago, that he was in such poor health that torture would bring death, and that the escribano for the audiencia was a close friend of Don Luis de Velasco, known enemy of the Cortés brothers. Furthermore, it was testified that Don Martín did not participate in the social affairs of the Marqués even though they lived under the same roof.

On January 8, 1568, Don Martín was put to torture by water and rope. His arms, legs, and feet were tied and stretched and several vessels of water were poured into his mouth. He refused to change earlier testimony and the officials ordered an end to the torture when they realized his physical weakness.

In January 1568 testimony about the last words of one Gómez de Vitoria, uttered just before his execution four days earlier, was presented. He had mentioned ties with conspirators in Peru and plans for protesting the curtailment of the succession of encomiendas, first to the King and that measure failing, for turning to the King of France for aid. Vitoria confirmed Don Martín's assertion that he had considered the talk of rebellion childish and meaningless. Cristóbal de Oñate retracted all charges that he had made in Madrid against Don Martín. Another statement, taken from Don Baltasar de Quesada as he awaited execution, also denied that Don Martín had been among the conspirators. Don Pedro de Quesada, executed on January 9, 1568, had confessed his own guilt but had said that many had been unjustly arrested and that Don Martín was innocent.

On January 10, 1568, Don Martín was sentenced to perpetual exile from the Indies and ordered to depart promptly for Spain; he was also ordered to pay a fine of 1,000 ducats. The fiscal appealed the sentence because it was not harsh enough and Don Martín's defenders appealed because he was innocent. The judgment was confirmed in the category of review, with the fine reduced to 500 ducats.

The record indicates that the sequestration of the goods of Don Martín was lifted but that more than 500 ducats was collected. The records appear to be incomplete, but it is apparent that Don Martín was still in Mexico on March 17, 1568, when he requested an extension of the time in which he could remain in his home under house arrest. A later document among the records is a petition, read before the audiencia on November 16, 1568, for a certificate showing that cotton belonging to Don Martín had been confiscated.[1]

---

[1] For extracts and summaries of these proceedings see Orozco y Berra, *Noticia histórica,* p. 217–246.

HC – M 17

LICENTIATES CONTRERAS Y GUEVARA AND CÉSPEDES DE CÁRDENAS, FISCALES, VS. DON MARTÍN CORTÉS, MARQUÉS DEL VALLE, ACCUSED OF TREASON AND INCITING REBELLION AGAINST THE KING. Records (incomplete) of a lawsuit before the Audiencia of Mexico, Sept. 18, 1566—Mar. 20, 1567. 388 leaves (1 title page, 377 written, 10 blank).

The first portion of this trial record is missing,[1] but it is known that the Marqués was arrested, charged, and imprisoned on July 16, 1566, at the same time that many other suspects were arrested. The two questionnaires of 42 and 10 questions, respectively, were drawn up and presented by Licentiates Contreras y Guevara and Céspedes de Cárdenas, the first on September 18 and the second on November 29, 1566, to prove that an insurrection, with the Marqués as its principal figure and probable leader, had been planned. The general tenor of the accusation was that the audiencia was to be overturned and the oidores assassinated, after which the Marqués was to be proclaimed King of New Spain. Diplomatic relations with other nations and the Pope were then to be established and an economy that was not dependent upon Spain was to be developed.

Word had reached New Spain of a royal decree, not yet officially in effect, that encomiendas could not be inherited beyond two lives or generations and of a summons from the Council of the Indies challenging the Marqués concerning the number of Indians from whom he received tribute. Such news added to the general unrest.

Witnesses for the fiscales against the Marqués included Don Francisco and Don Luis de Velasco, knights of the Order of Santiago and brother and son of the late Viceroy; Don Hernando de Portugal, Ortuño de Ibarra, and Hernando de Villanueva, officials of the royal exchequer; Juan de Sámano, alguacil mayor of Mexico; Baltasar de Aguilar, Gonzalo Sánchez de Aguilar, Agustín de Villanueva, Baltasar de Quesada, Licentiate Cristóbal de Ayala Espinosa, Julián de Salazar, Jerónimo de la Mota, Captain Juan de Céspedes, Juan Gómez, Juan de Salazar, Alonso de San Vicente, Pedro de Aguilar, Pedro de Quesada, Alonso de Villanueva Cervantes, and Francisco de Velares. Some of the witnesses gave testimony more than once; others confirmed earlier statements.

The case of the Marqués was organized around 88 questions, presented on September 16, 1566, by Álvaro Ruiz. Through the questionnaire it was denied that the Marqués had any intention of committing treason; it was asserted that he had been loyal to the King, that he had tried to calm rebellious encomenderos, that he had aspired to no greater respect and prerogatives than were properly due him, and that the accusations came largely from persons who had become his enemies.

Witnesses who testified in behalf of the Marqués included Fray Miguel de Alvarado, provincial of the Augustine order; Antonio de Oliver, conquistador; Juan Bautista and

---

[1] Orozco y Berra, *Noticia histórica* p. 55–216. When Orozco y Berra published the documents in the form of summaries and extracts, a sixth cuaderno of 117 sheets, not in the Harkness collection, was part of this document. The opening portions of the records were then already missing. Part 6 contained an interrogatory presented by Licentiate Ayala de Espinosa, bringing out testimony about his learned background and moral qualities; proceedings regarding the sequestration of properties of the Marqués; a plea by Ruiz that the lawsuit be continued in the Council of the Indies with a delay on the sequestering of the property of the Marqués and the opposition of the fiscal to these pleas; reports of the administration of the marquesado and the payment, taken from the estate of the Marqués, of the guards required during the imprisonment of the Marqués; and the fiscal's proof of the good character and reliability of his witnesses and, on the part of some, evidence of their friendship with the Marqués.

Alonso Pereyra, musicians; García del Castillo; Leonel de Cervantes; Maestre Alonso, surgeon; Pedro Pacheco; Doctor Juan de la Fuente, abogado; Bartolomé Osorio, Hernando Rivadeneyra, Alonso Bazo de Andrada, Miguel de Solís, Gonzalo de Salazar, Lope de Sosa, Gabriel de Chávez, Antón García de Castro, Pedro de Requeno, Agustín de Bustamante, Luis Gómez, Juan Núñez Maldonado, Juan de Valdivieso, Antonio de Caravajal, Miguel de Ecija, Jerónimo de Bustamante, Cristina de la Rabia [?], all of Mexico; Pedro de Saucedo, silversmith; Fray Diego de Olarte and Fray Antonio Roldán, provincials of the Franciscan order; Fray Diego Valadez, Franciscan; Bernardino de Albornoz, alcaide; Gonzalo Gómez de Cervantes; Antonio and Isabel de Villarroel, son and wife of Gaspar de Villarroel, apothecary; and Margarida Perez, free black woman, ladina.

The three questionnaires are reproduced in full transcription and translation on p. 245. Depositions of witnesses replying to the three interrogatories were given between September 19, 1566 and March 20, 1567. Much of the testimony of the Marqués preceded that for the fiscal, but several denunciations which were confirmed in the questioning had been made initially in May, June, or July of 1566.

On February 22, 1567, the Viceroy Gastón de Peralta, Marqués de Falces, ordered that the Marqués, before going to Spain to present his case before the King, should make a pleito de homenaje, a form of oath of loyalty made before another knight, as a binding pledge that he would proceed to Spain and appear before the King. The Marqués del Valle took such an oath, promising to remain at his home until he could present himself in Vera Cruz in readiness to sail for Spain on March 20; he also promised to go before the King and the Council of the Indies within 50 days of his landing at a Spanish port.

Evidence was produced of a complaint made on June 28, 1565, by Julián de Salazar, alcalde ordinario of Mexico, because of an attack made upon him at the instigation of the Marqués in June 1565. Petitions were made for certificates of time spent in guarding the Marqués, for copies of a letter from Licentiate Ayala de Espinosa to Alonso de Ávila and of the latter's confession at the time of his execution, and for the so-called crowning garland and standard of the Marquesa and the Marqués, all of which were to be sent to Spain as part of the proceedings. Evidence was presented, recorded, challenged, and even deleted; certified copies of the testimonies were requested and, for the most part, granted. Ruiz presented evidence designed to discredit witnesses on grounds of their known enmity for the Marqués and their untrustworthy character.

Details about a letter written to King Philip and found in the streets in December 1566 by Pedro Gómez de Cáceres (described in HC—M 26, p. 21) appear in the testimony. The letter, signed by Licentiate Ayala de Espinosa, Pedro and Baltasar de Quesada, and Pedro de Aguilar and dated December 8, 1566, advised the King that the Viceroy, at the suspected urging of the Marqués, had prevented their departure for Spain where they wanted to report rebellious conditions in New Spain and urge that an investigation be undertaken. Other documents reveal that the Viceroy took steps to imprison Pedro de Aguilar in the custody of Bernardino de Albornoz, alcaide of the arsenal, and to deliver Licentiate Espinosa de Ayala, a cleric, to the Archbishop of Mexico for trial and imprisonment. Evidence showed that Pedro de Aguilar wrote to the licentiate, but after many demands and signed depositions, the Viceroy ordered the release of the four men involved in the writing of the letter.

The fiscal requested a copy of the letter from the Council of the Indies challenging the Marqués' count of his vassals and summoning him to appear and answer the accusation within six months. Other documents reveal that the Marqués had conferred power of attorney upon Diego Ferrer and Pedro de Villaverde, of Valladolid, in order to comply with the summons. They had been authorized to ask the King that the Marqués be granted property in Castile in exchange for his lands in New Spain. A statement

from the minutes of the ayuntamiento of Mexico for May 29, 1566, recorded the recommendation made by Don Luis de Castillo, at the suggestion of the Marqués, that a spokesman be sent to Spain to petition the King to confirm grants of encomienda in perpetuity.

Other documents in the suit concern a suit against Fray Luis Cal, a lawsuit in which Pedro de Aguilar had been accused of perjury, and the replies of March 1567 to a questionnaire by the fiscal that attempted to prove that the witnesses for the Marqués either were his close friends and associates or shared his guilt in the planned insurrection.

HC – M 18

LICENTIATE CÉSPEDES DE CÁRDENAS, FISCAL, VS. DIEGO ARIAS DE SOTELO AND BALTASAR DE SOTELO, ACCUSED OF CONSPIRACY. Records (incomplete) of a lawsuit before the Audiencia of Mexico, Nov. 18, 1566—July 30, 1567. 98 leaves (96 written, 2 blank).

Diego Arias de Sotelo, regidor of Mexico, and his brother Baltasar de Sotelo, formerly of Peru and more recently in the service of Tristán de Luna y Arellano in the province of Florida, were accused of taking part in the alleged conspiracy. In a petition of November 21, 1566, Baltasar de Sotelo denied his involvement. After a bond had been furnished by Hernando de Portugal, royal treasurer, and Luis Ramirez de Vargas, the home of Hernando de Portugal was designated the prison for Sotelo. Juan de Salazar presented a letter on his behalf, showing that Baltasar de Sotelo offered Captain General Francisco de Velasco his services in helping to prevent a rebellion.

Records of a suit in which Diego Arias de Sotelo had opposed the Marqués del Valle over the boundary between the pueblos of the Marqués and the city of Mexico were placed before the audiencia; evidence of another lawsuit in which he had acted for the Indians of Tarimbaro in a lawsuit against the Indians of Matalcingo, a pueblo under the charge of the Marqués, was also given.

Céspedes de Cárdenas, the fiscal, demanded that Diego Arias be put to torture in order to secure a full confession of the involvement attributed to him in the confession made by Alonso de Ávila at the gallows. Diego Arias de Sotelo was acquitted of the charges on January 28, 1567, and the fiscal protested the decision, attesting to the reliability of the secretary of the audiencia, Sancho López de Agurto, who had recorded Ávila's statement.

Testimony gathered in Guayangareo (now Morelia) in Michoacán in October 1566 was presented before the audiencia. The questions asked concerned Baltasar de Sotelo—his earlier sojourn in Peru and the circumstances that precluded his deep involvement in the rebellion led by Francisco Hernández Girón, his protection of loyal vassals of the King in Peru; his service as captain and maestre de campo in the expedition to Florida under Governors Tristán de Arellano and Angel de Villafañe, and his subsequent passage from Cuba to New Spain where he had offered his services to Viceroy Velasco. After the death of the Viceroy he had spent nearly all of his time at his brother's haciendas in Michoacán where he had led a quiet and peaceful life.

The incomplete records terminate with motions for the release from prison of Diego Arias de Sotelo for 60 days on provision of a bond of 10,000 ducats, which is furnished by Hernando de Portugal. Terms for the case were extended for additional time to the end of September 1567. Some of the missing portions of this record are represented by photocopies of supplementary records from the Biblioteca Conway.[1]

---

[1] For extracts and summaries of this lawsuit see Orozco y Berra, *Noticia histórica,* p. 247–277.

HC – M 19

CRIMINAL PROCEEDINGS AGAINST CRISTÓBAL DE OÑATE FOR CONSPIRACY AGAINST THE KING. Madrid and Mexico, May 5, 1567—Jan. 8, 1568. Part I: Record of proceedings before the Council of the Indies in Madrid, May 5-13, 1567. Part II: Record of proceedings before Licentiate Alonso Muñoz and Dr. Luis Carrillo, jueces comisarios in Mexico, Nov. 11, 1567—Jan. 8, 1568. 46 leaves (42 written, 4 blank).

Cristóbal de Oñate, who had first been in Lima with the Conde de Nieva, Viceroy of Peru, and had then proceeded to Mexico where a relative of the same name was living, appeared before the Council of the Indies on May 5, 1567. Word of the conspiracy against the crown had reached the council from the audiencia of Mexico, and Oñate, who testified that he had come to Spain to carry out a vow to enter the Church because he had been saved from drowning, had been taken into custody for questioning. He denied any knowledge of a plan for rebellion and said that although he knew many of the supposed conspirators, his only knowledge of the rebellion was based upon a letter received by the widow of the Conde de Nieva. He had been aware only of the general discontent among the colonists concerning the decree limiting the inheritance of encomiendas. Oñate was subjected to torture by water and rope and incriminated several of the accused, describing his conversations with them. He explained his change in testimony by saying that he had intended to come earlier and report the conspiracy but his own illness and the death of his mother had detained him.

Under torture or threat of torture, he described purported plans of the conspirators to turn to the King of France if the King of Spain would not yield on the issue of encomiendas, to attempt to secure papal support and investiture of a new king, and to secure French naval assistance through a Monsieur Juan de Bandoma of Bayonne. He also divulged specific plans to take over the royal headquarters and to kill the oidores. Each time he gave testimony, it was written down, and he was asked to sign an attestation as to the accuracy of the statement of what he had said.

On November 11, 1567, the case was resumed in Mexico by the fiscal, Dr. Francisco de Sande, who accused Oñate before Licentiate Alonso Muñoz and Dr. Luis Carrillo, jueces comisarios. The term for the case was limited to three days, and on the same day Oñate named Francisco de Escobar to act as his procurador. Another attorney, Licentiate Ledesma, acting for the poor, was named to aid Oñate and Bernaldino Maldonado. Oñate's lawyers were unable to obtain further delay and proceedings began. Oñate ratified his earlier testimony with the exception of his statement that he had delivered letters to Juan de Bandoma. He also added that on one of the occasions when he had overheard discussions of a rebellion, Bernaldino Maldonado, former soldier in Peru, had also been present.

Several pages of testimony given on December 26 that are not concerned principally with the case of Cristóbal de Oñate follow his initial testimony in this document and are described in HC—M 22, p. 18. Francisco de Escobar presented a questionnaire on behalf of Oñate, dwelling on his loyal and Christian character and the hardships and privations that he had undergone for the previous year and a half.

Oñate was sentenced to be carried through the streets on a beast of burden with his hands and feet tied and a town cryer proclaiming his crime and the justice of his sentence and then to be hanged and quartered. All appeals were denied, and he was executed on January 8, 1568. Oñate's confession at the gallows is included at the end of the records of the trial of Don Martín Cortés.[1]

---

[1] For extracts and summaries of these proceedings see Orozco y Berra, *Noticia histórica,* p. 279–328.

HC – M 20

DR. FRANCISCO DE SANDE, FISCAL, VS. DON BALTASAR AND DON PEDRO DE QUESADA, ACCUSED OF CONSPIRACY AGAINST THE KING. Records (incomplete) of a lawsuit before Licentiate Alonso Muñoz and Dr. Luis Carrillo, jueces comisarios, in Mexico, Nov. 7, 1567—Apr. 6, 1570. 43 leaves (1 title page, 37 written, 5 blank).

On November 13, 1567, Don Baltasar de Quesada appeared before the jueces comisarios and confirmed three earlier depositions that he had made to Oidores Ceynos and Villalobos. He had no information to add except that Alonso de Ávila had told him that Cristóbal de Oñate had reported that his uncle of the same name had stated that the King was about to lose New Spain; this had caused him much surprise as he had considered the elder Cristóbal a loyal subject.

Four days later Don Pedro de Quesada appeared before the judges and declared that he had told most of what he knew of the insurrection, adding only an incident involving one Lope de Sosa and ratifying his statement of July 15, 1566. He also reported the pleasure with which the Marqués had received news of the presence of the French at Punta de Santa Elena, adding that this news had also been pleasing to the friars. It was pointed out that he had mentioned Bernaldino Maldonado in this statement for the first time in connection with the insurrection, but he nevertheless ratified his earlier statement.

The fiscal accused the Quesadas of involvement in the insurrection, of keeping their knowledge of it secret for a year, of failing to give due warning to the authorities, and of thus being guilty of lese majesty. He asked that their goods be sequestered and their houses be torn down, that they be declared ignoble and vile persons to be stripped of all insignia of arms, and that they be put to torture. Juan de Salazar, on behalf of the accused, denied the charges. Letters written by Baltasar de Quesada in October 1567 are included in this record, following ratification of earlier depositions made by Pedro de Aguilar, Cristóbal de Oñate, Gabriel Chávez, Gonzalo Nuñez, and Angel de Villafañe. Bernaldino Maldonado did not at first ratify his earlier declaration, stating that it had been exacted under torture, but when he was again put to torture, he said that his earlier statements had been true.

The accused were defended on the grounds that as soon as they had suspected that there were plans for an insurrection, they had reported it to the oidores, thus doing a great service to the King. They had served loyally under Don Francisco de Velasco with their arms and horses, Don Pedro had taken part in the pacification of the Chichimecas and the natives of Copala, and both brothers were of noble blood and could not be considered traitors.

December 24, 1567, Juan de Salazar asked that they be allowed house arrest. This was denied and on January 8, 1568, Don Pedro was sentenced to death and the loss of his property. Don Baltasar was similarly sentenced on January 9. An appeal against these sentences was apparently received too late for consideration and the brothers were summarily executed. Their last statements, made on the scaffold, are included in the documents, as is a request dated April 4, 1570, by Lope de Miranda, alcalde del crimen, and Dr. Francisco de Sande, fiscal, for delivery of a copy of the confession of Pedro de Quesada.[1]

---

[1] For extracts and summaries of this lawsuit see Orozco y Berra, *Noticia histórica*, p. 329–345.

HC – M 21

ANTONIO MORALES DE MOLINA, BISHOP OF MICHOACÁN, VS. LICENTIATE RODRIGO DE CARAVAJAL, PRIEST OF THE TOWN OF SAN MIGUEL OF THE CHICHIMECAS, FOR HAVING RESISTED THE AUTHORITIES WHO WERE SENT TO ARREST BERNALDINO MALDONADO. Nov. 12, 1567—Jan. 10, 1567 (i.e., 1568). 45 leaves (1 title page, 43 written, 1 blank).

In the course of a lawsuit against Alonso de Castillo, the arrest of Bernaldino Maldonado had been ordered, and Alguacil Juan Gallego de Villapando, assisted by Diego Osorio, had been sent to make the arrest. Their efforts were blocked by the soldiers of Don Alonso de Castillo, particularly by one Francisco de Hinojosa. Maldonado was able to escape and took refuge in the church and adjacent living quarters of the priest Rodrigo de Carajaval, who was alleged to have come to the doorway in doublet and hose, bearing a broadsword which he kept for his self-defense.

Upon orders from the bishop of Michoacán, Rodrigo de Carajaval was arrested by the priest Juan Sánchez and his goods sequestered on November 20, 1567. He was taken to Mexico for a trial that opened on November 25, with Juan Nuñez pleading the case in his behalf. Rodrigo de Caravajal denied that he was a relative of Maldonado as the alguacil alleged and in reply to questions explained that he was a former member of the Dominican Order and had become a secularized priest in the mines of Guachinango, later in Purificación, and most recently in the town of San Miguel. He denied any knowledge of the conspiracy or acquaintance with the conspirators of 1566 and declared that he had only protected Maldonado in order to preserve the sanctity of his church, as violence against Maldonado had been threatened by the soldiers in pursuit.

The priest escaped from prison, and an inquiry into the responsibility for his escape was opened but not brought to a conclusion. Apparently the bishop's order for the pursuit and apprehension of the escaped priest could not be carried out, and the suit must have been dropped.[1]

HC – M 22

DR. FRANCISCO DE SANDE, FISCAL, VS. DON BALTASAR AND PEDRO DE QUESADA, BALTASAR DE AGUILAR, BERNARDINO MALDONADO, AND OTHERS. Record (incomplete) of testimony against these conspirators before the jueces comisarios, Licentiate Alonso Muñoz and Dr. Luis Carrillo, in Mexico, Nov. 26—Dec. 30, 1567. 9 leaves (7 written, 2 blank). Sewed into HC – M 19 between leaves 28 and 29.

Baltasar de Aguilar, Pedro de Aguilar, Baltasar de Quesada, and Pedro de Quesada confirmed statements that they had made before Oidores Ceynos and Orozco between April 17 and July 18, 1566, implicating persons involved in the conspiracy. Cristóbal de Oñate confirmed similar testimony that he had given in Madrid in May 1566 before Alonso Muñoz and Luis Molina of the Council of the Indies and had later ratified in December of the same year in Mexico. Gabriel Chávez and Jerónimo Nuñez also confirmed prior testimony. Among those named in the documents were Pedro and Baltasar de Quesada, Baltasar de Aguilar, Bernaldino Maldonado, Cristóbal de Oñate, Bernaldino Pacheco de Bocanegra, Pedro de Aguilar, Diego Arias and Baltasar de Sotelo,

---

[1] For extracts and summaries of these proceedings see Orozco y Berra, *Noticia histórica*, p. 347–362.

Francisco de Reynoso, Nuño de Chavez, Luis Ponce de León, Hernando de Córdoba, Don Francisco Pacheco, Bernaldino Pacheco de Bocanegra, Francisco Rodríguez Magarino, Diego Rodríguez Orozco, Martín Cortés (Marqués del Valle), Luis Cortés, and Alonso de Ávila Alvarado.

Bernaldino Maldonado gave contradictory evidence but was put to torture and gave evidence against the Bocanegras, whom he claimed to have sheltered previously out of friendship.[1]

HC – M 23

Dr. Francisco de Sande, fiscal, vs. Juan de Valdivieso, accused of conspiracy, before Licentiate Alonso Muñoz and Dr. Luis Carrillo, jueces comisarios, in Mexico, Dec. 3, 1567—Mar. 20, 1568. 271 leaves (1 title page, 266 written, 4 blank).

On December 3, 1567, the jueces comisarios initiated action against Juan de Valdivieso, accusing him of complicity in the conspiracy against the King. He was represented first by Juan Caro and then by Juan de Salazar, who denied allegations that Valdivieso had been associated with the person and activities of the Marqués del Valle. These charges stemmed largely from the fact that his sister Guiomar Vazquez de Escobar was the wife of Don Luis Cortés.

Juan de Salazar attempted to prove that Valdivieso was on bad terms with the Marqués and that he had objected violently to the marks of respect exacted by the Marqués and thus became involved in a street fight between partisans of the Marqués, notably the Bocanegras, and his own faction which included several of those who had denounced the Ávila brothers and the Cortés brothers. His own disagreements with Luis Cortés, who had strongly resented Valdivieso's actions, were also described. Further attempts to prove a close relationship to the Marqués were countered by statements that most of Valdivieso's dealings with the Cortés family had been in behalf of the interests of his sister. Statements made at the gallows by Alonso de Ávila and the Quesada brothers were introduced as evidence. An order issued by the audiencia on November 5, 1566, clearing Valdivieso and others from suspicion of conspiracy, was also cited.

A sentence of perpetual exile and a fine of 2,000 ducats was appealed by the fiscal as too lenient and by Salazar as unsupported by proof. The sentence was confirmed on January 28, 1568, with reduced penalties of 10 years of exile and a smaller fine, and on March 20, 1568, Valdivieso delivered 500 pesos or one third of the fine that he was to pay.

The final portion of the document concerns two outbreaks of street fighting that took place in Mexico in April and May 1565.[2]

---

[1] For extracts and summaries of this lawsuit see Orozco y Berra, *Noticia histórica*, p. 312–325.

[2] For extracts and summaries of this lawsuit see Orozco y Berra, *Noticia histórica*, p. 379–397.

HC – M 24

DR. FRANCISCO DE SANDE, FISCAL, VS. ANTONIO RUIZ DE CASTAÑEDA BEFORE LICENTIATE ALONSO MUÑOZ AND DR. LUIS CARRILLO, JUECES COMISARIOS, IN MEXICO, DEC. 6, 1567—MAY 26, 1568. 62 leaves (1 title page, 59 written, 2 blank).

Antonio Ruiz de Castañeda was accused of complicity in the conspiracy planned by the Ávila brothers and the Marqués del Valle and his brothers. Castañeda testified that he was of age, that he held an encomienda of half of the Indians of the pueblo of Tehuacán from which he received 2,000 pesos and that he held mines and neighboring lands with a total of 21 slaves. Gil González de Ávila had been married to his cousin, and at Ávila's execution Castañeda had sworn to avenge the death of an innocent person. He had offered to serve the King but had been excused from military service because he had just returned exhausted from fighting to pacify the Chichimecan Indians. The term for the case was extended several times, once because Castañeda was ill, and he was permitted to leave the jail and remain under house arrest for a short time.

The fiscal repeated earlier charges that Castañeda was to have taken part in the conspiracy, that he was related to and intimate with Gil González, and that he had openly tried to aid other conspirators and had asserted their innocence after their arrest. Testimony in favor of Castañeda was given by many witnesses but the jueces comisarios ruled that Castañeda must be exiled and pay costs and a fine. The sentence was appealed and confirmed in review, but with a less severe term of exile and a smaller fine. Castañeda's appearance to fulfill his exile was certified by the notary public of Puebla de los Angeles on May 26, 1568.[1]

HC – M 25

DR. FRANCISCO DE SANDE, FISCAL, VS. VICEROY GASTÓN DE PERALTA, MARQUÉS DE FALCES. Records of proceedings before Licentiate Alonso Muñoz and Dr. Luis Carrillo, jueces comisarios, and Pedro Farfán, oidor of the Audiencia of Mexico, Dec. 6, 1567—Feb. 14, 1568. 35 leaves (1 title page, 29 written, 5 blank).

After he had been ordered by the jueces comisarios to return to Spain, the Marqués de Falces presented a writ on December 6, 1567, outlining his actions in New Spain from the time of his arrival on September 17, 1566, and requesting permission to make a probanza of his services that he could present to the King. The fiscal asked that the probanza be withheld pending investigation by the Viceroy, who presented a second petition stating that he had not misrepresented the facts, had not showed any lack of respect for the oidores, and had treated the Marqués del Valle and the purported rebels not with partiality but with fairness.

Later in December the fiscal presented a questionnaire the intent of which was to accuse the Viceroy of both ignoring and concealing evidence of the uprising and of being too lenient toward the Marqués and others who were accused. The judges refused to allow the fiscal to interrogate witnesses and denied the Viceroy's petition, maintaining that these matters should be decided in Spain. Both petitioners appealed the decisions and on February 13, 1568, the records were ordered sent to the Council of the Indies in the category of review. A favorable ruling was made when the Viceroy petitioned

---

[1] For extracts and summaries of this lawsuit see Orozco y Berra, *Noticia histórica,* p. 399–410.

that he be given a copy of the testimony of Baltasar de Aguilar in which he had been accused.[1]

HC – M 26

LICENTIATE CÉSPEDES DE CÁRDENAS AND DR. FRANCISCO DE SANDE, FISCALES, VS. PEDRO GÓMEZ DE CÁCERES, ALCALDE MAYOR OF MICHOACÁN, ACCUSED OF PARTICIPATION IN THE CONSPIRACY AGAINST THE KING, BEFORE THE AUDIENCIA OF MEXICO AND LICENTIATE ALONSO MUÑOZ AND DR. LUIS CARRILLO, JUECES COMISARIOS. Records (incomplete) of lawsuits in Mexico, July 28, 1566—Mar. 4, 1568. 151 leaves (1 title page, 146 written, 4 blank).

These partial records are not consecutively bound and the earliest proceedings are described in the last 50 pages of the trial record.

On July 28, 1566, the audiencia ruled that Pedro Gómez de Cáceres, who had been accused, was to choose a residence for his prison upon furnishing a bond and under penalty of death if he should flee. He named the house of his brother, Cristóbal de Tapia, and a bond was furnished by his brother and Juan Velazquez de Salazar. The audiencia then proceeded to seek information about suspicious statements against civil and ecclesiastical authorities that had been attributed to the defendant.

Juan de Salazar, in the name of Cáceres, replied to accusations, denying the charges, and the prisoner, who had been granted a few days of freedom, was granted the city as his prison upon the payment of a bond of 10,000 ducats. On February 28, 1567, witnesses who had accused the defendant confirmed their previous denunciations.

The suit continued before the jueces comisarios. In January 1568 they ordered the sequestration of the property of all of those accused of conspiring in the insurrection, including the defendant who held property rights in Ataclán, Atotonilco, and Guazqueceloya. Juan Caro, in behalf of Cáceres, denied that the defendant had been involved in the rebellion or had wrongfully intercepted a letter from Espinoza and Aguilar to the King, delivering it instead to the Viceroy, the Marqués de Falces. The fiscal Francisco de Sande asked that Cáceres be put to torture in spite of Caro's presentation of a royal cedula of recommendation directed to the audiencia, attesting to the services to the crown given by Cáceres and his father, Andrés de Tapia. The fiscal again asked that Cáceres be put to torture; Caro introduced evidence of a sentence pronounced by the audiencia on September 17, 1566, against Baltasar de Bonilla because he had illegally imprisoned Gómez de Cáceres as a traitor.

A questionnaire by Caro attempted to prove that the denunciations were caused by personal animosities, that the defendant had rendered many services to the crown, and that he was not a friend of the Marqués, who had had nothing to do with the marriage of Cáceres to Francisca Ferrer, a member of the Marquesa's household. The sequestration of his goods and the living conditions of the prison were also protested by Caro. A sentence of perpetual exile from the Indies and a fine of 1,000 ducats was imposed; it was appealed but confirmed on January 28, 1568, with a shortened exile of 10 years. Gómez de Cáceres was refused permission to leave the prison before his departure for Spain and denied an extension of time for paying his fine. His brother Andrés de Tapia delivered a third of the fine to the royal exchequer on March 4, 1568, and presented a bond for the payment of the guards and alguacil, whereupon the sequestration of Cáceres' properties was lifted.[2]

---

[1] For extracts and summaries of these proceedings see Orozco y Berra, *Noticia histórica,* p. 411–440.

[2] For summaries and extracts from these proceedings see Orozco y Berra, *Noticia histórica,* p. 363–378.

HC – M 27

DR. FRANCISCO DE SANDE, FISCAL, VS. PEDRO HERNÁNDEZ PACHECO, ACCUSED OF PARTICIPATING IN THE CONSPIRACY. Fragment of the record of a lawsuit before Licentiate Alonso Muñoz and Dr. Luis Carrillo, jueces comisarios, in Mexico, Dec. 20, 1567. 1 leaf.

On behalf of the defendant, who was imprisoned under suspicion of participation in the conspiracy, Juan Caro petitioned that Pedro Hernández Pacheco de declared innocent, inasmuch as his guilt had not been proved and he had come to New Spain in 1561 only to take care of his inheritance. The fiscal was given a copy of the petition.

HC – M 28

DR. FRANCISCO DE SANDE, FISCAL, VS. DON GARCÍA DE ALBORNOZ, REGIDOR. Records of a lawsuit before Licentiate Alonso Muñoz and Dr. Luis Carrillo, jueces comisarios, in Mexico, Jan. 12—Mar. 30, 1576. 145 leaves (1 title page, 142 written, 2 blank).

Don García de Albornoz, who had been imprisoned after the jueces comisarios had received information against him, denied his participation in the rebellion on January 14, 1568. Those who had previously denounced the regidor for failure to respond to a call to arms and for appearing to be critical of the King and audiencia ratified their earlier statements and verified that a writ had been issued before Andrés Orejon, alcalde mayor, ordering Albornoz to appear at Acamalutla in the province of Acapulco with arms and horse. Cristóbal Pérez was named lawyer for the defendant and unsuccessfully petitioned for the release of the prisoner on grounds of illness.

Pérez introduced a questionnaire about the illness of Albornoz, his loyalty, and the enmity of the witnesses, incurred because of actions taken by Albornoz to protect the Indians. He presented evidence of suits in which Albornoz had accused Spanish merchants, the alcalde mayor, and some of the hostile witnesses of abusing and over-charging the Indians and of encouraging the harmful practice of the exchange of goods on credit.

On January 26, 1568, the jueces comisarios pronounced a sentence of exile for 10 years and a fine of 1,000 ducats. The sentence was appealed and Pérez and the fiscal continued their charges, Pérez presenting documents showing that the Indians of Acamalutla had conferred a power of attorney upon Albornoz as their defender.

Other items included in the records are ordinances of Viceroy Luis de Velasco about the treatment of the Acapulco Indians, denunciations by Albornoz of persons violating these ordinances, copies of regulations and decrees on the curtailment of vagabondage and discouraging the presence of unattached men and women in the Indian villages, a ruling that Spaniards should live in Acapulco, and measures against priests who neglected their Indian charges.

On January 30, 1568, Pérez introduced more questions to prove the greediness of the priests and to emphasize points made earlier. The fiscal produced evidence that Albornoz had been sued for exacting the illegal carrying of goods by the Indians. The sentence was confirmed in the category of review, with an exile reduced to six years and a fine of 500 ducats, which was deposited in the royal exchequer the same day. Controversy over the costs of the suit continued, May 30, 1576, being the latest date of any of the documents.[1]

---

[1] For extracts and summaries of this lawsuit see Orozco y Berra, *Noticia histórica,* p. 441–470.

HC – M 29

LICENTIATE ALONSO MUÑOZ AND DR. LUIS CARRILLO, JUECES COMISARIOS. Fragment concerning the sequestering of the property of Don Martín Cortés, Marqués del Valle, Mexico, Jan. 1568. ½ leaf (torn).

> Instructions by the jueces comisarios to the alguaciles of La Rinconada, ordering the sequestering of the marquesado and appointing as trustees Hernández and Baltasar Vezinecatl and as ecclesiastical constable, Martín Días.

HC – M 30

DR. CÉSPEDES DE CÁRDENAS, FISCAL OF THE AUDIENCIA OF MEXICO. Records of proceedings before the audiencia concerning the bonds required from royal officials appointed to administer the sequestered possessions of Don Martín Cortés, Marqués del Valle, Mexico, Mar. 8—May 12, 1569. 56 leaves (1 title page, 42 written, 13 blank).

> Don Martín Cortés' possessions were sequestered by the audiencia as a result of the Ávila-Cortés conspiracy of 1566. Gordián Casasano, factor; Bernardino de Albornoz, treasurer; and Lope of Villanueva, accountant, were appointed administrators of Cortés' possessions.
>
> Records include an order of the audiencia of March 8, 1569, that the royal officials furnish bond in the amount of 33,000 pesos each, guaranteeing the management of the possessions of Martín Cortés; a declaration of Casasano, Albornoz, and Villanueva stating they had little time for the management of Cortés' numerous properties and that the bond should be a lesser amount; the contention of the fiscal Cárdenas that it was the duty of the appointed officials to manage Cortés' properties for the Crown, emphasizing that the properties yielded 100,000 pesos annually and that the officials would be adequately compensated; and notarial acts for various bonds that were posted.

HC – M 31

GONZALO SALAZAR, GUARD. Fragment of petition to the Audiencia of Mexico for payment of salary, July 18–19, 1570. 1 leaf.

> Salazar had guarded Don Martín Cortés, Marqués del Valle, for seven months of the Marqués' imprisonment on charges of conspiracy. Before delivering his prisoner to Captain Juan de Céspedes, Salazar requested payment of his salary.

HC – M 32

INQUISITION. Mexico. Record of an inquiry of the purity of blood of Dr. Esteban de Portillo, vicar-general of the Archbishopric of Mexico. Mexico, Sept. 9, 1571— Apr. 5, 1577. 125 leaves (2 title pages, 116 written, 7 blank).

> Dr. Barbosa, precepter of the Cathedral, petitioned the inquisitor Pedro Moya de Contreras to initiate an investigation of the purity of Portillo's blood because Portillo was suspected of being a descendant of Moors or Jews.
>
> Included in the records are four letters of Portillo to the Inquisition complaining of rivalries and enmity towards him as the result of his successful career; interrogatories

and testimonies concerning the family of Portillo given in Mexico, Tlaxacala, and the town of Portillo in Spain; interrogatories and testimonies in the Audiencia of Mexico, dated in the 1550's, about the services rendered to the crown by Esteban de Portillo's father, the conquistador Francisco de Portillo; information provided by Portillo's brother, Bachiller Pedro Garces, secular priest; and certification of Esteban de Portillo's admission as ordinario to the Holy Office.

HC – M 33

INQUISITION. Mexico. Record (incomplete) of proceedings by the Inquisition concerning the granting of the title of familiar of the Holy Office to Pedro de Herrera, notary. Antequera [Oaxaca] and Mexico, Aug. 20, 1572 and Mar. 23, 1580. 8 leaves (7 written, 1 blank).

Includes results of an investigation undertaken on August 20, 1572, by Dr. de Alzoriz, archdeacon of the Cathedral of Mexico and inquisitor of the Holy Office, concerning the purity of blood of Maria de Bejarano, wife of Pedro de Herrera, and an order of Inquisitor Licentiate Bonilla, dated March 23, 1580, awarding the title of familiar to Herrera.

HC – M 34

ARTEAGA DE MENDIOLA, FISCAL, VS. DON MARTÍN CORTÉS, MARQUÉS DEL VALLE, TO RECOVER COSTS OF THE REBELLION OF 1566. Copy of the records (incomplete) of an investigation before the Audiencia of Mexico, Feb. 6—Aug. 7, 1574. 50 leaves.

The costs incurred by the rebellion had to be determined to collect what the Marqués was obligated to pay. Álvaro Ruiz in Mexico and Sebastián de Santander in Spain represented the Marqués. A questionnaire (missing from this record) was used to ascertain how many guards and arms were required to maintain order and to protect officials and prisoners, as well as to evaluate the cost of construction of specially fortified quarters in the prison, ordered by the jueces comisarios. The depositions of the witnesses showed that guards had regularly been employed at the royal palace where the Marqués was detained, that Captain Juan de Céspedes and guards were on duty when the conspirators were taken, that arms and gunpowder were regularly supplied from Mexico, and that the special strong wall continued to be of use after the rebellion. Witnesses included Diego López de Montalban, shopkeeper; Juan Navarro, interpreter for the royal exchequer; Ambrosio de Riberos, Spaniard; Jorge de Aranda, official of the contaduria; Pedro de Campos and Claudio de Arciniega, citizens of Mexico; Bartolomé de Ecija, artilleryman; and Cristóbal Gudiel, gunner in the royal palace.

The fiscal petitioned that he be given information about the number of new halberds returned by Don Francisco de Velasco and others, a record of Pedro de Aguilar's denunciation of the Marqués and others, and certified documents showing the amount paid to Pedro de Aguilar as an informer. Other records include copies of the orders dated July 6, 1567, given to the jueces comisarios, the cedula specifying the amount and source of their salaries, an affidavit showing the date of their departure for New Spain, statements of the dates of death of Licentiate Zaraba, Dr. Carrillo, and Pedro del Campo, and a receipt for 11,200 ducados paid to the comisarios by the Casa de Contratación. Permission to supply copies of the latter items was granted by the Council of the Indies in response to a request from Sebastián de Santander over the

opposition of the fiscal Licentiate Lopez de Sarria; Álvaro Ruiz presented them before the audiencia. Many certifications concerning the documentary evidence are included in the trial records; among the officials signing them are Gordián Casasano, escribano of the audiencia and chancilleria, Juan Serrano, and Juan de Ledesma, escribano de camara de governación in Spain.[1]

HC – M 35

DON MARTÍN CORTÉS, MARQUÉS DEL VALLE. Fragment of the record of the trial of the Marqués and others for conspiracy by the Audiencia of Mexico, July 5, 1574. 1 leaf (torn).

Cortés' attorney Alonso Bazo de Andrada petitioned the audiencia for copies of the accusations made first by the former fiscal and then by the fiscal Dr. Francisco de Sande against Diego Arias Sotelo, Bernaldino de Bocanegra, Antonio de Carvajal, and Pedro Gómez de Cáceres.[2] A copy of the order given to Sande to proceed against the Marqués was also requested.

HC – M 36

DON MARTÍN CORTÉS, MARQUÉS DEL VALLE. Fragment of the record of the trial of the Marqués for conspiracy by the Audiencia of Mexico, July 9–10, 1574. 1 leaf (torn).

Alonso Bazo de Andrada, attorney for Cortés, petitioned the audiencia that the fiscal comply with an order to deliver copies of some testimony to him. According to a note on this manuscript, Andrada was given copies of the accusations by Pedro Gómez de Cáceres and Antonio de Carvajal.[3]

HC – M 37

DON MARTÍN ENRÍQUEZ DE ALMANSA, VICEROY OF MEXICO. Letter of the alcalde mayor of Chalco and report of an investigation by the alcalde concerning a request by the Indians of Quitlabaca [Cuitláhuac] to use part of the tribute for construction and decoration of their church. Mexico and Quitlabaca, Feb. 19–25, 1578. 14 leaves (12 written, 2 blank).

Includes letter of the Viceroy to Suero de Cangas, alcalde mayor of Chalco, informing him of the petition of the Indians and ordering a report on the local situation; testimonies of the Indians, including that of Don Juan Marcos, Indian governor, concerning the state of their church and annual revenues; testimony of the vicar of the Dominican monastery, Fray Juan Crisóstomo, in favor of the petition; and a letter of the alcalde to the Viceroy reporting on the situation.

---

[1] For extracts and summaries of this investigation see Orozco y Berra, *Noticia historica,* p. 191–216.

[2] See also HC–M 36.

[3] See also HC–M 35.

HC – M 38

INQUISITION. Mexico. Records of the trial of Francisco Hernández, owner of an estancia in the valley of Guaychiapa [Huichapan?], accused of stating that fornication with an unmarried woman was not a sin and of having desired to seduce an Indian girl. Mexico, Sept. 2—Oct. 17, 1578. 26 leaves (23 written, 3 blank).

> Includes a denunciation of Hernández by Luis de Guzmán before the inquisitor Alonso Fernández de Bonilla; confessions of the defendant and his denial of guilt on the grounds that he had referred to carnal relations wherein a woman is paid; investigation by and testimonies before Miguel Izquierdo, priest; sentence of Hernández to hear Mass with a rope around his neck, to be led through the street on a horse accompanied by a public crier announcing his crimes, and to receive two hundred lashes.

HC – M 39

DON MARTÍN CORTÉS, MARQUÉS DEL VALLE, VS. DOÑA INES DE LEÓN. Records (incomplete) of a lawsuit to recover possession of Juana, a black slave, and her two children. Mexico, July 9, 1585—July 21, 1587. 75 leaves (1 inserted vellum, 3 blank, 71 written).

> Diego de Mendoza, on behalf of the Marqués, presented a claim for the recovery of the slave Juana and her two children before the oidor Diego Garcia de Palacio, juez de provincia. The claim was against Doña Ines de León who had assumed possession of Juana as part of her marriage pledge and dowry when she married Diego Perez de Algava, an overseer for the Marqués.
>
> Pedro de la Barrera, in the name of Ines de León, disputed the validity of Diego de Mendoza's power to act for Cortés, as his power of attorney had been delegated to him through Hernan Gutierrez Altamirano, the person originally empowered to act by Cortés. He alleged that Juana had been bought by the late husband of Doña Ines from Don Martín Cortés, brother (of the same name) of the Marqués and that Algava had gained the right of peaceful possession by virtue of having held her for 20 years and that Algava also had freed one of her children by a clause in his will. Diego de Mendoza claimed that the slave had never truly belonged to the husband of Doña Ines and that the matter had been brought up many times by the Marqués, but his agents had never pressed the matter because of Algava's poverty.
>
> Both attorneys asked for delays between October 1585 and February 10, 1586. Witnesses for the Marqués were questioned in October 1585; their testimony verified the contentions of Mendoza that Juana properly belonged to the Marqués. Similar testimony gathered for Doña Ines in January 1586 corroborated her claims.
>
> On April 29, 1568, the oidor Dr. Garcia Palacio, juez de provincia, ruled in favor of the Marqués, ordering that Juana and her two children be delivered to him. An appeal was made and the case went before the audiencia, where Juan de Palencia acted in the name of Doña Ines and Álvaro Ruiz was the advocate for the Marqués.
>
> On June 13, 1586, Juana produced evidence that she and her husband had paid the equivalent of 200 pesos de oro de minas in return for which she had been freed, and she submitted a deed of manumission executed by Doña Ines de León on September 14, 1585.[1] She asked for protection of her freedom, and her suit was joined to that of the

---

[1] Stella R. Clemence, "Deed of emancipation of a Negro woman slave, dated Mexico, September 14, 1585," *Hispanic American Historical Review*, v. 10 (Feb. 1930): 51–57.

Marqués. Francisco de Herrera pleaded in her behalf, alleging that she had been bought by the brother of the Marqués, who had paid for her through a deduction from the sum permitted him for subsistence, as shown in the account books of the marquesado.

Doña Ines was asked to post bond to prevent Juana's loss of 200 pesos, should she be deprived of her freedom. Although Álvaro Ruiz repeatedly asked that the evidence in the accounts be copied and brought to the court, no such action is recorded in the documents, which close with a plea of July 21, 1587, requesting a decision. It must therefore be concluded that the case was either abandoned or concluded in favor of the Marqués.

HC – M 40

INQUISITION. Mexico. Decree by Francisco López de Rebolledo, commissary of the Holy Office of Vera Cruz and the Port of San Juan de Ulúa, concerning the inspection of books and images brought in by ship. Vera Cruz, Oct. 27–28, 1586. 2 leaves.

This decree, dated October 27, ordered that all packages of books and images arriving by ship were to be inspected by the Inquisition. A certificate of the public proclamation of the decree on the following day was prepared by Juan de V[illa]seca, notary.

HC – M 41

FRANCISCO LÓPEZ DE REBOLLEDO, COMMISSARY OF THE HOLY OFFICE OF VERA CRUZ AND THE PORT OF SAN JUAN DE ULÚA. Records of inspection by the commissary of 14 ships arriving in San Juan de Ulúa from Cádiz and Seville. Vera Cruz, Nov. 5, 1586—Jan. 28, 1587. 86 leaves (55 written, 31 blank).

Includes answers to eight questions concerning details of the voyage, meetings with foreign ships, the crew's observation of religious practices, books and images carried, and whether the latter were inspected by officials of the Inquisition;[1] and testimonies of personnel of each vessel.

HC – M 42

DON JUAN DE VELASCO, CACIQUE AND GOVERNOR OF HUEXUAPA [HUAJUAPAN] IN THE MIXTECA BAJA, AND OTHER INDIANS. Petition to José de Solís, alcalde mayor of the province of Acatlán, Sept. 9—Oct. 6, 1592. 6 leaves (5 written, 1 blank).

On September 9, 1592, the Indians asked for assistance from the royal exchequer to furnish ornaments for the church.

Includes testimony concerning the poverty of the Indians and a request that this petition be forwarded to the Viceroy, acknowledgment of receipt of the petition by the alcalde mayor, and an annotation by Licentiate Herver de Corral, fiscal, requesting additional information as to the sums required.

[1] See HC – M 40.

HC – M 43

INQUISITION. Mexico. Records of the trial of Sebastián Suárez, black slave of Maestre Pedro, surgeon, for blasphemy. Mexico, Aug. 16, 1594—Dec. 10, 1596. 36 leaves (27 written, 9 blank).

> Includes testimonies before Inquisitor Lobo Guerrero concerning blasphemies pronounced by Sebastián while in prison; charges made by Martos de Bohorques, fiscal of the Holy Office, against the defendant for blasphemy; confessions of the defendant; and sentence of Sebastián to hear Mass holding a wax candle, wearing a rope around his neck and a clamp on his tongue, to be led through the streets on a horse, and to receive 200 lashes.

HC – M 44

DR. DON JUAN DE SALAMANCA, TREASURER, JUEZ PROVISOR, AND VICAR OF THE CATHEDRAL OF MEXICO. Marriage applications and licenses issued. Mexico, Jan. 14— July 19, 1604. 20 leaves.

> Marriage applications (including petitions and testimonies of freedom to marry) and licenses for:
> 1. Pedro Díaz and Francisca Martínez, Jan. 14–19, 1604.
> 2. Agustín de Soberanes and Ursula de la Cruz, mestizos, Jan. 27–31, 1604.
> 3. Domingo and Polonia, black slaves, Feb. 10–14, 1604.
> 4. Bartolomé de San Juan and Catalina de Melgarejo, Feb. 28—Mar. 1, 1604.
> 5. Pedro Gonzáles and Magdalena de Salcedo, July 14–17, 1604.
> 6. Juan and Juana, black slaves, July 16–19, 1604.

HC – M 45

DON JUAN DE MENDOZA Y LUNA, VICEROY OF MEXICO. Fragment of record of the residencia undertaken by the new Viceroy, Don Juan de Mendoza y Luna, Marqués de Montesclaros, concerning his predecessor, Viceroy Gaspar de Zuñiga y Acevedo, Conde de Monterrey. Mexico, Jan. 29, 1604. 2 leaves.

> Record of bond posted by Melchor de Legazpi and Alonso de Guzmán.

HC – M 46

INQUISITION. Mexico. Records (incomplete) of an investigation of a complaint by Cristina Tsipaqua, Tarascan Indian woman, that Juan Durán, Augustine friar, pueblo of San Felipe, made amorous advances to her after confession. Aranzán and Mexico, Feb. 29, 1608—Nov. 8, 1612. 18 leaves, loose (16 written, 2 blank).

> Includes a letter from Licentiate Cristóbal Plancarte, beneficiado of Aranzán, to Fray Diego Muñoz, Franciscan friar, informing him of the Indian woman's complaint and Fray Diego's response and requesting more details; report of the alleged amorous advances by Juan Durán; denunciation of the affair to the Inquisition and further investigation including testimony of Cristina Tsipaqua given in June 1608; summons of wit-

nesses by Fray Diego, dated October 22, 1612; and a report from Plancarte that Cristina Tsipaqua had died the previous year.[1]

HC – M 47

INQUISITION. Mexico. Records of the investigation of Diego Díaz, Portuguese, accused of bigamy. Mexico and Puebla de los Angeles, July 5, 1608—Feb. 26, 1610. 34 leaves (1 title page, 22 written, 11 blank).

Includes accusations before Alonso Fernández de Santiago, commissary of the Inquisition, against Díaz by Manuel Home for having married Maria de Cardilla, even though he had already been married in Spain; transmittal of records to the Inquisition in Mexico and return of the records to Puebla for further investigations; testimonies taken in Puebla of witnesses, including Juan Sanchez Muñoz, who had come from Avila, Spain, to New Spain with Díaz; report of the escape of Díaz from an obraje where he had been a prisoner and his recapture in Puebla; investigation and report of Fray Juan de Lazcano, superior of the Franciscan monastery in Tlaxcala; and release of Díaz on bond, pending receipt of more information about his first marriage.

HC – M 48

INQUISITION. Mexico. Records of the trial of Diego Alonso Cepero, soldier, for blasphemy. Vera Cruz and Mexico, Sept. 14, 1608—Mar. 23, 1609. 56 leaves (1 title page, 43 written, 12 blank).

Includes testimonies before Fray Baltasar de Morales, superior of the Franciscan monastery and commissary of the Holy Office in Vera Cruz, concerning blasphemies pronounced by Diego Alonso Cepero; orders of the inquisitors Licentiate Alonso de Peralta and Gutierre Bernardo de Quirós and of Dr. Martos de Bohorques, fiscal for the Inquisition, to imprison the defendant and transfer him to Mexico for trial; confessions of Cepero, who maintained he had uttered the blasphemies in a fit of rage; and sentence given to Cepero of exile to China for five years.

HC – M 49

INQUISITION. Mexico. Record of an investigation of Lorenzo López Iñiguez, native of Mexico, for blasphemy. Xochimilco and Mexico, May 16–27, 1609. 34 leaves (1 title page, 16 written, 17 blank).

Includes the accusations of blasphemy made by Dr. Martos de Bohorques, fiscal of the Holy Office, against Lorenzo López Iñiguez and the demand that he be imprisoned in the secret prison of the Inquisition; the voluntary self-denunciation of the defendant for uttering blasphemies when he was in a fit of rage; and testimonies of others, given before Fray Juan de Lazcana in Xochimilco, confirming the blasphemies.

---

[1] Documentation for the period July 1608—Oct. 21, 1612 is missing.

HC – M 50

ALONSO DE AGUILAR CERVANTES, ALCALDE MAYOR OF TLAPA. Records relating to the July 13, 1609, insurrection of the Indians of Tlapa. Tlapa and Mexico, July 14–27, 1609. 8 leaves (1 title page, 7 written).

Includes the alcalde's description of the events of July 13, 1609, when the Indians gathered at the government headquarters voicing offensive comments in Nahuatl, throwing stones, and urging other Indians to come armed with bows and arrows; testimonies of Alonso de Benavides, Alonso de Alabés Avendaño, Antonio López, and Álvaro de Escobar supporting the alcalde's statements; remittance of the report to the Viceroy Don Luis de Velasco; and the Viceroy's request of July 27 for additional information.

HC – M 51

FRANCISCO DE QUINTANADUEÑAS, BOOKKEEPER OF THE MARQUESADO OF OAXACA. Memoranda and extract of an unidentified account book. [1589–1591?]. 13 leaves. (12 written, 1 blank).

Includes memorandum of some items mentioned in a lawsuit between the Marqués del Valle and Francisco de Quintanadueñas, extracts from a Libro Largo, and a memorandum of the Marqués' objections to Quintanadueñas' annotations in the books.

Transcriptions and Translations of Selected Documents

By J. Benedict Warren

Introduction

Four 16th-century documents are presented in transcription and translation in the following pages. Even though they are all related to Hernando Cortés and his son Martín, they are quite varied in character. Two of them are royal decrees. The earlier one, issued by Charles I, granted a coat of arms to Hernando Cortés; the other, from the court of Philip II, renewed and clarified the grant of the Marquesado del Valle to Martín Cortés, son and heir of the conqueror of Mexico. In regard to their physical form, both of these documents were engrossed in calligraphic form on parchment. The headings are illuminated, and the texts are handprinted in a style that is similar to that of the published books of the time.

The most lengthy of the four documents is the record of a lawsuit initiated in 1531 by the attorneys of Hernando Cortés against the Licentiates Juan Ortiz de Matienzo and Diego Delgadillo, oidores or judges of the First Audiencia of New Spain, over the tributes of the Indian town of Huejotzingo, situated across the mountains from Mexico City, toward the east. This document, or more correctly this file of documents, is written in the cursive hand of the attorneys and court clerks of the early 16th century. The quality of the writing varies from the rather careful script of the judicial acts and sentences to the scribbled annotations that the clerks made on the backs of petitions during the hearings. These annotations were later written out in full, a fact which explains the duplication which is apparent in the text. In this court record were placed eight paintings by the Indians of Huejotzingo, which enumerate the tributes they gave to the royal authorities in Mexico City.

The fourth item included here consists of the questionnaires of the prosecution and defense from the trial of Martín Cortés, second Marqués del Valle, on charges of treason in 1566. These questionnaires are part of an extensive trial record concerning a supposed conspiracy to overthrow Spanish royal power in New Spain and to make the young Marqués king. A number of sections from this trial record are contained in the Harkness Collection, although it is far from a complete file. The handwriting of these questionnaires is a comparatively clear cursive hand of the period.

In transcribing these items we have followed the moderately paleographic model established by Stella R. Clemence in her published transcriptions of documents from the Peruvian section of the Harkness Collection.[1] Abbreviations are written out,

---

[1] *The Harkness Collection in the Library of Congress. Documents from Early Peru, the Pizarros and the Almagros, 1531–1578,* translated and edited by Stella R. Clemence (Washington, 1936).

eliminating the use óf superscript letters, but the supplied letters are not italicized. Where a tilde was used over a vowel in the manuscript to indicate an "n" following the vowel, the "n" has been supplied in the text and the tilde has been dropped. In most cases the elisions of the manuscript have been retained (e.g., "della" for "de ella", and "questa" for "que esta"). Exceptions to this rule have been made, however, for cases in which particular confusion might arise. For example, "en el" is used rather than "ẽl", and "mi el" where it was elided to "mil".

Punctuation and capitalization have not ordinarily been supplied within the text unless they seemed to be clearly indicated in the manuscript, but capital letters have been used at the beginning of paragraphs and periods at the end, even when they are not used in the original. Further, proper names have been capitalized, even though this rarely occurs in the manuscript.

In translating the documents, it was sometimes difficult to make an easily readable translation and at the same time remain true to the tone and sense of the original. The documents vary from the polished but ponderous style of the formal royal decrees to the on-the-spot translation of the judicial testimony of Indians. Some of the material is not in good Spanish and thus cannot be accurately translated into good English. Breaks and changes in direction of the thought occur in midsentence, for example, and these must be reflected in the translation. The secretarial notes of the court clerks have been translated as notes, rarely in complete sentences.

The description of Cortés' coat of arms was translated into ordinary English rather than the technical language of heraldry to make it understandable to a wider audience, at the risk of possibly losing a degree of precision.

Because of limitations of time, it was decided that the text should not be annotated any further than absolutely necessary. Such commentary as seemed necessary has been included in the text in brackets.

I wish to acknowledge the support and assistance of Earl J. Pariseau, acting chief of the Latin American, Portuguese, and Spanish Division, and the staff of the division, as well as the staff of the Manuscript Division of the Library of Congress. Special recognition and thanks are due to my wife Patricia for her assistance and advice, to G. Micheal Riley of Marquette University for his help with place names, and to Mary Ellis Kahler, assistant chief of the Latin American, Portuguese, and Spanish Division, for her long hours of painstaking editorial work.

J. Benedict Warren
University of Maryland

Grant of Coat of Arms to Hernando Cortés
1525

[*Cover*]

59

Titulo de armas que su Magestad dio al Illustrisimo señor don Hernando Cortes, Marques del Valle.

[*a few illegible words*]

[*rubrica*]

Fue expedida esta merced en 7 de Marzo de 1525.

1°

[*60*] Don Carlos por la divina clemencia i emperador semper agusto rey de Alemaña, Doña Juana su madre y el mismo Don Carlos por la gracia de Dios rreyes de Castilla de Leon de Aragon de las dos Secilias de Jerusalem de Nabarra de Granada de Toledo de Valencia de Galizia de Mallorcas de Sebilla de Cerdeña de Cordoua de Corcega de Murcia de Jaen de los Algarbes de Algezira de Gibraltar E de las yslas de Canaria y de las Yndias yslas tierra firme de Mar Oceano condes de Barcelona Señores de Biscaya e de Molina duques de Athenas y de Neopatria condes de rruisellon y de Cerdania, marqueses de Oriztan y de Gociano archduques de Avstria duques de Borgoña y de Bravante Condes de Flandes y de Tirol, Etcetera; Por quanto por parte de vos Hernando Cortes nuestro governador y capitan general de la Nueva España y provincias della nos fue hecha rrelacion que entre muchos y grandes seruicios que uos aveys hecho en la pacificacion y poblacion de la dicha Nueva España y provincias della que dizque en tiempo de tress años sujetastes y aplicastes a nuestro Seruicio y señorio mas de ocho cientas leguas de tierra poblada de mucha gente que nos rreconocen por supremos i vniversales señores que vos el dicho Hernando Cortes fuistes desde la ysla Fernandina con vn armada a la dicha Nueva España con los españoles que con vos llevabades los quales siendo ynformados que en ella avia vn gran Señor y mucha multitud de gente ovieron temor y contradixeron vuestro proposito que hera entrar la tierra adentro afirmando ser mejor estar en la costa de la mar y cerca de los nabios que llevastes para os socorrer dellos y que viendo vos que los nabios serian cabsa de ympedir vuestra yntencion y los españoles con las espaldas dellos no poner todas sus fuerças en los peligros

Patent of arms which His Majesty gave to the Most Illustrious Lord Don Hernando Cortés, Marqués del Valle.

[*rubric*]

This grant was issued on March 7, 1525.

Don Carlos, by the divine clemency, Emperor ever august and King of Germany; Doña Juana and the same Don Carlos, by the grace of God, Kings of Castile, of León, of Aragon, of the two Sicilies, of Jerusalem, of Navarre, of Granada, of Toledo, of Valencia, of Galicia, of the Majorcas, of Seville, of Sardinia, of Córdoba, of Corsica, of Murcia, of Jaén, of the Algarve, of Algeciras, of Gibraltar, and of the Canary Islands, and of the Indies, Islands and mainland of the Ocean Sea; Counts of Barcelona; Lords of Biscay and of Molina; Dukes of Athens and Neopatria; Counts of Roussillon and Cerdagne; Marqueses of Oristano and Gociano; Archdukes of Austria; Dukes of Burgundy and Brabant; Counts of Flanders and Tirol, et cetera:

On the part of you, Hernando Cortés, our governor and captain general of the New Spain and its provinces, a report was made to us that among the many and great services that you have done in the pacification and colonization of the said New Spain and its provinces, it is reported that in a period of three years you subjected and attached to our service and dominion more than eight hundred leagues of land, populated with many people who recognize us as supreme and universal lords. You, the said Hernando Cortés, went from the Fernandine Island [*Cuba*] with a fleet to the said New Spain with the Spaniards whom you took with you. They, upon being informed that in that land there was a great lord and a great multitude of people, became fearful and contradicted your intention of going into the land. They asserted that it would be better to be on the seacoast near the ships that you brought, in order to support yourselves from them. And you, seeing that the ships would be an obstacle to your intention and that as long as the Spaniards had them at their backs they

que se ofreciesen hezistes dar con los nabios a la costa para que se deshiziesen y quebrasen y los españoles perdiesen esperança de ser socorridos dellos y que entrando quarenta leguas la tierra adentro con trezientos españoles a pie y quinze a cavallo y ocho cientos yndios amigos vuestros os salieron al camino de vna provincia mucho nu[*60v*]mero de henemigos Con los quales peleastes muchos dias y os tuvieron cercado y puesto en tan estrema necesidad que vos fue muchas vezes por los españoles rrequerido que os volviesedes a la costa de la mar diziendo que vuestra empresa hera muy temeraria y que vos por los aplacar hos haziades tan compañero y familiar de cada vno que determinaron que pues vos queriades morir que ellos tanbien se pornian a la muerte contra los henemygos y dizque peleastes de tal manera con ellos que al fin los traxistes a nuestro seruicio y obidiencia y que viendo los naturales desta provincia que se dize Tascala que vuestra yntencion hera de yr a la gran cibdad de Tenustican fuistes mucho ymportunado por ellos y por los españoles que no fuesedes a aquella cibdad porque estaba fundada sobre agua y tenia muchas puentes levadizas y el señor y naturales della heran gente que nunca tratavan ni guardavan verdad y con astucias y traiciones se havian hecho tan poderosos que casi todas aquellas provincias heran suyas y que no enbargante esto fuistes y entrastes en la dicha cibdad de Tenustitan y os distes tan buena manera que sin escandolo ni alboroto tomastes en vuestro poder al señor della y hezistes que el y sus vasallos nos diesen la obidiencia y señorio de la dicha tierra y estando asi trabaxando que todas aquellas provincias fuesen nuestros vasallos y vos dixesen y descubriesen otros secretos y cosas para nos lo escreuir y hazer saber tovistes nueva que en la costa de la mar avia ciertos nabios y dizque vos salistes de la dicha cibdad y venistes a la dicha costa a ver que gente heran y si llevauan provisiones nuestras y en saliendo luego los yndios de la cibdad se rrevelaron contra nos y con paz simulada os tornaron a rrecebir dentro con novecientos españoles que llevabades y siendo entrados levantaron todas las puentes y começaron a pelear con vos la qual pelea dizque duro seys dias en que fueron muertos y heridos muchos españoles y viendo vos el poco rremedio que avia para los que quedavan determinastes de rronper por los he[ne]migos y saliros de la dicha cibdad en la qual salida ovo tanto peligro que murieron de los dichos españoles que asi teniades con vos trezientos y cinquenta de cavallo y a los que quedaron les fue forçado yr peleando y defendiendose por tierra de los henemigos mas de veynte leguas en las quales siempre vos fueron dado alcance y que en todas ellas vos el dicho Hernando Cortes levastes la rretaguarda donde padecistes mucho peligro y vos hirieron a vos y al cavallo en que yvades tress o quatro vezes y el dia postrero que yvades a salir fuera de los

would not put forth their full efforts in the dangers that might arise, had the ships beached so that they would be destroyed and broken and the Spaniards would lose the hope of being supported by them.

Then you went inland for forty leagues with three hundred Spaniards on foot and fifteen on horseback and eight hundred Indians who were friendly to you, and in one province a great number of enemies came out against you on the road. You fought with them for many days, and they had you surrounded and placed in such extreme necessity that many times the Spaniards begged you to return to the seacoast, saying that your undertaking was very foolhardy. In order to quiet their fears you became such a companion and close friend of each one of them that they determined that, since you wished to die, they would also expose themselves to death against the enemy. It is reported that you fought with them in such a manner that you finally brought them to our service and obedience.

When the natives of that province, which is called Tlaxcala, saw that your intention was to go to the great city of Tenochtitlan, you were greatly importuned by them and by the Spaniards that you should not go to that city because it was built on the water and it had many drawbridges, and the lord and natives of it were people who never spoke nor kept the truth, and by acts of cunning and treachery they had made themselves so powerful that almost all of those provinces were theirs.

In spite of this you went and entered into the said city of Tenochtitlan. And you acted in such a good manner that, without public commotion or disturbance, you took the lord of it into your power and you brought it about that he and his vassals should give us their obedience and the dominion over the land. And while you were thus laboring that all of those provinces should become our vassals and should tell and reveal to you other matters and secrets so that you might write and make it known to us, you received news that along the seacoast there were certain ships, and you reportedly left the said city and came to the said coast to see what people they were and whether they carried writs from us.

And as soon as you left the city, the Indians of it rebelled against us, but with simulated peace they received you into the city once more with nine hundred Spaniards whom you brought with you. And after you had entered, they raised all of the bridges and began to fight with you. It is reported that this fight lasted for six days and that many Spaniards were killed and wounded in it. And when you saw what little help there was for those who were left, you determined to break through the enemy and leave the said city. During this departure there was such great danger that three hundred and fifty of the Spanish horsemen whom you had with you were killed, and those who were left had to make their way, fighting and defending themselves, through the land of the enemies for more than twenty leagues, during which you were always within their range. And during the whole twenty leagues you, the said Hernando Cortés, supported the rearguard where you underwent great danger, and they injured you and the horse on which you were riding three or four times.

terminos de los henemigos se junto todo el poder dellos creyendo que alli acabarian
a los españoles y vos començaron a cercar de todas partes y pelearon con vos muy
[61] osadamente y que vos el dicho Hernando Cortes peleastes de tal manera en
aquel rrecuentro que matastes vn capitan muy principal de los henemigos con la
muerte del qual luego afloxaron y dieron lugar a que vos fuesedes y vos y los dichos
españoles vos rretruxistes a la provincia de Taxcala a donde los naturales della vos
rreçibieron bien y llegados a esta provincia como vos y los españoles o[s — *between
lines*] vistes tan rronpidos y desbaratados y tantas provincia y barbaros contra vosotros
dizque de secreto los principales de vuestra compania os amonestaron y avn
rrequerieron que os volviesedes al puerto de la villa de la Vera Cruz donde vos
aviades començado a hazer vna fortaleza y con ella y con los nabios terniades
seguridad de las vidas porque haziendose otra cosa creyan que en ninguna manera
escaparia ninguno dellos especialmente que dizque temiades que los naturales desta
provincia de Taxcala donde estabades se confederarian con los de Tenustitan y asi
seriades mas presto destruidos a lo qual vos nuca distes lugar poniendoles delante
rrazones y cabsas por donde no conbenia salir de alli mas antes volber sobre los
henemigos porque dizque si a la costa de la mar os fuerades nuca aquellas partes
se pudieran tornar a rreduzir porque ydo vos y los españoles oviera mas oportunidad
para la confederacion de todos los naturales y estando ellos conformes no bastara
ningun poder para los entrar y de aqui fuistes luego a vna provincia que se dize
Tepeaca que confinaba con esta otra porque los naturales della estaban Revelados
y que precediendo primeramente todo lo necesario para los ynducir a paz y seruicio
nuestro les hecistes la guerra y conpelidos por ella nos dieron la obidiencia y que
despues de rreducida esta provincia rrebolvistes sobre las provincias de Mexico y
Tenustitan que estan en torno de la laguna y con quarenta de cavallo y seiss cientos
a pie y con jente de los amigos entrastes por las dichas provincias y en este camino
hezistes muchas cosas en nuestro seruicio vos y la dicha gente que llevauades y por
yndustria vuestra se rreduzieron a nuestra obidiencia muchas provincias y poblaciones
de la laguna y comarca della y despues de las aver rreduzido dizque luego determinastes de poner cerco sobre la cibdad de Tenustitan porque ya teniades alguna
mas copia de gente y cavallos y aviades hecho treze fustas para la conbatir por el
agua que fue muy gran ardid e ynbencion vuestra para se poder tomar aquella
cibdad en que estaba toda la paz y sosiego de aquellas partes E que puesto el cerco
por la tierra vos el dicho Hernando Cortes vos metistes por el agua en las dichas
fustas con trezientos españoles [61v] y fuistes rrequerido que en ninguna manera lo
hiziesedes porque contra ellas se esparaba la mayor rresistencia y peligro y que no lo
quesistes hazer por ser cosa lo de las fustas muy ymportante y seguistes con ellas

And the next day, as you were preparing to leave the territory of the enemy, they brought together all of their forces, believing that here they would finish off the Spaniards, and they surrounded you on all sides and fought with you very boldly. And you, the said Hernando Cortés, fought so well in that encounter that you killed a very outstanding captain of the enemy. With his death they immediately lost heart and gave way so that you could go on. And you and the said Spaniards withdrew to the province of Tlaxcala, where the natives received you well.

When you arrived in that province and when you and the Spaniards saw that you were so routed and defeated and that there were so many provinces and barbarians against you, it is reported that the leaders of your company secretly exhorted you and even demanded that you should return to the port of the town of Vera Cruz, where you had begun to build a fortress and because of it and the ships you would have safety for your lives, because they thought that if you did anything else, in no way would any of them escape. They thought this especially because reportedly you were afraid that the natives of this province of Tlaxcala, where you were, would unite with those of the province of Tenochtitlan and thus you would be the more easily destroyed.

To this you never gave way, but you placed before them causes and reasons why it would not be good to leave there but that rather you should turn upon your enemies, because you felt that if you were to go away to the seacoast, those regions could never again be subjected, because once you and the Spaniards had left, there would be greater opportunity for a confederation of all of the natives, and if they were in agreement, no force would be adequate for entering among them.

From there you went to a province that is called Tepeaca, which borders upon this other one, because the natives of it had rebelled. And after first doing everything necessary to bring them to peace and our service, you made war on them. Compelled by this, they gave us their obedience.

After this province had been subjugated, you turned once more against the provinces of Mexico and Tenochtitlan which are around the lake. And with forty horsemen and six hundred foot soldiers and with warriors from among the friendly nations, you entered through the said provinces. And along this way you and the soldiers whom you took with you did many things in our service. And by your industry many provinces and settlements of the lake and its region were subjected to our obedience.

After you had subjugated them, it is reported that you immediately determined to lay siege on the city of Tenochtitlan because by now you had a greater number of men and horses and you had constructed thirteen lateen-rigged lighters in order to fight them on the water. This was a very great stratagem and invention on your part in order to be able to take that city in which was all the peace and tranquility of those regions. And having laid siege by land, you, the said Hernando Cortés, attacked by water in the said lighters with three hundred Spaniards. And you were urgently requested not to do it by any means because the greatest resistance and danger were expected against the boats. But you were not willing to do this, because the action of

y vos fuistes a meter entre los henemigos y con muy gran pelygro desenbarcastes junto a la cibdad donde muchos dias peleastes mano a mano con los henemigos muy peligrosamente y que de esta vez tuvistes cercada la dicha cibdad de Tenustitan setenta y cinco dias donde vos y los espanoles y los yndios nuestros vasallos que os ayudavan padecistes ynfenitos travajos y peligros a los quales dizque vos siempre hallastes delante y fueron heridos y muertos muchos dellos y puestos en tanto estremo que platicavan muchas vezes que darian por bien sufrido todo el trabajo pasado si levantasedes el cerco porque les parecia cosa ymposible poder se tomar la cibdad y que vos hovistes en el dicho cerco en tal manera que ni por necesidad de manteni- mientos ni porque vna vez fuistes rronpido y desbaratado y vos mataron cinquenta españoles y otras vezes vos herian y matavan la gente no dexastes de conbatir a los de la cibdad hasta tanto que a cabo de los setenta y cinco dias prendistes al señor y principales y capitanes de la cibdad la qual juntamente con otras muchas provincias fueron rreduzidas a nuestro seruicio y distes fin y conclusion a ello.

E nos suplicastes y pedistes por merced vos diesemos y señalasemos armas para que las podais traher y traigais demas de las armas que al presente teneis de vuestros predecesores y nos acatando los muchos trabajos y peligros y aventuras que en lo Suso dicho pasastes y porque de vos y de vuestros seruicios quede perpetua memoria y vos y vuestros descendientes seais mas honrrados por la presente vos hazemos merced y queremos que demas de las armas que asi teneis de vuestro linaje podais tener y traher por vuestras armas propias y conocidas vn escudo que en el medio del a la mano derecha en la parte de arriba aya vna aguila negra de doss cabeças en campo blanco que son las armas de nuestro ymperio y en la otra meitad del dicho medio escudo a la parte de abaxo vn leon dorado en campo colorado en memoria que vos el dicho Hernando Cortes y por vuestra yndustria y esfuerco truxistes las cosas al estado arriba dicho y en la meytad del otro medio escudo de la mano yzquierda a la parte de arriba tress coronas de oro en campo negro la vna sobre las dos en memoria de tress Señores de la gran cibdad de Tenustitan y sus provincias que vos vencistes que fue el primero Motecçuma que fue muerto por los yndios teniendole vos preso y Cuetaoacin su hermano que sucedio en el señorio y se rrevelo contra nos y os echo de la dicha cibdad [62] y el otro que sucedio en el dicho señorio Guauctemucin y sostubo la dicha rrevelion hasta que vos le vencistes y prendistes y en la otra meytad del dicho medio escudo de la mano yzquerda a la parte de abaxo podais traher la cibdad de Tenustitan armada sobre agua en memoria que por fuerça de armas la ganastes y sujetastes a nuestro señorio y por orla del dicho escudo en campo amarillo siete capitanes y señores de siete provincias y poblaciones que estan en la laguna y en torno della que se ·rrevelaron contra nos y los vencistes y prendistes en la dicha cibdad de Tenustitan apresionados y atados

the boats was a matter of great importance. And you continued with them and proceeded to plunge in among the enemy, and with great danger you disembarked next
to the city where for many days you fought very dangerously hand-to-hand with the
enemy.

And starting from this time, you had the said city of Tenochtitlan under siege for
seventy-five days. There you and the Spaniards and the Indians, our vassals, who
helped you, suffered infinite labors and dangers in which reportedly you were always
in the forefront. And many of them were killed and wounded and brought to such an
extreme that many times they expressed the fact that they would consider all of the
past labors as well suffered if you would raise the siege, because it seemed impossible
to them that the city could be taken. But you conducted yourself in the said siege in
such a way that, neither for need of provisions nor because they broke through and
defeated you once and killed fifty of your Spaniards and other times they killed and
wounded your men, you did not leave off fighting with the men of the city until
finally at the end of the seventy-five days you captured the lord and leading men and
captains of the city. And the city and many other provinces were subjected to our
service, and you brought it all to an end and conclusion.

And you asked and entreated us that as a favor we would give and set aside for
you a coat of arms so that you could bear it besides the coat of arms of your ancestors
which you have at the present. And we, respecting the many labors, dangers, and
adventures which you underwent as stated above, and so that there might remain a
perpetual memorial of you and your services and that you and your descendants
might be more fully honored, by the present letter we grant to you, and it is our will,
that besides the coat of arms of your lineage which you have, you may have and bear
as your coat of arms, known and recognized, a shield on which, on the upper part of
the half on the right-hand side, there will be a black eagle with two heads on a white
field, which are the arms of our empire; and on the other half of the said half shield,
on the lower part, a golden lion on a red field, in memory of the fact that you, the
said Hernando Cortés, by your industry and effort brought matters to the state
described above. And on half of the other half shield, the upper part on the left-hand
side, are three gold crowns on a black field, one above the other two, in memory of the
three lords of the great city of Tenochtitlan and its provinces whom you conquered,
of whom the first was Moctezuma, who was killed by the Indians while you held him
prisoner, then Cuitláhuac, his brother who succeeded him in his authority and
rebelled against us and cast you out of the said city, and Cuauhtémoc, the other who
succeeded in the said authority and who sustained the said rebellion until you
defeated and apprehended him. And on the other half of the said half shield, on the
lower part of the left-hand side, you may bear the city of Tenochtitlan fortified on
the water, in memory of the fact that by force of arms you conquered it and
subjected it to our dominion; and for the border of the said shield, on a yellow field,
seven captains and lords of the seven provinces and settlements which are in and
around the lake, who rebelled against us and whom you defeated and captured in the
said city of Tenochtitlan, to be shown as prisoners bound with a chain which shall be

con vna cadena que se venga a cerrar con vn candado debaxo del dicho escudo y encima del vn yelmo cerrado con su tinble en vn escudo a tal como este las [*the coat of arms is painted in the middle of the page, beginning here*] quales dichas armas vos damos por vuestras armas conocidas y senaladas demas de las armas que asi teneys de vuestros predecesores y queremos y es nuestra merced y voluntad que vos y vuestros hijos y descendientes y dellos y de cada vno dellos las ayais y tengais por vuestras armas conocidas y señaladas y como tales las podais y puedan traher en vuestros Reposteros y casas y en los de cada vno de los dichos vuestros hijos y descendientes y en las otras partes que vos y ellos quisieredes y por bien tovieredes y por esta nuestra carta o por su traslado siñado de scrivano publico mandamos a los ylustrisimos ynfantes nuestros muy caros y amados hijos y hermanos y a los ynfantes duques marqueses condes rricos homes maestres de las hordenes priores comendadores y sub comendadores alcaides de los castillos y casas fuertes y llanas e a los del nuestro consejo y oydores de las nuestras abdiencias y a todos los corregidores asistentes y governadores y alcaldes y alguaziles de la nuestra casa y corte y chancelleria y a todos los concejos rregidores alcaldes y alguaziles de la nuestra casa y corte y chancelleria y a todos los concejos rregidores alcaldes y alguaziles merinos prevostes y otras justicias E juezes qualesquier asi de estos nuestros Reynos y señorios como de la dicha [*62v*] Nueva España E yndias y yslas y tierra firme del mar oceano asy a los que agora son como a los que seran de aqui adelante y a cada vno y qualquier dellos en sus lugares y juredizciones que vos guarden y cumplan y hagan guardar y cumplir a vos y a los dichos vuestros hijos y descendientes dellos la dicha merced que vos hazemos de las dichas armas E las ayan y tengan por vuestras armas conocidas y señaladas y como tales vos las dexen y consientan poner y traer y tener a vos y a los dichos vuestros hijos y descendientes y dellos: y contra ello ni contra cosa alguna ni parte dello enbargo ni contrario alguna vos no pongan ni consientan poner en tiempo alguno ni por alguna manera So pena de la nuestra merced y de cinquenta mill maravedis para la nuestra camara a cada vno que lo contrario hiziere. E demas mandamos al ome que les esta nuestra carta mostrare que los emplaze que parescan ante nos en la nuestra Corte do quier que nos seamos del dia que los emplazare hasta quinze dias primeros siguientes So la dicha pena so la qual mandamos a qualquier escribano publico que para esto fuere llamado que de ende al que ge[*sic-se*] la mostrare testimonio Sinado con su sino porque nos sepamos en como se cumple nuestro mandado dada en la villa de Madrid a siete dias del mes de março año del nascimiento de nuestro Salvador Ihu Xpo [*Jesu Christo*] de mill y quinientos E veynte E cinco años.

YO EL RREY

closed with a lock beneath the shield, and above it a closed helmet with its crest, on a shield like the one shown here.

This coat of arms we give you as your own, acknowledged and specified as yours, besides the coat of arms that you have from your ancestors. And we desire, and it is our will and pleasure, that you and your children and descendants and their descendants and those of each and every one of them should have and hold them as your acknowledged and specified arms. And as such you and they can bear them on your ornamental trappings and houses and on those of each of your said children and descendants and in other places where you and they may wish and consider it good. And by this our letter or by a copy of it signed by a notary public, we command the most illustrious infantes, our very dear sons and brothers, and the infantes, dukes, marquesses, counts, grandees, masters of the orders, knight-commanders and sub-commanders, wardens of castles and of houses with moats and of country houses, and the members of our council and oidores of our audiencias, and all of the corregidores, assistants, governors, alcaldes, and constables of our house, court and chancery, and all of the councils, aldermen, alcaldes, and constables *of our house, court and chancery, and all of the councils, aldermen, alcaldes, and constables* [*the italicized words appear to be an unintentional repetition by the scribe*], judges of the sheepwalks, provosts, and other justices and judges of whatever kind, both of these our realms and dominions and of the said New Spain and Indies and islands and mainland of the Ocean Sea, both those who are at the present and who will be henceforth and to each and every one of them in their places and jurisdictions, that they observe and fulfill for you and see to it that for you and your said sons and their descendants the said grant that we make to you of the said coat of arms be observed and fulfilled and that they have and hold them as your acknowledged and specified coat of arms, and that as such they allow and consent that you and your said sons and descendants and their descendants place, bear, and have them.

And against this or against any part or matter of it they shall not place nor consent that there be placed any obstacle or impediment for you at any time or in any manner, under penalty of our favor and of fifty thousand maravedís for our exchequer for everyone who may do the contrary. And moreover, we command the man who shows them this our letter that he summon them to appear before us in our court, wherever we may be, within the first fifteen days immediately following the day on which he shall have summoned them under the said penalty. Under the same penalty we command to whatever notary public may be called upon for this purpose that when he is shown it he must give an affidavit signed with his sign, so that we may know to what extent our command is fulfilled. Given in the town of Madrid on the seventh day of the month of March in the year of the birth of Our Savior Jesus Christ one thousand five hundred and twenty-five.

I THE KING

Yo Francisco de los Couos secretario de sus cesarea y catholicas Magestades la fize
screuir por su mandado [*rubicra*]
Registrada. Joan de Samano [*rubrica*]
             Fr. G. Episcopus Oxomensis [*rubrica*]
             Doctor Caruajal [*rubrica*]
             Horbyna por Chanciller [*rubrica*]
Derechos de sello cl [*rubrica de Horbyna*]

[*In a later hand, on unnumbered leaf following 62*] En 11 de noviembre de 1733,
Por mandado del señor Don Juan Esteuan de Yturbide Cauallero del orden de
Santiago Gouernador del Estado, saque vn testimonio de este titulo: Y para que
conste pongo esta Razon.

I Francisco de los Cobos, secretary of His Imperial and Their Catholic Majesties, had it written by their command. [*rubric*]
Registered. JUAN DE SAMANO [*rubric*]

        FR. G[ARCÍA] BISHOP OF OSMA [*rubric*]

        DOCTOR CARVAJAL [*rubric*]

        URBINA PRO-CHANCELLOR [*rubric*]

Fees for the seal 150 [*rubric of Urbina*]

On November 11, 1733, by the command of the Lord Don Juan Estevan de Iturbide, a knight of the Order of Saint James, Governor of the Estate, I made a copy of this patent; and so that there may be evidence of it, I place this note here. [*Written in a later hand*]

The Harkness 1531 Huejotzingo Codex

Introduction

Document no. 2 of the Mexican Manuscripts in the Harkness Collection is a portion of a lawsuit which the conqueror of Mexico, Hernando Cortés, Marqués del Valle, brought against members of the first audiencia, Nuño de Guzmán, president, and Licentiates Juan Ortiz de Matienzo and Diego Delgadillo, oidores, in 1531–32. The manuscript is particularly significant because it contains testimony by Aztec Indians from the community of Huejotzingo, accompanied by eight native drawings, the contents of which they explained in the course of the judicial hearing.

First mention of this particular Indian pictorial material appeared in an article by Alfonso Toro in 1925, in which he discussed the "Códice del archivo de los Duques de Monteleone y Marqueses del Valle." Because Toro mentioned the Monteleone family in passing, the scattered and generally unpublished technical literature on Mexican Indian pictorial documents adopted a shortened form of his title, "Codex Monteleone." To honor the donor and to provide a more descriptive name, this codex will henceforth be designated by a title giving the place and date of composition: Harkness 1531 Huejotzingo Codex.

Previously its pictorial elements have been only partially published. The transcription of one small portion of the document made by Francisco Fernández del Castillo has appeared in print, but there have been no extended published commentaries or scholarly discussions. The Harkness 1531 Huejotzingo Codex is of special significance not only because it dates from extremely early in the post-Conquest period but also because it is within a context of detailed, native explanatory material, often, if not usually, lacking for such documents.

Provenance

Among those who were called as witnesses in this lawsuit were Indians. To aid in their testimony, Cortés' lawyer entered into the record eight Indian drawings, which they explained through an interpreter.

The colonial Spanish system of justice differed greatly from judicial practices in

the Anglo-Saxon tradition. In Hispanic procedures, charges were brought, and a questionnaire was devised by the plaintiff, to be answered by witnesses whom he or his lawyers chose. The testimony was taken from them without the defendants necessarily being present. When the scribe had recorded the testimony, it was then forwarded to the defendants, who were given a stipulated period of time to formulate a questionnaire of their own and bring in witnesses to answer their queries. When the judges were satisfied that both sides had presented sufficient testimony, they rendered judgment in Mexico City, but if the case involved a substantial sum of money or land or an important public official, they could allow the case to be sent to the Council of the Indies in Spain, which rendered final judgment in the name of the King.

The present document is fragmentary in that only the testimony from the witnesses favorable to the Cortés side of the suit was recorded. It is not known whether the defendants actually called witnesses, but judgment was rendered against them and was immediately appealed to the Council of the Indies. The final determination of the case is unknown. Although the outcome would be of some interest to historians, the lack of further information on the case does not materially affect the value of the native Indian materials.

For many years these rich and important materials were housed in the Hospital de la Inmaculada Concepción y de Jesús Nazareno in Mexico City, together with other documents related to the Cortés family and estates. The documents passed as legacies to Cortés' direct descendants, the Italian dukes of Monteleone. Their agents in Mexico City from time to time permitted properly introduced scholars to use the manuscripts. Thus the great, early 19th-century Mexican historian Lucas Alamán was given access to the papers, and much of his important work on the period just after conquest is based on them. He correctly described and published a version of the Cortés coat of arms, the original of which is in the Harkness Collection.

The materials forming the Harkness 1531 Huejotzingo Codex remained in these private archives until at least 1925 when Toro saw them and published his brief note, accompanied by Fernández del Castillo's transcription, which has been found paleographically defective when compared with the original document. The collection was acquired for Mr. Harkness by the well-known dealer A. S. W. Rosenbach in 1927 and 1928.

The Mexican Government acquired the remainder of the Cortés papers, which at present are housed in the Archivo General de la Nación, under the title "Papeles de Hospital de Jesús" (papers of the Hospital of Jesus). They are, of course, freely available to scholars, although they have not been extensively exploited. The materials in Mexico also contain native pictorial documents, but of a later date.

The Indian Paintings

A general description of Document no. 2 has been provided above. The Codex itself consists of eight native paintings of various sizes, all on amatl, probably a fig-based, native paper, with symbols principally in black and red ink. These papers, which are in a good state of preservation, are grouped together and sewed between

leaves 38 verso and 39 recto in the 79 leaves of the total document. On the reverse of each the Spanish clerk of the court, Alonso Valverde, placed his rubric, as well as numbers I through VIII, with a Spanish language note or gloss. Only painting VI has a minor gloss on the obverse. The paintings do not follow the order in which they are mentioned in the manuscript. Table 1 provides detailed descriptions of the paintings.

In an unpublished summary of these materials, Miss Stella Clemence indicated that paintings I, II, and VIII show the cost to the Indians for their own food and for material they supplied in daily work on construction in Mexico City during the regime of the defendants. The services included work on the irrigation ditch, the houses and monasteries of Saint Dominic, and the houses where Matienzo and Delgadillo were living, later occupied by Licentiates Juan de Salmeron and Francisco de Ceynos. The Indians not only supplied the stone, lumber, lime, and other materials but also transported them on their backs. Shown in these three paintings are the symbols for clothing, red chile peppers, sage, maize, turkeys, lumber, stone, and some unidentified objects.

Painting III shows 20 items of fine cotton clothes ordered by Nuño de Guzmán and delivered to Licentiate Matienzo. Painting IV depicts the fine fabrics made from red rabbit fur for Licentiate Matienzo. Paintings V and VI indicate warrior's equipment and other items which were furnished by Huejotzingo for Nuño de Guzmán's expedition of conquest in New Galicia. Painting VII records the tributes of maize which the Indians of Huejotzingo brought to the officials of the royal treasury in Mexico City in 1529 and 1530.

HOWARD F. CLINE

Summary Description

Scribe's Number	Order in Manuscript	Size in inches	Reverse side Spanish gloss	Colors
I	1	17½ x 18	[Una cruz]. Donde aqui empieça lo q. han dado a hoy dos e presidente asta este papel [illegible word] q. es de las obras q. han hecho a Santo Domingo. I de Guaxucingo. [Rubric]	
II	6	10 x 15	De Guaxucingo. II. dos. [Rubric]	Peppers; red, 6 triangles: tan.
III	4	7¾ x 19	Tres de Guaxucingo. [Rubric]	Designs: red, with combinations of yellow, blue, green, and red.
IV	5	8¾ x 16½	de Guaxucingo IV cuatro [Rubric]	Designs: red, Pantli: black, edged with red.
V	7	16¼ x 19	de Guaxucingo. V. cinco. [Rubric]	Blue, red, yellow, green, tan, black.
VI	8	16½ x 17	de Guaxucingo. VI. seys	black only

VII	3	9½ x 17	[una cruz] Aqui vera V.S. el maiz q. llevaron a los oydores q. son cxvi çotli en. q. se montan 6300 cargas. Este fue todo del maiz de V.S. Lo q. esta colorado es otra quenta y porq. yo lo avia sacado y lo dexe con las comidas dos oydores pasados no vamos otros papeles. VII siete de Guaucingo. [Rubric]	Maize: red and black; Granary: tan.
VIII	2	10 x 15	[una cruz] Este es la memoria y escrito q. han hecho en las hobras de Santo Domingo. y no ay hotro papel sino [illegible word] Santo Domingo y todos estos son el presidente e oydores. Ocho. VIII de Guaxucingo. [Rubric]	

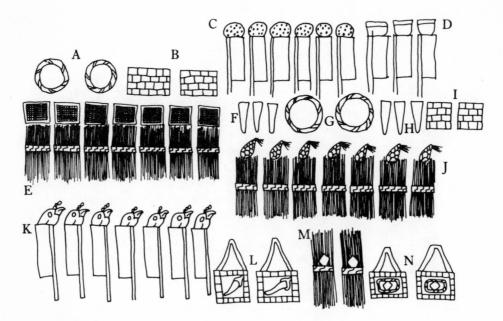

Painting I (scribe's number), no. 1 in manuscript

A.   2 loads of lime
B.   2 piles of adobe bricks for construction
C.   6 x 20 = 120 loads of beans (frijoles?)
D.   3 x 20 = 60?
E.   7 x 400 = 2,800 loads of cloth at 20 each
F.   3 loads of stones
G.   2 loads of lime
H.   3 loads of stones
I.   2 piles of adobe bricks
J.   7 x 400 = 2,800 loads of maize
K.   7 x 20 = 140 turkeys
L.   2 x 8,000 = 16,000 chile peppers
M. 2 x 400 = 800 ?
N.   2 x 8,000 = 16,000 ?

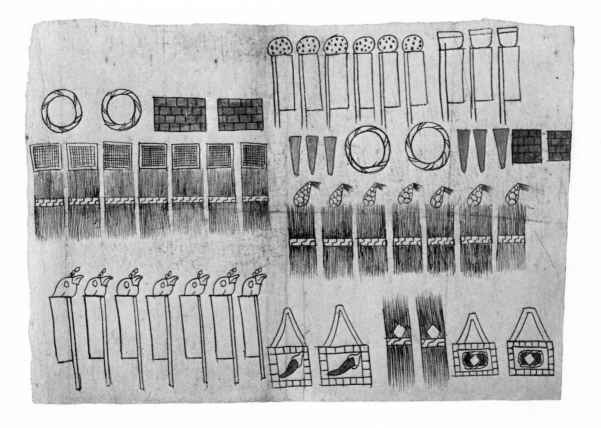

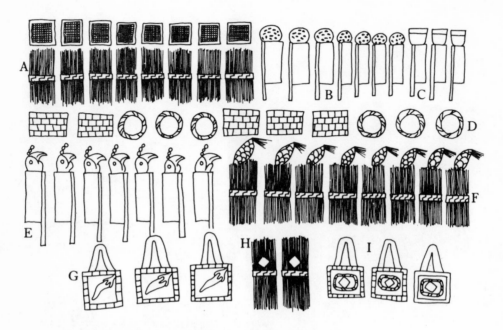

Painting II (scribe's number), no. 6 in manuscript

A. 8 x 400 = 3,200 loads of cloths at 20 each

B. 7 x 20 = 140 loads of beans (frijoles?)

C. 3 x 20 = 60 ?

D. 5 piles of adobe bricks, 6 loads of lime

E. 7 x 20 = 140 turkeys

F. 8 x 400 = 3,200 loads of maize

G. 3 x 8,000 = 2,400 chile peppers

H. 2 x 400 = 800 ?

I. 3 x 8,000 = 24,000 ?

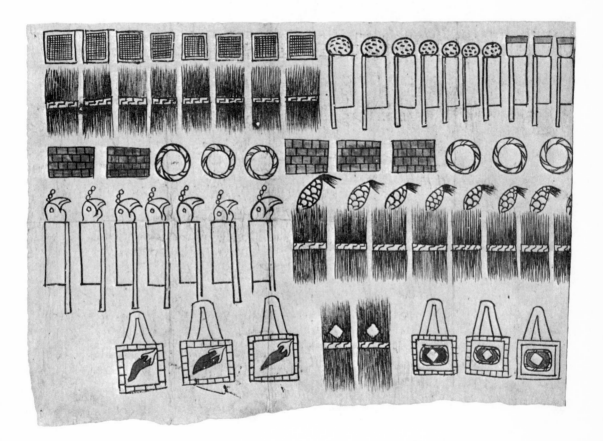

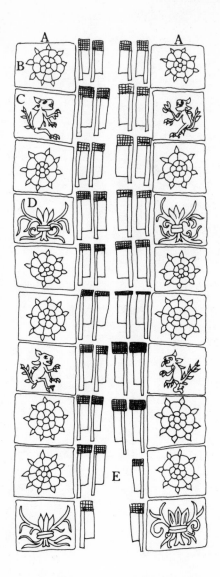

Painting III (scribe's number), no. 4 in manuscript

A. 20 cloths with designs, each 8 piernas (16'?) x 5 brazas (30')

B. Flower design

C. Rabbit design

D. Reed design

E. Cost 37 x 20 = 740 smaller cloths. Costs distributed as follows:
    Flower, 460; Rabbit, 160; Reed, 120

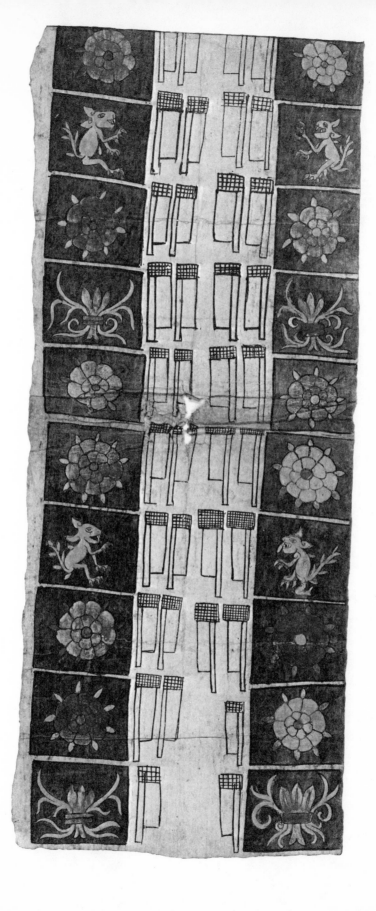

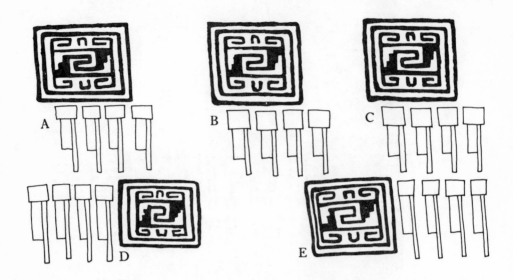

Painting IV (scribe's number), no. 5 in manuscript

A-E.   5 cloths of woven, red rabbit fur, each costing
          4 x 20 = 80 mantles, a total of 400 mantles

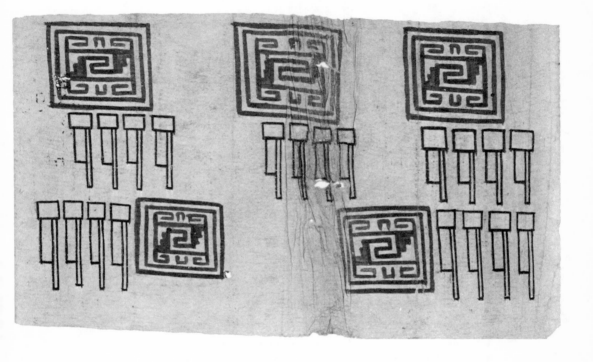

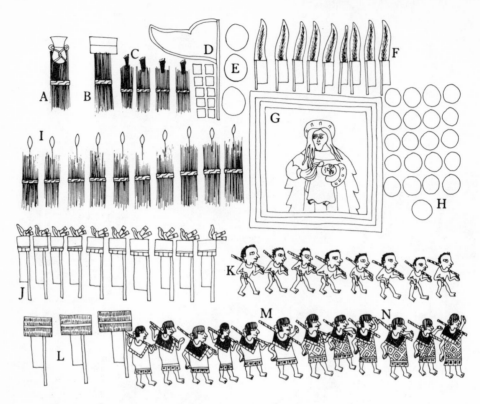

Painting V (scribe's number), no. 7 in manuscript

A.   400 pots of liquidambar

B.   400 small mantles to purchase food en route

C.   4 x 400 = 1,600 pairs of sandals, for same purpose

D.   1 banner for Don Tomé (see H) to carry; cost 10 loads of small
     mantles at 20 per load

E.   3 fine gold plaques used in the standard of the Madonna

F.   9 plumages, each containing 20 large green feathers at a cost of
     9 loads of 20 mantles each

G.   Madonna standard for Nuño de Guzmán (About 16" x 16", gold leaf.
     One of earliest native productions related to Catholicism.)

H.   21 small gold plaques, the thickness of 3 fingernails or a silver real, to purchase
     a horse for Don Tomé, a principal and brother of Don Juan, lord of Huejotzingo

I.   10 x 400 = 4,000 metal-tipped darts

J.   10 x 20 = 200 loads of loincloths, total 4,000

K.   8 male slaves sold to Indian merchants to pay for gold for the Madonna
     standard

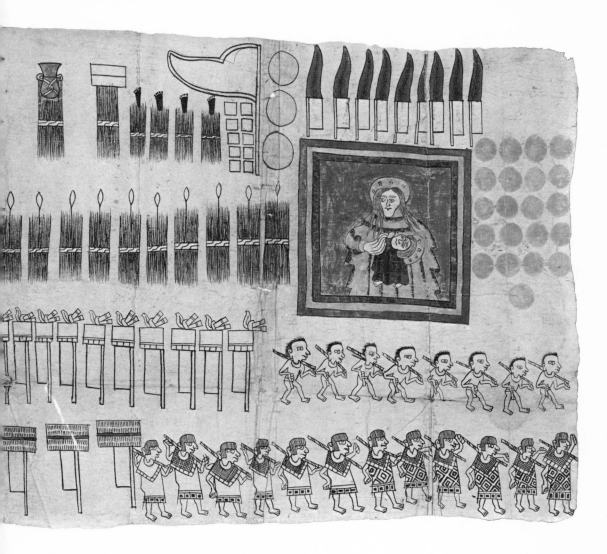

L. 3 x 20 = 60 leather-covered chests

M. 6 female slaves, sold to pay for gold for Madonna standard

N. 6 female slaves, dressed differently from M., sold to pay for gold for Madonna standard

Painting VI (scribe's number), no. 8 in manuscript

A. 2 Aztec war leaders from Huejotzingo, with different shield design

B. 11 houses or lineages, who contributed warriors

C. Scribal note: Honze casas de principales [*rubric*]

D. 16 x 20 = 320 warriors

E. 3 x 400 = 1,200 woven bags

F. 9 x 400 = 3,600 small blankets

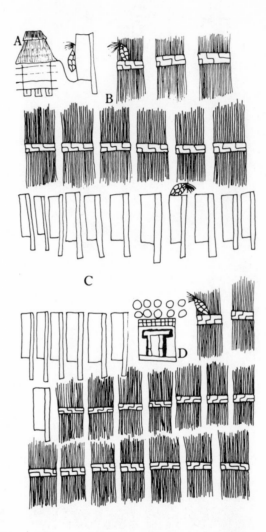

Painting VII (scribe's number), no. 3 in manuscript

A. Native granary holding maize, paid in 1529 and 1530

B. 9 x 400 = 3,600, plus 20 paid in 1529 and 1530

C. 16 x 400 = 6,400, plus 18 x 20 = 360, total 6,760 loads
    of maize paid in 1529

D. 10 houses or lineages who contributed maize

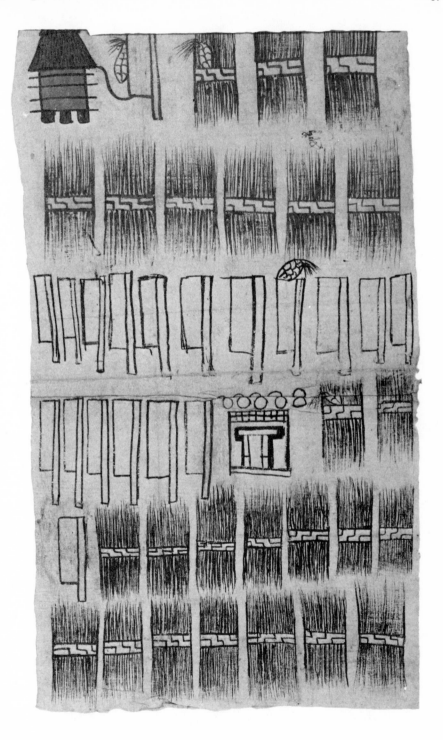

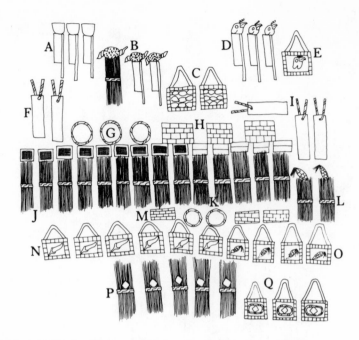

Painting VIII (scribe's number), no. 2 in manuscript

A. 3 x 20 = 60 ?

B. 400 plus 2 x 20 = 440 loads of beans (frijoles?)

C. 2 x 8,000 = 16,000 eggs

D. 3 x 20 = 60 turkeys

E. 8,000 turkeys or quail

F. 2 loads of lumber

G. 3 loads of lime

H. 3 piles of adobes

I. 3 loads of lumber

J. 9 x 400 = 3,600 blankets

K. 5 x 400 = 2,000 small cloths

L. 2 x 400 = 800 loads of maize

M. 2 loads of lime and 3 piles of adobes

N. 6 x 8,000 = 48,000 chile peppers

O. 4 x 8,000 = 32,000 ears of corn

P. 5 x 400 = 2,000 ?

Q. 3 x 8,000 = 24,000 ?

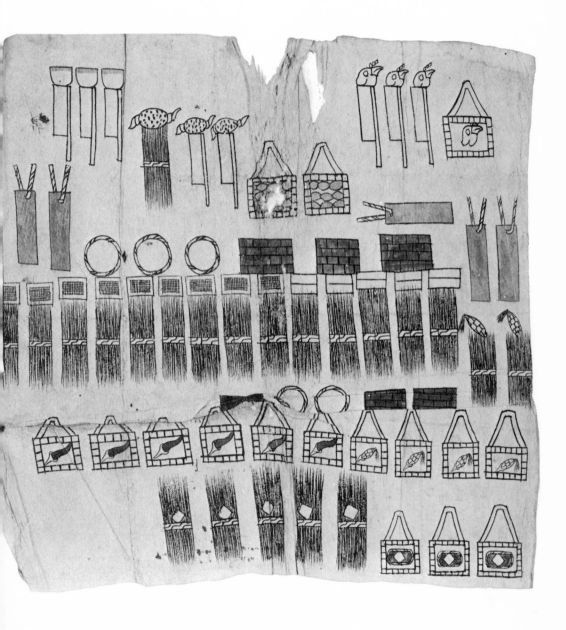

145

[1]

L 4

legajo xiiii°

Proceso del Marques del Valle

contra

Nuño de Guzman e los licenciados Matienço e Delgadillo

sobre los yntereses del pueblo e probincia de Vagoçingo.

sacado

.11: [*modern*]

Al liçençiado en xv de noviembre de yUdxxxi.

[*a word illegibly blotted*]

sacado

[*Partially torn off*] [*re*]çibio a prueba en primera estancia y en segunda sy y no se

hizo[   ] por ninguna parte.

lxv hojas

xxxiii hojas y
las siguientes.

145

L 4

file 14

Lawsuit of the Marqués del Valle

against

Nuño de Guzmán and the Licentiates Matienzo and Delgadillo concerning the interests of the town and province of Huejotzingo.

copied

11

To the licentiate, November 15, 1531.

copied

[*It was*] brought to proof in the first instance and also in the second and [   ] was not done by either party.

65 leaves.

33 leaves and

those that follow.

[*lv*] En la cibdad de Tenuxtitan desta Nueva España a catorze dias del mes de febrero año del nascimiento de Nuestro Salvador Ihu Xpo [*Iesu Cristo*] de myll e quinientos e treynta e un años ante los magnificos senores liçençiados Juan de Salmeron e Alonso Maldonado e Francisco de Ceynos e Vasco de Quiroga presidente e oydores de la abdiencia e chancilleria Real que por mandado de su Magestad en esta Nueva Espana Reside e por ante my Jeronimo Lopes escribano de camara de su Magestad y de la dicha abdiencia e de Sancho Lopes de Agurto my aconpanado nombrado por los dichos señores presidente e oydores para en esta cabsa e en otras que en esta Real abdiencia se tratan c[*on*] ny contra los licenciados Juan Ortis de Matienço e Diego Delgadil[*lo*] presidente e oydores que fueron desta Real abd[*iencia*] parecio presente Gonçalo de Herrera en nombre dé[*l*] Marques del Valle e por virtud del poder que d[*el*] tiene presento un escripto de querella su thenor de[*l*] qual es este que se sigue.

[*2*] El Marques contra los liçençiados sobre lo de Guaxeçingo.

xiiii°   catorze

MUY PODEROSOS SENORES

Gonçalo de Herrera en nombre del Marques del Valle me querello de Nuño de Guzman e de los liçençiados Juan Ortiz de Matienço e Diego Delgadillo vuestro presydente e oydores que fueron, digo que teniendo el dicho mi parte y poseyendo por justos y derechos titulos e merçed de vuestra Magestad que justifican e han justificado la posesyon huso y aprovechamiento de los yndios del pueblo de Guaxuçingo que es en la provincia [*lacuna in the text*] llevando los frutos e aprovechamientos del dicho pueblo, los dichos Nuño de Guzman e liçençiados de hecho y contra todo derecho y syn cabsa ni Razon alguna quitaron al dicho mi parte el dicho pueblo e aprovechamientos del e lo tomaron e apropiaron el dicho pueblo para si llevando los frutos e Rentas del como lo han llevado del año de veynte e nueve que paso a esta parte aprovechandose del dicho pueblo en todas las granjerias que han podido e serviçios e otras cosas nesçesarias; y lo que peor es que al tiempo que el dicho pueblo quitaron al dicho mi parte publicaron e dixeron que lo ponian en cabeça de vuestra Magestad para que de las granjerias e aprobechamientos del dicho pueblo se sirbiesen; y en la verdad vuestra Majestad ha gozado del nombre y ellos se llevaron e gozaron del probecho; y pues por las leyes e derechos de vuestros Reynos esta mandado e defendido a los juezes hazer tales tomas y tener tales tratos y granjerias aviendo de tener en todo las manos linpias, los dichos Nuño de Guzman e liçençiados en hazer lo que hizieron cometieron fuerça delito e despojo e notoria barateria ques avida en derecho por cavsa capital; y de lo que mas my parte se tiene por agraviado es que aviendo le sydo noteficadas por mi parte a los dichos Nuño de Guzman e liçençiados e a cada vno dellos vuestras Reales probisiones para quel dicho pueblo no se quitase al dicho my parte y que si le fuese quitado le fuese buelto no quisieron obedeçer ni complir vuestras Reales provisyones y en vuestro descato y en perjuizio de mi parte se an serbido del dicho pueblo el dicho tiempo en que han llevado del dicho

In the city of Tenochtitlan of this New Spain on the fourteenth day of the month of February in the year of the birth of Our Savior Jesus Christ one thousand five hundred and thirty-one, before the magnificent Lords Licentiates Juan de Salmerón, Alonso Maldonado, Francisco de Ceynos, and Vasco de Quiroga, president and oidores of the audiencia and royal chancery which by command of His Majesty resides in this New Spain, and in the presence of me, Jerónimo López de Agurto, clerk of the high court of His Majesty and of the said audiencia, and of Sancho López de Agurto, my assistant, appointed by the said lords president and oidores to serve in this case and in others which are conducted in this royal audiencia [*with*] or against the Licentiates Juan Ortiz de Matienzo and Diego Delgadillo, former president and oidores of this royal audiencia, Gonzalo de Herrera appeared present in the name of the Marqués del Valle and in virtue of a power of attorney which he has from him, he presented a writ of complaint, the tenor of which is that which follows.

The Marqués versus the licentiates over the matter of Huejotzingo.

14 Fourteen

VERY POWERFUL LORDS

I, Gonzalo de Herrera, in the name of the Marqués del Valle, present a complaint against Nuño de Guzmán and the Licentiates Juan Ortiz de Matienzo and Diego Delgadillo, your former president and oidores. I say that while my said party held and possessed by just and right titles and grant of Your Majesty which justify and have justified the possession, use, and utilization of the Indians of the town of Huejotzingo which is in the province of [*lacuna*], taking the fruits and profits of the said town, the said Nuño de Guzmán and licentiates did in fact and against all right and without any cause or reason take from my said party the said town and the utilization thereof. And they took and appropriated the said town for themselves, taking the fruits and incomes of it, as they have taken them from the year twenty-nine past up to the present, making use of the said town in all the enterprises they could as well as services and other necessary things. And what is worse is that at the time when they took the said town from my said party, they published and said that they were placing it under tribute to Your Majesty [*literally: placing it in the head of your Majesty*] in order that they might make use of the incomes and profits of the said town. And in truth Your Majesty has enjoyed the name, and they have taken for themselves and enjoyed the profit. And since by the laws of your realms it is prohibited that judges should make such seizures and carry on such dealings and enterprises because they must keep their hands clean in everything, the said Nuño de Guzmán and licentiates, in doing what they did, committed violence, crime, spoliation, and notorious fraud, which in law is considered as a capital case. And the matter about which my party feels himself most aggrieved is that after my said party had notified the said Nuño de Guzmán and licentiates and each one of them about your royal decrees to the effect that the said town should not be taken away from my said

pueblo en cada vn año mas cantidad [*2v*] de seis myll castellanos de oro de minas, y por lo que asy an cometido son obligados a padeçer las penas çibiles e criminales e capitales que segund fuero e derecho de vuestros Reynos estan determinadas e puestas contra los semejantes delinquentes, las quales porque a ellos sea castigo y a otros enxenplo.

Pido e suplico a vuestra Magestad las mande por todo Rigor de derecho esecutar en sus personas e vienes o en qualquiera dellos; e ynçidenter de vuestro Real oficio el qual para ello ymploro les condene a que den y Restituyan al dicho my parte los dichos seis mill castellanos de oro de minas en cada vn año [*que no — cancelled*] con mas la pena del derecho condenando les mas en las otras penas e desacatos e desynobediençias, sobre todo lo qual pido me sea echo entero conplimiento de justicia e juro a Dios y a esta + [*cruz*] que lo que pido no es de malicia.

LICENCIADO TELLEZ [*rubrica*]

Querella de Gonçalo de Herrera en nombre del Marques del Valle sobre el pueblo de Guaxaçingo, contra Nuño de Guzman e los liçençiados Matienço y Delgadillo.

En xiiii de hebrero de 31. Traslado. que Responda a la primera.

Y asy presentado el dicho escripto en la manera que dicha es los dichos señores pueblo de Guaxaçingo, contra Nuño de Guzman e los liçençiados Matienço y parte e que por la primera abdiençia Responda.

Y despues de lo suso dicho quinze dias del dicho mes de hebrero e del dicho año ante los dichos señores e en presençia de mi el dicho escribano e acompanado paresçio presente Gregorio de Saldaña en nombre de los [*liçençiados — canceled*] dichos liçençiados Matienço e Delgadillo e presento vn escripto queste que se sigue.

[*3*]   MUY PODEROSOS SEÑORES

Los liçençiados Juan Ortiz de Matienço y Diego Delgadillo Respondiendo a vna querella que contra nosotros puso Gonzalo de Herrera en nonbre del Marques del Valle en que en efeto dize que teniendo el e poseyendo el pueblo de Guaxoçingo, nos servimos del y llevamos los tributos, segund que esto y otras cosas en la dicha su demanda se contienen cuyo thenor avido aqui por Repetido, dezimos que vuestra Magestad no deve hazer cosa alguna de lo pedido por la parte contraria, su querella no proçede ni a lugar de derecho por lo siguiente:

Lo primero porque no es puesta por parte ny en tiempo ny en forma careçe de

party and that if it had been taken away from him it should be returned to him, they did not wish to obey nor fulfill your royal decrees. And in disrespect to you and in prejudice to my party they have made use of the said town during the said time, during which they have taken from the said town each year an amount greater than six thousand castellanos of mined gold. And for what they have thus committed they are obliged to suffer the civil and criminal and capital penalties which are determined and established by the statutes and laws of your realms against such offenders, so that it may be a punishment for them and an example for others.

I beg and entreat Your Majesty that you command that the penalties be executed with the full rigor of the law on their persons and goods and on any one of them. And incidentally, I call upon your royal authority to condemn them to give and restore to my said party the said six thousand castellanos of mined gold for each year, besides the penalty of the law, condemning them moreover to other penalties for their irreverences and disobediences. Concerning all of this I ask that complete fulfillment of justice be made to me, and I swear to God and this † [cross] that what I ask is not from malice.

LICENCIATE TELLEZ [rubric]

Complaint of Gonzalo de Herrera in the name of the Marqués del Valle concerning the town of Huejotzingo, against Nuño de Guzmán and the Licentiates Matienzo and Delgadillo.

February 14, '31. Transcript. That they respond at the first.

And the said brief having been presented in the manner which is stated, the said lords president and oidores said that they commanded and command that a transcript be given to the other party and that they respond during the first session.

And after the abovesaid, on the fifteenth day of the said month of February of the said year, before the said lords and in the presence of me, the said clerk and assistant, Gregorio de Saldaña appeared present in the name of the said Licentiates Matienzo and Delgadillo and presented a brief which is as follows.

VERY POWERFUL LORDS

We, the Licentiates Juan Ortiz de Matienzo and Diego Delgadillo, respond to a complaint which Gonzalo de Herrera made against us in the name of the Marqués del Valle in which in effect he says that while he held and possessed the town of Huejotzingo, we made use of it and took the tributes, according as this and other things are contained in his said demand, the content of which is considered as repeated here. We say that Your Majesty must not do anything requested by the contrary party; his complaint is not in conformity with nor acceptable in the law because of the following:

First, because it is not presented by the party, nor on time, nor in proper form and

lo sustançial e de verdadera Relaçion, negamos la.

Lo otro porque el dicho Marques nunca tuvo ni poseyo el dicho pueblo de Guaxoçingo ni del tuvo titulo ni çedula de su Magestad, y caso negado quel dicho Marques en algund tiempo se servia del dicho pueblo nosotros no nos serviriamos ni servimos en aquel tiempo del dicho pueblo ny en otro [al — *canceled*] tiempo alguno ny llevamos del tributo alguno como la parte contraria dize.

Lo otro porque si nosotros alguna mahiz y aves huvimos del dicho pueblo, que negamos, aquello seria y fue como de pueblo de vuestra [*su — written over*] Magestad y estando como estava puesto en vuestra Real cabeça, y de lo qual hezimos relaçion a vuestra Magestad, y no se hallara ni provara con verdad nosotros aver avido ni Resçibido los tributos del dicho pueblo, ni aver nos del servido en nuestras granjerias como la parte contraria dize, antes esta la verdad en contrario, y asi es publico e notorio, porque el dicho pueblo se puso en cabeça de vuestra Magestad y vuestros ofiçiales pusieron en el calpixque, el cojia e cojio los tributos quel dicho pueblo hera obligado dar, y los entrego a vuestros ofiçiales, y esto no se puede dezir barateria ny lo es, como la parte contraria menos bien dize, y nosotros emos thenido las manos linpias y emos hecho todo lo que buenos juezes devieren hazer asi en estos cargos como de otros que de vuestra Magestad emos thenido, y en tal possesion emos sido e somos avidos e tenidos.

[*3v*] Lo otro porque nosotros sienpre emos obedeçido las çedulas e mandamientos de vuestra Magestad y sobre esto articulo devria el dicho Marques ver la virga de su ojo pues presume ver la paja en el ajeno, como protesto articular, en la proçecuçion desta cabsa, y si en algo se dexaron de cumplir por entero las çedulas de vuestra Magestad, que negamos seria porque el dicho Marques las ganaria con falsas Relaçiones y porque de aquello vuestra Magestad hera mas servydo, y ansi nos lo tenya mandado vuestra Magestad.

Por las quales Razones y por cada vna dellas pedimos e suplicamos a vuestra Magestad nos mande dar e de por libres e quitos de lo pedido e demandado por parte del dicho Marques para lo qual y en lo neçesario vuestro Real ofisçio ynploramos e pedimos justiçia e costas.

Liçençiado Delgadillo [*rubrica*]

Gregorio de Salda en nonbre de los liçençiados Matienço y Delgadillo Responde a la querella que dellos dio el Marques del Valle sobre lo de Guaxoçingo.

En xv de hebrero. Traslado. A la primera diga e concluya. [*rubrica*]

E asi presentado el dicho escripto en la manera que dicha es los dichos senores presidente e oydores dixieron que para la primera abdiencia diga e concluya.

it is lacking substantial elements and a truthful report, we deny it.

Further, the said Marqués never had nor possessed the said town of Huejotzingo, nor did he have title to it nor a decree from His Majesty, and if at some time the said Marqués did make use of the said town, which we deny, we would not have nor did we make use of the said town at that time nor at any other time, nor did we take any tribute from it as the contrary party asserts.

Further, if we accepted any corn and fowls from the said town, which we deny, that would have been and was as from a town of Your Majesty, it being, as it was, placed under your royal tribute, concerning which we made a report to Your Majesty. And it will not be found nor proven with truth that we have had or received the tributes of the said town, nor that we have made use of it in our enterprises as the contrary party says. Rather the contrary is the truth, as is public and well known, because the said town was placed under tribute to Your Majesty and your officials [*of the treasury*] placed in it an overseer who collected the tributes which the said town was obliged to give, and he gave them to your officials. This cannot be called fraud nor is it such, as the contrary party says less than well, and we have kept our hands clean and we have done everything that good judges should do, both in these duties and in others that we have had from Your Majesty, and we have been and are considered to be in possession of such a reputation.

Further, we have always obeyed the decrees and commands of Your Majesty, and concerning this article, the said Marqués should see the beam in his own eye, since he presumes to see the thatch in that of his neighbor, as I affirm that I will bring out by questioning in the prosecution of this case. And if in anything the decrees of Your Majesty were not entirely fulfilled, which we deny, it would be because the said Marqués gained them through false reports and because from our action, Your Majesty was better served, and thus Your Majesty had commanded us.

For these reasons and for each one of them we ask and beseech Your Majesty that you command us to be considered as free and relieved of what is asked and demanded by the party of the said Marqués and that you so consider us. For this matter and in whatever is necessary we implore your royal authority, and we ask justice and the costs.

LICENTIATE DELGADILLO [*rubric*]

Gregorio de Saldaña, in the name of the Licentiates Matienzo and Delgadillo, answers the complaint which the Marqués del Valle brought against them concerning the matter of Huejotzingo.

On February 15. Transcript. At the first let him make a statement and conclude.

And the said brief having been presented in the manner which is stated, the said lords president and oidores said that for the first session he should make a statement and conclude.

E despues de lo suso dicho en veynte e siete dias del dicho mes de hebrero e del
dicho año ante los dichos señores e en presençia de mi el dicho escribano e de
Martin de Castro mi acompañado pareçio presente el Gonçalo de Herrera e
presento vn escripto que se sigue.

[4]   Muy poderosos señores

Gonçalo de Herrera en nonbre del Marques del Valle en el pleyto que trato
con los liçençiados Juan Ortiz de Matienço e Diego Delgadillo, digo Respondiendo
a vn escryto presentado por parte de los dichos liçençiados el qual aqui syendo
Resumido vuestra Magestad a de proçeder en el caso conforme a lo pedido por
el dicho mi parte ansy por lo que dicho e alegado tengo a que me Refiero como
por lo que se sygue.

Lo uno porque es puesta por parte el dicho Marques puede seguir este juyzio
por procurador por ser como es persona ylustre pido en el ynteresçe de my parte,
porque el dicho Marques syenpre tuvo e poseyo el dicho pueblo de Guaxaçingo
des [p — *canceled*] del principio questa tierra conquisto por consentimiento de
vuestra Magestad el qual consta e paresçe pues manda por su Real cedula e
provisyon que no se le quiten los pueblos quel a tenido e poseydo e tenia e poseya
al tiempo que fue en vuestros Reynos de Castylla e sy algunos le fuesen quitados
e Removidos se los mandasen bolver e Restituyr segun que a vuestra Magestad les
[*i.e., le es*] notorio, los dichos liçençiados no solamente no quisieron Restytuyr los
dichos pueblos al dicho mi parte ni cunplir vuestras provisyones e çedulas Reales,
mas avn gozaron e an gozado de los frutos e Rentas del dicho pueblo del tiempo
contenido en mi demanda so color que lo ponian en vuestra Real cabeça.

No haze al caso decir que lo enbiaron a hacer saber a vuestra Magestad y que
para ello pedian liçençia como lo confiensan en el dicho su escryto cuya confisyon
açevto en quanto haze por mi parte porque ellos no pidieron tal liçençia y en caso
que lo enbiaran a hacer saber a vuestra Magestad no les fue conçedida, de donde
se ynfiere que sy vuestra Magestad fuera servido [e — *canceled*] que gozaran del
dicho pueblo e se aprovecharan del se lo mandara e pues no se les mando ni
Respondio a su Relaçion fue visto serle denegado el vso e aprovechamiento del
dicho pueblo e por consyguiente los dichos liçençiados aver yncurrido en las
penas e desacatos e sinobidyençias que se deven a vuestra Magestad y estar
o[*4v*]bligados como estan a Restituçion de lo por mi pedido y ansy se escluye todo
lo dicho e alegado de contrario.

Lo otro en quanto dizen los dichos liçençiados que el dicho mi parte avia de
ver e considerar la viga de su ojo y no mirar la paja en el ajeno, digo que el dicho
mi parte a obedesçido [*la* — *canceled*] vuestras provisyones y mandamientos Reales
como muy obidiente e leal vasallo e que syenpre a tenido Respeto a vuestro Real
seruiçio y al bien publico de vuestra Republica e a avmentado e acresentado
vuestros Reinos, a Remunerado a vuestros vasallos en vuestro nonbre no a[*n* —
canceled] sydo desacatado a vuestros Reales mandamientos ni a tenido su propio

And after the abovesaid, on the twenty-seventh day of the said month of February of the said year, before the said lords and in the presence of me, the said clerk, and of Martín de Castro my assistant, Gonzalo de Herrera appeared and presented a brief which follows.

VERY POWERFUL LORDS

I, Gonzalo de Herrera in the name of the Marqués del Valle in the lawsuit which I am carrying on with the Licentiates Juan Ortiz de Matienzo and Diego Delgadillo, say in response to a brief presented by the party of the said licentiates, which is here repeated, that Your Majesty must proceed in the case in conformity with the petition of my said party both because of what I have said and affirmed, to which I refer, and because of what follows.

First, because it is presented by the party. The said Marqués can prosecute this case through an attorney because of the fact that he is an illustrious person. I present the petition in the interest of my party because the said Marqués always had and possessed the said town of Huejotzingo by consent of Your Majesty since the beginning when he conquered this land. This is clear and apparent since you command by your royal decree and writ that he should not be deprived of the towns which he has had and possessed and did have and possess at the time when he went to your realms of Castile, and if any were taken from him, it should be commanded that they be returned and restored to him, as is well known to Your Majesty. The said licentiates not only did not wish to restore the said towns to my said party nor fulfill your royal writs and decrees, but they even enjoyed and have enjoyed the fruits and incomes of the said town for the time contained in my claim under the pretext that they were placing it under your royal tribute.

It does not affect the case to say that they sent Your Majesty notification of it and that they asked permission for it, as they confess in their said brief, and I accept their confession insofar as it is of benefit to my party. They did not request such permission, and in case they did send Your Majesty notification, it was not conceded to them. From this it is inferred that if Your Majesty had been pleased that they should make use of the said town and profit from it, such would have been commanded, but since it was not commanded nor was there any answer to their report, it was evident that the use and utilization of the said town was denied them and that consequently the said licentiates have incurred the penalties and irreverences without the obediences which are due to Your Majesty and that they are obliged to restitution of what I have asked. Thus is excluded everything stated and alleged to the contrary.

Further, insofar as the said licentiates say that my said party should see and consider the beam in his own eye and not look at the thatch in another's eye, I say that my said party has obeyed your royal writs and commands as a very obedient and loyal vassal and that he has always had respect for your royal service and for the public good of your state and has augmented and increased your realms. He has rewarded your vassals in your name, he has not been disrespectful to your royal

ynteresse en mas que el vuestro y de vuestra Republica como los dichos liçençiados lo an hecho e procurado e a vuestra Magestad les notorio segund paresçe por las ynformaçiones que en el caso se an dado contra los dichos liçençiados e porque del dicho libelo mi parte es ynfamada y del Resulta sy ansy fuese culpa contra el dicho mi parte protesto de querellar e pedir su ynjuria en su tiempo e lugar.

Porque pido e suplico a vuestra Magestad proçeda en el caso contra los dichos liçençiados e contra cada vno dellos como tengo pedido e para ello vuestra Real ofiçio ynploro e las costas pido e protesto e pido sobre todo cumplimiento de justiçia e las costas pido e protesto e negando lo perjudiçial concluyo; e pido ser Resçibido a prueva.

LIÇENÇIADO TELLEZ [*rubrica*]

El Marques del Valle con los liçençiados Matienço e Delgadillo sobre lo de Guaxaçingo Responde e concluye.

En xxvii de febrero. Traslado e Responda e concluya en la primera en haz de Saldaña.

Y asi presentado el dicho escripto los dichos señores dixieron que mandavan e mandaron que Respondan e concluyan para la primera abdiençia.

Y despues de lo suso dicho en seys dias del mes de março e del dicho año ante los dichos señores e [*en presençia de mi Alonso Lucas—between lines*] pareçio Gonçalo de Herrera e presento el escripto syguiente.

[5]   MUY PODEROSOS SEÑORES

Gonçalo de Herrera en la denunçiaçion que tengo fecha contra los liçençiados Matienço e Delgadillo sobre lo de Guaxaçingo digo que les a sydo puesto termino que Respondan e concluyan y no lo an fecho yo les acuso la primera Rebeldia, e concluyo e pido a vuestra Magestad aya el pleyto por concluso e Reçiba a prueva anbas partes.

[5v] Gonçalo de Herrera contra el liçençiado Delgadillo e Matienço sobre la denunçiaçion que tiene fecha de Guaxaçingo acusa la primera Rebeldia e concluye e pide ser Reçibido a prueba anbas partes, por no aver concluydo los liçençiados.

En vi de março. Traslado a la parte a la primera.

E asi presentado el dicho escripto en la manera que dicha es los dichos señores dixieron que mandavan e mandaron que para la primera abdiençia Responda.

commands, nor has he placed his own interest ahead of your interests and those of your state, as the said licentiates have done and attempted, and this is well known to Your Majesty, as is apparent from the judicial inquiries which have been presented in this case against the said licentiates. Because my party has been defamed by the said libel and if perchance any guilt results from it against my said party, I protest that I will present a complaint and petition regarding his injury at the proper time and place.

Therefore I ask and beseech Your Majesty that you proceed in the case against the said licentiates and against each one of them as I have petitioned and for this I implore your royal authority, and I ask and protest the costs, and above all I ask the fulfillment of justice, and I ask and protest the costs, [*sic*] and denying what is prejudicial, I conclude. And I ask to be received to proof.

LICENCIATE TELLEZ [*rubric*]

The Marqués del Valle with the Licentiates Matienzo and Delgadillo concerning the matter of Huejotzingo responds and concludes.

On February 27. Transcript—and let him respond and conclude at the first—in the face of Saldaña.

And the said brief having been thus presented, the said lords said that they commaned and do command that they should respond and conclude for the first session.

And after the abovesaid on the sixth day of the month of March of the said year before the said lords and in the presence of me Alonso Lucas, Gonzalo de Herrera appeared and presented the following brief.

VERY POWERFUL LORDS

I, Gonzalo de Herrera, in the denunciation which I have made against the Licentiates Matienzo and Delgadillo concerning the matter of Huejotzingo, say that a time limit has been placed upon them within which they should respond and conclude, and they have not done so. I accuse them of the first default, and I conclude and ask that Your Majesty consider the proceedings as concluded and receive both parties to proof.

Gonzalo de Herrera, against the Licentiates Delgadillo and Matienzo concerning the denunciation which he has made about Huejotzingo, accuses them of the first default and concludes and asks that both parties be received to proof because the licentiates have not concluded.

On March 6. Transcript to the party—at the first.

And the said brief having been thus presented in the manner which is stated, the said lords said that they commanded and do command that they respond for the first session.

E despues de lo susodicho en seys dias del dicho mes de março e del dicho año
ante los dichos señores presidente e oydores e en presençia de mi el dicho escribano
[*e del dicho aconpanado—canceled*] paresçio presente Gonçalo de Herrera e presento
el escripto syguiente.

[*6*]   Muy poderosos señores

Gonçalo de Herrera en el pleyto que trato con los liçençiados Matienço e Delgadillo sobre el aprouechamiento del pueblo de Guaxaçingo digo que les a sydo
puesto termino en que Respondan e concluyan e no lo an fecho e le a sydo acusada
la primera Rebeldia; yo le acuso la segunda Rebeldia e concluyo e pido a vuestra
Magestad aya el pleyto por concluso y Reçiba a prueva anbas partes e sobre todo
pido justiçia.

Gonçalo de Herrera en el pleyto que trata con los liçençiados Matienço e Delgadillo sobre el aprouechamiento del pueblo de Guaxeçingo acusa la segunda
Rebeldia e concluye e pide Reçiba a prueva anbas partes.

En vi de março. A prueba [*en h — canceled*] de consentimiento de partes e en su
haz con ix dias.

E asi presentado el dicho escripto en la manera que dicha es los dichos señores
presidente e oydores dixieron que de consentimiento de partes Resçibian a prueva
[*e dieron la sentençia syguiente — canceled*] a anbas las dichas partes con termino
de nueve dias e dieron la sentençia syguiente.

[*6v*]   Muy poderosos señores

Gonçalo de Herrera en nombre del Marques del Valle [*Nothing follows the introduction*]

[7] En el pleyto que es entre partes de la una abctor demandante El Marques del
Valle E su procurador En su nonbre E de la otra rreos defendientes los liçençiados
Juan Ortiz de Martienço E Diego Delgadillo E su procurador En su nombre sobre
las cabsas e rrazones en el proçeso del dicho pleyto contenidas Fallamos que devemos
rreçebir E rreçebimos a anbas las dichas partes conjuntamente a la prueva de lo
por ellas E por cada vna dellas dicho E alegado E de aquello que provado les podria
E puede aprovechar salvo jure ynpertinençiun et non admitendorun para la qual
prueva hacer E traer E presentar ante nos les damos y asyñamos termino de nueve
dias primeros siguientes E apercebimos a las dichas partes E a cada vna dellas que
vengan E parezcan ante nos a ver presentar jurar E conosçer los testigos provanças
y escrituras que la vna parte presentare contra la otra E la otra contra la otra E
por esta nuestra sentençia juzgando asy lo pronunçiamos E mandamos.

And after the abovesaid on the sixth day of the said month of March of the said year before the said lords president and oidores and in the presence of me the said clerk, Gonzalo de Herrera appeared present and presented the following brief.

VERY POWERFUL LORDS

I, Gonzalo de Herrera, in the lawsuit which I am conducting with the Licentiates Matienzo and Delgadillo concerning the utilization of the town of Huejotzingo, say that a time limit has been set for them in which they should respond and conclude and they have not done it, and they have been accused of the first default; I now accuse them of the second default, and I conclude; and I ask that Your Majesty consider the proceedings as concluded and receive both parties to proof; and above all I ask justice.

Gonzalo de Herrera, in the lawsuit which he is conducting with the Licentiates Matienzo and Delgadillo concerning the utilization of the town of Huejotzingo, accuses them of the second default, and he concludes and asks that both parties be received to proof.

On March 6. To proof with the consent of both parties and in their presence—with nine days.

And the said brief having been thus presented in the manner which is stated, the said lords president and oidores said that with the consent of the parties they received both the said parties to proof with a time limit of nine days, and they gave the following sentence.

In the lawsuit which is being conducted between the parties of, on the one hand, the Marqués del Valle and his attorney in his name as plaintiff and, on the other hand, the Licentiates Juan Ortiz de Matienzo and Diego Delgadillo and their attorney in their name as defendants, concerning the causes and reasons which are contained in the proceedings of the suit, we find that we must and do receive both of the said parties conjointly to proof of what has been stated and alleged by them and by each one of them and of that which when proven could and can be of help to them *salvo jure impertinentium et non admittendorum* [*observing the law regarding impertinent and inadmissable matters*], and in order to make this proof and to bring it and present it before us, we give and assign them a limit of the next nine days immediately following, and we summon the said parties and each one of them that they should come and appear before us to see the presentation, swearing and acknowledgement of the witnesses, evidence, and instruments which the first party may present against the second or the second against the first, and we pronounce and command it by this our sentence, judging it to be thus.

EL LIÇENÇIADO SALMERON [*rubrica*]
LICENCIATUS ALONSO MALDONADO [*rubrica*]
EL LICENCIADO CEYNOS [*rubrica*]
LICENCIADO QUIROGA [*rubrica*]

Dada en vi de março iUdxxxi años

[*7v*] E despues de lo susodicho en treynta dias del dicho mes de março del dicho año ante los dichos señores presidente e oydores e en presençia de mi el dicho escribano [*e del dicho aconpañado—canceled*] pareçio presente Garçia de Llerena e presento el escripto syguiente.

[*8*]   MUY PODEROSOS SEÑORES

   Garçia de Llerena en nonbre del Marques del Valle en el pleito que trato con los liçençiados Juan Ortiz de Matienço e Diego Delgadillo sobre los yntereses del pueblo de Vaxoçingo, digo que a my notiçia ha venido que en esta çivdad estan çiertos prençipales del dicho pueblo, los quales thienen las figuras de lo que a los dichos liçençiados el dicho pueblo dio, suplico a vuestra Magestad les mande y conpela que las den al secretario porque dellas hago presentaçion e pido que se tomen sus dichos por ellas e por el ynterrogatorio que en la dicha cavsa tengo presentado e para ello si neçesario pido quartoplazo con protestaçion de pedir Reçebtor para en el dicho pueblo de Vaxoçingo hazer mas copiosamente my probança para en todo lo qual su Real ofiçio ynploro e pido justiçia.
                     GARÇIA DE LLERENA [*rubrica*]

[*8v*] El Marques del Valle contra los liçençiados sobre los yntereses de Vaxoçingo. A se de ler.

En xxx de março. Que se le proRoga el termino sy ha jurado por x dias que sea comun e se notifique a la otra parte, e que Resçiba el secretario las figuras que presenta. [*rubrica*]

   E asi presentado el dicho escripto en la manera que dicha es los dichos señores presidente e oydores dixieron que se le proRoga el termino sy ha jurado por otros diez dias y sea comun a las partes e se notifique a la otra parte e que Resçiba el secretario las figuras que se presentaren.

   E despues de lo susodicho en veynte e dos dias del mes de abril e del dicho año ante los dichos señores presidente e oydores e en presençia de mi el dicho escribano [*e aconpanado—canceled*] pareçio [*p—canceled*] Garçia de Llerena en abdiençia publica e presento el escripto siguiente.

LICENTIATE SALMERÓN [*rubric*]
LICENTIATE ALONSO MALDONADO [*rubric*]
LICENTIATE CEYNOS [*rubric*]
LICENTIATE QUIROGA [*rubric*]

Given on March 6, the year 1531.

And after the abovesaid on the thirtieth day of the said month of March of the said year before the said president and oidores and in the presence of me the said clerk, García de Llerena appeared present and presented the following brief.

VERY POWERFUL LORDS

I, García de Llerena, in the name of the Marqués del Valle in the lawsuit which I am conducting with the Licentiates Juan Ortiz de Matienzo and Diego Delgadillo concerning the interests of the town of Huejotzingo, say that it has come to my notice that in this city there are certain of the leading men of the said town who have the paintings of what the said town gave to the said licentiates. I beseech Your Majesty that you command and compel them to give the paintings to the secretary because I make presentation of them; and I ask that their statements be taken by means of the paintings and by the questionnaire which I have presented in the said case, and for this, if necessary, I request an extension of the time limit with a protestation that I will ask for a secretary to go to the said town of Huejotzingo to take testimony for me more fully; and for all of this I implore your royal authority, and I ask for justice.

GARCÍA DE LLERENA [*rubric*]

The Marqués del Valle versus the licentiates concerning the interests of Huejotzingo. It must be read.

On March 30. That the limit is extended for ten days if he has sworn—that it be common to both parties and that the other party be notified and that the secretary receive the paintings which he presents. [*rubric*]

The said brief having been thus presented in the manner which is stated, the said lords president and oidores said that the limit is extended for him for another ten days if he has sworn and that it should be common to the parties and that the other party should be notified and that the secretray should receive the paintings which may be presented.

And after the abovesaid, on the twenty-second day of the month of April of the said year, before the said lords president and oidores and in the presence of me the said clerk, García de Llerena appeared in public session and presented the following brief.

[9]   MUY PODEROSOS SEÑORES

Garçia de Llerena en nonbre del Marques del Valle en el pleyto que el dicho mi parte trata contra los liçençiados Matienço e Delgadillo sobre los yntereses de Vexoçingo, digo que porque al presente han venido a esta çibdad çiertos testigos que en la dicha cavsa han de dezir sus dichos pido quarto plazo de quinçe dias suplico a vuestra Magestad me lo otorgue, e juro a Dios etç en anyma de mi parte que no lo pido maliçiosamente, sino porque mi parte thiene neçisidad de presentar los dichos testigos en la dicha cavsa e para lo neçisario el Real offiçio de vuestra Magestad ynploro.

[9v] El Marques contra los liçençiados sobre los yntereses de Vexoçingo pide quarto-plazo de xv dias. Verlo.

xxii de abril 1531. Jurolo. Otorganle de x dias en haz de Saldana.

E asi presentado el dicho escripto en la manera que dicha es los dichos presidente e oydores dixieron que le otorgavan e otorgaron el dicho quarto plazo de diez dias el qual lo juro e se dio en haz de Saldana procurador de los dichos liçençiados.

E despues de lo suso dicho en quinze dias del mes de mayo del dicho año ante los dichos señores presidente e oydores e en presençia de mi el dicho Alonso Lucas escribano pareçio presente Garçia de Llerena en la dicha abdiençia e presento el escripto syguiente.

[10]   MUY PODEROSOS SEÑORES

Garçia de Llerena en nonbre del Marques del Valle en el pleito que trato con los liçençiados Juan Ortiz de Matienço e Diego Delgadillo sobre los yntereses del pueblo de Vaxoçingo e su sujeto, digo que porque allende de las probanças que por mi parte estan fechas tengo neçesidad de poner e presentar en la dicha cavsa ciertos dichos e depusiçiones que en la pesquisa secreta fueron tomados que solamente declararon en lo que particularmente en que cosas e como los dichos yndios de Vaxocingo avian seruido e contribuido a los dichos liçençiados suplico a vuestra Magestad mande al escribano en cuio poder la dicha pesquisa esta me de vn traslado avturiçado de lo tocante a los seruicios e tributos que los dichos liçençiados del dicho pueblo vbieron, que yo estoy presto e aparejado de le pagar por ello su justo e devido salario que por ello deve aver e pido justiçia e en lo neçesario el Real ofiçio de vuestra Magestad ynploro, porque de las dichas escripturas para en la dicha cavsa hago presentaçion.

[10v] El Marques contra los liçençiados sobre los ynteresses de Vaxoçingo. A se de ler.

VERY POWERFUL LORDS

I, García de Llerena, in the name of the Marqués del Valle in the lawsuit which my said party is conducting against the Licentiates Matienzo and Delgadillo concerning the interests of Huejotzingo, say that because at the present time there have come to this city certain witnesses who must make their statements in the said case, I ask for an extension of fifteen days. I beseech Your Majesty to grant it to me, and I swear to God etc., on the soul of my party that I do not ask it maliciously but because my party needs to present the said witnesses in the said case. And in as far as it is necessary, I implore the royal authority of Your Majesty.

The Marqués versus the licentiates concerning the interests of Huejotzingo asks for an extension of 15 days. Look at it.

April 22, 1531. He swore to it. They grant him 10 days in the face of Saldaña.

And the said brief having been presented in the manner which has been stated, the said president and oidores said that they granted and do grant him the said extension of ten days, and he swore to it, and it was given in the face of Saldaña, the attorney of the said licentiates.

And after the abovesaid, on the fifteenth day of the month of May of the said year, before the said lords president and oidores and in the presence of me the said Alonso Lucas, clerk, García de Llerena appeared present in the said session and presented the following brief.

VERY POWERFUL LORDS

I, García de Llerena, in the name of the Marqués del Valle in the lawsuit which I am conducting with the Licentiates Juan Ortiz de Matienzo and Diego Delgadillo concerning the interests of the town of Huejotzingo and its subject region, say that besides the proofs that have been presented by my party, I need to place and present in the said case certain statements and depositions which were taken in the secret investigation, but only those declarations which they made in particular regarding how and in what things the said Indians of Huejotzingo have served and contributed to the said licentiates. I beseech Your Majesty that you command the clerk in whose possession the said investigation is that he give me a notarized copy of whatever refers to the services and tributes which the said licentiates received from the said town. I am ready and prepared to pay him for it the just and due salary which he should have for it. And I ask justice, and in necessary matters, I implore the royal authority of Your Majesty because I make presentation of the said documents to be placed in the said case.

The Marqués versus the licentiates concerning the interests of Huejotzingo. It must be read.

xv de mayo. Que se lo de pagando.

E asi presentado el dicho escripto en la manera que dicha es los dichos señores presidente e oydores dixieron que mandaban e mandaron que se le de pagandolo etc.

E despues de lo susodicho en veynte e syete dias del dicho mes de mayo e del dicho año ante los dichos señores presidente e oydores e en presençia de mi el dicho escriuano pareçio presente Garçia de Llerena en abdiençia publica e presento el escripto siguiente.

[*11*]   MUY PODEROSOS SEÑORES

Garçia de Llerena en nonbre del Marques del Valle en el pleito que trato contra los liçençiados Matienço e Delgadillo sobre los yntereses del pueblo de Vazoçingo que ynjustamente despojaron al dicho mi parte hago presentaçion de la primera çedula e probision de vuestra Magestad con que los dichos liçençiados fueron Requeridos e con la Respuesta que a ella dieron la qual esta originalmente en poder de Miguel Lopez escriuano publico suplico a vuestra Magestad le mande que citada la parte de los dichos liçençiados me del testimonio de la dicha cedula e avtos porque del hago presentaçion para en esta dicha cavsa.

Otrosi hago presentaçion de la sobrecarta de la dicha çedula de vuestra alteza con que los dichos liçençiados fueron Requiridos por testimonio de Alonso Lucas y de Geronimo de Medina en el tiempo que fueron escribano desta Real avdiençia suplico a vuestra Magestad mande al dicho Alonso Lucas me de vn traslado en publica forma para en la dicha cavsa porque del dende agora hago presentaçion çitada la parte de los dichos liçençiados para que lo vean corregir e conçertar con el dicho testimonio original e pido justicia e en lo neçesario el Real ofiçio de vuestra Magestad ynploro.

[*11v*] El Marques contra los liçençiados sobre los yntereses del pueblo de Vaxoçingo. A se de ler.

Por presentado lo que dize trayendolo e que se çiten los liçençiados para los ver coRegir e conçertar Alonso Lucas que le de io que pide en forma en haz de Saldaña. **xxvii de mayo.**

E asy presentado el dicho escripto en la manera que dicha es los dichos señores dixieron que lo avian por presentado trayendolos e que se çite a Gregorio de Saldaña en nonbre de los dichos liçençiados para que los vea corregir e Alonso Lucas que de lo que pide en forma lo qual se mando en haz del dicho Saldaña.

May 15. That it should be given to him upon payment.

And the said brief having been presented in the manner which is stated, the said lords president and oidores said that they commanded and do command that it be given to him provided that he pays for it, etc.

And after the abovesaid, on the twenty-seventh day of the said month of May of the said year, before the said lords president and oidores and in the presence of me the said clerk, García de Llerena appeared present in public session and presented the following brief.

Very powerful lords

I, García de Llerena, in the name of the Marqués del Valle in the lawsuit which I am conducting against the Licentiates Matienzo and Delgadillo concerning the interests of the town of Huejotzingo of which they unjustly despoiled my said party, make presentation of the first decree and writ of Your Majesty, of which the said licentiates were notified, and with it the reply which they gave to it, which in the original, is in the possession of Miguel López, notary public. I beseech Your Majesty to command him that having cited the party of the said licentiates, he should give me the notarized copy of the said decree and acts because I make presentation of it for inclusion in this said case.

Further, I make presentation of the covering letter of the said decree of Your Highness, of which the said licentiates were notified, through a notarized copy of Alonso Lucas and Jeronimo de Medina, made at the time when they were clerks of this royal audiencia. I beseech Your Majesty to command the said Alonso Lucas to give me a copy in public form for inclusion in this case. As of the present I make presentation of it, the party of the said licentiates being cited to see it corrected and set in agreement with the said original official copy. And I ask justice, and in what is necessary, I implore the royal authority of Your Majesty.

The Marqués versus the licentiates concerning the interests of the town of Huejotzingo. It must be read.

As presented what he says when he brings it—and that the licentiates be cited to see them corrected and set in agreement—Alonso Lucas that he should give him what he asks in form—in the face of Saldaña. **May 27.**

And the said brief having been presented in the manner which is stated, the said lords said that they would accept the documents as presented when he brings them and that Gregorio de Saldaña be cited in the name of the said licentiates to see them corrected and that Alonso Lucas give him what he asks in proper form, all of which was commanded in the face of the said Saldaña.

E despues de lo susodicho en veynte dias del mes de março e del dicho año ante los dichos señores presidente e oydores e en presençia de mi el dicho escriuano en abdiençia publica pareçio presente Garçia de Llerena el ynterrogatorio syguiente.

[12] El Marques contra los liçençiados Matienço e Delgadillo sobre Guaxoçingo.

Por las preguntas siguientes sean preguntados los testigos que son o fueren presentados por parte del Marques del Valle en el pleito que trata con los liçençiados Juan Ortiz de Matienço e Diego Delgadillo en el pleito que contra ellos trata i sobre los yntereses del pueblo e probinçia de Vaxoçingo de que despojaron al dicho Marques.

i   Primeramente sean preguntados si conoçen al Marques del Valle a los liçençiados Matienço e Delgadillo e a Nuño de Guzman e si thienen notiçia del pueblo e probinçia de Vaxoçingo.

ii   Yten si saben e han visto que el dicho Marques del Valle tubo e poseyo el dicho pueblo e probinçia de Vaxoçingo en su encomienda e administraçion llevando e aprobechandose dellos en los tributos seruiçios e aprobechamientos que tenian por costunbre de dar despues que esta Nueva España conquisto para su Magestad hasta que los dichos liçençiados e Nuno de Guzman vinieron a ella.

iii   Yten si saben e vieron e dello thienen notiçia y sabiduria que en todo el tiempo que el dicho Marques tubo el dicho pueblo e probinçia en su encomienda fueron los señores e naturales del muy vien tratados e mandados tratar e Relevados de seruiçios e tributos con que Reçibiesen vejaçion, y endustriados en las cosas de nuestra santa fe, porque luego trabaxo de fundar e poner en el dicho pueblo e probinçia vn monesterio de franciscanos de donde han tenido pedricaçion, conoçimiento de las cosas de nuestra santa fe.

iiii°   Yten si saben e vieron que luego como los liçençiados Juan Ortiz de Matienço e Diego Delgadillo y Nuno de Guzman llegaron a esta çivdad enbiaron a llamar a los señores e prinçipales del, e les pidieron que les diesen e traxesen cierta cantidad en mas de mill pesos de oro en texuelos e joyas e asimismo en piedras e plumas e Ropa y esclavos en mas cantidad de valor de otros mill pesos de oro, digan los testigos que oro, piedras, plumas, Ropa esclavos e otras cosas luego que llegaron los dichos presidente e oydores les dieron y en el camino antes que a esta çivdad llegasen.

v   Yten si saben e vieron etç que asimismo los dichos Nuño de Guzman e liçençiados Matienço e Delgadillo mandaron luego a los señores e prinçipales del dicho pueblo e probinçia que sirbiesen en esta çivdad a los dichos liçençiados Matienço e Delgadillo de lena yerba, mahiz axi, aves pescado codorniçes vebos e otros muchos seruiçios de probision e bastimento para sus casas que cada dia cotidianamente les davan en esta çivdad, digan lo que davan cada dia cotidianamente.

[12v] vi   Yten si saben e vieron etç que antes que los dichos Nuño de Guzman e

And after the abovesaid, on the twentieth day of the month of March of the said year, before the said lords president and oidores and in the presence of me the said clerk, García de Llerena appeared present in the public session [*and presented*] the following questionnaire.

The Marqués versus the Licentiates Matienzo and Delgadillo concerning Huejotzingo.

By the following questions let the witnesses be interrogated who are or may be presented by the party of the Marqués del Valle in the lawsuit which he is conducting with the Licentiates Juan Ortiz de Matienzo and Diego Delgadillo in the lawsuit which he is conducting against them concerning the interests of the town and province of Huejotzingo of which they despoiled the said Marqués.

1. First let them be asked whether they know the Marqués del Valle and the Licentiates Matienzo and Delgadillo and Nuño de Guzmán and whether they have knowledge of the town and province of Huejotzingo.

2. Also, whether they know and have seen that the said Marqués del Valle had and possessed the said town and province of Huejotzingo in his charge and administration, taking and making use of them in the tributes, services, and profits which they were accustomed to give, from the time that he conquered this New Spain for His Majesty up to the time that the said licentiates and Nuño de Guzmán came to it.

3. Also, whether they know and saw and have information and knowledge of the fact that during the whole time that the said Marqués had the said town and province under his charge, the lords and natives of it were very well treated; and it was commanded that they be well treated and relieved of services and tributes from which they might receive vexation and that they be instructed in the matters of our holy faith; and for this reason he labored at once to found and place in the said town and province a monastery of Franciscans, whence they [*the Indians*] have received preaching and the knowledge of the matters of our holy faith.

4. Also, whether they know and have seen that as soon as the Licentiates Juan Ortiz de Matienzo and Diego Delgadillo and Nuño de Guzmán arrived in this city, they summoned the lords and leading men of the town and asked that they give and bring a certain quantity, more than six thousand pesos, of gold in ingots and jewels and also stones and feathers and clothing and slaves in an amount worth more than another thousand gold pesos; and let the witnesses say what gold, stones, feathers, clothing, slaves, and other things they gave to the said president and oidores immediately upon their arrival and on the road before they arrived in this city.

5. Also, whether they know and saw, etc., that the said Nuño de Guzmán and Licentiates Matienzo and Delgadillo also immediately commanded the lords and leading men of the said town and province that as a service to the said Licentiates Matienzo and Delgadillo they should bring to this city wood, hay, maize, chile pepper, fowl, fish, quail, eggs, and many other services in provisions and supplies for their houses which they gave them every day in this city; let the witnesses say what they gave every day.

6. Also, whether they know and saw, etc., that before the said Nuño de Guzmán and

liçençiados Matienço e Delgadillo se començasen a serbir de los yndios del dicho
pueblo por parte del dicho Marques sus procuradores les mostraron e notificaron
e presentaron vna çedula e probision de su Magestad ante escriuano que dello dio
fe, por la qual su Magestad mando a los dichos presidente e oydores que no quitasen
tocasen ni Removiesen al dicho don Fernando Cortes yndios hazienda ni otra cosa
alguna de la manera quel lo avia dexado hasta que su alteza otra cosa probeyese,
e la dicha çedula se presento antellos y por testimonio de Juan Fernandez del
Castillo escriuano.

vii Yten si saben e vieron que despues por los procuradores del dicho Marques
fue notificado presentado y Requeridos los dichos Nuño de Guzman e liçençiados
Matienço e Delgadillo con otra segunda sobrecarta de la dicha çedula, e no ostante
que dixeron que la obedeçian no la guardaron ni cunplieron antes dixeron quel
dicho pueblo e probinçia lo avian señalado para su Magestad llevandosellos los
seruiçios cotidianos de cada vn dia hasta el dia que vinieron los señores presidente
e oydores que agora en esta Real avdiençia Residen.

viii° Yten si saben e vieron e dello thienen notiçia que los dichos Nuño de Guzman,
Matienço e Delgadillo han avido e llevado del dicho pueblo e probinçia dendel
comienço del año de quinientos e veynte e nueve hasta el fin del año de quinientos
e treynta años ellos para si mas de diez mill hanegas de mahiz e de treynta mill aves
e de quarenta mill codorniçes e de treçientos mill vebos e çient cargos de axi e
dozientos esclavos e tres o quatro mill pieças de Ropa e piedras Ricas e plumas e
muchas obras de pinturas e texidos e otros muchas seruiçios e aprobechamientos que
del dicho pueblo han avido en los dichos dos años en valor de mas de quatro mill
pesos de oro de minas, digan los testigos lo que saben e an visto que los dichos yndios
han dado a los susodichos.

ix Yten si saben e vieron etç que allende de los dichos seruiçios e cosas que dieron
a los dichos Nuno de Guzman e liçençiados Matienço e Delgadillo dieron los dichos
yndios despues que heran pasados çinco o seys meses que los susodichos se seruian
e aprobechavan dellos en toda manera de seruiçio e tributo a los ofiçiales de su
Magestad ochoçientos pesos de oro que salia de ley de treçe e catorçe quilates cada
seys meses e dos mill pieças de Ropa en cada tributo e diez mill hanegas de mahiz
e con esto se acudia a los ofiçiales de su Magestad por manera que an dado los
dichos yndios allende de lo que los liçençiados Matienço e Delgadillo e Nuño de
Guzman dellos se han aprobechado en los dichos dos años tres mill e dozientos pesos
en oro, e ocho mill pieças de Ropa, digan los testigos lo que saben.

[*13*] **x** Yten si saben e vieron que sirviendose los dichos Matienço e Delgadillo del
dicho pueblo e probinçia asi en los dichos seruiçios cotidianos como en obras de sus
casas e huertas que hazian, el dicho liçençiado Delgadillo escribio çiertas cartas a
calpisques e personas que tenian en los dichos pueblos diziendo que bien sabian que
los yndios e señores del dicho pueblo le devian tantas mill hanegas de mahiz del
tiempo e tributo pasado que luego les hesecutasen e aprisionasen por la paga dello

the Licentiates Matienzo and Delgadillo began to use the services of the Indians of the said town, on the part of the said Marqués, his attorneys showed, notified, and presented to them a decree and writ of His Majesty in the presence of a notary who authenticated it, by which His Majesty commanded the said president and oidores that they should not take away, lay hands on, or remove Indians, property or anything else from the said Don Hernando Cortés from the way that he had left it, until His Highness should decree something else; and the said decree was presented before them also through a notarized copy to Juan Fernández del Castillo, notary.

7. Also, whether they know and saw that later, by the attorneys of the said Marqués, the said Nuño de Guzmán and Licentiates Matienzo and Delgadillo were notified, presented, and summoned with another second covering letter of the said decree, and in spite of the fact that they said that they would obey it, they did not observe or fulfill it, but rather they said that they had set aside the said town and province for His Majesty, while they took for themselves the daily services up to the day of the arrival of the lords president and oidores who now reside in this royal audiencia.

8. Also, whether they know and saw and have knowledge of the fact that the said Nuño de Guzmán, Matienzo, and Delgadillo have had and taken for themselves from the said town and province since the beginning of the year 1529 up to the end of the year 1530 more than ten thousand fanegas of maize and thirty thousand fowl and forty thousand quail and three hundred thousand eggs and a hundred loads of chile and two hundred slaves and three or four thousand pieces of clothing and rich stones and feathers and many works of painting and weaving and many other services and profits which they have had from the said town during the said two years, worth more than four thousand pesos of mined gold; let the witnesses say what they know and have seen that the said Indians have given to the abovementioned.

9. Also, whether they know and saw, etc., that besides the said services and things which they gave to the said Nuño de Guzmán and Licentiates Matienzo and Delgadillo, after five or six months had passed when the abovementioned were making use of them in every kind of service and tribute, the said Indians gave to the official [*of the treasury*] of His Majesty every six months eight hundred pesos of gold which was assayed at thirteen and fourteen carats and two thousands pieces of clothing in each tribute and ten thousand fanegas of maize; and with this they went to the officials of His Majesty, so that besides what the Licentiates Matienzo and Delgadillo and Nuño de Guzmán have exploited from them, the said Indians during the said two years have given three thousand and two hundred pesos in gold and eight thousand pieces of clothing; let the witnesses say what they know.

10. Also, whether they know and saw that while the said Matienzo and Delgadillo were availing themselves of the said town and province both in the said daily services and in the construction of their houses and gardens which they were making, the said Licentiate Delgadillo wrote certain letters to the overseers and persons whom they had in the said towns, saying that they well knew that the Indians and lords of the said town owed him so many thousand fanegas of maize from the tribute of past times and that they should immediately enforce it upon them and imprison them for

e sobre pagarlo e traherlo a esta çivdad fueron los señores e naturales de los dichos pueblos e probinçia muy maltratados.

xi   Yten si saben e vieron y es publico e notorio que a cavsa de las vejaçiones e malos tratamientos que los dichos liçençiados e Guzman mandavan hazer e hazian a los yndios de la dicha probinçia de Vaxoçingo, e las molestias e amenaças que a los señores contino hazian que los avian de ahorcar les mandaron que traxesen en vn camino dos o tres mill yndios cargados de mahiz e no ostante que hera tiempo de ynbierno e muy peligroso con las amenaças e grandes temores que a los señores hazian los enbiaron, y en el puerto de Chalco pereçieron vna noche con las dichas cargas mas de çiento e çinquenta yndios de la dicha probinçia finalmente que murieron por el maltratamiento e agrabios que por ellos les hera hecho.

xii   Yten si saben e vieron oyeron dezir que los dichos Nuño de Guzman Matienço e Delgadillo traxeron en esta çivdad cotidianamente en las obras de sus casas huertas molinos vatanes [*huertas — canceled*] e tierras mas mill e quinientos onbres haziendoles traher la piedra madera cal a su costa e los maestros e ofiçiales que podria mereçer e mereçia mas de tres mill castellanos la obra que con los dichos yndios hizieron durante el tiempo de los dichos dos años.

xiii   Yten si saben y es publico e notorio quel dicho Nuño de Guzman e los dichos liçençiados Matienço e Delgadillo luego que a esta tierra llegaron se mostraron publicos e capitales henemigos del Marques del Valle e de sus criados e amigos e que como tales henemigos les hazian las obras asi en le tomar su hazienda como en prisiones como en vejaçiones e malos tratamientos.

Yten si saben que todo lo suso dicho es publica voz e fama.

Yten de ofiçio etç.

EL LIÇENÇIADO TELLEZ [*rubrica*]

[*13v*] Ynterrogatorio del Marques del Valle contra los liçençiados Matienço e Delgadillo sobre los yntereses de Vaxoçingo.

En xx de março. Por presentado.

E asi presentado el dicho ynterrogatorio en la manera que dicha es los dichos señores dixieron que lo avian por presentado e que se ponga en el proçeso.

A Balverde [*rubrica*]

[*14*] El Marques sobre lo de Guaxoçingo.
Testigo. El dicho Alonso Galeote testigo presentado en la dicha rason aviendo jurado en forma de derecho e siendo preguntado dixo lo siguiente.
i   A la primera pregunta dixo que conosçe los en ella contenidos e sabe e tiene

the payment of it; and concerning the matter of paying it and bringing it to this city the lords and natives of the said towns and province were very badly treated.

11. Also, whether they know and saw and it is public and well known that, by reason of the vexations and maltreatments which the said licentiates and Guzmán commanded to be done and did do to the Indians of said province of Huejotzingo and by reason of the disturbances and threats which they [*the licentiates and Guzmán*] were constantly making to the lords to the effect that they were going to hang them, they [*also*] commanded the lords that they should bring two or three thousand Indians at one time loaded with maize; and in spite of the fact that it was winter and very risky, because of the threats and the resultant fear which they were causing the lords, they sent the Indians; and one night in the pass of Chalco with the said burdens, more than one hundred and fifty Indians of the said province were hurt and finally died from the mistreatment and injuries which were done to them by the said authorities.

12. Also, whether they know and saw or heard it said that the said Nuño de Guzmán, Matienzo, and Delgadillo, for the labor on their houses, gardens, mills, fulling mills, and lands, brought to this city every day a thousand and five hundred more men, making them bring the stone, wood, and lime at their own cost and also [*brought*] masters and craftsmen; and the work which they did with the said Indians during the course of the said two years could have been worth and was worth more than three thousand castellanos.

13. Also, whether they know and whether it is public and well known that as soon as the said Nuño de Guzmán and the said Licentiates Matienzo and Delgadillo arrived in this land, they showed that they were public and capital enemies of the Marqués del Valle and of his servants and friends and that as enemies they did such things to them as to take their possessions and put them in prison, as well as other vexations and ill treatment.

Also, whether all the abovesaid is a matter of public knowledge.

Also, officially, etc.

THE LICENTIATE TELLEZ [*rubric*]

Questionnaire of the Marqués del Valle versus the Licentiates Matienzo and Delgadillo concerning the interests of Huejotzingo.

March 20. As presented.

The said questionnaire having been presented in the manner which is stated, the said lords said that they accepted it as presented and that it should be placed in the proceedings.

To Valverde [*rubric*]

The Marqués, concerning the matter of Huejotzingo.

Witness. The said Alonso Galeote, a witness presented in the said case, having sworn in the legal form and being questioned, said the following.

1. To the first question he said that he knows those who are named in it and that he

notiçia del dicho pueblo porque lo a visto.

Preguntado por las preguntas generales dixo que no es pariente de ninguna de las partes ni su enemigo ni le enpeçe otra cosa de las generales e ques criado del dicho Marques e queria que vençese el pleito la parte que tubiere justiçia e ques de hedad de treynta e e [*sic*] siete años poco mas o menos.

ii A la segunda pregunta dixo que la sabe como en ella se contiene porque lo vido y este testigo estubo en el dicho pueblo por el dicho Marques seys o siete años hasta que vinieron los dichos presidente e oydores.

iii A la terçera pregunta dixo que la sabe como en ella se contiene porque como dicho tiene este testigo estubo en el dicho pueblo e tuvo cargo del seys o siete años e lo bido asi e a la continua el dicho Marques mandaba fuesen bien tratados e yndustriados e para ello procuro de poner los dichos frayles e monesterio a seys años donde estan hasta oy.

iiii° A la quarta pregunta dixo que no la sabe.

v A la quinta pregunta dixo que lo que desta pregunta sabe es que luego como los dichos liçençiados Matienço e Delgadillo vinieron estando este testigo en Guaxoçingo le [*14v*] escrivio Pilar naguatato vna carta a este testigo desde esta çibdad en que le dezia como los dichos liçençiados abian tomado el dicho pueblo de Guaxoçingo para que les diese de comer a anbos que este testigo no lo estorbase e que antes mandase a los dichos yndios que lo traxesen e lo hiziesen e que dende en adelante [*has—canceled*] durante todo el tiempo del cargo de los dichos liçençiados vido este testigo como los yndios del dicho pueblo cotidianamente proveyeron en esta çibdad a los dichos liçençiados de mayz aves gallinas codornices pescado e otras muchas cosas y esto cotidianamente, e estaban en esta çibdad en su seruiçio a la continua yndios del dicho pueblo e que en este tiempo estando este testigo en el dicho pueblo porque los yndios del faltaron a los dichos liçençiados çiertos dias de no dalles el mayz que solian, el dicho liçençiado Delgadillo escrivio a este testigo vna carta en que le dezia que los dichos yndios devian a el e a Matienço çierta cantidad de mayz que le avian faltado de dar queste testigo hiziese con ellos que se lo traxesen y este testigo lo dixo asi a los dichos yndios e los dichos yndios [*lo—canceled*] dixeron que lo trayan.

vi A la [*quinta—canceled*] sesta pregunta dixo que oyo deçir lo contenido en la pregunta a muchas personas de que no se acuerda.

vii A la setena pregunta dixo que dize lo que dicho tiene en la quinta e sesta preguntas e que vido que los dichos liçençiados Matienço e Delgadillo se sirvieron de los dichos yndios como dicho tiene hasta que vinieron los señores presidente e oydores.

[*15*] **viii°** A la octaba pregunta dixo que dize lo que dicho tiene en la quinta pregunta e lo demas que lo no sabe.

ix A la novena pregunta dixo que lo que desta pregunta sabes que desde a dos meses poco mas o menos tiempo a lo queste testigo se acuerda que los dichos presidente e oydores vinieron e que se sirvian como dicho tiene de los dichos yndios, este

has knowledge of the said town because he has seen it.

When he was asked the general questions, he said that he is not a relative of any of the parties nor their enemy nor does anything else of the general questions affect him and that he is a servant of the said Marqués and that he would wish that the party which has justice on its side would win the suit and that his age is approximately thirty-seven years.

2. To the second question he said that he knows it as it is contained in the question because he saw it, and this witness was in the said town for the said Marqués for six or seven years until the said president and oidores came.

3. To the third question he said that he knows it as it is contained in the question because, as he has stated, this witness was in the said town and had charge of it for six or seven years, and he saw that it was thus, and the said Marqués continually commanded that they should be well treated, and he labored to put friars and a monastery in it six years ago, and they are there to the present day.

4. To the fourth question he said that he does not know it.

5. To the fifth question he said that what he knows about this question is that as soon as the said Licentiates Matienzo and Delgadillo arrived, while this witness was in Huejotzingo, the interpreter Pilar wrote a letter to this witness from this city. In it he told him that the said licentiates had taken the said town of Huejotzingo to supply the two of them with food and that this witness should not hinder it, but rather he should command the said Indians that they should bring it and do it. From that time forward, during the whole term of office of the said licentiates, this witness saw that the Indians of the said town daily supplied the said licentiates in this city with maize, fowl, chickens [*turkeys*], quails, fish, and many other things, and this daily. And Indians of the said town were in this city in their service continuously. During this time, while this witness was in the same town, because the Indians of it missed certain days in giving the licentiates maize as they were accustomed, the said Licentiate Delgadillo wrote this witness a letter in which he said that the said Indians owed to him and Matienzo a certain quantity of maize which they had failed to give him [*sic*] and that this witness should deal with them so that they would bring it to him. This witness told this to the said Indians, and the said Indians said that they would bring it.

6. To the sixth question he said that he had heard the contents of the question stated by many people whom he does not remember.

7. To the seventh question he said that he reaffirms what he has stated in the fifth and sixth questions and that he saw that the said Licentiates Matienzo and Delgadillo made use of the said Indians, as he has said, until the arrival of the lords president and oidores.

8. To the eighth question he said that he reaffirms what he has stated in the fifth question and that he does not know the rest.

9. To the ninth question he said that what he knows about this question is that as far as this witness remembers, approximately two months after the said president and oidores arrived and took the services of the said Indians, as he has said, this witness

testigo sabe e vido quel dicho pueblo se puso en cabeça de su Magestad e pusieron en el dicho pueblo por calpisque de su Magestad a vn Gibaja el qual Recogia los tributos por su Magestad y queste testigo pasando por el dicho pueblo vido en poder del dicho calpisque cierto oro en tejuelos el qual dixo a este testigo como andava Recogendo el tributo e que le avian de dar oro e Ropa e que no tiene memoria quantos tejuelos de oro e Ropa le dixo que le davan avnquel dicho Gibaja se lo dixo a este testigo.

x   A las diez preguntas dixo que dize lo que dicho tiene en la quinta pregunta, e quel dicho Gibaja e vn Segura coxo dixeron a este testigo como por mandado del dicho presidente Nuno de Guzman avian atados e traydo los presos a esta çibdad [*con(?) por que los yndios—canceled*] a los señores del dicho pueblo porque no avian venido aviendolos enbiado a llamar e que los avian traydo con çepillos a los pies hasta Estapalapa.

xi   A las honze preguntas dixo que este testigo oyo dezir a vn Vargas estançiero de Baltasar Rodrigues como viniendo de Guaxoçingo a esta çibdad [*15v*] çiertos yndios cargados de mayz para los dichos liçençiados Delgadillo e Matienço en el puerto de Chalco les avia tomado vn yelo de que se avian elado dos o tres yndios e que de los mismos yndios de Guaxoçingo dixeron a este testigo que se avian elado e muerto treynta o quarenta yndios trayendo el dicho mayz para los dichos liçençiados.

xii   A las doze preguntas dixo que no la sabe mas de que [*co—canceled*] cotidiana-mente estavan en esta çibdad cantidad de yndios en seruiçio de los dichos liçençiados, a los quales beya acarrear e traer madera e piedra pero que no sabe para lo que hera.

xiii   A las treze preguntas dixo que lo contenido en esta pregunta fue e a sido y es muy publico e notorio en esta çibdad e tierra e por tal este testigo los a tenido en todo lo que a visto.

xiv°   A las catorze preguntas dixo que dize lo que dicho tiene en que se afirma lo qual es verdad e lo que sabe para el juramento que hizo e firmolo.

ALONSO GALEOTE [*rubrica*]

[*16*] El dicho Juan Valençiano testigo presentado en la dicha Razon aviendo jurado segund derecho dixo lo syguiente.

i   A la primera pregunta dixo que conoçe a los en la dicha pregunta contenidos e que tiene notiçia del dicho pueblo de Guaxoçingo porque le a visto y estado en el mucho tiempo.

Preguntado por las preguntas generales dixo ques de hedad de quarenta e çinco años poco mas o menos e que no le enpeçe ninguna de las generalidades e que vença el pleyto quien toviere justiçia e que a sido criado del dicho Marques e agora no lo es.

ii   A la segunda pregunta dixo que la sabe como en ella se contiene porque asi lo vido este testigo de nueve anos a esta parte queste testigo a estado y esta en esta

knows and saw that the said town was placed under tribute to His Majesty; and they placed in the town as overseer for His Majesty one Gibaja who collected the tributes for His Majesty. This witness, passing through the said town, saw certain gold in ingots in the possession of the said overseer, and he told this witness how he was going around collecting the tribute and that they had to give him gold and cloth. He does not remember what amount of gold ingots and cloth he said that they gave, although the said Gibaja did tell it to this witness.

10. To the tenth question he said that he reaffirms what he has said in the fifth question, and that the said Gibaja and one Segura, a cripple, told this witness how, by command of the said president Nuño de Guzmán, they had tied up the lords of the said town and had brought them as prisoners to this city because they had not come when he had summoned them and that they had brought them with hobbles [*cepillos*] on their feet as far as Istapalapa.

11. To the eleventh question he said that he had heard a certain Vargas, overseer of Baltasar Rodríguez' farm, say how when certain Indians were coming from Huejotzingo to this city burdened with maize for the said Licentiates Delgadillo and Matienzo, a freeze had overtaken them in the pass of Chalco, from which three or four Indians had been frozen. The Indians of Huejotzingo themselves told this witness that thirty or forty Indians had frozen and died when they were bringing the said maize for the said licentiates.

12. To the twelfth question he said that he does not know anything more than that daily there was a quantity of Indians in this city in service of the said licentiates, and he saw them transport and bring wood and stone, but he does not know what it was for.

13. To the thirteenth question he said that the contents of this question were and have been and are very public and well known in this city and land, and this witness has considered them as such in everything that he has seen.

14. To the fourteenth question he said that he reaffirms what he has stated and that he stands fast in it. It is the truth and what he knows by the oath which he made, and he signed it.

ALONSO GALEOTE [*rubric*]

The said Juan Valenciano, a witness presented in the said case, having sworn according to the law, said the following.

To the first question he said that he knows those named in the said question and that he has knowledge of the said town of Huejotzingo because he has seen it and been in it at length.

1. When he was asked the general questions, he said that he is approximately forty-five years old and that none of the generalities affect him; and may he who has justice win the suit; and he has been a servant of the said Marqués, but he is not so anymore.

2. To the second question he said that he knows it as it is contained in the question, because this witness has seen that it is thus for the past nine years that this witness

tierra y este testigo estuvo en el dicho pueblo teniendo cargo de la hazienda por el dicho Marques seys o siete años.

iii   A la terçera pregunta dixo que en todo el tiempo queste testigo estuvo en el dicho pueblo como dicho tiene sabe e vido este testigo que los señores e naturales del dicho pueblo de Guaxoçingo fueron muy bien tratados e administrados syn vexaçion ni eçesivos [*tr—canceled*] seruiçios porque asi lo vido este testigo e el dicho Marques sienpre mandava que asi se hiziese e que los yndios fuesen yndustriados en las cosas de nuestra fee e vido como hizo haçer el dicho monesterio de frayles en el dicho **monesterio.**

iiii°   A la quarta pregunta dixo que no la sabe.

v   A la quinta pregunta dixo que despues que los dichos liçençiados Matienço e Delgadillo vinieron a esta tierra este testigo estuvo en el dicho pueblo çierto tiempo que le paresçe que fue año e medio poco mas o menos e que en todo el dicho tiempo vido este testigo que los yndios del dicho pueblo sirvieron [*16v*] a los dichos liçençiados Matienço e Delgadillo en provelles de las cosas contenidas en la pregunta porqueste testigo lo vido traer a la continua estando en el dicho pueblo e despues queste testigo salio del dicho pueblo supo asymismo de los yndios como todavia hasta que los dichos liçençiados dexaron los dichos cargos los yndios les sirvieron proveyendoles de las dichas cosas e este testigo los veya a los dichos yndios entrar y estar en casa de los dichos liçençiados.

vi   A la sesta pregunta dixo que no la sabe.

vii   A la setena pregunta dixo que no la sabe mas de lo que dicho tiene en las preguntas antes desta.

viii°   A la otava pregunta dixo que sabe e vido este testigo que los dichos yndios daban e dieron a los dichos liçençiados de las cosas contenidas en la pregunta en muncha cantidad [*pero que la—canceled*] e que los yndios se quexavan dello a este testigo pero que no sabe que cantidad fue.

ix   A la novena pregunta dixo que este testigo oyo dezir a Gibaxa calpisque que estava en el dicho pueblo por su Magestad que los dichos yndios davan de tributo a los ofiçiales de su Magestad cada seys meses dozientos pesos de oro e mill mantas e lo demas no lo sabe mas de que quando Nuño de Guzman quiso yr a la guerra los yndios del dicho pueblo traxeron mucha cantidad de cotaras que dezian los dichos yndios que heran para el dicho Nuño de Guzman.

x   A las diez preguntas dixo que este testigo oyo deçir [*lo conte—canceled*] en Guaxoçingo a yndios del e a [*vn—canceled*] fray Toribio del monesterio questa en el dicho pueblo [*17*] lo contenido en esta pregunta, e que avian traydo presos a los dichos yndios [*a este cib—canceled*] a la casa del calpisque del dicho pueblo e en lo demas dize lo que dicho tiene.

xi   A las honze preguntas dixo que dize lo que dicho tiene e queste testigo [*e quel dicho—canceled*] oyo dezir al dicho fray Toribio como por mandado de los dichos liçençiados Matienço e Delgadillo avian salido de Guaxoçingo mucha cantidad de yndios cargados de mayz para los dichos liçençiados e que se avian muerto en el camino çiertos de los dichos yndios e lo demas que no lo sabe.

has been and is in this land; and this witness was in the said town in charge of the properties of the said Marqués for six or seven years.

3. To the third question he said that during all the time that this witness was in the said town, as he has stated, he knows and he saw that the lords and natives of the said town of Huejotzingo were very well treated and administered without vexation or excessive services because this witness saw it thus. And the said Marqués always commanded that it should be done thus and that the Indians should be instructed in the matters of our faith, and he saw how he had the said monastery of friars built in the same monastery [*sic—town*].

4. To the fourth question he said that he does not know it.

5. To the fifth question he said that after the said Licentiates Matienzo and Delgadillo came to this land, this witness was in the said town for a certain time—it seems to him that it was a year and a half, slightly more or less—and this witness saw that during that whole time the Indians of the said town served the said Licentiates Matienzo and Delgadillo in supplying them with the things mentioned in the question, because this witness saw them bring these things continuously while he was in the said town. And after this witness left the said town he knew also from the said Indians how they still served the said licentiates up to the time that they left their offices, supplying them with the said items. And this witness saw the said Indians enter and remain in the house of the said licentiates.

6. To the sixth question he said that he does not know it.

7. To the seventh question he said that he does not know it except for what he has said in the questions before this one.

8. To the eighth question he said that this witness knows and saw that the said Indians gave to the said licentiates some of the things mentioned in the question in great quantity and that the Indians complained about it to this witness, but he does not know what amount it was.

9. To the ninth question he said that he heard Gibaja, the overseer who was in the said town for His Majesty, state that the said Indians gave as tribute to the officials of His Majesty two hundred pesos of gold and a thousand blankets every six months. As to the rest, he does not know it except that when Nuño de Guzmán wanted to go to the war, the Indians of the said town brought a great quantity of footgear which the said Indians stated were for the said Nuño de Guzmán.

10. To the tenth question he said that he heard the Indians in Huejotzingo and Fray Toribio from the monastery in the said town say what is contained in this question; and they had brought the said Indians as prisoners to the house of the overseer of the said town; and as to the rest he asserts what he has already stated.

11. To the eleventh question he said that he reaffirms what he has stated and that this witness heard the said Fray Toribio say how, by command of the said Licentiates Matienzo and Delgadillo, a great number of Indians had left Huejotzingo loaded with maize for the said licentiates and that certain of the said Indians had died on the road, and as to the rest, he does not know anything.

xii A las doze preguntas dixo que a sido muy notorio en este tierra que los dichos liçençiados han sido enemigos del dicho Marques e asy lo a visto este testigo por la obra en las cosas que han tocado al dicho Marques.

xiii A las treze preguntas dixo que dize lo que dicho tiene en que se afirma y es la verdad para el juramento que hizo e firmolo.

        MARTIN DE CASTRO [*rubrica*]
        escriuano

Testigo. Baltasar yndio prinçipal natural del pueblo de Guaxoçingo que dixo ques xpiano [*cristiano*] babtizado abiendo jurado sobre la señal de la cruz e prometido de deçir verdad siendo preguntado por lengua de Albaro de Çamora ynterpetre con juramento en forma que del se Resçibio dixo lo siguiente.

i A la primera pregunta dixo que conosçe a los en ella contenidos e sabe el dicho pueblo porques su tierra.

    Preguntado por las preguntas generales dixo que no es [*pariente — canceled*] enemigo de ninguna de las [*17v*] partes ni a sido ynduzido por ninguna de las partes para dezir cosa alguna mas de la verdad.

ii A la segunda pregunta dixo que la sabe como en ella se contiene porque asi es verdad e lo vido.

iii A la terçera pregunta dixo que la sabe porque asi pasa y es verdad e paso por este testigo como vno de los naturales del dicho pueblo.

iiii° A la quarta pregunta dixo que lo que sabe es que luego que los dichos Nuño de Guzman e liçençiados Matienço e Delgadillo vinieron bido este testigo como [*los dichos — canceled*] Gibaja questava por calpisque en el dicho pueblo de Guaxoçingo dixo al señor e prinçipales del dicho pueblo e a este testigo como vno dellos que los dichos oydores les enbiavan a deçir con el que les enbiasen oro e que se lo pedian en nombre de su Magestad e quel señor e prinçipales del dicho pueblo traxeron çiertos tejuelos de oro e los dieron al contador e lo demas no sabe.

v A la quinta pregunta dixo que sabe e vido que [*l—canceled*] desde a çiertos dias que los dichos presidente e oydores vinieron mandaron a los dichos señor e prinçipales de Guaxoçingo que les sirviesen en esta çibdad de Aves e huevos e codornizes e que destas cosas probeyeron a los dichos presidente e oydores durante todo el tiempo de sus cargos e no de otra cosa de lo contenido en la pregunta.

vi A la sesta pregunta dixo que no la sabe.

[*18*] **vii** A la setena pregunta dixo que no la sabe.

viii° A la otaba pregunta dixo que no dieron a los dichos liçençiados mayz ninguno pero que le dieron muchas aves porque todo el dicho tiempo le dieron cada dia seys aves mayores e seys codornizes e veynte e cinco huebos y esto todo el dicho tiempo, e les dieron asymismo axi e que a los dichos liçençiados no les dieron otra cosa de lo contenido en la pregunta porque lo demas lo davan a los ofiçiales de su Magestad.

ix A la novena pregunta dixo que dieron a su Magestad dos tributos de oro e

12. To the twelfth question he said that it has been very well known in this land that the said licentiates have been enemies of the said Marqués, and this witness has seen that it is thus by their deeds in the matters which have touched on the said Marqués.
13. To the thirteenth question he said that he reaffirms what he has stated, on which he stands firm, and it is the truth by the oath that he made, and he signed it.

> MARTÍN DE CASTRO [*rubric*]
> *notary*

Witness. Baltasar, an Indian leader, native of the town of Huejotzingo, who said that he is a baptized Christian, having sworn on the sign of the cross and promised to tell the truth, and being questioned through Álvaro de Zamora, an interpreter, from whom an oath was taken in legal form, made the following statement.
1. To the first question he said that he knows those who are named in it and that he knows the town because it is his land.

When he was asked the general questions, he said that he is not an enemy of any of the parties nor has he been induced by any of the parties to say anything other than the truth.
2. To the second question he said that he knows it as it is contained in the question because it is the truth and he saw it.
3. To the third question he said that he knows it because it happens thus and is the truth; and it happened to this witness as one of the natives of the said town.
4. To the fourth question he said that what he knows is that as soon as the said Nuño de Guzmán and Licentiates Matienzo and Delgadillo arrived, this witness saw how Gibaja, who was in the said town of Huejotzingo as overseer, said to the lord and leading men of the said town and to this witness as one of them, that the said oidores sent them a message saying that they should send gold and that they were asking for it in the name of His Majesty; and the lord and leading men of the said town brought certain gold ingots and gave them to the accountant, and he does not know the rest.
5. To the fifth question he said that he knows and saw that a few days after the arrival of the said president and oidores, they commanded the said lord and leading men of Huejotzingo that they should do service to them in this city with birds, eggs, and quail, and they provisioned the said president and oidores with these things during their whole term of office and not with anything else mentioned in the question.
6. To the sixth question he said that he does not know it.
7. To the seventh question he said that he does not know it.
8. To the eighth question he said that they did not give any maize to the said licentiates, but that they gave him [*sic*] many birds, because during all of the said time they gave him [*sic*] daily six major birds [*turkeys*] and six quail and twenty-five eggs, and this during the whole period; and they also gave them chile; and they did not give to the said licentiates any other thing of those mentioned in the question because they gave the rest to the officials of His Majesty.

Ropa que fueron en ellos çiento e treynta tejuelos de oro e [*ot — canceled*] mill e
quatroçientos pieças de Ropa en ambos tributos.

x A las diez preguntas dixo que es verdad que los dichos liçençiados enbiaron a
que los prendiesen por el dicho mayz pero que no hera para ellos syno para su
Magestad e que por ellos prendieron a don Juan e a otros señores e prinçipales
del dicho pueblo e los echaron de cabeça en vn çepo.

xi A las honze preguntas dixo que no se acuerda de que se obiesen muerto los
yndios pero ques verdad que fueron molestados e maltratados por mandado de
los dichos presidente e oydores.

xii A las doze preguntas dixo que es verdad que por mandado de los dichos
presidente e oydores los yndios del dicho pueblo hizieron obras en el caño del agua
[*18v*] [*pasa adelante — in the upper margin*] y en las casas donde posavan los
dichos presidente e oydores poniendo para ello piedra madera cal e otros materiales
e trayendolo e llevandolo los yndios a cuestas e que asimismo quando Nuño de
Guzman fue a la guerra les llebo muchos yndios adereçados de guerra a su costumbre
e muchos bastimentos, e al dicho presidente dieron vn penacho con chapas de
oro e quatroçientas mantas e otras mantas Ricas de tochomill, e otras cosas de
todo lo qual mostraron çiertas figuras pintadas e dixeron que todo lo en ellas
pintado dieron a los dichos presidente e oydores.

xiii A las treze preguntas dixo que no sabe el nada desto y esto es la verdad para
el juramento que hizo e lo declaro el dicho ynterpetre so virtud del dicho juramento
e lo firmo.

> [*rubrica*]

[*20; 19 and 19v are blank*]   Testigo. E despues de lo susodicho en la dicha çibdad
de Mexico primero dia del mes de março e del dicho año de mill e quinientos e
treinta e un años fue Resçibido su dicho de Lucas yndio que antes se dezia
Tamavaltetle vesyno e prinçipal de Guaxoçingo por lengua de Pedro [*d — canceled*]
Garcia [*z — canceled*] ynterpetre estante en esta çibdad del qual dicho testigo por
la dicha lengua abiendo jurado en forma de derecho e asymesmo el dicho ynterpetre
que declararya verdad de lo que le fuese preguntado e el dicho yndio Respondiese
e dixese a las dichas preguntas del dicho ynterrogatorio por donde fueron preguntados dixeron lo siguiente.

i A la primera pregunta dixo que conosçe a los contenidos en la dicha pregunta
a los dichos liçençiados Matienço e Delgadillo e Nuño de Guzman de dos años
a esta parte e al dicho Marques del Valle despues que vyno a esta tierra.

Fue preguntado por las preguntas generales dixo ques de hedad de çinquenta
e dos años poco mas e que no es pariente de ninguna de las partes e que el Marques
y los otros contenidos en la pregunta son caballeros y el un maçegual E quel dicho
Marques a sydo su amo deste testigo e de todos los otros yndios de Guaxoçingo

9. To the ninth question he said that they gave to His Majesty two tributes of gold and cloth and that in them there were a hundred and thirty gold ingots and a thousand and four hundred pieces of cloth in the two tributes.

10. To the tenth question he said that it is true that the said licentiates sent a command that they should imprison them because of the said maize but that it was not for them but for His Majesty; and for them [*sic—i.e., this*] they imprisoned Don Juan and other lords and leading men of the said town and they put their heads in stocks.

11. To the eleventh question he said that he does not remember that the Indians died but that it is the truth that they were molested and maltreated by the command of the said president and oidores.

12. To the twelfth question he said that it is true that by command of the said president and oidores the Indians of the said town did construction work on the water conduit and on the houses where the said president and oidores lived, supplying for it the stone, wood, lime, and other materials, which the Indians carried on their backs; and likewise when Nuño de Guzmán went to the war, he took from them many Indians outfitted for war after their fashion and many provisions; and they gave to the said president a piece of featherwork with plates of gold and four hundred blankets and other rich blankets of woven rabbit fur and other things; and of all of this they showed certain painted figures and said that they gave to the said president and oidores everything that is painted on them.

13. To the thirteenth question he said that he does not know anything of this; and this is the truth by the oath that he made; and the said interpreter expounded it by virtue of the said oath, and he signed it.

[*rubric*]

Witness. And after the abovesaid, in the said city of Mexico on the first day of the month of March of the said year of one thousand five hundred and thirty-one a statement was received from Lucas, an Indian who was formerly called Tamavaltetle, a citizen and leading person of Huejotzingo, through an interpreter Pedro García, a resident in this city; after the said witness had sworn in legal form through the said interpreter and the said interpreter had also sworn that he would explain the truth of the questions and of what the said Indian would respond and state to the said questions of the said interrogatory by which they were questioned, they said the following.

1. To the first question he said that he knows those who are mentioned in the question—the said Licentiates Matienzo and Delgadillo and Nuño de Guzmán for the past two years, and the said Marqués del Valle since he came to this land.

When he was asked the general questions, he said that he is a little more than fifty-two years old and that he is not a relative of any of the parties and that the Marqués and the others mentioned in the question are knights and he is a commoner and that the said Marqués has been the master of this witness and of all of the other Indians of Huejotzingo and that he has not been bribed nor asked nor frightened to

E que no a sydo dadivado ni Rogado ni atemoryzado para decir su dicho contra verdad e fue avisado por el dicho ynterpetre que diga verdad e que si no la dixere que Dios Nuestro Señor todopoderoso questa en el çielo le castigara por ello y los señores presydente e oydores tambien muy cruelmente e Respon[*dyo quel es*] xpistiano e que dyra verdad etc. [*e solo la dira que*] lo lleve los vnos o los otr[*os e que les dieron los*] tributos e cosas conten[*idos en(?) vnos papeles*] e dallos a quien es(?) [*Requerido(?) e que lo lleve o vença*] el vno o los otros. [*A corner of this leaf is missing. The text has been reconstructed as far as possible from a microfilm copy which was made before the complete loss of the fragment.*]

[*20v*] **ii** A la segunda pregunta dixo que sabe quel dicho Marques del Valle dende que vino a estas partes e hasta quel dicho Marques se fue dellas para los Reinos de Castilla heran suyos del dicho Marques e le trybutavan e davan todos los tributos que les pedian asi de seruiçios e otros aprovechamientos que dellos el dicho Marques se [*ser — canceled*] queria dellos servir y que despues de partido desta Nueva España el dicho governador don Hernando Cortes el fator Gonzalo de Salazar dixo a este testigo e a otros muchos de los yndios prinçipales del dicho pueblo que ya no heran del dicho governador sino del Rey e que a el abian de trybutar. Fue preguntado como lo sabe dixo que porque lo vydo e este testigo fue uno de los yndios que trybutavan al dicho Marques e los adminitrava e faboresçia mucho en sus cosas que a todos les cumplia e que oy en dia les llora el coraçon porque lo tenyan e queryan como a madre e a padre, e vido quel dicho fator dixo las palabras que dicho tiene.

iii A la tercera pregunta dixo que sabe e vido todo lo contenido en la dicha pregunta porque como dicho tiene en la pregunta antes desta ellos heran tan byen tratados e Relevados e yndustriados del dicho Marques que oy dia le aman e quieren e lloran por el, E se hizo el dicho monesterio de Sant Francisco donde los frayles los yndustriavan e administravan en las cosas de la santa fee catolica de los xptianos e que los tributos que le davan no heran demasyados e los podian [*muy*] bien dar e questo es asy verdad.

[**iiii°** *A la quarta pregun*]ta dixo que lo queste testigo sabe de la dicha [*pregunta lo o*]yo decir a otros yndios e parientes [*e gente del dicho pueblo*] al tiempo que los dichos Nuño [*rubrica*] [*21*] de Guzman e Matienço e Delgadillo vinieron a esta çibdad que abyan enbiado a llamar al Señor y prynçipales del dicho pueblo con vn xpistiano e que esto fue todo muy publico entre chicos e grandes, E que al dicho llamado abyan venido el dicho señor del dicho pueblo E çiertos prinçipales e parientes suyos deste testigo dende en veinte dias que les fueron a llamar pero queste testigo no vino con ellos E queste testigo [*sabe de çierto E oyo deçir — canceled*] no sabe ni oyo deçir que a la sazon los susodichos les pidiesen ni demanda- sen cosa ninguna pero que despues dende a çierto tiempo queste testigo no tiene memorya mas de quanto antes quel dicho Nuño de Guzman fue a la guerra [*Mando llamar E que — canceled*] vn xpistiano español que a la sazon hera calpisque en el dicho pueblo de Guaxoçingo pidio al señor e principales del dicho pueblo le diesen [*oro — between lines*] para comprar vn cavallo para que [*vn —*]

give his statement contrary to the truth; and through the said interpreter he was admonished that he should tell the truth and that if he did not tell it, Almighty God Our Lord who is in Heaven (and the lords president and oidores also) would punish him very cruelly; and he answered that he is a Christian and that he will tell the truth, etc., and that he will tell it alone, and let either the one or the others win it, and that they gave them the tributes and things contained on some papers, and he will give them to whom he is told and let the one or the others gain or win it.

2. To the second question he said that he knows that they belonged to the Marqués del Valle from the time that he came to these parts up until he left them for the realms of Castile, and they paid tribute to him and gave him all the tributes which they asked of them, both in services and in other uses which the said Marqués wished to make of them and that after the said Governor Don Hernando Cortés left this New Spain, the Factor Gonzalo de Salazar told this witness and many of the other leading Indians of the said town that they no longer belonged to the said governor but to the King and that they would have to pay their tribute to him. He was asked how he knew it, and he said that it was because he saw it and this witness was one of the Indians who paid tribute to the said Marqués, who administered and favored them greatly in their affairs, and he performed his duty in regard to all of them; and today their heart weeps, because they held and loved him as their mother and father; and he saw that the said factor said the words that he has said.

3. To the third question he said that he knows and saw everything contained in the said question because, as he has said in the question before this one, they so were well treated and relieved and instructed by the said Marqués, that today they love and want and weep for him; and the said monastery of Saint Francis was built, where the friars administered and instructed them in the matters of the holy Catholic faith of the Christians; and the tributes which they gave him were not excessive and they could very well give them; and this is the truth.

4. To the fourth question he said that what this witness knows about the said question he heard said by other Indians and relatives and people of the town at the time that the said Nuño de Guzmán and Matienzo and Delgadillo came to this city, namely, that they had sent a Christian to summon the lord and leading men of the town, and this was very public among young and old. And at the said summons the said lord of the said town and certain of the leading men and relatives of this witness had come, within twenty days of the summons, but this witness did not come with them, and this witness does not know nor did he hear that at this time the abovementioned men demanded or asked anything. But later after a certain time— this witness does not remember when it was except that it was a while before the said Nuño de Guzmán went to the war—a Christian Spaniard who was at the time overseer in the said town of Huejotzingo asked the lord and leading men of the said town to give

canceled] don Tome señor del dicho pueblo fuese a la guerra cavalgando con el
dicho Nuño de Guzman porque no podia yr a pie e asy buscaron veinte e un
tejuelos de oro pequeños e no gordos de gordor e cantydad de tres uñas de dedo o
de canto de vn Real de plata e porque el dicho su caçique asymęsmo desya quel
no podia yr a la guerra a pie que le buscasen en que fuese e asy le buscaron vn
cavallo e se compro del valor del dicho oro el dicho cavallo e fue con el dicho
Nuño de Guzman e questo es la verdad e quel dicho Nuño de Guzman ni los
dichos liçençiados nunca les pidieron otro oro ny Ropa ni plumas eçebto que
quando el dicho Nuño de Guzman quiso yr [*21v*] [*a la*] guerra [*e — canceled*] les
pidio al dicho señor e prinçipales que le diesen una ymagen de Santa Maria fecha
de oro para la llevar consygo a la guerra porqueste testigo lo vydo y que dende
a çiertos dias los dichos señor e prinçipales a cabsa de no thener oro para hacer
la dicha ymagen e para aver las plumas o plumajes que en ella se avian de poner
[*E —canceled*] vendieron a yndios mercaderes veynte esclavos por [*e — canceled*]
los quales les dieron tres tejuelos de oro e nueve plumajes verdes grandes e los
dichos tejuelos buenos e gordos no sabe que podian pesar e que de los dichos tres
tejuelos se habia hecha la dicha ymagen de Santa Maria E se hizo tan ancha e
tan grande de mas de media braço; e que los dichos nueve plumajes heran çiento
e ochenta plumas Rycos e grandes de los que los dichos yndios tienen en mucho las
quales dichas plumas le pusyeron todo alRededor de la dicha ymagen a manera
de çeradura E que asi hecha desta manera el dicho señor e prinçipales del dicho
pueblo y este testigo con ellos la traxeron al dicho Nuño de Guzman con el dicho
calpisque que se dezia Gibaja, e la dieron al dicho Nuño de Guzman presente este
testigo el qual la Resçibio e que asymesmo al tiempo que les pidio la dicha imagen
el dicho Nuño de Guzman les [*pi—between lines*]dyo [*mantas—canceled*] diez
vanderas pintadas para llevar a la guerra las quales les dieron e tanbien les pidyo
mill e seisçientos pares de çapatos quellos se calçan que se llaman qutaras e mas
[*quatro — between lines*] çientos toldillos e tanbien quatroçientos cantaros de
ocuçotle que huele que [*22*] que se dize liquidanbar entre xpistianos e quatro mill
flechas e otros quatro mill masteles e [*otros — canceled*] mantas los dos mill masteles
e los otros dos mill mantas pequeñas delgadas de las quellos se suelen cobrir e mas
sesenta petacas Encoradas e mas otras dos mill e ochoçientas mantillas otras estas
dichas dos mill e ochoçientas mantillas dixo este dicho testigo [*E los dichos—
canceled*] que los dichos señor e prinçipales las avian dado a los mill onbres yndios
quel dicho Nuño de Guzman llevo del dicho pueblo a la guerra E mas los dichos
quatro mill masteles e mantillas para que se cobriesen e conprasen sus comidas e
los dichos çapatos e cutaras se dieron para su vestir e gasto de los dichos mill yndios
de guerra e que solamente se dyo al dicho Nuño de Guzman la dicha ymagen de
Santa Maria con las dichas plumas e mas vna cama Rica para el dicho Nuño de
Guzman que dieron por ella a mercaderes veynte e dos cargas de Ropa cada carga
de veinte mantas e que [*asymesmo — canceled*] este testigo no se la vido dar syno
que otros prinçipales se la dieron fuee preguntado que quienes fueron los que la
dieron e torno a decir que este testigo se la vido dar al dicho Nuño de Guzman

him gold to buy a horse so that Don Tomé, the lord of the said town, could go to the war on horseback with the said Nuño de Guzmán, because he could not go on foot. And so they sought out twenty-one ingots of gold, small and not fat, of the thickness and quantity of three fingernails or of the edge of a silver real, and because their said chieftain also said that he could not go to the war on foot and that they should seek something on which he might go, they sought a horse and it was purchased for the value of the said gold and he went with the said Nuño de Guzmán, and this is the truth. And neither the said Nuño de Guzmán nor the said licentiates ever asked them for any other gold or cloth or feathers, except that when the said Nuño de Guzmán wanted to go to the war, he asked the said lord and leading men to give him an image of Saint Mary, made of gold, to take with him to the war, because this witness saw it. And after a few days, because they did not have the gold to make the said image and to get the feathers or featherworks to put on it, they sold twenty slaves to Indian merchants for whom they [*the merchants*] gave them three gold ingots and nine great green plumages. And he does not know how much the said good thick ingots might weigh. And from the said three ingots the said image of Saint Mary was made, and it was made as broad and as long as more than half an arm. And the said nine plumages were a hundred and eighty feathers of the long and rich kind [*quetzal feathers*] which the said Indians value very highly, and they placed the said feathers all around the said image after the manner of an enclosure. And when it had been made after this fashion, the said lord and leading men of the said town, and this witness with them, brought it to the said Nuño de Guzmán with the said overseer, who is named Gibaja. And they gave it to the said Nuño de Guzmán in the presence of this witness, and he received it. And at the same time that he asked them for the said image, the said Nuño de Guzmán asked them for ten painted banners to take to the war, and they gave them to them. And he also asked them for a thousand and six hundred pairs of the shoes which they wear, which are called cutaras, and also four hundred small awnings [*toldillos*] and also four hundred pitchers of fragrant ocuço-tle, which is called liquidambar among the Christians, and four thousand arrows, and another four thousand breeches and blankets, two thousand of them breeches and the other two thousand the small thin blankets with which they are accustomed to cover themselves, and also sixty leather-covered chests and also another two thousand eight hundred small blankets. This witness said that the said lord and leading men had given these two thousand eight hundred small blankets to the thousand Indian men whom the said Nuño de Guzmán took from the said town to the war, as well as the said four thousand breeches and little blankets, so that they might cover themselves and buy their food, and the said shoes and cutaras were given for the clothing and expenses of the said thousand Indian warriors. And they gave to the said Nuño de Guzmán only the said image of Saint Mary with the said feathers, plus one rich bed for the said Nuño de Guzmán, for which they gave to some merchants twenty-two loads of cloth, with twenty blankets in each load. This witness did not see it given to him, but other leading men gave it to him. He was asked who were those who gave it to him and he corrected himself to say that this witness had seen it given to the said

e otros prinçipales se la dieron juntamente con este testigo E que mas dieron al calpisque del dicho pueblo veinte paños pintados de algodon de a çinco braças en largo de a ocho piernas cada una que les costaron la hechura e paños [*22v*] treinta e syete carguillas de mantillejas de las malas quellos se cobren de algodon chiquitas de a veynte mantyllejas cada carga; fue preguntado sy sabe por cuyo mandado le dieron al dicho calpisque los dichos veinte paños dixo que no lo sabe mas de quanto el dicho calpisque se los pidio al señor del dicho pueblo antes que fuese a la guerra e a [*sic*] a los prinçipales y este testigo se los vido dar e questo sabe y es verdad de la dicha pregunta.

v A la quinta pregunta dixo que lo que sabe de la dicha pregunta e vido es que dende que los dichos liçençiados Matienço e Delgadillo vynieron a esta çibdad que podra aver dos años [*c — canceled*] poco mas o menos que el señor e prinçipales E yndios del dicho pueblo de Guaxoçingo servian a los dichos liçençiados Matienço e Delgadillo cada vn dia ordynariamente [*dandoles — between lines*] a cada vno dellos diez gallinas e seys codornizes E a Antonio Velazquez naguatato ynterpetre con dos gallinas e vna fanega de maiz cada dia e veinte huebos e que demas desto las vezes quel dicho Antonio Velazquez pidia Ropa que tambien se la davan e algund pescado [*e agy e frisoles—canceled*] e que asymesmo daban e servian a los dichos liçençiados ordinariamente a cada vno dellos [*quarenta — between lines; ochenta — canceled*] huebos en los dias de carne con las dichas gallinas e codornizes y los dias de pescado les davan los dichos huebos e pescado E que de cada syete dias les davan a cada vno de los dichos liçençiados çinquenta cargas de mayz E que [*demas de lo que dicho tiene — canceled*] [*rubrica*] [*23*] quel dicho maiz hera [*del serviçio — canceled*] del mayz de los propios yndios maçeguares del dicho pueblo de Guaxoçingo e su probinçia [*e que demas de — canceled*] fue Repreguntado que si este dicho testigo vido traer el dicho maiz e gallinas [*que — badly blotted*] que dicho tiene dixo que algunas vezes fue en lo traer e dar en las dichas casas de los dichos liçençiados e a ellos fue preguntado que diga e declare por cuyo mandado trayan lo que dicho tiene a los dichos oydores dixo quel dicho calpisque les mandava traer lo susodicho e al dicho Antonio Velazques e questo sabe e vido desta pregunta.

vi A la sesta pregunta dixo que no la sabe ni lo oyo decir.

vii A la setena pregunta que la no sabe Eçebto que los dichos seruiçios e comida que ordinariamente davan los dichos yndios [*del dicho — between lines; e — canceled*] pueblo e su provinçia a los dichos oydores se la dieron todo el tiempo que dicho tiene hasta quel dicho Marques del Valle governador susodicho vyno despaña a estas partes e nunca mas les dieron la dicha comyda ni otra cosa e que a los oydores pasados como dicho tiene le dieron la dicha comida los dichos dos años hasta quel dicho Marques vyno [*a Tezcuco — between lines*] e questo es verdad e que venido el dicho Marquez a Tescuco hasta entonçes les dieron la dicha comida e hasta diez o onze dias despues que dixeron que no tenian que les dar a los dichos oydores.

viii° A la otava pregunta dixo que dize este testigo [*rubrica*] [*23v*] lo que dicho

Nuño de Guzmán, and other leading men had given it to him together with this witness. And moreover, they gave to the overseer of the said town twenty painted cloths of cotton, each one of them about five fathoms in length by eight legs [*piernas*] in width. The cloths and the workmanship cost them thirty-seven small loads of little blankets, of the poor, little cotton ones with which they cover themselves, and there were twenty little blankets in each load.

He was asked if he knows by whose command they gave the said twenty cloths to the said overseer. He said that he did not know more than that the said overseer asked them of the lord and leading men of the said town before he went to the war, and this witness saw them given to him, and this is the truth regarding the said question.

5. To the fifth question he said that what he knows and saw of the said question is that from the time that the said Licentiates Matienzo and Delgadillo came to this city, possibly two years ago, a little more or less, the lord, leading men, and Indians of the said town of Huejotzingo served the said Licentiates Matienzo and Delgadillo, ordinarily giving to each one of them every day ten hens and six quail, and to the interpreter Antonio Velázquez they gave two hens and a fanega of maize every day and twenty eggs, and besides this when the said Antonio Velázquez would ask them for clothing, they would give it to him, and some fish. And as a service to the said licentiates they ordinarily gave to each of them forty eggs with the said hens and quail on days of meat, and on fish days they gave them the said eggs and fish. And every seven days they gave to each of the said licentiates fifty loads of maize, and the said maize was from the maize of the common Indians of the said town of Huejotzingo and its province. He was cross-examined as to whether this said witness saw them bring the said maize and hens which he has mentioned. He said that sometimes he was present when it was brought and given to the said licentiates in their houses. He was asked that he state and declare by whose command they brought what he has mentioned to the said oidores. He said that the said overseer commanded them to bring the abovementioned and also what was given to Antonio Velázquez. And this is what he knows and saw concerning this question.

6. To the sixth question he said that he does not know it nor has he heard it said.

7. To the seventh question, that he does not know it, except that regarding the said services and food which the said Indians of the said town and its province ordinarily gave to the said oidores, they were given to them during the whole time that he has mentioned until the said Marqués del Valle, the abovesaid governor, came from Spain to these parts, and never again did they give them the said food nor anything else. And as he has said, they gave the said food to the past oidores for the said two years until the said Marqués came to Texcoco, and this is the truth. And when the said Marqués came to Texcoco, up until then they gave them the said food and for ten or eleven days afterwards, when they told them that they did not have to give it to the said oidores.

8. To the eighth question he said that this witness reaffirms what he has stated in the

tiene eɪ. la quarta e setena pregunta antes desta e que demas de lo contenido en
ellas sabe e vido este testigo que traxeron a [*la c*]asa [*la casa—badly blotted*] de los
dichos liçençiados Matienço e Delgadillo otras diez myll e tresyentas e veinte cargas
de mayz lo qual hera de los mayzales que solian senbrar para dar e davan al dicho
Marques antes que se fuese a Castylla e que lo demas contenido en la pregunta
este testigo no lo sabe.

ix A la novena pregunta dixo que lo queste testigo sabe e vido de la dicha
pregunta es que en todo el dicho tiempo quel dicho Marques fue a Castylla e
vyno a esta Nueva España los dichos yndios del dicho pueblo de Guaxoçingo e su
provinçia traxeron al contador Rodrigo de Albornoz çiento e veynte tejuelos de
oro no sabe que cosa es quilates pero que dize que hera cada uno de gordor de la
punta del dedo meñique e de anchor del [*primero ded—canceled*] segundo dedo
dende la coyuntura hasta toda la uña, lo qual se les traxo en dos vezes e estava
presente quando se le dyo el dicho oro vn christiano español que dezian que hera
fator para el fator pero que no sabe su nonbre E que asymesmo les davan [*de çiento
E veinte dias a otros çiento e veinte dias — canceled*] cada çiento e veinte dias
[*rubrica*] [*24*] ocho çientas pieças de Ropa de toldillos de a quatro piernas cada
vno de lo que se compran e venden en la tianguez E otros ocho çientas mantyllas
blancas de cobryr de indios de algodon, E que [*no tiene no — canceled*] sabe e
vido que asymesmo trayan a los dichos ofiçiales contador e fator mucho mayz En
muchas vezes cada vez çient cargas pero que no tiene memoria ni sabe que tanta
cantydad Es fue preguntado como sabe lo que dicho tiene e a quien se entregava
de los dichos ofiçiales, dixo que como dicho tiene todo lo suso dicho lo trayan al
dicho contador e antel e que despues de lo aver visto el dicho contador lo mandava
llevar en casa del fator fue preguntado que personas lo Resçibian en casa del
dicho factor, dixo quel que lo Resçibia hera vn español xpistiano baxico de cuerpo
estando presentes otros xpistianos e questo es lo que sabe e vido desta pregunta
e al presente se le acuerda.

x A la deçima pregunta dixo que la no sabe mas de que los calpistes questavan
en el dicho pueblo de Guaxoçingo al tiempo [*que les o — canceled*] y antes que
traxesen a casa de los dichos liçençiados el mayz que tiene declarado en la [*ocho —
between lines*] pregunta les dixeron a los dichos yndios que lo traxesen pues heran
de las tierras del Marques e lo tenian Recogido.

xi A la honzena pregunta dixo que la no sabeçebto que al tiempo que los dichos
yndios del dicho pueblo [*rubrica*] [*24v*] de Guaxoçingo traxeron el mayz contenido
en la dicha otava pregunta que fueron muchos de quebrantamiento hecharon mucha
sangre por las naryzes y en el puerto de Chalco en la pregunta contenido muryeron
algunos de los dichos yndios fue preguntado como lo sabe dixo que porqueste
testigo les vido salir de las dichas naryzes la dicha sangre e la carga que trayan
que hera tambien grande e venia con ellos [*este testigo — between lines*] e que
despues de bueltos al dicho pueblo de Guaxoçingo del dicho quebrantamiento
muryeron como dicho tiene pero queste testigo no los vido morir mas de que le
dixeron que heran muertos otros yndios e questo sabe desta pregunta e vido.

fourth and seventh questions before this. And besides what is contained in them this witness knows and saw that they brought to the house of the said Licentiates Matienzo and Delgadillo another ten thousand three hundred and twenty loads of maize. It was from the maize fields which they used to sow in order to give it to the said Marqués before he went to Castile. And as to the rest contained in the question, this witness does not know it.

9. To the ninth question he said that what this witness knows and saw concerning the said question is that during the whole time while the said Marqués went to Castile and returned to this New Spain, the said Indians of the said town of Huejotzingo and its province brought to the Accountant Rodrigo de Albornoz a hundred and twenty ingots of gold. He does not know what carats are, but he says that each one of them was as thick as the tip of his little finger and as broad as the second finger from the joint to all of the fingernail. They brought it to them in two deliveries, and he was present when the said gold was given to a Christian Spaniard who they say was factor for the factor, but he does not know his name. And also every hundred and twenty days they gave them eight hundred pieces of cloth in small awnings of about four legs each, of the kind that they buy and sell in the market place. And they gave another eight hundred small cotton blankets of the kind with which the Indians cover themselves. And he also saw and knows that they also brought to the said officials, the accountant and factor, much maize at many different times, each time a hundred loads, but he does not remember or know what amount it is. He was asked how he knows what he has said and to which of the officials was it given. He said that, as he has stated, they brought all the abovementioned to the accountant and into his presence, and after the said accountant had seen it, he commanded that it be taken to the house of the factor. He was asked what person received it in the house of the said factor. He said that the one who received it was a Spanish Christian, quite short in stature, while other Christians were present. And this is what he knows and saw and recalls at the present concerning this question.

10. To the tenth question he said that he does not know it, except that the overseers who were in the said town of Huejotzingo before and at the time that they brought to the house of the said licentiates the maize that he has spoken of in the eighth question told the said Indians that they should bring it, since they were from the lands of the Marqués and they had it gathered already.

11. To the eleventh question he said that he does not know it except that at the time when the said Indians from the said town of Huejotzingo brought the maize mentioned in the eighth question, many were very fatigued, and their noses bled badly, and in the pass of Chalco which is mentioned in the question some of the said Indians died. He was asked how he knows it. He said that it was because this witness saw the said blood come from their said noses, and the load that they carried was also great, and this witness came with them. And after they returned to the said town of Huejotzingo they died from the said fatigue, as he has said, but this witness did not see them die, except that other Indians told him that they were dead. And this is what he knows and saw about this question.

xii A la dozena pregunta dixo que lo queste testigo sabe e vido de la dicha
pregunta es que en todo el tiempo [*cont — canceled*] queste dicho testigo tiene dicho
en las preguntas antes desta a la continua andavan en esta çibdad en la obra
quel dicho liçençiado Matienço hasia en sus casas que son en dondel dicho
liçençiado posava antes que veniesen los señores presidente e oydores, trayendo para
la obra de las dichas casas cal e madera e piedra e otros materyales e cosas
nesçesaryas a la dicha obra a su costa de los dichos yndios e su comida quellos
asymesmo trayan, porqueste testigo lo vido e andava en la dicha obra muchas
vezes mandando los dichos yndios e que vna vez porque no querian haçer la dicha
obra enbyaron [*rubrica*] [25] presos a quatro dellos dichos yndios e estuvieron en la
dicha carçel diez dias, e questo es lo que sabe e vido desta pregunta e quel no sabe
apreçiar lo que vale la dicha obra ni lo que alli gastaron pero que vale mucho.
xiii A las treze preguntas dixo que no la sabe ni vido nada desto.
xiiii° A la catorze pregunta del dicho ynterrogatorio dyxo que dize lo que dicho
tiene en que se afirma y es la verdad e lo que dello sabe e vido e al presente se le
acuerda, lo qual que dicho es el dicho Pedro Garçia ynterpetre dixo e depuso so
cargo del dicho juramento que hecho tiene segund quel dicho yndio se lo dixo e
declaro e el lo a podido pronunçiar e declarar, e firmolo de su nombre fuele
encargado el secreto.

     Pedro Garçia [*rubrica*]

Testigo. E despues de lo susodicho en la dicha çibdad de Mexico [*dos—canceled*]
tres dias lunes de dicho mes de abril del dicho año de mill e quinientos e treynta
e vn años por lengua e ynterpetre de Juan de Ledesma veçino desta dicha çibdad
fue Resçibido su dicho e depusiçion de Estevan yndio que antes se dezia Tochel
que en xpistiano quiere decir conejo del qual dicho testigo por la dicha lengua fue
Resçibido juramento en forma devida de derecho so cargo del qual prometio decir
e declarar verdad e lo que dixo e depuso es lo siguiente.
i A la primera pregunta dixo que conosçe [*a los — between lines*] en la pregunta
contenidos al dicho Marques del Valle de [*rubrica*] [25v] diez años a esta parte e a
los dichos liçençiados Matienço e Delgadillo e Nuño de Guzman dende que vinieron
e les mandaron hacer lo que hasyan.
    Fue preguntado por las preguntas generales dixo ques de hedad de quarenta
e syete años poco mas o menos e que no es pariente de ninguna de las dichas partes
e fue abysado por el dicho ynterpetre diga e declare verdad so cargo del juramento
que tiene hecho e fue abysado que sy no la dize que Dios Nuestro Señor le
castigara y los señores tytuanes muy cruelmente dixo quel es xpistiano e sabe que
si dize mentyra que Nuestro Señor le castigara e los señores tytuanes tanbien [*el qual
dixo que si — canceled; E — between lines*] que bien sabe que yra al enfierno e

12. To the twelfth question he said that what this witness knows and saw concerning the said question is that during the whole time which this witness has mentioned in the questions preceding this one, they were continually in this city in the construction work which the said Licentiate Matienzo was doing on his houses, which are where the said licentiate lived before the lords president and oidores came. For the work on the said houses they brought lime, stone, wood, and other materials and things necessary for the said work at the cost of the said Indians, and they likewise brought their food, because this witness saw it and frequently he was present at the said works, commanding the said Indians. And once, because they did not want to do the said work, they sent four of the said Indians to prison, and they were in the said jail for ten days. And this is what he knows and saw concerning this question. And he does not know how to evaluate how much the said work is worth nor what they expended there, but it is worth a great deal.

13. To the thirteenth question he said that he does not know it nor has he seen anything of this.

14. To the fourteenth question of the said interrogatory he said that he reaffirms what he has stated, and he stands firm in it, and it is the truth and what he knows and saw and recalls at the present about it. All of what has been said the said interpreter Pedro García spoke and deposed under the obligation of the oath which he has made, according as the said Indian said and declared it to him and as he has been able to articulate and explain it, and he signed it with his name. He was put under the obligation of secrecy.

PEDRO GARCÍA [rubric]

Witness. And after the abovesaid in the said city of Mexico on Monday the third day of the said month of April of the said year of one thousand five hundred and thirty-one, through the interpreter Juan de Ledesma, citizen of this city, a statement and deposition was received from Esteban, an Indian who was previously named Tochel, which in the Christian language means rabbit. From the said witness through the said interpreter an oath was received in due legal form, under the obligation of which he promised to tell the truth; and what he said and deposed is the following.

1. To the first question he said that he knows those mentioned in the question—the said Marqués del Valle for the past ten years and the said Licentiates Matienzo and Delgadillo and Nuño de Guzmán from the time that they arrived and commanded them to do what they did.

He was asked the general questions. He said that he is forty-seven years of age, a little more or less, and that he is not a relative of any of the said parties; and he was advised through the said interpreter that he should speak and declare the truth under the obligation of the oath that he has made, and he was advised that if he does not speak the truth God Our Lord will punish him, as will also the lords tituanes [*i.e., the president and oidores—possibly from tlatoani, a Nahuatl title for a local ruler*] very cruelly. He said that he is a Christian and he knows that if he tells a lie Our Lord will punish him, and the lord tituanes also, and he knows well that he will go to

promete dezir verdad fue preguntado sy es henemigo de los dichos liçençiados
Matienço e Delgadillo e Nuño de Guzman e sy es amigo del dicho Marques dixo
que al dicho Marques tiene este testigo e todos los maçeguares del dicho pueblo
de Guaxoçingo por padre de todos ellos e que no quiere bien a los dichos
liçençiados e Nuño de Guzman porque un dia los dichos liçençiados mandaron
hechar preso a este testigo en la carçel de cabeça en çepo porque no traya yndios
para hacer en el caño del agua e que queria quel dicho Marques vençese este plito
porque le paguen lo que le an llevado e a toda Guaxoçingo e su provinçia.

ii A la segunda pregunta dixo que sabe e a vysto que del dicho tiempo de los
dichos diez años a esta parte que ha dicho que conosçe al dicho Marques a visto
hasta que los dichos oydores venieron a esta çibdad que servian e seruieron al dicho
Marques teniendole por señor e dando le sus tributos e los tenia en su encomienda
[*rubrica*] [*26*] e administraçion porqueste testigo lo vido e algunas vezes venia con
los maçeguares que trayan el dicho tributo e otras vezes venian otros e otras vezes
Recogia este testigo los yndios que los abian de traer.

[*There is no answer to the third question.*]

iiii° A la quarta pregunta dixo que luego como llegaron a esta çibdad los dichos
liçençiados Matienço e Delgadillo e Nuño de Guzman los yndios del dicho pueblo
de Guaxoçingo e su provinçia ni veniendo a ella no los salieron a Resçibir salvo
quel señor e prinçipales de los dichos yndios y este testigo con ellos vino a esta
çibdad a los ver e conosçer e que no les dieron ningund oro ni Ropa ni otra cosa
salvo que les traxeron comida gallinas e codornizes que podrian ser hasta quarenta
gallinas e veinte codornizes e vna canastilla de huebos, E que dende a un año que
los dichos oydores e Nuño de Guzman heran venidos a esta çibdad el calpiste del
dicho pueblo que se dize Gibaja que dizque es ydo a Guatymala les dixo que
diesen algo a Nuño de Guzman quando queria yr a la guerra y ellos les dixeron
que que le darian y el dicho Gibaja les dixo que [*una ymagen — canceled*] lo
quellos quisiesen y ellos ordenaron de hacer un paño con una hoja de oro [*en medio
— between lines*] de ymagen de Santa Maria toda la dicha hoja e ymagen la qual
le dieron al dicho Nuño de Guzman ellos y el dicho [*cos — canceled*] calpiste que
se la traxeron a esta çibdad, e que para la obra e gasto de lo que la dicha ymagen
costo vendieron veinte esclavos ocho onbres e doze mugeres y para mas tres
tejuelos de oro [*rubrica*] [*26v*] que entraron en la dicha ymagen, y que [*el d —
canceled*] Ençima del paño donde yva asentada la dicha ymagen yvan nueve
plumajes cada plumaje veinte plumas que les costaron nueve cargas de toldillos
de a veinte toldillos cada carga, e que este testigo vido quel dicho Nuño de Guzman
dixo al señor de Guaxoçingo que le diese gente para yr a la guerra con el seys
çientos onbres aparejados a vso de guerra como ellos lo solian hacer e que se los
dieron e con ellos e çierta Ropa e aparejos que tienen pintados en çiertos papeles
e pydio que le fuesen mostrados los dichos papeles e le fue mostrado vn papel de
çiertas pinturas la qual va señalada de una señal de mi el escribano e Reçebtor

hell, and he promises to tell the truth. He was asked whether he is an enemy of the said Licentiates Matienzo and Delgadillo and Nuño de Guzmán and whether he is a friend of the said Marqués. He said that this witness and all the common people of the said town of Huejotzingo consider the said Marqués as the father of all of them and that he does not well like the said licentiates and Nuño de Guzmán because one day the said licentiates commanded that this witness should be thrown into the prison with his head in the stocks because he did not bring Indians to work on the water conduit. And he would like for the said Marqués to win this lawsuit so that they will pay him for what they have taken from him and from all of Huejotzingo and its province.

2. To the second question he said that he knows and has seen that during the period of the past ten years during which, as he has said, he has known the said Marqués, he has seen that until the said oidores came to this city they served the said Marqués, considering him as their lord and giving him their tributes, and he had them in his charge and administration, because this witness saw it, and sometimes he came with the commoners who brought the tribute, and at other times others came, and at other times this witness gathered the Indians who would bring it.

[*There is no answer to the third question*]

4. To the fourth question he said that when the said Licentiates Matienzo and Delgadillo and Nuño de Guzmán arrived in this city, the Indians of the said town of Huejotzingo and its province did not come to it nor did they go out to receive them, except that the lord and leading men of the said Indians, and this witness with them, came to this city to see and know them. And they did not give them any gold or cloth or anything else, except that they brought food, hens, and quail, possibly as many as forty hens and twenty quail and a little basket of eggs. And about a year after the said oidores and Nuño de Guzmán had come to this city, the overseer of the said town, who is named Gibaja, who has reportedly gone to Guatemala, told them that they should give something to Nuño de Guzmán when he wanted to go to the war. And they asked what should they give. And the said Gibaja told them, whatever they wished. And they determined to make a cloth with a sheet of gold, and the whole sheet of gold would be an image of Saint Mary. This they gave to the said Nuño de Guzmán, they and the said overseer, and they brought it to him in this city. And for the workmanship and expense of what the said image cost, they sold twenty slaves— eight men and twelve women—and also for the three ingots of gold which went into the said image. And on top of the cloth on which the image was placed there were nine plumages, each plumage consisting of twenty feathers, and these cost them nine loads of little awnings, with twenty awnings in each load. And this witness saw that the said Nuño de Guzmán said to the lord of Huejotzingo that he should give him men to go to the war with him—six hundred men outfitted for war after the manner in which they are accustomed to do it. And they gave them and with them also certain clothing and gear which they have painted on certain papers. And he asked that the said papers be shown to him, and he was shown one paper of certain paintings, which is signed with a sign of me the undersigned notary and secretary.

ynfrascripto, e vista por el las dichas pynturas el dicho ynterpetre dixo que en aparejos de la dicha gente abian gastado treinta e dos mill e quatroçientas pieças de Ropa de toldillos y luego torno a decir que heran veinte e syete mill e seyscientas pieças de toldillos e que entre los dichos onbres que asy llevo a la guerra fueron honze prinçipales de honze casas de Guaxoçingo y que despues que fue el dicho Nuño de Guzman partido desta çibdad porque don Tome yndio [*señor — canceled*] hermano del dicho señor de Guaxoçingo yva con el a la guerra e no podya yr a pie le dieron para en que fuese vn cavallo el qual les costo veynte e vn tejuelos En oro pequeños segun que lo vido e pidyo que le fuese mostrado otro papel donde los tenian pintados en el qual esta el dicho [27] la dicha ymagen E pintura de Santa Maria que dicho tiene y esclavos que les costo e que les dieron a los yndios que yvan a la guerra con el dicho Nuño de Guzman dosientos masteles e quatro mill arquillos de saeta de tepuzque o metal de la tierra e mill e seysçientos pares de cutaras e les dieron mas para la comyda del dicho camino ochoçientas mantillas a los dichos yndios para con que la conprasen e mas les dieron [*quatro — between lines; ocho — canceled*] çientas ollillas de Resyna lo qual todo que dicho es esta pintado en el dicho papel En que esta figurada la dicha ymagen de Nuestra Señora e señalada de my señal otrosy dixo que [*le — canceled*] dieron mas a los dichos yndios para yr a la dicha guerra nueve cargas de mantas delgadas de a veynte mantas cada carga de las con que los dichos yndios se cubren segund que lo tenian pintado en la dicha pintura, e que para hacer una vandera que dizque esta pintada en la dicha pintura para que los dichos yndios llevasen diez cargas de mantillas delgadas de cobryr de a veynte mantas cada carga luego torno a decir que la dicha vandera la llevava don Tome fue preguntado que como sabe lo que dicho tiene dixo que porque este testigo lo vido e estuvo presente al tiempo que se lo dieron para que lo llevasen a la guerra e se gastase en lo que dicho tiene e otrosi dixo mas este dicho testigo que le fuese mostrados otros dos papeles de pynturas e visto por el testigo uno dellos dixo quel dicho papel En que traen pintados çinco paños [*rubrica*] [27v] dixo que los dichos çinco paños se hisyeron de tochumy colorado en que gastaron en cada vno de los dichos çinco paños ochenta pieças de Ropa delgada pequeñas dellas y de las otras, y queste testigo vydo quel dicho calpiste que se dezia Gibaja los pidio al dicho don Juan caçique del dicho pueblo diziendo que lo mandavan Matienço e Delgadillo e que los dichos paños heran para Matienço y este testigo vydo que se hisieron los dichos paños e despues vido [*quel dicho cal — canceled*] que los prinçipales del dicho pueblo venieron a esta çibdad e dezian que venian a dar los dicho paños al dicho Matienço porqueste testigo los vido partyr para esta çibdad con los dichos paños e despues de bueltos los dichos prinçipales y el dicho don Juan este testigo les pregunto sy se los abian dado e que le Respondio el dicho don Juan que avia venido con los dichos prinçipales e que se los abya dado el qual dicho papel va asymesmo señalado de my Rubryca, e [*el dicho — canceled*] el otro dicho papel de pinturas que asymesmo va señalado de my señal, dixo que veynte paños de pinzel que en el estan fygurados

And when he had looked at the said pictures, the said interpreter said that in gear for the said warriors they had spent thirty-two thousand and four hundred pieces of cloth of small awnings, and then he corrected himself to say that they were twenty-seven thousand and six hundred little awnings. And among the said men whom he took to the war there were eleven leading men of eleven houses of Huejotzingo. And after the said Nuño de Guzmán had left this city, because Don Tomé, Indian, brother of the said lord of Huejotzingo, was going with him to the war and he could not go on foot, they gave him a horse on which to ride. It cost them twenty-one small gold ingots, according to what he saw. And he asked to be shown another paper where they have them painted, on which is the said image and painting of Saint Mary which he has mentioned and the slaves which it cost them. And they gave to the Indians who went to the war with the said Nuño de Guzmán two hundred breeches [*masteles*] and four thousand small bows with arrows of tepuzque, or the metal of the land, and a thousand and six hundred pairs of cutaras. And also for their food along the said road, they gave eight hundred small blankets to the said Indians so that they might buy the food with them, and they also gave them four hundred small pots of resin. All this that has been stated is painted on the said paper on which is depicted the said image of Our Lady and which is signed with my sign. Further, he said that to the said Indians who were going to the said war they gave nine loads of thin blankets, with twenty blankets in each load, of the kind with which the said Indians cover themselves, according as they have painted it in the said painting. And in order to make a banner which he says is painted in the said painting, so that the said Indians could carry it, they spent ten loads of the thin little blankets for covering, with twenty blankets in each load. He then corrected himself to say that Don Tomé carried the said banner. He was asked how he knows what he has said. He said that it was because this witness saw it and was present at the time when they gave it to them so that they could take it to the war and spend it on what he has said. And, further, this witness asked that he should be shown two other papers of paintings, and when the witness saw one of them he said that the said paper on which they have five cloths painted—he said that the said five cloths were made of red rabbit fur, and that on each one of the said five cloths they spent eighty small pieces of thin cloth of the one kind and the other. And this witness saw that the said overseer who is named Gibaja requested them of the said Don Juan, the cacique of the said town, saying that Matienzo and Delgadillo commanded it and that the said cloths were for Matienzo. And this witness saw that the said cloths were made, and later he saw that the leading men of the said town came to this city and they said that they were coming to give the said cloths to the said Matienzo, because this witness saw them leave for this city with the said cloths. After the said principal men and the said Don Juan had returned, this witness asked them whether they had given the cloths to him, and the said Don Juan answered him that he had come with the said leading men and that they had given them to him. This said paper is also signed with my rubric. And as to the other said paper of paintings, which is also signed with my sign, he said that the twenty painted cloths which are depicted on it were made

se hisyeron en el dicho pueblo e provinçia de Guaxoçingo por mandado del dicho
calpiste el qual les dixo que heran para el dicho Nuño de Guzman e quel les
mandava y los dichos liçençiados que se hisiesen e asy las hysyeron los dichos veinte
paños que costaron los diez e syete dellos hacer cada vno a quarenta mantas y los
otros tres a [28] veynte mantas porque no heran tales e queste testigo vydo quel
dicho don Juan con çiertos prinçipales los enbyo a esta çibdad al dicho liçençiado
Matienço e despues supo que los abya Resçibido el dicho Matienço.

v   A la quinta pregunta dixo que lo queste testigo sabe e vydo de la dicha pregunta
es que luego como a esta çibdad vinieron les mandaron al dicho don Juan que les
hisyese seruir [*de — between lines; ca de leña e — canceled*] abes [*e yerba —
canceled*] gallinas e codornizes e agi e tomatles fue preguntado como entendyo el
que se lo dezia al dicho don Juan [*dixo—canceled*] E en que lengua se lo abya
dicho dixo que Velazquez que entonçes hera su naguatato lo dixo al dicho don Juan
presente este testigo e otros prinçipales E que dende en adelante cada dia les
seruian En les traer a los dichos liçençiados para amos a dos syete gallinas e quatro
codornizes e veynte huebos lo qual davan a los cozineros de los dichos liçençiados e
queste testigo fue en lo traer algunas vezes e otras vezes en lo Recoger en el dicho
Guaxoçingo para lo enbiar; luego dixo que nunca este testigo vyno con las dichas
gallinas e codornizes syno que lo enbiaba y lo Recogia fue preguntado que pues
como sabe que los cozineros de los dichos liçençiados lo Resçibian dixo que lo
supo e sabia de los prinçipales que lo venian a traer E questo sabe desta pregunta.
[*rubrica*]

[*28v*] **vi**   A la sesta pregunta dixo que la no sabe.

vii   A la setena pregunta dixo que dize lo que dicho tiene en la quinta pregunta
e que los dichos liçençiados Matienço e Delgadillo e Nuño de Guzman les mandaron
que diesen los tributos al fator del Rey e que asy se lo dieron dos vezes en oro e
Ropa, e que los dichos serviçios hordinarios de comyda lo daban a los dichos
liçençiados Matienço e Delgadillo e se lo dieron quantia de dos años dende que se
lo enpeçaron a dar hasta que venieron a este çibdad los señores presidente e
oydores e luego dixo que se lo dexaron de dar quando el dicho Marques del Valle
vyno e al dicho Marques se lo davan el dicho seruiçio ordinario todo el tiempo
questovo en Tezcuco torno a decir que nunca dieron nada al dicho Marques salvo
que dende a obra de diez dias despues que los dichos señores oydores llegaron a
esta çibdad el dicho Marques les dixo que seruiesen a Francisco Verdugo al qual
syrven.

A la otava pregunta dixo que dize lo que dicho tiene en la quinta pregunta e
setima preguntas [*dixo — canceled*] e quel mayz que les an dado para sy [*demas(?)
— canceled*] a los dichos liçençiados Matienço e Delgadillo no lo tienen debujado
mas de quanto de ocho a ocho dias les davan a cada vno dellos cinquenta cargas
de mayz que no sabe quanto valdrian ni lo que pueden montar los gallinas e
co[*r — canceled*]dorni[*29*]zes, e huebos, e agi e tomatles e que no sabe que les ayan
dado otra cosa mas de lo que tiene dicho en la quarta pregunta que se dyo asy
para el dicho liçençiado como para los yndios que yvan con el dicho Nuño de

in the said town and province of Huejotzingo, by the command of the said overseer, who said that they were for the said Nuño de Guzmán and that he and the said licentiates commanded them to make them. And thus they made the said twenty cloths, and to make seventeen of them it cost forty blankets apiece, and the other three cost twenty blankets apiece because they were not as good. And this witness saw that the said Don Juan sent them to this city with certain leading men to the said Licentiate Matienzo, and later he knew that the said Matienzo had received them.

5. To the fifth question he said that what this witness knows and saw concerning the said question is that as soon as they came to this city, they commanded the said Don Juan that he should see to it that they were supplied with birds, hens, and quail, and chile and tomatoes. He was asked how he understood the person who said that to the said Don Juan and in what language he had said it. He said that Velázquez, who was at that time his interpreter, told it to the said Don Juan in the presence of this witness and of the other leading men. And from that time onward they served them by bringing to the two licentiates together seven hens and four quail and twenty eggs, which they gave to the cooks of the said licentiates. And sometimes this witness took part in bringing them, and sometimes in collecting them in the said Huejotzingo in order to send them. Then he said that this witness never came with the said hens and quail but that he sent them and he collected them. He was asked, then, how does he know that the cooks of the said licentiates received them. He said that he knew it from the leading men who came to bring them. And this is what he knows about this question.

6. To the sixth question he said that he does not know it.

7. To the seventh question he said that he reaffirms what he has said in the fifth question and that the said Licentiates Matienzo and Delgadillo and Nuño de Guzmán commanded them that they should give the tributes to the King's factor and that thus they gave them to him twice in gold and cloth. And the said ordinary services of food they gave to the said Licentiates Matienzo and Delgadillo, and they gave them for a period of two years, from the time that they began to give it until the arrival of the lords president and oidores in this city. And then he said that they left off giving it when the said Marqués del Valle came and they gave the said ordinary service to the said Marqués all the time that he was in Texcoco. He corrected himself to say that they never gave anything to the said Marqués, except that, about ten days after the arrival of the said oidores in this city, the said Marqués told them that they should serve Francisco Verdugo, whom they now serve.

To the eighth question he says that he reaffirms what he said in the fifth and seventh questions. And as to the maize that they have given to the said Licentiates Matienzo and Delgadillo for themselves, they do not have it depicted, but regarding the amount, they gave to each of them every eight days fifty loads of maize. He does not know how much they would all be worth nor what the hens, quail, eggs, chile, and tomatoes would amount to. And he does not know that they have given anything else besides what he has said in the fourth question, which was given both for the said licentiate and for the said Indians who were going with the said Nuño de

Guzman a la guerra; e questo sabe des[*ta*] pregunta.

ix A la novena pregunta dixo que lo que sabe desta pregun[*ta*] es que dende a obra de seys meses poco ma[*s*] o menos que los dichos yndios del dicho pueblo de Guaxoçingo e su provinçia en dar la comida ordinaria que dicho tiene a los dichos liçençiados Matienço e Delgadillo que dieron en dos vezes [*a — canceled*] los dichos señor e prinçipales del dicho pueblo a los ofiçiales de su Magestad la una vez setenta tejuelos e la otra sesenta que este testigo no sabe que tanto podian valer entre xpistianos syno que heran buenos e del tamaño e anchor de los tres tejuelos questan pintados en [*el*] dicho papel donde esta pintada Santa Maria de gordor cada vno como la punta del dedo de la mano meñique ni tanpoco sabe de que ley o quilates podian ser mas de que los dichos tejuelos tocava el dicho calpiste en el dicho pueblo e quel se contentava de la color quel oro e tejuelos tenian e asi lo trayan fue preguntado como sabe lo que dicho tiene dixo que porqueste testigo Recogio el dicho oro en el dicho pueblo e provinçia de [*29v*] Guaxoçingo y el señor e prinçipales dello dieron a çiertos prinçipales para que lo traxesen a esta çibdad e que despues supo este testigo que abyan venido con ello antel contador de su Magestad Rodrigo de Albornoz con e con [*sic*] mill e dozientas pieças de Ropa que asymesmo este testigo recoxo para que traxesen e que visto por el dicho contador lo abya enbiodo a la casa del fator de su Magestad e quo lo abya alli Resçibido no tiene memoria quien e quel mayz que al dicho fator an dado lo tienen pintado en una pyntura que pydio le[*s — canceled*] fuese mostrado e vista por el dixo por la dicha lengua que diez e seys pinturas negras de pintura de manera de peynes de indios cada pintura es quatroçientas cargas de mayz e otros diez e syete Rayas negras a manera de vanderyllas de yndios derechas, que cada vna dellas es veinte cargas, dixo que todo el dicho mayz enbiaron del dicho pueblo de Guaxoçingo a esta çibdad con yndios tamenes que lo trayan e çiertos prinçipales con ellos lo qual es del maiz del tributo del año pasado de veynte e nueve E que del tributo del año de quinientos e treinta les enbyaron todo el maiz que se montan nueve Rayas coloradas a manera de peynes de yndios [*30*] que cada bna de las dichas Rayas es quatrocientas e otra Raya colorada pintada de manera de vandera derecha, dize que son veinte cargas todo el qual dicho mayz dixo que abian sacado de una trox que alli en la dicha pyntura trayan pintada, fue preguntado que a quien se dyo y entrego el dicho mayz dixo que lo traxeron al dicho contador a que lo viese a que de alli lo llevaron a casa del fator porque asy se lo dixo otros prinçipales del dicho pueblo que abyan venido con los dichos tamemes lo qual les mandavan que traxesen los dichos liçençiados Matienço e Delgadillo, e questo sabe desta pregunta el qual dicho papel de pyntura va señalado de mi el dicho escribano e Reçeptor.

x A la decima pregunta dixo que la no sabe.

xi A la honzena pregunta dixo que del quebrantamiento que los yndios tovieron

Guzmán to the war. And this is what he knows about this question.

9. To the ninth question he says that what he knows about this question is that it was a matter of six months, a little more or less, after the said Indians of the said town of Huejotzingo and its province began to give to the said Licentiates Matienzo and Delgadillo the ordinary food which he has mentioned, that on two occasions the said lord and leading men of the said town gave to the officials of His Majesty seventy ingots the first time and sixty the second. This witness does not know how much they might be worth among Christians, but that they were good and of the form and breadth of the three ingots that are painted on the said paper where Saint Mary is painted. Each one was of the thickness of the end of the little finger. Neither does he know of what quality or carats they might be except that in the said town the said overseer touched the said ingots and that he was content with the color that the gold in the said ingots had, and so they brought it. He was asked how he knows what he has said. He said that it was because this witness collected the said gold in the said town and province of Huejotzingo, and the lord and leading men gave it to certain leading men to bring it to this city, and later this witness knew that they had come with it before Rodrigo de Albornoz, the accountant of His Majesty, together with a thousand and two hundred pieces of cloth which this witness likewise collected so that they might bring it. And after the said accountant had seen it, he had sent it to the house of the factor of His Majesty, and there someone whom he does not remember received it. And as to the maize which they have given to the said factor, they have it painted in a painting which he asked to be shown. And when he saw it he said through the said interpreter, regarding the sixteen black pictures painted after the fashion of the combs of the Indians, that each picture represents four hundred loads of maize and the other sixteen black bands, after the fashion of outstretched banners of the Indians, each one of them is twenty loads. He said that they sent all of the said maize from the said town of Huejotzingo to this city by Indian bearers who brought it, and there were certain leading men with them. This is concerning the maize of the tribute of the past year of twenty-nine. And concerning the tribute of the year of [*one thousand*] five hundred and thirty, they sent them all the maize which amounts to nine red bands after the fashion of Indian combs, and each of the said bands is four hundred, and of the other red band, painted after the fashion of an outstretched banner, he says that they are twenty loads. All of this said maize he says that they had taken from a granary which they have depicted there in the said painting. He was asked to whom they gave and delivered the said maize. He said that they brought it to the said accountant so that he might see it and that from there they took it to the house of the factor, because that is what he was told by the other leading men of the town who had come with the said bearers. The said Licentiates Matienzo and Delgadillo commanded them that they should bring it. And this is what he knows about this question. The said paper of painting is signed by me, the said notary and secretary.

10. To the tenth question he said that he does not know it.

11. To the eleventh question he said that from the fatigue which the Indians suffered

en traer el dicho maiz que dicho tiene a los ofiçiales de su Magestad de cansados e quebrantados [*quan—canceled*] despues de bueltos a sus casas [*adoleçieron e— between lines*] muryeron algunos dellos porqueste testigo lo vidos [*sic—los vido*] enterrar.

xii A la dozena pregunta dixo que nunca labraron en los hedifiçios e obras contenidas en la pregunta salvo en las casas donde posava el dicho liçençiado Matienço en que [*rubrica*] [*30v*] agora posan los señores liçençiados Juan de Salmeron e Ceynos E no[?]en la casa donde posava el dicho liçençiado Delgadillo, y en las obras de la casa e monesterio de Santo Domingo desta çibdad las quales obras que asy hisyeron en las dichas casas e monesterio dixo que tienen pintadas en tres papeles la Ropa e agy e chian que gastaron en mayz en la hacer y en la piedra e madera que supo pero que no sabe quanto puede valer porqueste testigo vido que los dichos oydores lo mandaron al dicho don Juan y el dicho calpiste tambien disiendo que los dichos oydores pasados se lo mandaban, los quales dichos tres papeles van señalados asymesmo del señal de mi el dicho Reçebtor.

xiii A las treze preguntas dixo que no sabe mas de quanto este dicho testigo oyo deçir que los liçençiados quitavan al dicho Marques que no le syrviesen e tributasen los dichos pueblos de Guaxoçingo e su provinçia.

xiiii° A la cartorze preguntas dixo que dize lo que dicho tiene en ques verdad por el juramento que tiene fecho en que se afirma lo qual todo que dicho es el dicho Juan de Ledesma ynterpetre dixo e declaro so cargo del dicho juramento que tiene hecho e que lo abya declarado de la manera quel dicho yndio se lo abya dicho e firmolo de su nombre.

JUAN DE LEDESMA [*rubrica*]

[*31*] Testigo. El dicho Rodrigo de Almonte estante en esta dicha çibdad e vesyno de la villa de Sant Luys testygo suso dicho aviendo jurado en forma debyda de derecho e syendo preguntado por las preguntas del dicho ynterrogatorio dixo e depuso lo siguiente.

i A la primera pregunta dixo que conosçe a los contenidos en la dicha pregunta al dicho Marques del Valle demas de quinze años a esta parte e a l[*os—canceled*] dichos liçençiado[*s—canceled*] Matienço demas de diez e seys años e al dicho Nuño de Guzman e Delgadillo en tiempo que usaron en esta çibdad los dichos ofiçios e cargos de presydente e oydor, e que tiene notiçia e sabe el pueblo contenido en la dicha pregunta porque a estado en el muchas vezes.

Fue preguntado por las preguntas generales dixo ques de hedad de treynta e çinco años e mas e que no es paryente de ninguno de los contenidos en la dicha pregunta ni henemigo de ninguno dellos ni es criado ni alegado de ninguna de las dichas partes ni lleva interese en esta cabsa e que vença este plito la parte que tuviere[?] justicia.

ii A la segunda pregunta dixo que la sabe como en ella se contiene porqueste testigo vido quel dicho Marques se seruia e seruio del dicho pueblo e yndios del e lo tenia

in bringing the said maize to the officials of His Majesty, as he has mentioned, from among those who were broken with fatigue after they returned to their houses, some of them grew sick and died, because this witness saw them buried.

12. To the twelfth question he said that they never labored on the buildings and works contained in the question, except in the houses where the said Licentiate Matienzo lived, in which the lords Licentiates Juan de Salmeron and Ceynos now live, and not [?] in the house where the said Licentiate Delgadillo lived, and on the works on the house and monastery of Saint Dominic of this city. Regarding the works which they did on the said houses and monastery, he said that they have painted on three papers the cloth, chile, and sage which they spent for maize and for the stone and wood. He knew, but he does not know now, how much it might be worth, because this witness saw that the said oidores commanded it to the said Don Juan, and the said overseer did so likewise, saying that the said past oidores commanded it. The said three papers are also signed with the sign of me, the said secretary.

13. To the thirteenth question he said that he does not know anything more than that this said witness heard it said that the licentiates took away from the said Marqués the said towns of Huejotzingo and its province so that they should not serve him or give him tribute.

14. To the fourteenth question he said that he reaffirms what he has stated, and the truth is in it by the oath that he has made, and he stands firm in it; and everything that has been said the said Juan de Ledesma, interpreter, stated and explained under the obligation of the oath which he has made, and he said that he had interpreted it after the manner that the said Indian had said it, and he signed it with his name.

JUAN DE LEDESMA [*rubric*]

Witness. The said Rodrigo de Almonte, resident in this city and a freeholder of the town of San Luis—the aforesaid witness having sworn in the due legal form and being questioned by the questions of the said questionnaire, said and deposed the following.

1. To the first question he said that he knows those who are mentioned in the said question—the said Marqués del Valle for more than the past fifteen years and the said Licentiate Matienzo for more than sixteen years and the said Nuño de Guzmán and Delgadillo during the time that they have exercised their said offices and duties of president and oidor in this city, and he knows and has information concerning the town mentioned in the question, because he has been in it many times.

He was asked the general questions. He said that he is thirty-five years old and more and that he is not a relative of any of those mentioned in the said question nor is he an enemy of any of them, nor is he a servant or ally of any of the said parties, nor does he have any special interest in this case, and may the party who has justice win this suit.

2. To the second question he said that he knows it as it is contained in the question because he saw that the said Marqués had the service of the said town and the

e tuvo en su encomienda e administra[*31v*]çion llevando los tributos e aprovechamientos del hasta tanto que le fueron quitados los dichos yndios por el dicho
presydente e oydores pasados e queste testigo vido quel dicho Marques tenya en el
dicho pueblo por su calpisque a Alonso Galeote e a Juan Valençiano por estançiero
o porquero que le criava e tenia cargo la granjeria e criança de los dichos puercos
que tenia en una estançia del dicho pueblo e a bna legua del.

iii   A la terçera pregunta dixo que sabe la dicha pregunta segund e como en ella
le [*sic—se*] contiene fue preguntado como la sabe dixo que porqueste testigo lo bydo
estando este testigo en el dicho pueblo de Guaxoçingo hablando con los señores e
prinçipales del le dezian que heran muy bien tratados del dicho Marques e de los
que por el estavan e que heran mandados tratar muy bien e Alonso Galeote por su
mandado los tratava muy bien e porque este testigo nunca vido ni supo que los
dichos yndios en tiempo quel dicho Marques los tuviese en su comienda e administraçion se quexasen ni quexaban como despues aca lo an hecho disiendoles a este dicho
testigo los dichos señores e prinçipales que los dichos presydente e oydores pasados
les fatigaban e molestaban mucho hechandodoles [*sic*] muchos tributos e en hacer los
venir a labrar a esta çibdad e que en el dicho monesterio de Sant Françisco del dicho
pueblo de Guaxoçingo los veya e vido que [*los—between lines*] yndustriavan [*32*] E
administraban los frayles del dicho monesterio en las cosas de nuestra santa fe catolica
veniendo al dicho monesterio a misa los señores e prinçipales del dicho pueblo e
[*prinçipales—canceled*] maçiguares del e questo es asy verdad.

iiii°   A la quarta pregunta dixo que oyo decir lo contenido en la dicha pregunta
que abia pasado asy a muchas personas de cuyos nonbres al presente no se acuerda.

v   A la quinta pregunta dixo que lo oyo decir como la pregunta lo declara a personas de cuyos nonbres no se acuerda.

vi   A la sesta pregunta dixo que oyo decir lo en la pregunta contenido a muchas
personas de cuyos nonbres no se acuerda.

vii   A la setena pregunta dixo que lo queste testigo sabe e vido de la dicha pregunta
es que los yndios del dicho pueblo de Guaxoçingo servian e syrvieron al dicho presidente e oydores pasados en los seruiçios [*ordinarios—canceled*] de comyda trayen-
doles mayz e gallinas e otras cosas de bastimento hasta tanto que venieron los señores
presidente e oydores desta Real abdiençia que agora son e porqueste testigo vydo
questaba en el dicho pueblo por calpiste Hernando de Gibaja en nombre e a boz
de su Magestad por mandado de los dichos presidente e oydores pasados enbiando
los tributos de oro e Ropa e otras cosas a esta çibdad para su Magestad e que oyo
decir publicamente que por parte del dicho Marques [*32v*] se avya presentado en la
dicha abdiençia vna sobrecarta de su Magestad e que no se abia conplido e questo
es lo que sabe e vido desta pregunta.

viii°   A la otava pregunta dixo que lo queste testigo sabe e vido de la dicha pregunta es lo que dicho tiene en la pregunta antes desta e que lo demas no sabe.

ix   A la novena pregunta dixo queste testigo vido quel dicho Hernando de Gibaja

Indians of it, and he had it in his charge and administration, taking the tributes and advantages of it up to the time that the said Indians were taken from him by the said former president and oidores. And this witness saw that the said Marqués had Alonso Galeote in that said town as his overseer and Juan Valenciano as his farmer or swineherd who raised and was in charge of the farming and raising of the said pigs which he had on a farm of the said town about a league from it.

3. To the third question he said that he knows the said question just as it is stated in it. He was asked how he knows it. He said that it was because this witness saw it when he was in the said town of Huejotzingo talking with the lords and leading men of it. They habitually said that they were very well treated by the said Marqués and by those who were there for him and that they were commanded to be treated well, and Alonso Galeote by his command treated them very well. Also, this witness never saw nor did he know that during the time that the said Marqués had the said Indians in his charge and administration they complained as they have complained since that time, when the said lords and leading men tell this said witness that the said former president and oidores fatigued and molested them a great deal, imposing many tributes on them and making them come to labor in this city. And in the said monastery of Saint Francis of the said town of Huejotzingo he saw that the friars of the said monastery instructed and administered them in the matters of our holy Catholic faith. The lords and leading men of the said town and the commoners of it come to the said monastery for Mass. And this is the truth.

4. To the fourth question he said that he had heard people say what is contained in the said question and that it had happened thus to many people whose names he does not remember at the present.

5. To the fifth question he said that he had heard people, whose names he does not remember, say what the question states.

6. To the sixth question he said that he has heard the content of the question stated by many people whose names he does not remember.

7. To the seventh question he said that what this witness knows and saw concerning the said question is that the Indians of the said town of Huejotzingo served the said former president and oidores in the services of food, bringing them maize and hens and other provisions up until the arrival of the present lords president and oidores of this royal audiencia. And this witness saw that Hernando de Gibaja was in the said town as overseer in the name and authority of His Majesty by command of the said former president and oidores, sending the tributes of gold and cloth and other things to this city for His Majesty. And he heard it said publicly that on the part of the said Marqués, a covering letter of His Majesty had been presented in the said audiencia and that it had not been fulfilled. And this is what he knows and saw concerning this question.

8. To the eighth question he said that what this witness knows and saw concerning the said question is what he has said in the question preceding this one and that he does not know the rest.

9. To the ninth question he said that this witness saw that the said Hernando de

calpiste del dicho pueblo en nonbre de su Magestad hasia Recoger el oro e Ropa
del tributo del dicho pueblo disiendo ser para [*la—canceled*] su Magestad e que lo
enbiaba a esta çibdad al presidente e oydores pasados pero que no sabe en que
cantydad e questo es lo que desta pregunta sabe e vido.

x   A la deçima pregunta dixo que lo queste testigo sabe de la dicha pregunta es
quel dicho Hernando de Gybaja calpiste del dicho pueblo de Guaxoçingo mostro
a este testigo muchas cartas del presidente Nuño de Guzman en que le mandava
que cobrase los tributos mayz Ropa e otras cosas y que este testigo vido que [*por
ello—canceled*] tuvo preso vn dia o dos a Juan Suares señor e prinçipal E governador del dicho pueblo un dia o dos en la posada del dicho Gibaja pero que no sabe
sy hera por los dichos tributos pero que cree por lo que dicho tiene que serya por
los dichos tributos e questo sabe desta pregunta.

xi   A la honzena pregunta dixo que lo queste testigo sabe de la dicha pregunta es
que oyo decir a fray Torybyo e a otro Religyoso frayles de la orden del dicho monesterio de Sant Françisco de Gua[*33*]xoçingo que trayendo el mayz contenido en la
pregunta en tiempo de ynbierno les abya nebado en el puerto de Chalco e que se
abian muerto çiento e treze yndios e questo sabe desta pregunta.

xii   A la dozena pregunta dixo que lo queste testigo sabe e vido de la dicha pregunta
es que venian para este dicha çibdad del dicho pueblo de Guaxoçingo e su probinçia
e dezian que venian para seruir e labrar en las obras desta çibdad que los dichos
oydores e presidente pasados les mandaban e questo sabe desta pregunta.

xiii   A la trezena pregunta dixo queste testigo oyo decir publicamente en esta çibdad
e fuera della a muchas personas de cuyos nonbres no se acuerda que los dichos Nuño
de Guzman Matienço e Delgadillo tenian e mostravan mucho Rigor en las cosas
que se ofresçian contra el dicho Marques e sus cosas e questo sabe desta pregunta.

xiiii°   A la catorze pregunta dixo que dize lo que dicho tiene de suso en que se
afirma y es la verdad e lo que de lo suso dicho sabe e vido e al presente se le acuerda
para el juramento que fize e firmolo de su nombre fuele encargado el secreto.

RODRIGO DE ALMONTE [*rubrica*]

[*En xxvi de abril de iUdxxxi juro el padre fray Torybio—canceled*]

Paso ante mi.

ALONSO DE VALVERDE [*rubrica*]

Gibaja, overseer of the said town in the name of His Majesty, had them collect the gold and fabrics of the tribute of the said town, saying that it was for His Majesty and that he sent it to this city to the former president and oidores, but he does not know in what amount. And this is what he knows and saw concerning this question.

10. To the tenth question he said that what this witness knows about the said question is that the said Hernando de Gibaja, overseer of the said town of Huejotzingo, showed this witness many letters from the president Nuño de Guzmán in which he commanded him that he should collect the tributes of maize and cloth and other things. And this witness saw that for a day or two he imprisoned Juan Suares, lord and leading man and governor of the said town, for a day or two in the dwelling of the said Gibaja, but he does not know if it was for the said tributes, but because of what he has said, he thinks that it would have been because of the said tributes. And this is what he knows about this question.

11. To the eleventh question he said that what this witness knows concerning the said question is that he heard Fray Toribio and another religious, friars of the order of the said monastery of Saint Francis of Huejotzingo, say that while they were bringing the maize mentioned in the question in the wintertime, it had snowed on them in the pass of Chalco and that a hundred and thirteen Indians had died. And this is what he knows concerning this question.

12. To the twelfth question he said that what this witness knows and saw concerning this question is that they came to this said city from the said town of Huejotzingo and its province, and they said that they were coming to serve and work in the construction works of this city and that the said former oidores and president had commanded them. And this is what he knows about this question.

13. To the thirteenth question he said that this witness heard many people in this city and outside of it, whose names he does not remember, say publicly that the said Nuño de Guzmán, Matienzo, and Delgadillo held and showed much severity in matters which presented themselves against the said Marqués and his affairs. And this is what he knows about this question.

14. To the fourteenth question he said that he reaffirms what he has stated above, in which he stands firm, and it is the truth and what he knows and saw and remembers at the present concerning the abovesaid by the oath that he made, and he signed it with his name. He was put under the obligation of secrecy.

> RODRIGO DE ALMONTE [*rubric*]

[*on April 26, 1531, Father Toribio took the oath—canceled*]
It took place in my presence.

> ALONSO DE VALVERDE [*rubric*]

[*33v*] Derechos desta probança que son treze fojas

y media -   cccc°   v

De tres juramentos -   xx   iiii°

De la ocupaçion que me ocupe de todo el tiempo

que en toda ocupaçion desta probança vn dya no

mas çiento e ochenta -   c   lxxx°

---

dc   ix

[*34, 34v, and 35 blank; 35v*] E despues de lo suso dicho en catorze dias del mes de junio e del dicho añn ante los dichos señores presidente e oydores e en presençia de mi el dicho escriuano pareçio presente en abdiençia publica Garçia de Llerena e presento vn escripto el qual es este que se sigue.

[*36*]   MUY PODEROSOS SEÑORES

Garçia de Llerena en nonbre del Marques del Valle en el plito que trato contra los liçençiados Matienço e Delgadillo sobre los yntereses del pueblo de Vexoçingo de que ynjustamente despojaron al dicho mi parte, digo quel termino probatorio e quartos plazos que nos dieron en la dicha cavsa son pasados pido publicaçion suplico a vuestra Magestad la mande hazer, e pido justicia e en lo neçesario el Real ofiçio de vuestra Magestad ynploro.

[*36v*] El Marques contra los liçençiados sobre los yntereses del pueblo de Vexoçingo pide publicaçion.

xiiii° de junio 1531. Treslado a la parte que para la primera abdiençia Responda porque no se deva hacer la publicaçion con aperçibimiento que se mandava hacer en haz de Saldaña.

E asi presentado el dicho escripto en la manera que dicha es los dichos señores dixieron que mandavan dar treslado e que Responda para la primera abdiençia e diga porque no se deva haçer publicaçion con aperçibimiento que se mandava haçer lo qual se mando en haz de Saldaña.

E despues de lo suso dicho en diez e seis dias del dicho mes de junio e del dicho año ante los dichos señores presidente e oydores e en presençia de mi el dicho escriuano pareçio Garçia de Llerena e presento vn escripto syguiente

The fees for this inquiry, which consists of thirteen and
and a half sheets _____   405

For three oaths _____   24

For the time which I spent fully occupied in making
this inquiry—one day and no more—one hundred and
eighty _____   180

                                              609 [*maravedís*]

And after the abovesaid, on the fourteenth day of the month of June of the said year, before the said lords president and oidores and in the presence of me the said clerk, García de Llerena appeared present in public audience and presented a brief which is as follows.

VERY POWERFUL LORDS

I, García de Llerena, in the name of the Marqués del Valle in the lawsuit which I am conducting against the Licentiates Matienzo and Delgadillo over the interests of the town of Huejotzingo of which they unjustly deprived my said party, say that the time limit for the proof and the extensions which they gave us in the said case have expired. I request publication. I beseech Your Majesty to command it to be done, and I ask for justice, and in all that is necessary I implore the royal authority of Your Majesty.

The Marqués versus the licentiates over the interests of the town of Huejotzingo, requests publication.

June 14, 1531. Copy to the party—that for the first session he respond why the publication should not be made—with the summons which is commanded to be made —in the face of Saldaña.

When the said brief was thus presented in the manner which is stated, the said lords said that they commanded that a copy be given and that he should answer for the first session and should say why the publication should not be made, with the summons which is commanded to be made, and this was commanded in the face of Saldaña.

And after the abovesaid, on the sixteenth day of the said month of June of the said year, before the lords president and oidores and in the presence of me the said clerk, García de Llerena appeared and presented a brief which follows.

[*37*]   Muy poderosos señores

Garçia de Llerena en nonbre del Marques del Valle en el pleito que trato contra
los liçençiados Matienço e Delgadillo sobre los yntereses del pueblo de Vexoçingo
de que ynjustamente despojaron al dicho my parte digo que yo en la dicha cavsa
pedi publicaçion y vuestra Magestad mando a las partes contrarias que dixesen
porque no se debia hazer, no dixeron, pido a vuestra Magestad la mande aver por
fecha e para ello el Real ofiçio de vuestra Magestad ynploro e pido justiçia.

[*37v*] El Marques contra los liçençiados sobre los yntereses de [*Vxo—canceled*] Vaxoçingo, dize que pidio publicaçion e las partes contrarios no dixeron porque no se
deviese hazer, pide se de por fecha.

xvi de junio de xxxi. Sy llevo termino e no dixo por fecha la publicaçion en haz
de Saldaña.

Publicaçion. E asi presentado el dicho escripto en la manera que dicha es los dichos
señores dixieron que sy la parte contraria llevo termino e no dixo que la avian por
fecha la publicaçion, lo qual se mando en haz de Saldaña procurador de los dichos
liçençiados e mandaron que se de traslado a cada una de las partes de los testigos e
probanças en esta cabsa presentados para que se alegue de su derecho.

[*38*] Los liçençiados Matienço e Delgadillo contra el Marques sobre los tributos del
pueblo de Guaxoçingo.

Por las preguntas siguientes e por cada vna dellas sean preguntados los testigos
que son o fueren presentados por parte de los liçençiados Juan Ortiz de Matienço
e Diego Delgadillo en el pleyto que con ellos trata el Marques del Valle sobre los
tributos del pueblo de Guachoçingo.

Primeramente sean preguntados si conosçen a los dichos liçençiados Matienço y
Delgadillo e si conosçen al dicho Marques e si tienen notiçia e conosçimiento del
pueblo de Guaxoçingo.
ii Yten si saben creen vieron oyeron deçir que los dichos liçençiados por mandado
de su Magestad y por su provision Real a ellos dirigida pusieron el dicho pueblo de
Guaxoçingo en cabeça de su Magestad, e asi se puso e se asento en los libros de sus
ofiçiales los cuales pusieron en el en nonbre de su Magestad calpisques e mayordomos, los quales cobraron e cojieron los tributos y serviçios del dicho pueblo para
su Magestad e los dieron y entregaron a sus ofiçiales, digan los testigos lo que saben.
iii Yten si saben etc. que si los dichos liçençiados algun mahiz o aves huvieron del
dicho pueblo lo huvieron despues destar puesto en cabeça de su Magestad y como
de pueblo suyo, lo qual fue en poca cantidad, y dello hizieron Relaçion a su Magestad
para que dello fuese servido digan los testigos lo que saben.

VERY POWERFUL LORDS

I, García de Llerena, in the name of the Marqués del Valle in the lawsuit which I am conducting against the Licentiates Matienzo and Delgadillo over the interests of the town of Huejotzingo of which they unjustly deprived my said party, say that in the said case I have requested publication and Your Majesty commanded the contrary parties that they should say why it should not be done. They have not made a statement. I petition Your Majesty that you command that the publication be considered made. And for this I implore the royal authority of Your Majesty and I ask for justice.

The Marqués versus the licentiates over the interests of Huejotzingo. He says that he requested publication and the contrary parties have not said why it should not be made. He asks that it be considered made.

June 16, '31. If he exceeded the time and he did not make a statement—the publication as made—in the face of Saldaña.

Publication. And the said brief having been thus presented in the manner which is stated, the said lords said that if the contrary party exceeded the time and did not make a statement, they consider the publication as made, and this was commanded in the face of Saldaña, the attorney of the said licentiates, and they commanded that a copy of the witnesses and proofs presented in this case be given to each of the parties so that they may make statements regarding their rights.

The Licentiates Matienzo and Delgadillo versus the Marqués over the tributes of the town of Huejotzingo.

By the following questions and by each one of them let the witnesses be questioned who are or may be presented by the party of the Licentiates Juan Ortiz de Matienzo and Diego Delgadillo in the lawsuit which the Marqués del Valle is conducting with them over the tributes of the town of Huejotzingo.

First let them be asked whether they know the said Licentiates Matienzo and Delgadillo and whether they know the said Marqués and whether they have information and knowledge concerning the town of Huejotzingo.

2. Also, if they know, believe, saw, or heard it said that the said licentiates by command of His Majesty and by his royal decree addressed to them, placed the said town of Huejotzingo under tribute to His Majesty, and thus it was placed and written down in the books of his officials who in the name of His Majesty placed overseers and majordomos in it, who collected and gathered the tributes and services of the said town for His Majesty and then gave and delivered them to his officials; let the witnesses say what they know.

3. Also, if they know, etc., that if the said licentiates had any maize or birds from the said town, they had it after it was placed under tribute to His Majesty, as from his town, and that it was in a small amount and that they made a report of it to His Majesty so that it might be for his service; let the witnesses say what they know.

iiii° Yten si saben etc. que los dichos liçençiados an sido muy buenos juez y usado bien y limpiamente sus ofiçios ansi en estas partes como en las otras donde an tenido cargo de justiçia y en esta tierra sienpre an procurado el bien e pro comun y poblaçion y perpetuaçion della, dando de comer a los conquystadores y casados y haziendo otras munchas obras de perpetuaçion y benefisçio de la tierra como buenos governadores y juezes digan los testigos lo que saben.

v Yten si saben etc. que todo lo suso dicho e cada cosa e parte dello sea publica boz e fama.

EL LICENCIADO DELGADILLO [*rubrica*]

[*38v*] Ynterrogatorio de los liçençiados Matienço y Delgadillo en el pleyto que con ellos trata el Marques del Valle sobre los tributos del pueblo de Guaxoçingo.

En ix de março. Presentado e presente.

En Mexico a nueve dias del mes de março del dicho año ante los dichos señores presidente e oydores e por ante mi el dicho escribano pareçio presente Gregorio de Saldaña en nombre de los dichos liçençiados e presento este ynterrogatorio E pidio que por el sean examinados sus testigos que en esta cabsa presentare.

E asi presentado los dichos señores dixeron que lo avian por presentado en quanto es pertinente e que por estar ocupados en cosas del serviçio de sus Magestades cometian la Reçibiçion e juramento de los dichos testigos a mi el dicho escribano o a qualquier de los Reçeptores desta Real abdiençia.

[*Eight Indian paintings are set in between leaves 38 and 39. They are reproduced, with explanatory notes, on p. 55.*]

[*39*] Despues de lo suso dicho en catorze dias del dicho mes de agosto del dicho año ante los dichos señores presidente e oydores e por ante mi el dicho escriuano pareçio presente el dicho Garçia de Llerena e presento el escripto e escriptura syguientes.

MUY PODEROSOS SEÑORES

Garçia de Llerena en nonbre del Marques del Valle en el pleito que trato con los liçençiados Matienço e Delgadillo sobre los yntereses del puebo de Vaxoçingo de que ynjustamente despojaron al dicho Marques hago presentaçion destos testimonios de la probision e sobrecarta de vuestra Magestad con que los dichos liçençiados fueron Requeridos para que al dicho Marques no se le quitase ni Remobiese cosa alguna de las que tenia al tiempo que partio desta Nueva España suplico a

4. Also, if they know, etc., that the said licentiates have been very good judges and have used their offices well and faithfully, both in these parts and in the others where they have had charge of justice, and in this land they have always sought the common good and welfare and the colonization and perpetuation of the land, giving food to the conquerors and married men and doing many other works for the perpetuation and development of the land as good governors and judges; let the witnesses say what they know.

5. Also, if they know etc., that all of the abovesaid and every thing and part of it may be public knowledge and information.

LICENTIATE DELGADILLO [*rubric*]

Questionnaire of the Licentiates Matienzo and Delgadillo in the lawsuit which the Marqués del Valle is conducting with them over the tributes of the town of Huejotzingo.

On March 9. Presented and let him present them.

In Mexico on the ninth day of the month of March of the said year, before the said lords president and oidores and in the presence of me the said clerk, Gregorio de Saldaña appeared present in the name of the said licentiates and presented this questionnaire and he asked that the witnesses whom he may present in this case be examined by it.

And it being thus presented, the said lords said that they accepted it as presented insofar as it is pertinent and that because they are occupied in matters of the service of Their Majesties, they committed the swearing-in and examination of the said witnesses to me the said clerk or to any of the secretaries of this royal audiencia.

[*Eight Indian paintings are set in between leaves 38 and 39. They are reproduced, with explanatory notes, on p. 55–68.*]

After the abovesaid, on the fourteenth day of the said month of August of the said year, before the said lords president and oidores and in the presence of me the said clerk, the said García de Llerena appeared present and presented the following brief and document.

VERY POWERFUL LORDS

I, García de Llerena, in the name of the Marqués del Valle in the lawsuit which I am conducting with the Licentiates Matienzo and Delgadillo over the interests of the town of Huejotzingo of which they unjustly deprived the said Marqués, make presentation of these notarized copies of the decree and covering letter of Your Majesty by which the said licentiates were notified that they should not take or remove from the said Marqués anything that he had at the time that he left this New Spain. I beseech Your Majesty that you accept them as having been presented and command them to

vuestra Magestad las aya por presentadas e las mande poner en el dicho proçeso e pido justiçia e en lo neçesario el Real ofiçio de vuestra Magestad ynploro.

[*39v*] El Marques contra los liçençiados sobre los yntereses de Vaxoçingo haze presentaçion destos testimonios de las probisiones de vuestra Magestad con que los dichos liçençiados fueron Requeridos.

xiiii° de agosto 1531. Por presentado e treslado de la petiçion en haz de Saldaña.

[*E asi presentado el dicho escripto en la manera que dicha es los dichos señores dixeron que la avian por presentado e que mandavan dar treslado de la petiçion—canceled.*]

[*40*]   Yo Miguel Lopez de Legazpe escriuano publico e del consejo desta çibdad de Tenuxtitan doy fee e testimonio a todos los que la presente vieren como en los Registros que paresçe que pasaron ante Juan Fernandez del Castillo escriuano publico que fue de la dicha çibdad en cuyo ofiçio yo sucedi esta un Requerimiento que paresçe que fue hecho por Pedro Gallego en nonbre del Marques del Valle a los señores presidente e oydores del abdiençia Real que en estas partes Resyde por birtud de vna çedula Real de su Magestad con çiertos abtos e Respuestas que los dichos señores dieron firmado del dicho Juan Fernandez del Castillo su thenor del qual vno en pos de otro es este que se sigue.

En la gran çibdad de Tenuxtitan desta Nueva España del mar oçeano miercoles nueve dias del mes de diziembre año del nasçimiento de Nuestro Saluador Ihu Xpo [*Iesu Cristo*] de mill e quinientos e veynte e ocho años en este dicho dia podia ser ora de bisperas dichas ante los muy nobles señores liçençiados Juan Ortiz de Matienço e Diego Delgadillo juezes e oydores del abdiençia Real que por mandado de su Magestad Resyde en esta dicha çibdad e Nueva España e en presençia de mi Juan Fernandez del Castillo escriuano de su Magestad e escriuano publico del numero desta dicha çibdad paresçio presente Pedro Gallego veçino desta dicha çibdad e en nonbre de don Hernando Cortes e por birtud del poder que dixo que del tenia syñado de escriuano publico e presento ante los dichos señores liçençiados juezes e oydores susodichos vn escripto de Requerimiento escripto en papel e vna çedula de su Magestad escripta en papel e firmada de su Real nonbre e Referendada de Francisco de los Cobos su secretario segund por ello paresçia el thenor de la qual de berbo and berbum uno en pos de otro es este que se sygue.

Sepan quantos esta carta vieren como yo don Hernando Cortes capitan general destas partes de la Nueva España por su Magestad otorgo e conozco que doy e otorgo todo mi poder conplido [*rubrica*] [*40v*] segund que lo yo he e tengo e segund que mejor e mas conplidamente lo puedo e devo dar e otorgar e de derecho mas puede e deve valer a vos Pedro Gallego veçino desta çibdad de Tenuxtitan generalmente para en todos mis plitos e abtos e negoçios asy çibiles como criminales que yo he e tengo e espero aver e tener e mover contra todas e qualesquier personas de

be placed in the said proceedings, and I ask for justice, and insofar as it is necessary I implore the royal authority of Your Majesty.

The Marqués versus the licentiates over the interests of Huejotzingo, makes presentation of these notarized copies of the decrees of Your Majesty by which the said licentiates were notified.

August 14, 1531. As having been presented, and copy of the petition—in the face of Saldaña.

I, Miguel López de Legazpi, notary public and notary of the council of this city of Tenochtitlan, give certification and testimony to all those who see the present document that in the registers of acts which appear to have taken place in the presence of Juan Fernández del Castillo, formerly notary public in this city, in whose office I succeeded, there is a demand which appears to have been made by Pedro Gallego in the name of the Marqués del Valle to the lords president and oidores of the royal audiencia which resides in these parts. It was made by virtue of a royal decree of His Majesty, with certain acts and replies which the said lords gave, and is signed by the said Juan Fernández del Castillo. Their content, one after the other, is what follows.

In the great city of Tenochtitlan of this New Spain of the Ocean Sea, Wednesday, the ninth day of the month of December, the year of the birth of Our Savior Jesus Christ one thousand five hundred and twenty-eight, on this said day at possibly the time of the completion of vespers, before the very noble lords Licentiates Juan Ortiz de Matienzo and Diego Delgadillo, judges and oidores of the royal audiencia which by the command of His Majesty resides in this said city and New Spain, and in the presence of me, Juan Fernández del Castillo, notary of His Majesty and notary public of the number of this city, Pedro Gallego, a freeholder of this said city, appeared present, and in the name of Don Hernando Cortés and by virtue of the power of attorney which he said that he has from him, signed by a public notary, he presented before the said lords licentiates, judges, and oidores abovesaid a brief of demand written on paper and a decree of His Majesty, written on paper and signed with his royal name and countersigned by Francisco de los Cobos, his secretary, according as it appears. Its tenor *de verbo ad verbum* [*word for word*] one after the other is that which follows.

Let all men who see this letter know that I, Don Hernando Cortés, captain general of these regions of the New Spain for His Majesty, grant and acknowledge that I give and grant all my complete power, according as I have and hold it and according as I can and should give and grant it most completely and as it can and should be most binding legally, to you, Pedro Gallego, freeholder of this city of Tenochtitlan, generally for use in all my lawsuits and acts and business, both civil and criminal, which I have and maintain and expect to have and maintain and institute against all and any

qualquier estado o condiçion que sean sobre qualquier cabsa e Razon e para que
las tales o otras qualesquier an o esperan aver e tener e mover contra mi en
qualquier manera e para que sobre Razon de los dichos mis plitos e de qualquier
dellos podays paresçer e parezcays ante todas e qualesquier justiçias e juezes de
qualquier fuero e juridiçion que sean e ante ellos e ante qualquier dellos pedir e
demandar querellar e Responder defender e negar e conosçer pedir e Requerir
protestar testimonio o testimonios de escriuanos e notarios publicos pedir e tomar
e sacar e todas otras buenas Razanos [*sic — razones?*] exebiçiones e defensyones por
mi e en mi nonbre poner e deçir e alegar e para demandar e Reçibir aver e [*co —
canceled*] cobrar todos e qualesquier bienes que sean mios e me pertenezcan e
qualesquier debdas que me son o fueren devidas en qualquier manera e dar e
otorgar dello que ansy Reçibieredes e cobraredes vuestra carta o cartas de pago e
de fin e quito las quales valan e sean firmes como sy yo mismo las diese e otorgase
e a ello presente fuese e para dar e presentar testigos e provanças e escripturas e
ver presentar jurar e conosçer los testigos e provanças que contra mi fueren dadas
e presentadas e las tachar e contradeçir en dichos e en fechos e en personas e haçer
qualquier juramento o juramentos asy de calunya como de çensorio e otros qualesquier que convengan de se haçer [*rubrica*] [*41*] en mi anima sy acaheçiere porque
e concluyr e çerrar Razones e pedir e oyr sentençia o sentençias asy ynterlocutorias
como difinitivas e consentyr e apelar delles e pedir e tomar e seguir e dar quien
syga el apelaçion alçada o vista o suplicaçion alli o donde con derecho se deva
haçer e deçir e Razonar e conplidamente tratar todas las otras cosas e cada una
dellas que convengan e menester sean de se hacer e que yo haria e hacer podria
presente seyendo avnque sean tales e de tal calidad que segund derecho devan e
Requieran aver en si otro mi mas espeçial poder e mandado e presençia personal
e otrosy para que en vuestro lugar e en mi nonbre podays haçer e sostituyr vn
procurador o dos o mas quales e quantos quisyeredes e por bien tovieredes e aquellos
Revocar e tornar a tomar e tener en bos el prinçipal poder desta procuraçion e
quan conplido e bastante poder yo he e tengo para lo suso dicho e para cada vna
cosa e parte dello otro tal e tan complido bastante e ese mismo lo doy e otorgo a
vos Pero Gallego e a los por bos fechos e sostituydos con todas sus ynçidençias e
dependençias anexidades e conexidades e con libre e general Renunçiaçion en
Razon de lo suso dicho e vos Relievo a vos e a ellos de toda carga de satisdaçion
e fiaduria e Ratum judicatum solvi con todas las clabsulas espeçiales e generales
e me obligo de aver por firme todo quanto por bos fuere fecho e Razonado so
obligaçion que hago de todos mis bienes muebles e Rayzes avidos o por aver fecha
la carta en este dicha çibdad de Temuxtitan a veynte e syete dias del mes de

persons whatsoever and of whatever state or condition they may be, and concerning any cause or reason whatsoever, and for what they or any others whatsoever have or hope to have and maintain and institute against me in any manner whatsoever. And I give it so that concerning the matter of my said lawsuits and of any one of them in order to demand and receive, to have and collect all and any goods whatsoever of whatever forum and jurisdiction they may be, and before them and before any one of them you may make petitions and demands, complain and respond, defend and deny and acknowledge, ask and require, protest testimony or affidavits of clerks and notaries public, to request and take and remove and all the other good acts and expositions and defenses for me and in my name, to adduce and state and allege, and in order to demand and receive, to have and collect all and any goods whatsoever that are mine and pertain to me and any debts whatsoever that are or may be due to me in any manner whatsoever, and to give and grant from what you thus may receive and collect your letter or letters of payment and quittance, which shall be valid and firm as though I myself gave and granted them and were present at it. I give it to you in order that you may bring and present witnesses and proofs and documents and see presented, sworn in, and identified the witnesses and evidences which may be given and presented against me, and to challenge and contradict them in their words and deeds and persons and to make any oath or oaths whatsoever both as to calumny and as to censoriousness and any other whatsoever which it is befitting that they be made, by my soul, if there is any reason to do so, and to conclude and close proceedings, and to request and hear a sentence or sentences, both interlocutory and definitive, and to consent or appeal from them, and to ask and take and follow the appeal, or to supply someone who will follow up the appeal which has been instituted or seen or make a petition for reversal there or where it should be done by law, and to speak and reason and treat completely of all the other matters and each one of them which it is right and necessary that they be done and that I would and could do if I were present, even though they be such and of such a nature that according to law they should have and require another more special power of attorney and command from me and my personal presence. And, further, I give it to you so that in your place and in my name you may appoint and substitute an attorney or two or more, of whatever rank and number you may wish or think best, and revoke and take back and keep in your hands the principal power of attorney. And as complete and adequate a power as I have and hold for the abovesaid and for each matter and part of it, another such and equally complete and adequate and the power itself I give and grant to you, Pedro Gallego, and to those appointed and substituted by you, with all its incidents and dependents, appurtenances, and annexed rights and with free and general renunciation in relation to the abovesaid, and I relieve you and them from all burden of surety and bond and *ratum judicatum solvi* [*a firm judgment to be paid*] with all the special and general clauses. And I obligate myself to accept as binding everything that shall be done and attested by you, under the obligation which I make of all my goods, movable and immovable, which I possess or shall possess. The letter was issued in this said city of Tenochtitlan on the

setiembre año del nasçimiento de Nuestro Saluador Jhu Xpo de mill e quinientos
e veynte e syete años e por mayor firmeza firme esta carta de mi nonbre en el
Registro della testigos que fueron presentes Diego Pache-[*rubrica*] [*41v*]co e Juan
de Jaso veçinos de la dicha çibdad E yo Gregorio de Saldaña escriuano publico
desta dicha çibdad lo fize escrevir e sacar de los Registros que paresçe que pasaron
ante Pedro del Castillo escriuano publico e del consejo que fue desta dicha çibdad
que fue por ende fize aqui este mio syno en testimonio de verdad.

MUY PODEROSOS SEÑORES

Pedro Gallego en nonbre de don Hernando Cortes digo que despues quel dicho
mi parte fue a los reynos de Castilla a besar los pies e manos a vuestra Magestad que
fue por el mes de mayo deste año presente vuestra Magestad avida consyderaçion
a los grandes e muy señalados seruiçios que a la corona avia hecho ansy en ganar
esta Nueva España como en descobrir e ganar otras muy grandes e muchas tierras
poniendo para ello su hazienda e aventurando su persona e vida muchas e ynfinitas
vezes de propio motu le hizo merçed e proveyo de vna çedula firmada de vuestro
Real nonbre para que los oydores de vuestra Magestad desta Nueva España e otras
qualesquier justiçias no le quitasen ni tocasen los yndios e pueblos quel dicho mi
parte tenia e poseya al tiempo que desta Nueva España partyo ni ansymismo en
hazienda ni en otra cosa que al dicho tiempo tenia e poseya antes lo dexasen libre
e desenbargadamente en el punto ser y estar que al dicho tiempo estava e a las
personas a quien lo dexava encargado e segund e como el dicho mi parte lo dexava
proveydo segund en la dicha çedula de vuestra Magestad mas largamente se contyene
a que me Refiero a vuestra Alteza vmilmente suplico vea la dicha çedula e la
guarde e mande guardar segund e como en ella se contiene e hago presentaçion de
la dicha çedula e provisyon de vuestra Magestad e pido lo por testimonio.
Licenciatus Altamirano.

EL REY

Presidente e oydores de la nuestra abdiençia de la Nueva España e otras [*rubrica*]
[*42*] qualesquier justiçias dellas porque don Hernando Cortes es venido a estos
Reynos e yo he sydo seruido dello e mi voluntad es que hasta tanto que otra cosa
mande no se le haga novedad en los yndios e pueblos e otras cosas que tenia en la
Nueva España por ende yo vos mando que hasta que como dicho es yo otra cosa
mande no hagays ni consyntays ni deys lugar que al dicho don Hernando Cortes
se le haga novedad ni mudança alguna en los yndios e pueblos e otras qualesquier
cosas que tenia e poseya al tiempo que partyo de la dicha Nueva España para
venir en estos nuestros Reynos syno que lo dexeys todo a las personas que en su

twenty-seventh day of the month of September in the year of the birth of Our Savior Jesus Christ one thousand five hundred and twenty-seven, and so that it might be more binding, I signed this letter with my name in the register of it. Witnesses who were present, Diego Pacheco and Juan de Jaso, freeholders of the said city. And I, Gregorio de Saldaña, notary public of this city had it written out and taken from the registers of acts which apparently took place in the presence of Pedro de Castillo, formerly notary public and notary of the council of this said city. Therefore I affixed here this my sign in testimony of the truth.

VERY POWERFUL LORDS

I, Pedro Gallego, in the name of Don Hernando Cortés, say that after my said party went to the realms of Castile to kiss the feet and hands of Your Majesty, which was during the month of May of this present year, Your Majesty took consideration of the great and very distinguished services which he had done for the crown both in conquering this New Spain and in discovering and conquering other very great and numerous lands, risking for it his possessions and hazarding his person and life many and infinite times; and Your Majesty *de motu proprio [of your own impulse]* showed favor to him and issued a decree signed by your royal name to the effect that the oidores of Your Majesty in this New Spain and any other justices whatsoever should not take away from him nor touch the Indians and towns which my said party held and possessed at the time when he left this New Spain, nor likewise should they bother his possessions nor any other thing that he held and possessed at the said time; rather they should leave them free and unencumbered, in the state of being in which they were at the said time and in the hands of those people whom he left in charge of them and in the manner and way in which my said party left it arranged, according as is contained more at length in the said decree of Your Majesty, to which I refer. I humbly beseech Your Highness that you look at the said decree and observe it and command that it be observed, just as it is expressed in it; and I make presentation of the said decree and writ of Your Majesty and I ask for a notarized record. Licentiate Altamirano.

THE KING

President and oidores of our audiencia of the New Spain and any other justices whatsoever of those parts: Because Don Hernando Cortés has come to these realms and I have been pleased by it and it is my will that until such a time as something else is commanded, no innovation should be made in regard to the Indians and towns and other things that he had in the New Spain, I therefore command you that until, as has been said, I may command something else, you shall not do nor consent nor allow that to the said Don Hernando Cortés there be made any innovation or change in the Indians and towns and any other things whatsoever which he held and possessed at the time that he left the said New Spain to come to these our realms, but you shall leave it all to the persons who stayed on in his name or who have his au-

nonbre quedaron o que su poder vbieren en aquella manera e en aquel punto y estado que entonçes estava porque asy cumple a mi seruiçio e no hagadas ende al, fecha en Monçon a veynte e nueve dias de junio de quinientos e veynte e ocho años, yo el Rey por mandado de su Magestad, Francisco de los Cobos, e en las espaldas de la dicha çedula de su Magestad estava una señal de firma e escripto e firmado lo syguiente.

Asentose esta çedula de sus Magestades en los libros de la Casa de la Contrataçion de las Yndias de Sevilla en beynte e tres dias del mes de jullio de mill e quinientos e veynte e ocho años Pero Xuarez Juan de Aranda.

El qual dicho Requerimiento e çedula de su Magestad de suso encorporada yo el dicho escribano publico ley e notyfique delante a los dichos señores juezes e oydores de su Magestad de berbo ad berbum como en ello se contiene e asy leydo e notyficado los dichos señores juezes e oydores dixeron quellos lo verian testigos el liçençiado Altamirano y el secretario Rodrigo de Albornoz, contador de su Magestad en esta Nueva España, Juan Fernandez del Castillo escriuano publico.

E despues de lo suso dicho en la dicha çibdad de [*rubrica*] [*42v*] Tenuxtitan sabado doze dias del dicho mes de diziembre e del dicho año de mill e quinientos e veynte e ocho años los dichos señores liçençiados oydores suso dichos en presençia de mi el dicho escriuano publico dixeron Respondiendo a la dicha çedula de su Magestad e Requirimiento a ellos fecho por parte del dicho don Hernando Cortes que ellos obedesçian e obedesçieron la dicha çedula de su Magestad e la ponian sobre su cabeça con el acatamiento que deven asy como a carta e mandado de su Rey e señor e quanto en el cumplimiento della dixeron questavan prestos e aparejados de hacer todo aquello que al seruiçio de su Magestad convenga e esto dixeron que Respondian e Respondieron a la dicha çedula de su Magestad e Requerimiento.

El qual dicho Requerimiento e abto de suso contenido yo el dicho escribano lo fize sacar del dicho Registro donde esta de pedimiento de Garçia de Llerena en nonbre del Marques del Valle e de mandamiento de Garçia Holguin alcalde hordinario en esta çibdad por su Magestad que mando que se le diese en publica forma para en çiertos plitos que trata en nonbre del dicho don Hernando Cortes el qual fue hecho e sacado en esta dicha çibdad de Tenuxtitan en diez e seys dias del mes de junio año del nasçimiento de Nuestro Saluador Ihu Xpo de mill e quinientos e treynta e vn años testigos que fueron presentes a lo ver sacar e corregir e conçertar del dicho original.

E yo el dicho Miguel Lopez escriuano publico y del consejo desta dicha çibdad lo fiz sacar y escribir de los dichos Registros por mandado del dicho señor alcalde E por ende fiz aqui mi sygno a tal [*signo*] en testimonio de verdad.

MIGUEL LOPEZ ESCRIUANO PUBLICO Y DEL CONSEJO [*rubrica*]

thority, in that manner and in that state in which they were then, because thus it is fitting for my service, and you shall not go against it. Done in Monzon on the twenty-ninth day of June of the year [*one thousand*] five hundred and twenty-eight. I the King. By the command of His Majesty, Francisco de los Cobos. And on the back of the said decree of His Majesty there was the rubric of a signature and the following, written and signed.

This decree of Their Majesties was written down in the books of the House of Trade of the Indies in Seville on the twenty-third day of the month of July of the year one thousand five hundred and twenty-eight. Pero Xuarez. Juan de Aranda.

I, the said notary public, read and made known the said demand and decree of His Majesty above incorporated in the presence of the said lords judges and oidores of His Majesty *de verbo ad verbum* [*word for word*] as it is expressed in it. And after it was thus read and made known, the said lords judges and oidores said that they would see it. Witnesses, the Licentiate Altamirano and the secretary Rodrigo de Albornoz, accountant of His Majesty in this New Spain. Juan Fernández del Castillo, notary public.

After the abovesaid, in the said city of Tenochtitlan, Saturday, the twelfth day of the said month of December of the said year one thousand five hundred and twenty-eight, the said lords licentiates oidores abovementioned said in the presence of me, the said notary public, and in answer to the said decree of His Majesty and the demand made to them by the party of the said Don Hernando Cortés, that they obeyed and would obey the said decree of His Majesty, and they placed it above their heads with the respect that they thus owe as to a letter and command of their King and lord; and as to the fulfillment of it, they said that they are ready and prepared to do everything that is proper for the service of His Majesty; and they said that this is their response to the decree of His Majesty and the demand.

I, the said notary, had the said demand and act that is contained above copied from the said register where it is, at the request of García de Llerena, in the name of the Marqués del Valle and at the command of García Holguín, alcalde ordinario in this city for His Majesty, who commanded that it be given to him in public form for use in certain lawsuits which he is conducting in the name of the said Don Hernando Cortés. This was done and copied in the said city of Tenochtitlan on the sixteenth day of the month of June of the year of the birth of Our Savior Jesus Christ one thousand five hundred and thirty-one. Witnesses who were present to see it copied and corrected and compared with the original: [*No names are given.*]

And I, the said Miguel López, notary public and of the council of this said city, had it copied and written from the said registers by command of the said lord alcalde, and therefore I made here my customary sign [*there is a sign*] in testimony of the truth.

MIGUEL LÓPEZ, *notary public and of the council* [*rubric*]

[*43–43v blank; 44*] Este es traslado bien e fielmente Sacado de vn testimonio e abtos que pareçe que pasaron ante Alonso Lucas escriuano que fue de la Real abdiençia desta Nueva España e ante Nuño de Guzman e los liçençiados Juan Ortiz de Matyenço e Diego Delgadillo a pedimyento de Garçia de Llerena en nonbre de don Fernando Cortes Marques del Valle sobre çiertos pueblos que dizque quitaron al dicho Marques segund oreginalmente por ello pareçia su thenor de lo qual es este que se sygue.

En la gran çibdad de Tenuxtitan desta Nueva España treze dias del mes de setienbre año del nasçimiento de Nuestro Saluador Ihu Xpo de mill e quinientos e veynte e nueve años en presençia de mi Alonso Lucas secretario de la avdiençia rreal paresçia Garçia de Llerena en nonbre de don Hernando Cortes e en la dicha avdiençia Real ante los magnificos señores liçençiados Juan Ortiz de Matienço e Diego Delgadillo presydente e oydores presento e ler hizo por mi el dicho escribano vn escripto con vn treslado de vna prouision su thenor del qual es este que se sygue.

MUY PODEROSOS SEÑORES

Garçia de Llerena en nonbre de don Hernando Cortes digo que ya vuestra Magestad sabe la merçed que por Respeto de los muchos e muy senalados seruiçios que el dicho mi parte a vuestra Magestad hizo en esta tierra le otorgo e conçedio dandole vna çedula e sobrecarta della firmada de su Real nonbre para que el presydente e oydores desta Nueva España ni otra justiçia o persona alguna no le tocasen en los pueblos [*e — between lines*] yndios que el thenia en sy al tiempo que desta Nueva España partio para los Reynos de Castilla a vesar vuestros Reales pies e manos e a dar cuenta a vuestra Alteza de todas las cosas en esta Nueva España acaesçidas segund que en la dicha çedula e sobrecarta mas largamente a que me Refiero se contiene las quales yo presente en este Real avdiençia e como quiera que el dicho presidente e oydores las obedesçieron diziendo que en todo harian conforme a lo que vuestra Magestad mandava syn enbargo de lo suso dicho quitaron al dicho mi parte a Tezcuco con su subjeto e la provinçia de Guaxoçingo y el pueblo de Miçante que tenia Saavedra en nonbre del dicho don Hernando y la provinçia de Teguantepeque e Soconusco e la çibdad de Vchichila e otros muchos pueblos e finalmente el dicho mi parte no se sirve de pueblo alguno que tenga e agora a venido a mi notiçia que despues que el dicho presydente e oydores supieron que vuestra Magestad avia hecho merçed al dicho don Hernando del titulo de Marques del Valle de Guaxaca adonde [*rubrica*] [*44v*] el dicho mi parte tenia algunos pueblos al tienpo que se partio como dicho es que son los syguientes Cuylapa con su subjeto Guaxaca Hetla con Guaxulutitan Talistaca Teoçopatlan Çinatlan Tetequatlan Tavquilabaco Aestepeta Colula Ocotlan Chichicapa Ayvtibeque Los Peñoles Macuylsuchil e[?] Tecoquila, han dado e Repartido a personas particulares los mas de los dichos pueblos y estançias e porque no paresca que savian que heran del dicho don Hernando nonbran los dichos pueblos que asy dan por de las

This is a transcript, taken well and faithfully, of an attestation and acts which appear to have taken place before Alonso Lucas, former notary of the royal audiencia of this New Spain and before Nuño de Guzmán and the Licentiates Juan Ortiz de Matienzo and Diego Delgadillo, at the request of García de Llerena in the name of Don Hernando Cortés, Marqués del Valle, over certain towns which he says they took from the said Marqués, according as it appeared in the original, the content of which is as follows.

In the great city of Tenochtitlan of this New Spain, on the thirteenth day of the month of September of the year of the birth of Our Savior Jesus Christ one thousand five hundred and twenty-nine, in the presence of me, Alonso Lucas, secretary of the royal audiencia, García de Llerena appeared in the name of Don Hernando Cortés; and in the said royal audiencia before the magnificent lords Licentiates Juan Ortiz de Matienzo and Diego Delgadillo, president and oidores, he presented and had me, the said clerk, read a brief with a transcript of a decree, the tenor of which is as follows.

Very powerful lords

I, García de Llerena, in the name of Don Hernando Cortés, say that Your Majesty already knows the favor which Your Majesty granted and conceded to my said party out of regard for the many and very distinguished services which he did for Your Majesty in this land, when you gave him a decree and a covering letter for it, signed by your royal name, so that the president and oidores of this New Spain or any other justices or persons would not bother him in the towns and Indians which he held for himself at the time when he left this New Spain for the realms of Castile to kiss your royal hands and feet and to give an account to Your Highness of all the things that have happened in this New Spain, according as it is expressed more at length in the said decree and covering letter, to which I refer. I presented them in this royal audiencia, and in spite of the fact that the said president and oidores showed obedience to them, saying that in everything they would act in conformity with what Your Majesty commanded, in spite of the abovesaid, they took from my said party Texcoco with its subject area, and the province of Huejotzingo, and the town of Mizantla which Saavedra held in the name of the said Don Hernando, and the province of Tehuantepec and Soconusco, and the city of Uchichila and many other towns, so that in the end my said party does not have the service of any town which he might hold. And now it has come to my knowledge that, after the said president and oidores knew that Your Majesty had made a grant to the said Don Hernando of the title of Marqués del Valle de Oaxaca [*Marqués of the Valley of Oaxaca*] where at the time that he left, as has been said, my said party held some towns which are the following: Cuilapa with its subject area, Oaxaca, Etla with Guaxototilan, Talistaca, Teozapotlan, Zimatlan, Tetequatlan, Taquilavacoya, Aestepeta, Colula, Ocotlan, Chichicapa, Ayutibeque, Los Peñoles, Macuilsuchil, and Tecoquila, they have given and allotted to private persons most of the said towns and farms. And in order that it might not appear that they knew that they belonged to the said Don Hernando, they named the said towns which they thus gave out, as though they belonged

personas a quien los deposyto Gonçalo de Salazar e Pero Almildes al tienpo que
contra el dicho don Hernando governador que hera se levantaron; a vuestra
Magestad suplico no consyenta ni de lugar que lo suso dicho se haga por el dicho
presydente e oydores antes guarden e cumplan la voluntad de vuestra Magestad
conforme a la dicha çedula e sobrecarta pues es en tanto agrauio e perjuiçio del
dicho mi parte que gano para la corona Real toda esta tierra e le costo tanto e
tanto trabajo, mayormente pues vuestra Alteza se ha dado del por bien seruido
y estoy presto de dar ynformaçion de como los dichos pueblos tenia el dicho mi
parte al tienpo que [*se — between lines*] partio para los dichos Reynos e porque
vuestra Magestad sea ynformado de lo que se prove çerca de lo suso dicho e para
en guarda e conservaçion del dicho mi parte pido al secretario desta Real avdiençia
me lo de por testimonio con que protesto todo lo que al derecho del dicho mi
parte protestar convenga contra quien protestarlo devo e a mi derecho convega e
sobre todo pido testimonio. Licentiatus Altamirano.

Otrosy digo que por [*que vea — between lines*] vuestra Magestad el agravio
que el dicho mi parte Resçibe e no ay porque le quitar los dichos pueblos puesto
que se le quiten diziendo que se pueble la villa de la dicha prouinçia de Guaxaca
digo que hallara vuestra Magestad que en la dicha villa ay ochenta e tantos veçinos
e todos tienen Repartimientos muy buenos syn tocar en los dichos pueblos del
dicho mi parte e syn otros Repartimientos que ay de personas que no biven en la
dicha villa de lo qual dare entera ynformaçion, los quales dichos ochenta e tantos
veçinos segund la grandeza desta tierra e otras villas que se pueblan en otros
cavos que tienen a poco mas de quinze o veynte vezinos es numero eçesivo para
en la dicha villa porque los que son conpelidos a yr alli podrian yr a las otras
villas donde ay poca [*rubrica*] [*45*] cantidad de vezinos e ay tanta e mas neçesydad
e mejor dispusyçion de poblar syn dar lugar al dicho agrauio que al dicho mi
parte se haze e pido justiçia e testimonio para que de todo vuestra Magestad sea
ynformado.

Este es vn traslado bien e fielmente sacado de vna çedula e sobrecarta de su
Magestad escripto en papel e firmada de su Real nonbre e Refrendada de
Francisco de los Covos su secretario e señalada en las espaldas della de çiertas
firmas e señales de los del su Real consejo su thenor de la qual es este que se sygue.

El rrey

Nuestro presydente e oydores de la nuestra avdiencia e chancelleria Real de la
Nueva España bien sabeys como yo mande dar e di para vos una mi çedula fecha
en esta guisa: El rrey. Presydente e oydores de la nuestra abdiençia de la Nueva
España y otras qualesquier justiçias della porque don Hernando Cortes es venido
a estos Reynos e yo he seydo seruido dello e mi voluntad es que hasta tanto que

to the persons to whom Gonzalo de Salazar and Pero Almíndez entrusted them at the time when they revolted against the said Don Hernando, former governor. I beseech Your Majesty that you should not consent nor allow that the abovementioned be done by the said president and oidores. Rather, they should observe and fulfill the will of Your Majesty in conformity with the said decree and covering letter, since it is so bothersome and prejudicial to my said party, who gained all this land for the royal crown, and it was so costly and laborious for him, especially since Your Highness has considered yourself well served by him. And I am prepared to give evidence of how my said party held the said towns at the time that he left for the said realms of Castile, so that Your Majesty may be informed as to what disposition is being made concerning the abovesaid. And for the protection and conservation of my said party, I ask the secretary of this royal audiencia to give me a notarized record. And I protest all that it is becoming to the rights of my party that I should protest against whomever I ought, and it is proper for my rights to protest. And concerning it all I request a notarized record. Licentiate Altamirano.

Further, in order that Your Majesty may see the aggravation that my said party receives and the fact that there is no reason for taking the said towns from him on the excuse that the town of the said province of Oaxaca was to be settled, I say that Your Majesty will find that in the said town there are eighty-some freeholders and they all have very good allotments, without touching the said towns of my said party and without counting the other allotments that there are of persons who do not live in the said town. Of all of this I will give complete information. Considering the great size of this land and the other towns which are being colonized in other extremities of it which have a little more than fifteen or twenty freeholders, the said eighty-some freeholders are an excessive number to stay in the said town, because those who are compelled to go there could go to the other towns where there is a small number of freeholders and as great or greater need and better disposition to settle, without allowing the said aggravation which is caused to my party. And I ask for justice and for a notarized record so that Your Majesty may be informed of everything.

This is a transcript, copied well and faithfully, of a decree and covering letter of His Majesty written on paper and signed by his royal name, countersigned by Francisco de los Cobos, his secretary, and signed on the back of it with certain signatures and rubrics of the members of his royal council, the content of which is as follows.

THE KING

Our President and oidores of our audiencia and royal chancery of the New Spain: You know well how I commanded to be issued and did issue for you a decree from me, written in this manner: The King. President and oidores of our audiencia of the New Spain and any other justices whatsoever of that region: Because Don Hernando Cortés has come to these realms and I have been pleased by it and it is my will that,

otra cosa mande no se le haga novedad en los yndios e pueblos y otras cosas que
tenia en la Nueva España, por ende yo vos mando que hasta tanto que como dicho
es yo otra cosa mande no hagays ni consintays ni deys lugar que al dicho don
Hernando Cortes se le haga novedad ni mudança alguna en los yndios e pueblos
y otras qualesquier cosas que tenia e poseya al tienpo que partio de la dicha Nueva
España para benir a estos nuestros Reynos syno que lo dexeys todo a las personas
que en su nonbre quedaron o que su poder tuvieren en aquella manera y en aquel
punto y estado que entonçes estava porque ansy cunple a mi seruiçio e no fagades
ende al fecha en Monçon a veynte e nueve dias del mes de junio de mill e
quinientos e veynte e ocho años. Yo el Rey por mandado de su Magestad Francisco
de los Covos. E agora el dicho don Hernando Cortes me suplico e pidio por merçed
que porque la dicha çedula mejor fuese conplida e guardada le mandase dar
nuestra sobrecarta della o como la mi merçed fuese, e yo tove lo por bien por ende
yo vos mando que veades la dicha çedula que de suso va encorporada e la guardeys
e cunplays e executeys e hagays guardar e conplir [*rubrica*] [*45v*] como en ella se
contiene syn que en ello aya falta alguna e ansy mismo proveereys como las
personas que tienen cargo de sus haziendas e granjerias sean bien tratados y no
consyntays que se les haga agrauio contra justiçia fecha en Madrid a doze dias
de setiembre de mill e quinientos e veynte e ocho años yo el Rey por mandado
se su Magestad Francisco de los Covos. Va escripto sobre Raydo o diz que vala
e no enpesca.

Fecho e sacado corregido e conçertado fue este dicho treslado de la dicha çedula
e sobrecarta de su Magestad de donde fue sacado en esta gran çibdad de
Tenuxtitan a tres dias del mes de abril de mill e quinientos e veynte e nueve
años testigos que fueron presentes al ver corregir e conçertar este dicho treslado
segund dicho es Gregorio de Villafuerte e Juan de Çespedes estantes en la dicha
çibdad. E yo Luys de Sosto escribano de sus Magestades que en vno con los dichos
testigos presente fuy a lo suso dicho fize aqui este mio sygno en testimonio de
verdad. Luys de Soto escribano de sus Magestades. Va enmendado diz para vos vala.

E asy presentadas las dichas escripturas en la manera que dicha es los dichos
señores presydente e oydores dixieron que lo Remitian e mandavan llevar al acuerdo.

E despues de lo suso dicho los dichos señores Respondiendo al dicho Requerimiento dixieron que el pueblo de Guaxoçingo e Tezcuco e Teguantepeque e
Soconusco e Vchichila que el dicho Garçia de Llerena dize en su petiçion que
se han quitado al dicho don Hernando Cortes que es verdad que los dichos señores
presydente e oydores le quitaron los dichos pueblos y provinçias al dicho don
Hernando y las dieron a su Magestad cuyas son lo qual hizieron por mandado
de su Magestad segund paresçe por la ynstruçion que les fue dada y ansy por esto
como porque antes desto estuvieron puestas en cabeça de su Magestad y asentadas

until such a time as something else is commanded, no innovation should be made in regard to the Indians and towns and other things that he had in the New Spain, I therefore command you that until such a time that, as has been said, I may command something else, you shall not do nor consent nor allow that to the said Don Hernando Cortés there be made any innovation or change in the Indians and towns and any other things whatsoever which he held and possessed at the time that he left the said New Spain to come to these realms, but you shall leave it all to the persons who stayed on in his name or who have his authority, in that manner and in that state in which they were then, because thus it is fitting for my service; and you shall not go against it. Done in Monzon on the twenty-ninth day of the month of June of the year one thousand five hundred and twenty-eight. I the King. By command of His Majesty. Francisco de los Cobos. And now the said Don Hernando Cortés has besought and petitioned me as a favor, in order that the said decree might be better fulfilled and observed, that I should command that a covering letter be issued for it, or whatever my pleasure might be; and I considered it good. Therefore I command you that you see that said decree which is incorporated above, and you shall observe and fulfill and execute it and see to it that it is observed and fulfilled, as it is expressed in it, without allowing any negligence in it. Likewise you shall provide that the persons who have charge of his haciendas and farms shall be well treated and you shall not consent that any injury be done to them contrary to justice. Done in Madrid on the twelfth day of September of the year one thousand five hundred and twenty-eight. I the King. By command of His Majesty. Francisco de los Cobos. Written over an erasure where it says "que". Valid; let it not damage it.

This transcript was made and copied, corrected and compared, from the said decree and covering letter of His Majesty, from which it was copied in this great city of Tenochtitlan on the third day of the month of April of the year one thousand five hundred and twenty-nine. Witnesses who were present to see this said transcript corrected and compared, as has been said: Gregorio de Villafuerte and Juan de Céspedes, sojourners in the said city. And I, Luis de Soto, notary of Their Majesties, who was present together with the said witnesses at the abovesaid, made here this my sign in testimony to the truth. Luis de Soto, notary of their Majesties. It is amended where it says "for you". Valid.

The said documents having been presented in the manner which is stated, the said lords president and oidores said that they remitted it and commanded that it be taken to the assembled court.

And after the abovesaid, the said lords, responding to the said demand, said that regarding the towns of Huejotzingo, Texcoco, Tehuantepec, Soconusco, and Uchichila, concerning which the said García de Llerena says in his petition that they have taken them away from the said Don Hernando Cortés, it is the truth that the said president and oidores took away the said towns and provinces from the said Don Hernando, and they gave them to His Majesty, to whom they belong. This they did by command of His Majesty, as is apparent from the instruction which was given to them. And it was done both for this reason and because previously they were placed

en sus libros y el dicho don Hernando syn tener poder para ello ni aviendo causa
ni Razon alguna mirando mas su propio ynterese y provecho que el seruiçio de su
Magestad las quito a su Magestad y las tomo y aplico para sy syn dar un yndio
[*rubrica*] [*46*] dellos a muchos conquistadores que fueron en ganar la tierra que
morian de hanbre y a lo que dize del pueblo de Miçante que se quito al dicho don
Hernando la verdad esta en contrario porque el dicho pueblo se quito por setençia
a Luys de Saavedra en quien estava depositado por çierto delito que cometio
segund paresçe y consta por el proçeso que sobre ello se hizo a que se Refiriere
y el dicho pueblo se dio a Pablos Mexia cavallero e hijodalgo que a seruido en
estas partes a su Magestad mucho mejor que el dicho Saavedra que primo lo
tenia, y en quanto a lo que dize que despues de savido por los dichos señores
presidente e oydores que el dicho don Hernando hera Marques de Guaxaca
hezieron la villa de Antequera por le quitar los dichos pueblos, dixieron que al
tienpo que los dichos señores presidente e oydores vinieron a estas partes su
Magestad enbio vna su provision firmada de su Real nonbre por la qual les mando
que Reedificasen en el Valle de Guaxaca vna villa que muchos dias avia estava
poblada y se llamava Segura de la Frontera la qual el dicho don Hernando despoblo
y los dichos señores en el conplimiento de la dicha prouision enbiaron a Reedeficar
y poblar la dicha villa muchos dias antes que en esta tierra se dixiese lo contenido
en la petiçion del dicho Garçia de Llerena y hasta agora no han visto prouisyon
alguna de su Magestad por donde paresçe lo que el dicho Garçia de Llerena dize
quanto mas que don Hernando despoblo la dicha villa syn cavsa ni Razon alguna
que justa fuese syno por su propio ynterese por tomar para sy como tomo todos los
Repartimientos que los veçinos de la dicha villa tenian que heran conquistadores
desta tierra, no mirando el provecho y bien de la tierra y poblaçion della ni
descargo de la Real conçiençia de su Magestad y que para este efeto de la
Reedeficaçion de la dicha villa se han tomado y toma [d]el dicho don Harnando los
dichos pueblos de la dicha prouinçia que son los que el dicho don Hernando Cortes
quito a los conquistadores e pobladores de la dicha villa y que en esto no se haze
agravio al dicho don Hernando syno conplir lo que su Magestad manda y hazer
el [*rubrica*] [*46v*] bien y pro de la tierra y poblaçion della y en quanto a lo demas
contenido en la petiçion del dicho Garçia de Llerena dixieron que los dichos
señores haran aquello que vean que mas conviene al seruiçio de su Magestad y
bien e poblaçion de la tierra y que para que conste desto la verdad mandaron que
se Resçiba ynformaçion de lo conthenido en esta Respuesta y se ponga juntamente
con ella la prouisyon de su Magestad en que manda que se haga la villa y sy el
dicho Garçia de Llerena quisiere testimonio se le de todo junto y no de otra
manera y esto dieron por su Respuesta no consyntiendo etc.

under tribute to His Majesty and written down in his books, and the said Don Hernando, without having authority for it nor any reason or cause, looking more to his own interest and profit than to the service of His Majesty, took them away from His Majesty and took them and adjudged them for himself without giving one Indian of them to many conquerors who took part in conquering this land, who were dying from hunger. And regarding what he says about the town of Mizantla, that it was taken from the said Don Hernando, the truth is to the contrary; the said town was taken away by judicial sentence from Luis de Saavedra to whom it was entrusted, because of a certain crime which he committed, as is apparent and evident from the trial which was conducted concerning it, to which we refer. And the said town was given to Pablos Mejía, a knight and a hidalgo, who has served His Majesty in these parts much better than the said Saavedra who had it first. And in regard to his statement that it was after the said lords president and oidores knew that the said Don Hernando was Marqués of Oaxaca that they established the town of Antequera in order to take the said towns away from him, they said that at the time that the said lords president and oidores came to these parts, His Majesty sent a writ, signed with his royal name, by which he commanded them that they should rebuild in the Valley of Oaxaca a town which was settled a long time ago and was called Segura de la Frontera and which the said Don Hernando depopulated. And in fulfillment of the said writ the said lords sent people to rebuild and settle the said town a long time before anything was said in this land about what is contained in the petition of García de Llerena. And up to the present they have not seen any writ of His Majesty by which the statement of the said García de Llerena would seem verified. They had all the more reason for doing this because Don Hernando depopulated the said town without any just cause or reason but for his own interest in order to take for himself, as he did take, all of the allotments which the freeholders of the said town had, and they were conquerors of this land. And he did this, not looking to the improvement and well-being and settlement of the land nor to the unburdening of the royal conscience of His Majesty. And for the purpose of the rebuilding of the said town, the said towns of the said province have been taken from the said Don Hernando, and they are the towns which the said Don Hernando Cortés took away from the conquerors and settlers of the said town. And in this no injury is done to the said Don Hernando except to fulfill what His Majesty commands and to work for the good and welfare of the land and its colonization. And as to the rest that is contained in the petition of the said García de Llerena, the said lords said that they will do what they see as most becoming for the service of His Majesty and for the welfare and settlement of the land. And so that the truth of this may be evident, they commanded that a report should be made about what is contained in this response and that with it should be placed the writ of His Majesty in which he commands that the town should be built, and if the said García de Llerena should want a notarized record, let it all be given to him together and not in any other manner. And they gave this as their response, not consenting, etc.

El Rey

Nuestro presydente e oydores de la nuestra avdiençia Real que avemos mandado prover para la Nueva España por parte de los conquistadores e pobladores de la dicha tierra me fue fecha Relaçion que luego como se gano la dicha tierra se hizo vn pueblo de xpianos en el termino de Guaxaca que se llamava Segura de la Frontera porque hera muy buena comarca y poblada de muchos yndios e avia minas de oro e plata e fertil de mantenimientos e otras cosas de que se nos seguia y esperava seguir mucho seruiçio y bien general a la dicha tierra y provecho a nuestras Rentas y que Hernando Cortes por se quedar con la dicha tierra tuvo forma como la dicha villa e pueblo se deshiziese y despoblase de que ha venido much daño a la dicha tierra e veçinos della espeçialmente a los veçinos de la dicha villa que tenian en ella sus haziendas e granjerias e me fue suplicado e pedido por merçed mandase tornar a hazer e poblar la dicha villa e pueblo pues tanto convenia a nuestro seruiçio o como la mi merçed fuese por ende yo vos mando que veades lo suso dicho y proveays çerca dello como mas convenga a nuestro seruiçio y bien de la dicha tierra e vezinos e moradores della e no fagades ende al fecha en Valladolid a veynte e tres dias del mes de agosto de mill e quinientos e veynte e syete años. Yo el Rey por mandado de su Magestad Francisco de los Covos. [*rubrica del escribano*]

[47] E despues de lo suso dicho en diez e syete dias del dicho mes de setienbre e del dicho año ante los dichos señores presydente e oydores pareçio el dicho Garçia de Llerena en el dicho nonbre e presento este escripto que se sygue.

Muy poderosos señores

Garçia de Llerena en nonbre de don Hernando Cortes digo que por otra mi petiçion que en el dicho nonbre di en esta Real abdiençia en catorze dias deste presente mes en que estamos de setienbre, pedi e suplique a vuestra Magestad que su presydente e oydores no diesen ni Repartiesen los pueblos e yndios que el dicho mi parte tenia en la prouinçia de Guaxaca asy porque su Magestad por su provision Real que yo en el dicho nonbre tengo presentada en esta Real abdiençia de que hize Representaçion y agora tanbien la hago, tiene mandado e manda a su presydente e oydores que no le hiziesen novedad ninguna en los pueblos e yndios e otras cosas que el dicho mi parte en esta Nueva España dexo al tienpo que della se partio a besar sus Reales pies e le dar quenta destos nuevos Reynos e señorios que le dexava paçificos conquistados e poblados, y como porque en le quitar e Remover los dichos pueblos Resçibia mucho daño e perdida porque sy alguna grangeria el dicho don Hernando tenia y le avia quedado en esta Nueva España no hera otra mas de la

The King

Our president and oidores of our royal audiencia which we have commanded to be appointed for the New Spain: On the part of the conquerors and settlers of the said land, a report was made to me that immediately upon the conquest of that land, a town of Christians was established in the region of Oaxaca, which was called Segura de la Frontera, because it was a very good region and populated with many Indians, and there were mines of gold and silver, and it was fertile with provisions and other things. From this there resulted for us much service and general good for the said land and an increase in our incomes, and it was hoped that these results would continue, but Hernando Cortés, in order to have the said land for himself, saw to it that the said town should be undone and depopulated, from which has resulted much harm to the said land and its freeholders, especially to the freeholders of the said town who had their farms and enterprises in it. And I was asked and begged as a kindness that I should command that the said town be remade and resettled, because it would be so good for our service, or whatever my will might be. Therefore I command you that you look into the abovementioned and make a decision concerning it as may be best for our service and for the good of the said land and of the freeholders and residents of it. And you shall not go contrary to it. Done in Valladolid on the twenty-third day of the month of August of the year one thousand five hundred and twenty-seven. I the King. By command of His Majesty. Francisco de los Cobos.

And after the abovesaid, on the seventeenth day of the said month of September of the said year, before the said lords president and oidores, the said García de Llerena appeared in the said name and presented this brief which follows.

Very Powerful lords

I, García de Llerena, in the name of Don Hernando Cortés, say that by another petition of mine which I presented in the said name on the fourteenth day of this present month of September in which we now are, I asked and besought Your Majesty that your president and oidores should not give nor allot the towns and Indians which my said party held in the province of Oaxaca. I asked this both because His Majesty, by his royal decree, which I have presented in this royal audiencia in the said name and of which I made a second presentation and do so again now, has commanded and commands his president and oidores that they should not make any innovation in regard to the towns and Indians and other things which my said party left in this New Spain at the time that he left it in order to kiss your royal feet and to give you an account of these new realms and dominions which he left peaceful, conquered, and colonized for you, and also because of the fact that they took away and removed the said towns from him he received much damage and loss, because if the said Don Hernando possessed and continued to maintain any enterprise in this New Spain, it was not other than that which he had in the said province with his

que en la dicha prouinçia tenia con sus esclavos y por su presydente y oydores fue
Respondido a la dicha petiçion muchas cosas e muy adefiçios, e no estando ynformados del fecho de la verdad en el despoblar que dizen de la villa de Antequera e
todo ello porque no se me diese el testimonio de la dicha petiçion que yo en el
dicho nonbre presente para que su Magestad fuese ynformado [*rubrica*] [*47v*] y avnque por mi fue pedido no se le quitasen los pueblos de la dicha prouinçia de Guaxaca
por lo suso dicho e por otras muchas cavsas e razones que para ello avia su presydente e oydores no lo han querido hazer e le han Repartido e dado todos los yndios
e no estante tanto dapno quanto en lo suso dicho el dicho don Hernando Resçibe
por del todo le quitar [*le—canceled*] lo que tiene el dicho presidente e oydores no
lo pudiendo ni deviendo hazer e yendo contra el thenor e forma de la dicha çedula
e prouisyon, agora nuevamente es benido a my notiçia que su presydente e oydores
quitan e despojan al dicho mi parte del pueblo de Tlapa con lo a el subjeto que el
dicho don Hernando tiene e posee en la juridiçion e termino de la villa de San Luys
e asymismo del pueblo de Tustla que es en la prouinçia de la çibdad de la Vera
Cruz donde el dicho don Hernando mi parte tiene fecho vn yngenyo de açucar e
donde ha gastado mucha suma e cantidad de pesos de oro y porque en le quitar
los dichos pueblos al dicho don Hernando Resçibiria mucho agravio e dapno, porque a vuestra Magestad suplico mande a su presydente e oydores que vean la dicha
çedula e sobrecarta que asy tengo presentada e la guarden e cumplan y no quiten
ni despojen al dicho don Hernando de los dichos pueblos e yndios hasta que su
Magestad en ello provea lo que se deve hazer con que protesto sy asy no hazieren
todos los yntereses e granjerias tributos daños e menoscabos que sobre ello por se
los quitar al dicho mi parte se le Recreçieren contra quien de [*rubrica*] [*48*] derecho
protestarlo devo e para que vuestra Magestad sea ynformado, pido a vuestra Magestad mande al secretario me de testimonio deste mi escripto e presentaçion del con
lo que por su presydente e oydores fuere Respondido, para en todo lo qual y en lo
mas neçesario el Real ofiçio de vuestra Magestad ynploro e pido justiçia. Garçia
de Llerena.

E asi presentado El dicho escripto en la manera que dicha es los dichos señores
presidente e oydores dixieron que mandavan e mandaron a mi el dicho Alonso Lucas
secretario suso dicho que sy [*qui—canceled*] testimonio quisyere el dicho Garçia de
Llerena que le de vn traslado e del otro escrito todo debaxo de un syno e no lo
uno syn lo otro.

Fecho e sacado fue este dicho traslado del dicho testimonio y escritos y çedula
original con que fue conçertado en la çibdad de Tenuxtitan Mexico desta Nueba
España a doze dias del mes de mayo año del nasçimiento de nuestro Saluador Ihu
Xpo de mill e quinientos e treynta e un años testigos que fueron presentes a lo ver
corregir e conçertar este dicho traslado con el dicho original Garçia de Llerena e
Alonso Melendez estantes en este dicha çibdad.

slaves. And to the said petition your president and oidores answered many very absurd things, not being well informed regarding the truth of the matter in what they call "the depopulation" of the town of Antequera and all of that, as to why there should not be given to me a notarized record of the said petition which I presented in the said name, so that His Majesty might be informed. And although I petitioned that the towns of the said province of Oaxaca should not be taken away from him because of the abovementioned and many other reasons and causes which there were for it, your president and oidores have not wished to do so, and they have allotted and given out all his Indians. And, as though it were not enough that the said Don Hernando receives so much injury when the said president and oidores take away from him everything that he has, even though they cannot and should not do so and are going against the tenor and form of the said writ and decree, just now it has come to my attention that your president and oidores are depriving and despoiling my said party of the town of Tlapa and the area subject to it, which the said Don Hernando holds and possesses in the jurisdiction and boundary of the town of San Luis, and likewise the town of Tustla which is in the province of the city of Vera Cruz. There the said Don Hernando my party has built a sugar mill and has spent a great sum and quantity of gold pesos. And because the said Don Hernando would receive great harm and damage in being deprived of the said towns, I therefore beseech Your Majesty that you command your president and oidores to consider the said decree and covering letter which I have thus presented and to observe and fulfill it and not to deprive nor despoil the said Don Hernando of the said towns and Indians until His Majesty makes a decision as to what should be done in this matter. And so, if they do not do thus, I protest all the interests and profits, tributes, damages and losses which may develop over this matter because of taking them from my said party, and I protest them against whomever I should legally do so. And so that Your Majesty may be informed, I ask Your Majesty to command the secretary to give me a notarized record of this my brief and the presentation of it and the response of your president and oidores. For all of this and for the most necessary elements of it I implore the royal authority of Your Majesty, and I ask for justice. García de Llerena.

The said brief having been presented in the manner which is stated, the said lords president and oidores said that they commanded me, the said Alonso Lucas, the abovementioned secretary, that if the said García de Llerena should desire a notarized record, I should give him a transcript also of the other document, all under one sign and not the one without the other.

This said transcript of the said notarized record and briefs and original decree, with which it was compared, was made and copied in the city of Tenochtitlan Mexico of this New Spain on the twelfth day of the month of May of the year of the birth of Our Savior Jesus Christ one thousand five hundred and thirty-one. Witnesses who were present to see this said transcript corrected and compared with the original: García de Llerena and Alonso Melendez, sojourners in this said city.

Va entre Renglones o diz que vea e emendado o diz la vala.

E yo Alonso de Paz escriuano de sus cesarea e catolicas Magestades este traslado conçerte e fiz escriuir e fiz aqui mio sygno a tal [*signo*] en testimonio de verdad.

ALONSO DE PAZ ESCRIUANO DE SU MAGESTAD [*rubrica*]

[*48v*] E asy presentada la dicha petiçion e escripturas en la manera que dicha es los dichos señores dixeron que lo avian por presentado quanto a lugar de derecho, e que mandavan dar traslado a la otra parte lo qual paso en haz de Gregorio de Saldaña su procurador.

[*49 blank; 49v*] El Marques presento estos testimonios de las probisiones de su Magestad e sobrecarta con que fueron Requeridos Nuno de Guzman e los liçençiados Matienço e Delgadillo para el pleito de los yntereses de Vaxoçingo.

Despues de lo suso dicho en diez e seis dias de dicho mes de agosto del dicho año ante los dichos señores presidente e oydores e presente mi el dicho escribano pareçio presente el dicho Garçia de Llerena e presento la petiçion siguiente.

[*50*]   MUY PODEROSOS SEÑORES

Garçia de Llerena en nonbre del Marques del Valle de Guaxaca [*illegible cancellation*] en el plito que trata con los liçençiados Matienço y Delgadillo sobre los yntereses del pueblo de Guaxulçingo diguo [*sic — digo*] que por vuestra Magestad mandado ver y examinar el proçeso del dicho plito y las escripturas testigos e probanças fechos e presentados por el dicho Marques hallara que el dicho Marques probo bien e conplidamente su yntento y demanda e todo equello que probarle convenia ca probo que teniendo e poseyendo el dicho Marques el pueblo e prouinçia de Guaxulçingo y aviendo su Magestad por su çedula Real e sobrecarta [*mandado*] que no le fuesen Removidos los pueblos yndios e otras cosas que tenia al tiempo que partio destas partes para Castilla ni se hiziese mudança alguna de como los avia dexado e que siendo noteficada la dicha cedula al [*sic*] dichos licençiados Matienço e Delgadillo partes contrarias seyendo oydores no solo no las obedesçieron mas avn contra el thenor dellas quitaron el dicho pueblo de Guaxalçingo al dicho Marques e le despojaron de la posesyon del ynjusta e no devidamente syn ser çitado oydo e llamado pretermissa toda horden del derecho, e que se seruieron del dicho pueblo e lleuaron del cada dia cada seis gallinas e seys codornizes e axi e quarenta huevos e otros mantenimientos e cada semana cada vno cinquenta cargas de mayz, e allende desto se prueva que llevaron del dicho pueblo muchas cargas de Ropa Rica y plumages y otras joyas en grand cantidad, e que se siruieron de los yndios de los

Insertion between lines where it says "that he may see" and amended where it says "the." Valid.

And I, Alonso de Paz, notary of His Imperial and Their Catholic Majesties, compared this transcript and had it written, and I made here my sign to such [*there is a sign*] in testimony of the truth.

ALONSO DE PAZ, *notary of His Majesty* [*rubric*]

And the said petition and documents having been presented in the manner which is stated, the said lords said that they accepted it as presented insofar as it is acceptable in law, and that they commanded that a copy be given to the other party, all of which took place in the face of Saldaña, their attorney.

The Marqués presented these notarized copies of the writs of His Majesty and the covering letter, with which the demand was made to Nuño de Guzmán and the Licentiates Matienzo and Delgadillo, for the lawsuit concerning the interests of Huejotzingo.

After the abovesaid, on the sixteenth day of the said month of August of the said year, before the said lords president and oidores and in the presence of me the said notary, the said García de Llerena appeared present and presented the following petition.

VERY POWERFUL LORDS

I, García de Llerena, in the name of the Marqués del Valle de Oaxaca, in the lawsuit which he is conducting with the Licentiates Matienzo and Delgadillo concerning the interests of the town of Huejotzingo, say that if it is commanded by Your Majesty that the proceedings of the said suit and the documents, witnesses, and proofs presented and made by the said Marqués be seen and examined, you will find that the said Marqués proved well and completely his intent and demand and everything that it was needful for him to prove. He proved that while the said Marqués held and possessed the town and province of Huejotzingo and after His Majesty had commanded by his decree and covering letter that he should not be deprived of the towns, Indians, and other things which he had at the time when he left these parts for Castile and that no change should be made in the way in which he had left them. And after the contrary party, the Licentiates Matienzo and Delgadillo, being oidores, were notified of the said decree, they not only did not obey them but even went contrary to the tenor of them and took away the said town of Huejotzingo from the said Marqués and deprived him of its possession unjustly and unduly, without his being cited, heard, and summoned, bypassing all the order of law. And they made use of the said town and took from it every day six hens and six quail and chile and forty eggs and other provisions, and each week each one took fifty loads of maize. And besides this it is proven that they took from the said town many loads of rich fabrics and works of feathers and other valuables in great quantity. And they made use of the Indians of

dichos pueblos en las obras e edificios que hizieron, e que los maltrataron e dieron trabajos excesiuos de que morieron en sola vna jornada çiento y treze syn otras muchas vezes que murieron [*50v*] muchos dellos y los hazian prender y prendieron para que les diesen el mayz que de tributo pasado deuian al dicho Marques que tenian Recogido en una troxe e los hizieron que les truxesen dello diez mill e tantas fanegas, e se lo hizieron traer a cuestas en tiempo de ynvierno e nieve de que morieron los dichos ciento e treze onbres que de suso tenguo dicho, e allende de todo esto se prueva que los dieron de tributo a ellos e a los oficiales de su Magestad ciento e treynta tejuelos de gordor de un dedo mellique e de tamaño como la [*sic*] medio dedo desde la coyuntura a la uña que podia pesar a cinquenta pesos cada vno e mas, e con esto mucha Ropa y mayz que todo podia valer diez mill castellanos cada vn año, e se prueva que llevaron lo suso dicho por espacio de dos años poco mas o menos lo qual todo son obligados averiguar e Restituir al dicho Marques mi parte, demas de que devan ser condenados en las penas en que yncurrieron por aver fecho e cometido lo suso dicho, de lo qual no les escuso decir que [*los ofic—canceled*] que hizieron acudir a los oficiales de su Magestad con los tributos porque aquello no los Relieva que por aver despojado al dicho Marques [*syn orden des*[*?*]*—canceled*] de la posesyon del dicho pueblo syn tella [*tela ?*] ni orden de derecho, son obligados a la Restitucion dello asy y como qualquier otro prouado lo seria segun derecho, y por aver se acudido a los oficiales por su mandado, ellos son obligados por aver mandado lo tomar ynjusta y no deuidamente, porque a vuestra Magestad suplico [*51*] que pronunciado el dicho Marques mi parte aver probado su yntencion y demanda y los dichos licenciados Matienço e Delgadillo no aver probado sus excepciones ni cosa que les Relieve los condene en todo lo de suso por el dicho mi parte pedido para lo qual y en lo necesario el Real oficio de vuestra Magestad ynploro y pido conplimiento de justicia y las costas pido y protesto y concluyo.

EL DOCTOR VALDEUIESO [*rubrica*]

[*51v*] El Marques contra los liçençiados Matienço e Delgadillo, dize de bien probado sobre los yntereses de Vaxoçingo e concluye.

xvi de agosto 1531. A la otra parte que para la primera concluya en haz de Saldaña.

E asi presentado los dichos señores dixeron que mandavan dar traslado a la otra parte e que para la primera abdiençia Responda e concluya lo qual mandauan en haz de Gregorio de Saldaña procurador de los dichos liçençiados.

the said towns in the works and buildings which they constructed, and they mis-treated them and imposed excessive labors on them, from which a hundred and thirteen died in one journey alone, without counting the many other times when many of them died. And they had them arrested and they arrested them so that they would give them the maize which they owed to the said Marqués from the past tribute, which they had collected in a granary. And they made them bring ten thousand and some fanegas of it, and they made them carry it on their backs during the time of winter and snow, and from this there died the said one hundred and thirteen men whom I have mentioned above. And besides this, it is proven that they gave as tribute to them and to the officials of His Majesty a hundred and thirty ingots as thick as the little finger and as broad as the middle finger from the joint to the fingernail, which might weigh fifty pesos apiece or more, and with this, much cloth and maize, which might all be worth ten thousand castellanos every year. And it is proven that they took the abovementioned for a period of about two years, a little more or less. And they are obligated to ascertain all of this and restore it to the said Marqués, my party, besides which they should be condemned to the penalties which they incurred because of having done and committed the abovementioned. And it is no excuse for them to say that they made the Indians go to the officials of His Majesty with the tributes because this does not relieve them of the fact that because of having deprived the said Marqués of the possession of the said town without the form or order of law, they are obligated to the restitution of it just as any other guilty person would be according to law. And because the Indians went to the officials by their command, they are obligated for having commanded it to be taken unjustly and unduly. Therefore I beseech Your Majesty that, having pronounced that the said Marqués my party has proven his intent and demand and that the said Licentiates Matienzo and Delgadillo have not proven their defense nor anything which would relieve them, you condemn them in everything that has been requested above by my party. For this and in everything necessary I implore the royal authority of Your Majesty and I ask for the fulfillment of justice. And I ask and protest the costs, and I conclude.

DOCTOR VALDEVIESO [*rubric*]

The Marqués versus the Licentiates Matienzo and Delgadillo says it is well proven concerning the interests of Huejotzingo and he concludes.

August 16, 1531. To the other party—that he should conclude for the first—in the face of Saldaña.

When it was thus presented, the said lords said that they commanded that a transcript be given to the other party and that for the first session he should respond and conclude. This they commanded in the face of Saldaña, attorney of the said licentiates.

Despues de lo suso dicho en diez e ocho dias del dicho mes de agosto del dicho año ante los dichos señores presydente e oydores e por ante mi el dicho escribano paresçio presente el dicho Garçia de Llerena e presento el escripto siguiente.

[52]   MUY PODEROSOS SEÑORES

Garçia de Llerena en nonbre del Marques del Valle en el pleito que trato con los liçençiados Matienço e Delgadillo sobre los yntereses del pueblo de Vaxoçingo de que ynjustamente le despojaron, digo que por la parte contraria esta la dicha cavsa dicho de vien probado e por mi parte esta dicho de vien probado e concluido e a fin de dilatar no quieren concluir acuso les la primera Reveldia suplico a vuestra Magestad la aya por acusada e la cavsa por conclusa difinitibamente e para ello el Real ofiçio de vuestra Magestad ynploro e pido justiçia.

[52v] El Marques contra los liçençiados sobre los yntereses de Vaxocingo dize que ha dicho de vien probado danbas partes e por parte del Marques esta la dicha cavsa conclusa e por dilatar vbiendo dicho de bien probado no han querido concluir acusa les la primera Reveldia pide se aya la cavsa por conclusa difinitibamente.

xviii° de agosto 1531. Por acusada para la primera diga e concluya en haz de Saldaña.

Primera Rebeldia. E asi presentado los dichos señores dixeron que avian por acusada la dicha primera Rebeldia e que mandavan e mandaron [*dar tresla—canceled*] a la otra parte que para la primera abdiençia Responda e concluya lo qual mandaron en haz de Gregorio de Saldaña procurador de los dichos liçençiados.

Despues de lo susodicho en veinte e un dias del mes de agosto del dicho año ante los dichos señores presidente e oydores e por ante mi el dicho escribano paresçio presente el dicho Garçia de Llerena e presento el escripto siguiente.

[53]   MUY PODEROSOS SEÑORES

Garçia de Llerena en nonbre del Marques del Valle en el pleito que trato con los liçençiados Juan Ortiz de Matienço e Diego Delgadillo sobre los yntereses del pueblo de Vaxoçingo de que ynjustamente mi parte estubo despojado doss años, digo que yo he acusado a la parte contraria primera Reveldia para que concluia difinitibamente pues esta por mi parte conclusa la dicha cavsa acuso les la segunda Rebeldia, suplico a vuestra Magestad la aya por acusada e la cavsa por conclusa e pido justiçia.

After the abovesaid, on the eighteenth day of the said month of August of the said year, before the said lords president and oidores and in the presence of me the said notary, García de Llerena appeared present and presented the following brief.

Very powerful lords

I, García de Llerena, in the name of the Marqués del Valle, in the lawsuit which I am conducting with the Licentiates Matienzo and Delgadillo over the interests of the town of Huejotzingo of which they unjustly deprived him, say that by the contrary party it is stated that the said case is well proven and by my party it is stated that it is well proven and concluded, and for the purpose of delay they do not wish to conclude. I accuse them of the first default and I beseech Your Majesty to consider the accusation as made and the case as concluded definitively. And for this I implore the royal office of Your Majesty, and I ask for justice.

The Marqués versus the licentiates over the interests of Huejotzingo says that he has made a statement that it is well proven by both parties, and by the party of the Marqués the said case is concluded, and for the sake of delay, having said that it is well proven, they have not wished to conclude. He accuses them of the first default and asks that the case be considered as concluded definitively.

August 18, 1531. As accused—for the first let him say and conclude—in the face of Saldaña.

First default. It being thus presented, the said lords said that they accepted the accusation of the first default and that they commanded the other party that for the first session he should respond and conclude. They commanded this in the face of Gregorio de Saldaña, attorney of the said licentiates.

After the abovesaid, on the twenty-first day of the month of August of the said year, before the said lords president and oidores and in the presence of me the said notary, the said García de Llerena appeared present and presented the following brief.

Very powerful lords

I, García de Llerena, in the name of the Marqués del Valle in the lawsuit which I am conducting with the Licentiates Juan Ortiz de Matienzo and Diego Delgadillo concerning the interests of the town of Huejotzingo of which my party was unjustly deprived for two years, say that I have accused the other party of the first default so that he would conclude definitively, because the said case is concluded by my party. I now accuse them of the second default. I beseech Your Majesty that you consider the accusations as made and the case as concluded, and I ask for justice.

[*53v*] El Marques contra los liçençiados sobre los yntereses de Vaxoçingo acusa les segunda Reveldia para difinitiba.

xxi de agosto 1531. Por acusada e para la primera Responda en haz de Saldaña.

Segunda Rebeldia. E asi presentado los dichos señores dixeron que avian por acusada la segunda Rebeldia e que mandaron dar traslado a la otra parte e que para le primera abdiençia Responda e concluya lo qual mandaron en haz de Saldaña.

E despues de lo susodicho en veinte e çinco dias del dicho mes de agosto del dicho año ante los dichos señores presidente e oydores e por ante mi el dicho escribano paresçio presente el dicho Garçia de Llerena e presento el escripto s~~~iente.

[*54*]   MUY PODEROSOS SEÑORES

Garçia de Llerena en nonbre del Marques del Valle en el pleito que trato con los liçençiados Matienço e Delgadillo sobre los yntereses de Vaxoçingo digo que por mi parte esta la dicha causa conclusa e acusadas las partes contrarias primera e segunda Rebeldia para que viniesen concluiendo no lo han querido hazer acuso les la terçera Reveldia suplico a vuestra Magestad la aya por acusada e por la contumaçia de las partes contrarias la cavsa por conclusa e les mande çitar vuestra Magestad para la Relaçion e sentençia de la dicha cavsa e pido justiçia e en lo neçesario el Real ofiçio de vuestra Magestad ynploro.

[*54v*] El Marques contra los liçençiados sobre los yntereses de Vaxoçingo acusa terçera Rebeldia pide la cavsa por conclusa difinitibamente y que vuestra Magestad mande çitar a las partes contrarias para la Relaçion del dicho proçeso e para oyr sentençia en la dicha cavsa.

xxv de agosto 1531. Que concluso acusada la otra Rebeldia por acusada e para la primera concluya en haz de Saldaña.

Tercera Rebeldia. E asy presentado los dichos señores dixeron que avian por acusada la dicha Rebeldia e que concluso acusadas las tress Rebeldias en tiempo e en forma [*que avian el dicho pleito por concluso e que asignavan termino para dar sentençia para luego e dende (?) para cada dia que fenecido no sea para la qual oyr çitavan la parte—canceled*] que mandavan dar traslado a la otra parte e para la primera Responda e concluya en haz de Saldaña.

The Marqués versus the licentiates concerning the interests of Huejotzingo, accuses them of the second default for definitive conclusion.

August 21, 1531. As accused—and let him respond for the first—in the face of Saldaña.

Second default. It being thus presented, the said lords said that they accepted the accusation of the second default and that they commanded that a transcript be given to the other party and that he respond for the first session and conclude. This they commanded in the face of Saldaña.

And after the abovesaid, on the twenty-fifth day of the said month of August of the said year, before the said lords president and oidores and in the presence of me the said notary, the said García de Llerena appeared present and presented the following brief.

Very powerful lords

I, García de Llerena, in the name of the Marqués del Valle in the lawsuit which I am conducting with the Licentiates Matienzo and Delgadillo concerning the interests of Huejotzingo, say that by my party the said case is concluded and the contrary parties have been accused of the first and second default so that they would come and make their conclusion. They have not wished to do it. I now accuse them of the third default. And I beseech Your Majesty to consider the accusation as made and the case as concluded through the contumacy of the contrary parties, and I ask Your Majesty to command them to be cited for the summary and sentence of the said case, and I ask for justice, and insofar as necessary, I implore the royal authority of Your Majesty.

The Marqués versus the licentiates over the interests of Huejotzingo, accuses the third default, asks that the case be definitively concluded and that Your Majesty command that the contrary parties be cited for the summary of the said proceedings and to hear sentence in the said case.

August 25, 1531. Concluded, the other default accused, as accused—and let him conclude for the first—in the face of Saldaña.

Third default. It being thus presented, the said lords said that they accepted the accusation of the said default and that it is concluded, the three accusations of default having been made in proper time and form, and they commanded that a transcript be given to the other party and that he respond and conclude for the first session, in the face of Saldaña.

Despues de lo suso dicho en veinte e seys dias del dicho mes de agosto del dicho año ante los dichos señores presidente e oydores e por ante mi el dicho escribano paresçio presente el dicho Gregorio de Saldaña e presento el escripto [*siguiente — canceled*] e escripturas e çedulas syguientes.

[55]   Muy poderosos señores

Gregorio de Saldaña en nonbre de los liçençiados Juan Hortiz de Matienço e Diego Delgadillo en el plito que con mis partes trata el Marques del Valle sobre los yntereses del pueblo de Guaxoçingo, digo que mandado beer y examinar el presente proçeso e testigos probança en el tomados e Resçibidos, hallara mis partes aver probado su yntençion y aquello que probar les convino para aver vitoria en esta cabsa, y la parte contraria no aver probado cosa alguna que le aproveche, los testigos que presenta no hazen fee ni prueba son solos e singulares barios y no contestes contradizen se vnos a otros y en sus dichos, son criados de la parte contraria, y asi lo dizen en las preguntas generales los yndios presentados por la parte contraria no hazen fee ni se les deven de dar credito porque son yndios vasallos del dicho Marques y todos los yndios generalmente son malos xptianos borrachos mentirosos ydolatras comen carne vmana personas viles que por qualquier cosa se perjuraran y a las pinturas que presenta la parte contraria mucho menos se les debe de dar fee porque son hechas por los mesmos yndios ynfieles y barbaros y para ello no fueron çitados mis partes y asy pudieran pintar todo lo que mas quisieran, Rodrigo de Almonte testigo presentado por la parte contraria no haze fee ni prueba porque se perjura y depone falsamente en decir como dize en la setena pregunta que los dichos indios sirbian a Nuño de Guzman siendo la verdad en contrario y ansi lo dizen los mismos yndios, y que mis partes tenian puesto por calpisque en el dicho pueblo a Fernando de Gibaja estando como estaba puesto por el fator Gonzalo de Salazar y con su poder y no con el de mis partes y ansi mismo se perjura en deçir como dize en la nobena pregunta quel dicho Gibaja cobraba los tributos para Nuño de Guzman y para mis partes y se las enbiaba constando como consta por el dicho proçeso que se cobraban para su Magestad y a sus ofiçiales se enbiaban y ellos lo resçibian, de todo lo qual pido e suplico a vuestra Magestad mande castigar al dicho Rodrigo de Almonte; porque pido e suplico a vuestra Magestad mande pronunçiar la yntençion de mis partes por bien probada, y la parte contraria no aver probado cosa alguna, y avsolber y dar por libres e quitos a mis partes de lo pedido e demandado por el dicho Marques para lo qual y en lo neçesario vuestro Real ofiçio ynploro e pido justiçia e costas.

Otrosi digo que para que a vuestra Magestad le conste como el dicho pueblo estaba en vuestra Real cabeça por vuestro mandamiento se puso en ella, hago presentaçion de los capitulos de la probision por donde vuestra Magestad lo mando y una fee de los libros de los ofiçiales de vuestra Magestad de como se asentaron

After the abovesaid, on the twenty-sixth day of the said month of August of the said year, before the said lords president and oidores and in the presence of me the said clerk, the said Gregorio de Saldaña appeared present and presented the following brief, documents, and decrees.

VERY POWERFUL LORDS

I, Gregorio de Saldaña, in the name of the Licentiates Juan Ortiz de Matienzo and Diego Delgadillo in the lawsuit which the Marqués del Valle is conducting with my parties over the interests of the town of Huejotzingo, say that when you are commanded to see and examine the present proceedings and witnesses and proof which have been taken and received in it, you will find that my parties have proven their intention and that which it behooved them to prove in order to gain victory in this case. And the contrary party has not proven anything which may be of any use to him, the witnesses which he presents do not afford credence nor proof; they are alone and individual, at variance and not in agreement, they contradict one another and themselves, they are servants of the contrary party, and they say so in the general questions. The Indians presented by the contrary party lack credibility, and they should not be given credence because they are Indian vassals of the said Marqués, and all the Indians in general are bad Christians, drunks, liars, idolaters, eaters of human flesh, vile persons who will perjure themselves for anything whatsoever. And much less should the paintings which the contrary party presents be given credence, because they were made by the same infidel and barbarous Indians, and my parties were not cited for it and so they could have painted whatever they wished. Rodrigo de Almonte, presented as a witness by the contrary party, does not afford credibility nor proof because he perjures himself and testifies falsely in saying, as he does in the seventh question, that the said Indians served Nuño de Guzmán, the truth being to the contrary, as the Indians themselves admit, and in saying that my parties had placed Hernando de Gibaja in the town as overseer, for he was placed there by the Factor Gonzalo de Salazar and with his authority and not with that of my parties. And he likewise perjures himself in saying, as he does in the ninth question, that the said Gibaja collected and sent the tributes for Nuño de Guzmán and for my parties, since it is evident from the said trial that they were collected for His Majesty and were sent to his officials, and they received them. For all of this I ask and beseech Your Majesty that you command the said Rodrigo de Almonte to be punished. Therefore I ask and beseech Your Majesty to command that the intention of my parties be pronounced as well proven, and that the contrary party has not proven anything, and that you absolve and judge my party as free and quit of everything asked and demanded by the said Marqués. For this and for what is necessary I implore your royal authority, and I ask for justice and the costs.

Furthermore, I say that in order that it may be clear to Your Majesty that the said town was under tribute to you and was placed there by your command, I make presentation of the articles of the writ by which Your Majesty commanded it and an affidavit from the books of the officials of Your Majesty concerning the fact that they

en vuestros libros y de los [55v] tributos que dieron, y de dos capitulos de la ynstruyçion que vuestra Magestad mando dar a mis partes que ablen sobre la manera que devian tener en el cunplir de las probisiones de vuestra Magestad, todo lo qual presento en quanto por mis partes haze y no en mas, y pido segund de suso.

EL LIÇENÇIADO DELGADILLO [*rubrica*]

Saldaña en nonbre de los liçençiados dize[n — *canceled*] de bien probado en el plito con el Marques sobre lo de Guaxoçingo y presenta vna fee de los libros de su Magestad de los tributos que ha dado Guaxoçingo y otros pueblos y dos capitulos de la ynstruyçion y otro capitulo de una probision de su Magestad para tomar las cabeçeras.

xxvi de agosto 1531. Que se ha por presentado quanto de derecho ha lugar e traslado.

[56] Relaçion de los pueblos quel presidente e oydores pasados pusieron en cabeça de su Magestad e ansy mismo de los tributos que cada vno de los pueblos contribuyo los quales estan en los Registros del contador Rodrigo de Albornoz que son los siguientes

Mexico y Tatelulco dieron dos tributos
Tascala con su sujeto dio seys tributos
Tezcuco con su sujeto dio siete tributos
Guaxoçingo con su sujeto dio dos tributos
Çenpual dio quatro tributos
Guaxaca y Cuylapa dio quatro tributos
Vichichila dio dos tributos
Teguantepeque dio seys tributos
Tutupeque dio seys tributos
Tamaçola dio dos tributos
Tamaçula dio siete tributos
Soconusco dio quatro tributos
Tepezculula dio un tributo
Tatatetelco dio tres tributos
Los çinco pueblos de la laguna dieron un tributo
Çacatula no ha contribuydo

Los quales dichos pueblos de suso contenidos fueron puestos en cabeça de su Magestad por Nuño de Guzman y el liçençiado Juan Ortiz de Matienço y el liçençiado Diego Delgadillo lo qual pareçe por los libros e Registros del dicho contador Rodrigo de Albornoz los quales dichos pueblos pareçe por los dichos libros que fueron puestos en caveça de su Magestad desde onze dias del mes de mayo del año de mill e quinientos e veynte e nueve años en adelante ques fecha y sacada desta dicha copia e traslado en la casa del dicho contador en esta grand

were set down in your books with the tributes which they gave and two articles from the instruction which Your Majesty commanded to be given to my parties which may bespeak the manner which they were to maintain in fulfilling the decisions of Your Majesty. All of this I present insofar as it is helpful to my parties and not for anything more, and I ask according as above.

LICENTIATE DELGADILLO

Saldaña in the name of the licentiates makes a statement of "well proven" in the suit with the Marqués concerning the matter of Huejotzingo, and he presents an affidavit from the books of His Majesty concerning the tributes which Huejotzingo and other towns have given and two articles of the instruction and another article of a writ of His Majesty to take the capital towns.

August 26, 1531. That it is received as presented insofar as allowable in law, and a transcript.

Report of the towns which the past president and oidores placed under tribute to His Majesty, and likewise of the tributes which each one of them contributed, which are in the registers of the Accountant Rodrigo de Albornoz, and they are the following:

Mexico and Tlaltelolco gave two tributes.
Tlaxcala with its subject area gave six tributes.
Texcoco with its subject area gave seven tributes.
Huejotzingo with its subject area gave two tributes.
Cempoala gave four tributes.
Oaxaca and Cuilapa gave four tributes.
Uchichila [Tzintzuntzan] gave two tributes.
Tehuantepec gave six tributes.
Tututepec gave six tributes.
Tamazola gave two tributes.
Tamazula gave seven tributes.
Soconusco gave four tributes.
Tepezcolula gave one tribute.
Tlatetelco gave three tributes.
The five towns of the lake gave one tribute.
Zacatula has not contributed.

The said towns named above were placed under tribute to His Majesty by Nuño de Guzmán and Licentiate Juan Ortiz de Matienzo and Licentiate Diego Delgadillo. This appears from the books and registers of the said accountant Rodrigo de Albornoz. From the said books it appears that the said towns were placed under tribute to His Majesty beginning on the eleventh day of the month of May of the year one thousand five hundred and twenty-nine. This was made and copied from this said copy and transcript in the house of the said accountant in this great city of

çibdad de Tenuxtitan Mexico en veynte e vn dias del mes de julio año del naçimiento de Nuestro Salbador Ihu Xpo de mill e quinientos e treynta e vno testigos Juan Tofino e Leon criados del dicho contador. Y yo Sancho Lopez de Agurto escribano de sus catolicas çesaryas Magestades y su notario publico en la su corte y en todos los sus Reynos y señorios y su Reçevtor de la avdiençia Real que en esta Nueba España en la gran çivdad de Tenustytan Mexico por su Real mandado Reside saque e fiz escribyr y sacar esta dicha copya y traslado de las [*dichas — canceled*] suso dichas probynçyas y pueblos en la manera que dicha es de los dichos libros y Regystros del dicho contador a pedimiento de los liçençiados Juan Hortiz de Matienço y Diego Delgadillo oydodores que fueron en la dicha avdiençia y por virtud de vn mando de los señores presydente y oydores desta dicha Real avdiençia que agora son y por ende fize aquy este mio syg- [*signo*] no en testymonio de verdad.

SANCHO LOPEZ DE AGURTO [*rubrica*]

[*56v*] Los tributos que dieron los pueblos.

[*57*] Yo Alonso Dias de Gibraleon escribano de sus Magestades doy fee que pareçe por vna ynstruyçion firmada de su Magestad e Refrendada de Françisco de los Covos su secretario que dieron al presydente e oydores de la avdiençia e chançilleria Real que Reside en esta Nueva España entre los capitulos della esta vno con çiertos nonbres de pueblos al pie del su thenor de lo qual vno en pos de otro es este que se sigue.

EL REY

Nuestro presidente e oydores de la nuestra avdiençia e chançilleria Real de la Nueva España lo que demas de lo contenido en las ynstruçiones e provisiones que para el buen govierno e probision desa tierra llevays mas particularmente se os puede deçir lo qual aveys de tener en muy grand secreto sin lo confiar de otra persona alguna es lo siguiente.

Asi mismo por la probision general que se[*? — badly blotted*] endreça a vosotros e a los perlados e Religiosos de San Francisco e de Santo Domingo sobre el Repartimiento de las tierras e yndios desa prouinçia se os manda que señaleys para nos las cabeçeras de prouinçias e pueblos prinçipales que os pareçiere que conbiene e como quiera que yo aca tengo Relaçion de los que deven ser puso se aquello asi generalmente por ser tantos los que en ello aveys de entender pero vosotros aveys destar sobre aviso que las cabeçeras e pueblos que han de quedar señalados para nos han de ser los que se siguen:

La grand çibdad de Tenuxtitan Mexico con su termino

Tascaltecle e su tierra

Tezcuco e su tierra

Vchichila en Mechuacan ques la cabeçera de la prouinçia con su tierra

Tamazula donde ay las minas de la plata con su tierra

Çacatula e su tierra

Tenochtitlan Mexico on the twenty-first day of the month of July of the year of the birth of Our Savior Jesus Christ one thousand five hundred and thirty-one. Witnesses: Juan Tofino and León, servants of the said accountant. And I, Sancho López de Agurto, scribe of Their Catholic and Imperial Majesties and their notary public in their court and in all their kingdoms and dominions and their secretary of the royal audiencia which by their command resides in this New Spain in the great city of Tenochtitlan Mexico, transcribed and had this copy and transcript of the abovesaid provinces and towns written and copied in the stated manner from the said books and registers of the said accountant at the request of the Licentiates Juan Ortiz de Matienzo and Diego Delgadillo, former oidores in the said audiencia, and in virtue of a command of the present lords president and oidores of this said royal audiencia. And therefore I made here my sign [*there is a sign*] in testimony of truth.

SANCHO LÓPEZ DE AGURTO [*rubric*]

The tributes which the towns gave.

I, Alonso Díaz de Gibraleón, notary of Their Majesties, certify that it appears from an instruction signed by His Majesty and countersigned by Francisco de los Cobos, his secretary, which they gave to the president and oidores of the royal audience and chancery which resides in this New Spain, that among the articles of it there is one with certain names of towns at the bottom, and the contents of it, one after the other, are as follows.

THE KING

Our president and oidores of our royal audiencia and chancery of the New Spain: The following is that which, besides what is contained in the instructions and decrees which you are taking for the good government and regulation of that land, can be said to you more privately, which you must keep very much in secret without confiding it to any other person.

Likewise, by the general decree which is addressed to you and to the prelates and friars of Saint Francis and Saint Dominic concerning the allotment of the lands and Indians of that province, you are commanded that you set aside for us the capitals of the provinces and the principal towns which may seem to be best to you. And although I have a report here of those that must be set aside, there it was set down in a general way because the ones which you must attend to in this matter are so many. But you must be alert to the fact that the capitals and towns which must be set aside for us must be those that follow:

The great city of Tenochtitlan Mexico with its boundaries;
Tascaltecle and its land;
Texcoco and its land;
Uchichila in Michoacán, which is the capital of the province, with its land;
Tamazula, where the silver mines are, with its land;
Zacatula and its land;

Acapulco e su tierra donde hazen los nabios del sur

Çenpual e su tierra, para lo que fuere menester para los nabios que se hizieren en el norte

En la prouinçia de Guaxaca Cuylapa ques la cabeçera con su tierra donde dizen que son la[s] buenas minas de oro

La cabeçera de Teguantepeque

La cabeçera de Tututepeque en la costa del Sur

La cabeçera de Socunusco

La cabeçera de Guatimala

Los lugares despañoles questan poblados e se poblaren

Yten todos los puertos del mar

Y como quiera que hasta que benida vuestra Relaçion e yo mando prober çerca del dicho Repartimiento que conbenga no se ha de haçer mudança en cosa ninguna de lo que agora esta Repartido aunque sean destas mismas cabeçeras de suso contenidas que han de quedar para nos pero como veys es justo pues que nos tan poco provecho tenemos de la dicha tierra que los que asy tienen encomendados los yndios nos den algund seruiçio e tributo de lo que ellos llevan dellos este tiempo que asi los han de tener hasta que [*rubrica*] [*57v*] se determine lo que generalmente han de dar por febdo o por tributo conforme a la dicha prouision por ende yo vos mando que vosotros como de vuestro lo probeays e conçerteys para que en este medio tiempo seamos serbidos de la dicha tierra cobrando para nos aquella cantidad de tributo e seruiçio que en el memorial que nos aveys de enbiar obieredes puesto e vos pareçiere que adelante se nos ha de pagar asy de lo que oy en dia tienen encomendado como de lo que de nuevo encomendaredes de los yndios que bacaren que no sean de las cabeçeras de suso declaradas porque estas e las que mas os pareçiere conbenientes han de quedar para nos sin las encomendar de nuevo.

El qual dicho traslado yo el dicho escribano saque del dicho oreginal e lo coRe[*e — canceled*]gi e conçerte con el oreginal el qual va çierto e verdadero e lo fiz escrevir por mandado de los señores presydente e oydores e de pedimiento del Liçençiado Delgadillo e por ende fiz aqui este mio signo a tal [*signo*] en testimonio de verdad.

ALONSO DIAZ DE GIBRALEON ESCRIUANO [*rubrica*]

[*58*] Yo Alonso Diaz de Gibraleon escribano de sus Magestades doy fee que pareçe por vna ynstruçion firmada de su Magestad e Refrendada de Francisco de los Cobos su secretario que dieron al presydente e oydores de la avdiençia e chancilleria Real desta Nueva España entre los capitulos della estan dos el thenor de las quales es este que se sigue.

Acapulco and its land, where they make the ships of the South Sea;

Cempoala and its land, for what may be necessary for building ships in the north;

In the province of Oaxaca, Cuilapa, which is the capital, with its land, where they say the good mines of gold are;

The capital of Tehuantepec;

The capital of Tututepec on the coast of the South Sea;

The capital of Soconusco;

The capital of Guatemala;

The places of Spaniards which are settled and may be settled;

Further, all of the seaports.

But until your report arrives and I command the determination to be made concerning the said allotment which may be fitting, no change is to be made in anything from the way in which it is now allotted, although it be concerning these same capital towns named above which must be kept for us. But you can see that it is just, since we have so little profit from the said land, that those who have the Indians thus entrusted to them, should give us some service and tribute from that which they take from them during this time when they are to have them thus, until a determination is made in general as to what they have to give as fee or tribute in conformity with the said decision. Therefore I command you that you determine and regulate it as something of your own, so that in this meantime we may be served by the said land. You shall collect for us that amount of tribute and service which you shall have put down in the memorandum which you are to send us, an amount such as it may seem proper to you that they should pay us in the future, both from what they now have entrusted to them and from what you shall entrust in the future from among the vacant encomiendas, provided they are not among the capitals mentioned above, because these and those which may seem best to you must be kept for us and not be given out anew as encomiendas.

I, the said notary, copied this said transcript from the said original and I corrected it and compared it with the original, and it is trustworthy and authentic, and I had it written by the command of the lords president and oidores and at the request of Licentiate Delgadillo, and therefore I made my sign here to it as such [*notarial sign*] in testimony of the truth.

ALONSO DÍAZ DE GIBRALEÓN, *notary* [*rubric*]

I, Alonso Díaz de Gibraleón, notary of Their Majesties, certify that it is apparent from an instruction, signed by His Majesty and countersigned by Francisco de los Cobos, his secretary, which they gave to the president and oidores of the royal audiencia and chancery of this New Spain, that among its articles there were two whose content is as follows.

El Rey

Muchas vezes acaeçe que algunas personas nos suplican por descubrimientos e poblaçiones e nuevas e por merçedes de tierras e yslas y peñoles e asy porque somos dellas ynportunados como porque nos han serbido les mandamos dar nuestras çedulas para vosotros para que ayays ynformaçion çerca dello e la envieys ante nos para que vista [*que — canceled*] se probea lo que convenga y que entretanto les encomendeys las dichas conquistas e poblaçiones e merçedes e cosas e porque podria ser questo fuese en deseruiçio nuestro e daño de las tales tierras estareys sobre aviso de mirar mucho en esto e sin enbargo de las çedulas e probisiones que ovieremos dado e dieremos no enbargante que en ellas se diga entretanto que biene la dicha ynformaçion e se vee les encomendeys las dichas conquistas hareys en ello lo que mas convenga al seruiçio de Dios e nuestro e bien e poblaçion desa tierra porque si despues pareçiere aver vosotros probeydo cosa yndevida e no conbeniente nos terniamos de vos por deserbidos e lo mandariamos Rebocar.

Asimismo algunas personas que nos han serbido e van a esas partes e otras que estan en ellas nos suplican les hagamos merçed de tierras e solares e otras haziendas e cosas e damos nuestras çedulas para que ayays vuestra ynformaçion y las enbieys con vuestro pareçer y porque aunque vosotros se os diese ynformaçion por la qual costase questo se podria buenamente conçeder sin perjuyzio de terçero e por conplir con las partes e por aver serbido o por otros respetos diesedes vuestro pareçer conforme a las dichas ynformaçiones quando alguna cosa desta calidad se ofreçiere enbiarnos eys vuestro pareçer aparte largo e particular de lo que os pareçiere que se deve prover e que mas conbiene al seruiçio de Dios e nuestro para que se haga lo que conbenga, e asi mismo quando oviere votos diversos escribirnos eys aparte el boto de cada vno e las cabsas que le movieren a botar de aquella manera.

Fecho e sacado fue este dicho traslado de los dichos capitulos oreginales en la çibdad de Mexico a tres dias del mes de agosto año del nasçimiento de Nuestro Saluador Ihu Xpo de mill e quinientos e tre[*rubrica*] [*58v*]ynta e vn años. Testigos que fueron presentes a lo veer leer coRegir e conçertar con el oreginal Antonio Serrano de Cardona e Pedro rregidor vecinos desta dicha çibdad. E yo Alonso Diaz de Gibraleon escriuano de su çesarea e catholicas Magestades e su escriuano y notario publico en la su corte e en todos los sus Reynos e señorios presente fuy en vno con los dichos testigos al veer leer corregir e conçertar deste dicho traslado con el oreginal e de mandamiento de los señores presidente e oydores e de pedimiento del liçençiado Delgadillo lo fiz escrevir e porende fiz aqui este mio signo a tal [*signo*] en testimonio de verdad.

Alonso Diaz de Gibraleon escriuano [*rubrica*]

THE KING

Frequently it happens that various people beg us for the right to make new discoveries and settlements and for grants of lands, islands, and hills, and because we are importuned by them as well as because they have served us, we command our decrees to be issued for you, so that you may make an inquiry concerning it and send it to us, so that when it is seen, a determination may be made as to what is best, and that in the meantime you may commit to them the said conquests and settlements and grants and other things. And because it is possible that this could be to our disservice and to the harm of such lands, you shall be on guard to look into this carefully, and notwithstanding the decrees and writs which we may have issued or may issue, and in spite of the fact that it may say in them "until such a time as the said inquiry comes and is seen, you shall commit to them the said conquests," you shall do in this matter what is best for the service of God, for us, and for the welfare and settlement of that land, because if it later appears that you have made an inappropriate and unbecoming decision, we will consider ourselves disserved by you and we will command it to be revoked.

Likewise some persons who have served us and go to those parts and others who are in them entreat us to make grants of lands and building sites and other properties and things to them, and we issue our decrees that you should make your investigation and send it with your opinion. And therefore, although a report may be given to you through which it may be evident that such a thing could very well be granted without prejudice to a third party, and you, in order to satisfy the parties because they have served or for other reasons, would give your opinion in agreement with the said reports, nevertheless when something of this kind arises, you must send us your opinion, separately, at length, and individually, concerning what you think should be decreed and what seems best for God's service and ours, so that whatever is becoming may be done. And likewise, when the opinions are at variance, you must write us separately about the opinion of each one and the causes that led him to think in that way.

This said transcript of the said original articles was made and copied in the City of Mexico on the third day of the month of August of the year of the birth of Our Savior Jesus Christ one thousand five hundred and thirty-one. Witnesses who were present to see it read, corrected, and compared with the original: Antonio Serrano de Cardona and Pedro Regidor, freeholders of this said city. And I, Alonso Díaz de Gibraleón, notary of His Imperial and Their Catholic Majesties and their clerk and notary public in their court and in all of their realms and dominions, was present together with the said witnesses to see the reading, correction, and comparison of this said copy with the original, and at the command of the lords president and oidores and at the request of Licentiate Delgadillo, I had it written. And therefore I made here this my sign to it as such [*notarial sign*] in testimony to the truth.

ALONSO DÍAZ DE GIBRALEÓN [rubric]
notary

E asy presentado los dichos señores dixeron que lo avian por presentado e que mandavan dar traslado a la parte del dicho Marques.

Despues de lo suso dicho en veinte e ocho dias del dicho mes de agosto del dicho año ante los dichos señores presidente e oydores e por ante mi el dicho escriuano paresçio presente el dicho Garçia de Llerena e presento el escripto siguiente.

[59]   Muy poderosos señores

Garcia de Llerena en nonbre del Marques del Valle en el pleito que mi parte trata contra los liçençiados Juan Ortiz de Matienço e Diego Delgadillo sobre los yntereses del pueblo de Guajoçingo, digo que despues destar conclusa la cavsa por mi parte por contumaçia de las partes contrarias con tres Rebeldias que juridicamente le fueron acusadas las partes contrarias dixeron de vien probado en ella protesto que para en la dicha cavsa principal el dicho escripto tenga aquella validaçion y haga la fe estar puesta en el dicho proçeso que de derecho puede e no mas, por estar como ya la dicha casva estava conclusa difinitibamente e asy en el dicho nonbre lo pido e pido justiçia y en lo neçesario el Real ofiçio de vuestra Magestad ynploro.

[59v] El Marques contra los liçençiados sobre los yntereses de Vajxoçingo a se de ler.

xxviii° de agosto dxxxi. Que se oye e que se ponga en el proçeso en haz de Saldaña.

E asy presentado los dichos señores dixeron que lo oyan e que mandavan que se ponga en el proçeso lo qual paso en haz de Gregorio de Saldaña, procurador de los dichos liçençiados.

[60] En el pleyto que es entre partes de la vna don Hernando Cortes Marques del Valle e de la otra los liçençiados Juan Ortiz de Matienço e Diego Delgadillo oydores que fueron desta Real abdiençia e sus procuradores en sus nonbres sobre los intereses del pueblo de Guaxoçingo:
Fallamos atentos los actos e meritos deste proçeso que la parte del dicho Marques provo su yntençion e demanda segun e como prouarle convino para en lo que de yuso sera contenido, damos la e pronunçiamos la por bien prouada e los dichos liçençiados no prouaron sus exebçiones ni cosa alguna que les aproveche, damos las e pronunciamos las por no prouadas, por ende que devemos condenar e condenamos a los dichos liçençiados a que dentro de nueve dias primeros syguientes despues que

And when it was thus presented, the said lords said that they accepted it as presented and they commanded that a copy be given to the party of the said Marqués.

After the abovesaid, on the twenty-eighth day of the said month of August of the said year, before the said lords president and oidores and in the presence of me the said clerk, the said García de Llerena appeared present and presented the following brief.

VERY POWERFUL LORDS

I, García de Llerena in the name of the Marqués del Valle, in the lawsuit which my party is conducting against the Licentiates Juan Ortiz de Matienzo and Diego Delgadillo concerning the interests of the town of Huejotzingo, say that after the case was concluded by my party because of the nonappearance of the contrary parties with three defaults of which they were juridically accused, the contrary parties made a statement of "well proven'" in it. I protest that as to its effect on the principal case the said brief, when it is placed in the said proceedings, should have that validity and authenticity which it can legally have and no more, because the said case was already definitively concluded. And I make this petition in the said name, and I ask for justice, and insofar as necessary, I implore the royal authority of Your Majesty.

The Marqués versus the licentiates over the interests of Huejotzingo. It must be read.

August 28, 1531. That it is heard and that it be placed in the proceedings—in the face of Saldaña.

And when it was thus presented, the said lords said that they heard it and that they commanded that it be placed in the proceedings; this was done in the face of Gregorio de Saldaña, attorney of the said licentiates.

In the lawsuit which is between the parties of Don Hernando Cortés, Marqués del Valle on the one hand and, on the other hand, the Licentiates Juan Ortiz de Matienzo and Diego Delgadillo, former oidores of this royal audiencia, and their attorneys in their names, over the interests of the town of Huejotzingo:

We find, considering the acts and merits of this case, that the party of the said Marqués proved his intention and demand, just as it was proper for him to prove it for what will be contained below. We grant and pronounce it as well proven; and the said licentiates did not prove their defense pleas nor anything that would be of any use to them. We deliver and pronounce them as not proven, and therefore we find that we must condemn and we do condemn the said licentiates that within the first

con la carta executoria desta nuestra sentençia fueren Requeridos den e paguen al
dicho Marques o a quien su poder oviere los provechos e intereses que pudiera aver
avido e llevado justamente del dicho pueblo e naturales de Guaxoçingo en el tienpo
que los dichos liçençiados vsaron sus ofiçios, los quales moderamos en tres mill pesos
de oro de lo que corre, y en quanto a lo demas que los dichos liçençiados llevaron e
Reçibieron [*para prouision de sus casas—between lines*] de los naturales de los dichos
pueblos lo Reseruamos para la pesquisa secreta con la qual mandamos acomular este
dicho proçeso para que çerca dello se haga lo que sea justiçia e condenamos mas a los
dichos liçençiados en las costas en este proçeso justa e derechamente hechas, la tasaçion de las quales en nos Reseruamos e por esta nuestra sentençia difinitiua juzgando
asy lo pronunçiamos e mandamos en estos escriptos e por ellos. Va entre Renglones
do dize, para prouisyon de sus casas.

     Episcopus Sancti Dominici [*rubrica*]
     Licentiatus Alonso Maldonado [*rubrica*]
     El Licenciado Ceynos [*rubrica*]
     Licenciado Quiroga [*rubrica*]

Dada e pronusçiada fue esta dichas [*sic*] sentençia por los dichos senores presydente
e oydodores estando en abdiençia publica a veynte e tres dias del mes de diziembre
de mill e quinientos e treynta e vn años en fas de los procuradores de las partes.

Contra los liçençiados sobre los yntereses de Guaxoçingo.

[*60v blank; 61*]   Muy poderosos señores

 Gregorio de Saldaña en nonbre de los liçençiados Juan Ortiz de Matienço e
Diego Delgadillo sintiendome por muy agraviado de vna sentençia quel presidente
e oydores del abdiençia e chançilleria Real de la Nueva España dieron e pronunçiaron contra mis partes en fabor de el Marques del Valle por la qual condenaron
a mis partes en tres mill pesos de oro de lo que corre por Razon de çiertos yntereses
del pueblo de Guaxoçingo, [*e(?)—canceled*] por tanto apelo de la dicha sentençia
para ante vuestra Magestad y para antel presidente e oydores de vuestro Real
Consejo de las Yndias y para ante quien y con derecho devo y pido se me otorgue
esta dicha apelaçion y pido justiçia y testimonio.

 Otrosy digo que me presento ante vuestra Magestad en el dicho grado de apelaçion nulidad o agravio o en aquella via e forma que de derecho lugar aya de la
dicha sentençia, y pido y suplico a vuestra Magestad me aya por presentado y me
resçiba en el dicho grado, y para ello vuestro Real ofiçio ynploro y pido justiçia.

    El liçençiado Delgadillo [*rubrica*]

nine days after they shall have been summoned by the executory letter of this our sentence, they should give and pay to the said Marqués or to the person who has his power of attorney the profits and interests which he might justly have received and taken from the said town and natives of Huejotzingo during the time that the said licentiates exercised their offices. We assess these incomes at three thousand pesos of the kind of gold that is current; and as to the rest that the said licentiates took and received for the provisioning of their houses from the natives of the said towns, we reserve it for the secret inquiry with which we command this said lawsuit to be placed, so that concerning it justice may be done. Moreover, we condemn the said licentiates to the costs justly and rightly made in this case, the assessment of which we reserve to ourselves, and judging it thus, we pronounce this as our definitive sentence, and we command it in and through these writings.

It is written between lines where it says "for the provisioning of their houses."

BISHOP OF SANTO DOMINGO [*rubric*]

LICENTIATE ALONSO MALDONADO [*rubric*]

LICENTIATE CEYNOS [*rubric*]

LICENTIATE QUIROGA [*rubric*]

This said sentence was given and pronounced by the said lords president and oidores, being in public audience, on the twenty-third day of the month of December of the year one thousand five hundred and thirty-one, in the face of the attorneys of the parties.

Against the Licentiates over the interests of Huejotzingo.

VERY POWERFUL LORDS

I, Gregorio de Saldaña, in the name of the Licentiates Juan Ortiz de Matienzo and Diego Delgadillo, complain as one who is much aggrieved at a sentence which the president and oidores of the royal audiencia and chancery of New Spain gave and pronounced against my parties in favor of the Marqués del Valle, by which they condemned my party to pay three thousand pesos of the kind of gold that is current on account of certain interests of the town of Huejotzingo. Therefore I appeal from the said sentence to the presence of Your Majesty and of the president and oidores of your Royal Council of the Indies and to the presence of whomever I should appeal to legally, and I ask that this appeal be granted to me, and I ask for justice and request a notarized record.

Furthermore, I say that I present myself before Your Majesty in the state of appeal, nullity, or injury, or in whatever way and form is legally acceptable, from the said sentence, and I ask and beseech Your Majesty that you accept me as having presented myself and that you receive me in the said state. And for this I implore your royal authority and ask for justice.

LICENTIATE DELGADILLO [*rubric*]

[*61v*] Saldaña en nonbre de los liçençiados Matienço e Delgadillo apela de la sentençia que contra sus partes se dio en favor del Marques del Valle sobre los yntereses
del pueblo de Guaxoçingo y presenta se ante vuestra Magestad en el dicho grado
de apelaçion y pide le ayan por presentado, y pide justiçia y testimonio.

En xxvii de diciembre de iUdxxxi años lo presento ante mi el contenido con protesto de se Retificar el primer dia de abdiençia. [*rubrica*]

ix de henero 1532. Que se oye e para la primera esprese agravios e haga sus
diligençias conforme a la hordenança.

En veynte y syete dias del mes de diziembre de mill e quinientos e treynta e un
años ante mi el dicho escribano paresçio Gregorio de Saldaña en nombre de los
dichos liçençiados e presento este escripto con protestaçion que hiso de a la primera
avdiençia se retificar ante los señores presydente e oydores.

Despues de lo suso dicho en nuebe dias del mes de henero de mill e quinientos e
treynta e dos años paresçio el dicho Gregorio de Saldaña e dixo que se Retificaba e
Retifico en el escripto suso dicho e que agora tornaba a hacer presentaçion del, [*e
asy presentado—between lines*] los dichos señores [*pres—canceled*] dyxeron que lo
oyan e que para la primera avdiençia esprese los agrabios de que se syente por
agrabiado e haga sus diligençias conforme a la hordenança.

Despues de lo suso dicho en xxviii° de diziembre del dicho año ante mi el dicho
escribano paresçio el dicho Garçia de Llerena en nombre del Marques del Valle e
presento este escripto con protestaçion que hiso de se retificar a la primera avdiençia
ante los señores presydente e oydores.

[*62*]   MUY PODEROSOS SEÑORES

Garçia de Llerena en nonbre del Marque del Valle en el pleito que trato con los
liçençiados Matienço e Delgadillo sobre los yntereses del pueblo e sujeto de Vexoçingo de que los dichos liçençiados Matienço e Delgadillo tubieron despojado ynjustamente al dicho mi parte me aRimo a la apelaçion en la dicha cavsa ynterpuesta
por parte de los dichos liçençiados de la sentençia dada por el muy Reberendo presidente e oydores del avdiençia e chançilleria Real desta Nueva España en quanto
fue o es o ser puede en perjuizio del dicho mi parte, e pido justiçia y en lo neçesario
vuestro Real ofiçio ynploro e las costas protesto.
                    [*rubrica del Licenciado Altamirano*]

Saldaña in the name of the Licentiates Matienzo and Delgadillo appeals from the sentence which was given against his parties in favor of the Marqués del Valle concerning the interests of the town of Huejotzingo, and he presents himself before Your Majesty in the said state of appeal, and he asks that they accept him as having presented himself; and he asks for justice and a notarized record.

On December 27 of the year 1531, the one named in it presented this before me with a protest that he would rectify it on the first day of audience. [*rubric*]

January 9, 1532. That he is heard and that he express injuries for the first and carry out his judicial procedures in conformity with the ordinance.

On the twenty-seventh day of the month of December of the year one thousand five hundred and thirty-one, before me the said clerk, Gregorio de Saldaña appeared in the name of the said licentiates and presented this brief with the protestation that he would rectify it at the first audience before the lords president and oidores.

After the abovesaid, on the ninth day of the month of January of the year one thousand five hundred and thirty-two, the said Gregorio de Saldaña appeared and said that he rectified the irregularity in regard to the abovesaid brief and that now he makes presentation of it again; and when it had been thus presented, the said lords said that they heard it and that for the first audience he should express the injuries for which he feels himself aggrieved and that he should carry out his judicial procedures in conformity with the ordinance.

After the abovesaid, on December 28 of the said year, before me the said clerk, García de Llerena appeared in the name of the Marqués del Valle and presented this brief with the protestation which he made of rectifying it at the first audience before the lords president and oidores.

Very powerful lords

I, García de Llerena, in the name of the Marqués del Valle in the lawsuit which I am conducting with the Licentiates Matienzo and Delgadillo over the interests of the town and subject area of Huejotzingo of which the said Licentiates Matienzo and Delgadillo kept my said party unjustly deprived, join in the appeal interposed in the said case by the party of the said licentiates from the sentence given by the very reverend president and the oidores of the royal audiencia and chancery of this New Spain, insofar as it was or is or can be prejudicial to my said party; and I ask for justice, and in whatever is necessary, I implore your royal authority and I protest the costs.

[*rubric of Licentiate Altamirano*]

[*62v*] Garçia de Llerena en nonbre del Marques del Valle contra los liçençiados Matienço e Delgadillo sobre los yntereses de Vexoçingo se aRima a la apelaçion ynterpuesta en la dicha cavsa por parte de los dichos liçençiados.

xxviii° de diziembre dxxxi por la mañana. Presento la ante mi Garçia de Llerena con protestaçion de se Retificar para la primera abdiençia. [*rubrica*]

ix de henero dxxxii. Que se oye.

Despues de lo suso dicho en nuebe dias del mes de henero año de mill e quinientos e treynta e dos años [*par — canceled*] ante los dichos señores presydente e oydores [*par — canceled*] y ante mi el dicho escriuano pareçio el dicho Garçia de Llerena en el dicho nombre e dixo que se Retificava e Retifico en el escripto suso dicho, los dichos señores dixeron que lo oyan e que harian justiçia.

Despues de lo suso dicho en x dias del mes de henero e del dicho año ante los dichos señores presydente e oydores pareçio presente el dicho Garçia de Llerena e presento el escripto syguiente.

[*63*]   Muy poderosos señores

Gonçalo de Herrera en nonbre del Marques del Valle en el pleito que trato con los liçençiados Matienço e Delgadillo sobre los yntereses e seruiçios e tributos que vbieron E llebaron del pueblo de Vexoçingo que tenia en encomienda mi parte, digo que vuestra Magestad deve mandar a los dichos liçençiados que paguen o depositen la cantidad en que fueron condenados por el muy Reberendo presidente E oydores desta Real avdiençia sin enbargo de la apelaçion que dizen que ynterponen de la dicha condenaçion e de la sentençia que contra ellos fue dado pues fue mal llevado lo que del dicho pueblo llevaron E la çedula e carta de vuestra Magestad por el dicho liçençiado Delgadillo presentada, manda que hagan el dicho deposito e paguen a cantidad en que fueren condenado si vbieren llevado algo mal llevado o fuere de barateria o cohecho como lo es lo que asi llavaron, e pido justiçia.

Licentiatus Altamirano [*rubrica*]

[*63v*] Gonçalo de Herrera en nonbre del Marques del Valle en el plito con los liçençiados Matienço e Delgadillo se a de leer.

x de henero 1531. Que no ha lugar.

Asy presentado en la manera que dicha es los dichos señores presydente e oydores dixeron que no ha lugar lo que pide en su escripto.

García de Llerena, in the name of the Marqués del Valle versus the Licentiates Matienzo and Delgadillo concerning the interests of Huejotzingo, joins in the appeal interposed in the said case by the party of the said licentiates.

December 28, [1]531 in the morning. García de Llerena presented it before me with the protestation of rectifying it for the first audience. [*rubric*]

January 9, [1]532. That he is heard.

After the abovesaid, on the ninth day of the month of January of the year one thousand five hundred and thirty-two, before the said lords president and oidores and before me the said clerk, the said García de Llerena appeared in the said name and said that he rectified the irregularity in the abovesaid brief; the said lords said that they heard it and that they would do justice.

After the abovesaid, on the tenth day of the month of January of the said year, before the said lords president and oidores, the said Garciá de Llerena [*sic*] appeared present and presented the following brief.

Very powerful lords

I, Gonzalo de Herrera, in the name of the Marqués del Valle in the lawsuit which I am conducting with the Licentiates Matienzo and Delgadillo concerning the interests, services, and tributes which they had and took from the town of Huejotzingo which my party had as his encomienda, say that Your Majesty must command the said licentiates to pay or deposit the amount to which they were condemned by the very reverend president and the oidores of this royal audiencia, in spite of the appeal which they say that they have interposed from the said condemnation and from the sentence which was given against them, since what they took from the said town was ill-gotten, and the decree and letter of Your Majesty which is presented by the Licentiate Delgadillo, commands that they make the said deposit and pay the amount to which they were condemned if they had taken anything ill-gotten or if it were from fraud or bribery, as is true of what they took; and I ask for justice.

Licentiate Altamirano [*rubric*]

Gonzalo de Herrera in the name of the Marqués del Valle in the lawsuit with the Licentiates Matienzo and Delgadillo. It must be read.

January 10, 1531. That it is disallowed.

When it had been thus presented in the manner that is stated, the said lords president and oidores said that what he asks in his brief is disallowed.

Despues de lo suso dicho en xii dias del dicho mes de henero e del dicho año ante los dichos señores presydente e oydores e en presençia de mi el dicho escriuano pareçio presente el dicho Gregorio de Saldaña en el dicho nonbre e presento el escripto syguiente.

[*Muy podersos señores. Francisco Desquivel—inverted. Apparently the scribe had begun to write another petition on this sheet.*]

[*64*]   MUY PODEROSOS SEÑORES

Gregorio de Saldaña en nonbre de los liçençiados Matienço e Delgadillo, digo que mandado ver y esaminar vn proçeso de pleyto que pende ante vuestra Magestad en grado de apelaçion de vna sentençia quel presidente e oydores de la abdiençia e chançilleria Real de vuestra Magestad que Reside en la çibdad de Mexico dieron e pronunçiaron contra mis partes en favor del Marques del Valle por la[*s—canceled*] qual condenaron a mis partes en tres mill pesos de oro de lo que corre por los yntereses del pueblo de Guaxeçingo, hallara la dicha sentençia ser ninguna y do alguna ynjusta e muy agrauiada dina de se Revocar y enmendar por todas las Razones de nulidad e agravio que del proçeso Resultan que aqui por espresas, y por lo siguiente.

Lo primero porque la dicha sentençia no fue dada a pedimiento de parte el proçeso no estava en estado de se sentençiar.

Lo otro porque hallara vuestra Magestad quel dicho Marques vino a estas partes con çierta armada dende la ysla de Cuba para conquistar e conquisto esta Nuba España con los suditos e vasallos de vuestra Magestad que consigo traya por manera que todas las tierras y vasallos desta Nueve España heran y son de vuestra Magestad, y el dicho Marques en nonbre de vuestra Magestad como capitan y despues como governador las tuvo, y puesto que por vuestra Magestad le fue mandado y defendido que no las Repartiese, contra vuestro Real mandado y defendimiento Repartio çierta parte de la tierra entre los conquistadores, y todo lo demas de que yva Repartiendo, lo tenia y poseya en nonbre de vuestra Magestad, vuestra Magestad hera visto poseer en cuyo nonbre poseeya, y desta manera, y sin otro titulo ni deposito el dicho Marques se llevava e llevo los tributos de toda la tierra en mas cantidad de dos millones de pesos de oro ques obligado a dar e pagar a vuestra Magestad a quien perteneçian e perteneçen, y despues quel dicho Marques fue a España mis partes pusieron en cabeça de vuestra Magestad las cabeçeras prinçipales de algunos pueblos, y otros algunos que no heran de aquella calidad Repartieron entre conquistadores y personas que avian seruido a vuestra Magestad y en poblar la villa de Antequera ques en la prouinçia de Guaxaca, como por vuestra Magestad les fue mandado, y la çedula de vuestra Magestad quel dicho Marques presento fue ganada subrretiçiamente callada la verdad y espresado lo contrario diziendo quel tenia e poseya los dichos pueblos quando de aqui partio para España por donde vuestra Magestad le mando dar la dicha çedula para que se los Restituyesen, la qual mis partes obediçieron por la dicha Razon, y en quanto al conplimiento sobreseyeron hasta hazer

After the abovesaid, on the twelfth day of the month of January of the said year, before the said lords president and oidores and in the presence of me the said clerk, the said Gregorio de Saldaña appeared present in the said name and presented the following brief.

Very powerful lords

I, Gregorio de Saldaña, in the name of the Licentiates Matienzo and Delgadillo, say that if you are commanded to look at and examine the proceedings of a lawsuit which is pending before Your Majesty in the state of appeal from a sentence which the president and oidores of the royal audiencia and chancery of Your Majesty which resides in the city of Mexico gave and pronounced against my parties in favor of the Marqués del Valle, by which they condemned my parties to pay three thousand pesos of the kind of gold that is current for the interests of Huejotzingo, you will find that the sentence is invalid, and where it is valid it is unjust and very damaging, worthy to be revoked and amended for all of the reasons of nullity and injury which result from the suit which I consider expressed here and for the following.

First, because the said sentence was not given at the request of a party to the suit, and it was not in a state to have the sentence passed.

Further, because Your Majesty will find that the said Marqués came to these parts with a certain armada from the island of Cuba to conquer, as he did conquer, this New Spain, with subjects and vassals of Your Majesty whom he brought with him, so that all the lands and vassals of this New Spain did and do pertain to Your Majesty, and the said Marqués held them in the name of Your Majesty, as captain and later as governor, and although he was given a prohibitive command by Your Majesty that he should not parcel them out, he allotted a certain part of the land among the conquerors, contrary to your royal command and prohibition; and all the rest, which he continued to parcel out, he held and possessed in the name of Your Majesty. Your Majesty was seen to be the possessor in whose name he possessed it, and in this way and without any other title or commission, the said Marqués took for himself the tributes of the whole land in an amount greater than two million gold pesos, which he is obliged to give and pay to Your Majesty to whom they did and do belong. And after the said Marqués went to Spain, my parties placed the principal capitals of some of the nations under tribute to Your Majesty, and they allotted some others which were not of the same rank among conquerors and other people who have served Your Majesty, and they allotted some also to colonize the town of Antequera, which is in the province of Oaxaca, as Your Majesty commanded them to do. And the decree of Your Majesty which the said Marqués presented was gained surreptitiously, concealing the truth and expressing the contrary, saying that he held and possessed the said towns when he left here for Spain, and as a result, Your Majesty commanded that he be given the said decree so that they would be restored to him; and my parties showed obedience to it for the said reason. And in regard to the fulfillment of it they delayed action until they could make a report about it to your Majesty, as they did, and they are awaiting what you may send as your command,

Relaçion dello a vuestra Magestad como lo hizieron esperando lo que sobrello enbiase a mander [*64v*] porque hazer lo contrario perjudicavan a vuestro Real patrimonio en adjudicar derecho de posision al dicho Marques en lo que no lo tenia y si el dicho Marques presento ante mis partes sobreçedula no fue hazeendo Relaçion de la Respuesta de mis partes, y por ello, y por no ser vista en vuestro Real consejo conforme a las leyes de vuestros Reynos avia de ser obedeçida y no conplida, la qual por las cabsas dichas, y porque por las dichas leyes estan dadas por ningunas las dichas sobreçedulas no se cumplio, y porque cumpliendola hera visto conplir la primera de que mis partes tenian suplicado siendo en tanto perjuyzio de vuestro Real patrimonio, y ansi por esto, como porque vuestra Magestad se llevo las Rentas y tributos del dicho pueblo y de todos los otros, mis partes no serian ni son obligados a cosa alguna, lo qual todo alego por publico e notorio como lo es, y pido e suplico a vuestra Magestad mande a su promotor fiscal tome la boz deste pleyto, y de todos los otros que a mis partes estan movidos sobre esta Razon y siga las cabsas en nonbre de vuestra Magestad y los mande sacar a paz y a salvo de todos ellos pues no consiente Razon ni se premite de justiçia que lo que mis partes con tan buen zelo y tan juridicamente hizieron llevando vuestra Magestad los tributos en mucha [*mas— between lines*] cantidad de lo questan condenados, lo ayan mis partes de pagar, y no solamente mande al dicho fiscal siga estas cabsas, mas tanbien la de los otros yntereses que perteneçen a vuestra Magestad quel dicho Marques llevo en suma de los dichos dos millones de pesos de oro como consta por la pesquisa secreta y Residençia que se hizo.

Lo otro porquel dicho Marques en caso negado que pudiera depositar la tierra y los pueblos della, no pudo tomar ni depositar en si cosa alguna mayormente siendo como hera governador salariado por vuestra Magestad lo qual alego por publico e notorio.

Lo otro porque ya mis partes ovieran quitado el dicho pueblo al dicho Marques que niego, no aviendo preçedido, como no preçedio sentençia, mis partes avian de ser dados por libres e quitos conforme a derecho, y a vuestra Magestad avian de pedir la parte contraria pues llevo los frutos e tributos del dicho pueblo y es obligado a los pagar y ansi pido se pronunçie.

Lo otro porque mis partes pidieron que se castigasen los testigos que se presentaron por la parte contraria que depusieron falsamente en esta dicha cabsa lo qual no se hizo.

[*65*] Por las quales Razones y por cada vna dellas pido e suplico a vuestra Magestad mande Revocar e dar por ninguna la dicha sentençia y dar por libres e quitos a mis partes de lo pedido e demandado por la parte contrario [*sic*] para lo qual y en lo neçesario vuestro Real ofiçio ynploro y pido justiçia y costas.

EL LIÇENÇIADO DELGADILLO [*rubrica*]

[*65v*] Gregorio de Saldaña en nonbre de los liçençiados Matienço e Delgadillo espresa agravios contra la sentençia que contra [*mis—written over*] sus partes dieron sobre lo de Guaxeçingo [*y ofrese se a provar—canceled almost illegibly*].

because if they had done the contrary, they would have prejudiced your royal patrimony by adjudicating a right of possession to the said Marqués for something that he did not possess. If the said Marqués presented a covering letter before my parties, it was not after making a report of the reply of my parties, and for this reason and because it had not been seen in your royal council in accordance with the laws of your realms, it was to be obeyed and not fulfilled; for these said causes and because such covering letters are nullified by the said laws, it was not fulfilled, and also because it was seen that to fulfill it would be also to fulfill the first decree, from which my parties had appealed because it was so prejudicial to your royal patrimony; and for this reason as well as because Your Majesty collected the incomes and tributes of the said town and of all the others, my parties should not be nor are they obligated to anything, and this I allege as public and well known, as it is. And I ask and entreat Your Majesty to command your prosecutor that he take up the prosecution of this suit and of all the others that have been brought against my parties concerning this matter and that he follow up these cases in the name of Your Majesty, and that he command that my parties be taken out of all of them peacefully and safely, for reason does not allow nor does justice permit that what my parties did with such good zeal and so juridically, enabling Your Majesty to take the tributes in much greater quantity than that for which thy are condemned, that my parties should have to pay for it. And you should not only command the fiscal to follow these cases, but also that of the other interests pertaining to Your Majesty, which the said Marqués took in the amount of the said two million gold pesos, as is evident from the secret inquiry and residencia which was made.

Further, because in case the said Marqués could allot the land and its towns, which is denied, he could not take nor assign to himself anything at all, especially since he was a governor, salaried by Your Majesty, which I allege as public and well known.

Further, because even though my parties had taken away the said town from the said Marqués, which I deny because no sentence preceded it, my parties would have to be released as free and absolved in accordance with the law, and the contrary party must ask it of Your Majesty, since Your Majesty took the fruits and tributes of the said town and is obliged to pay them, and I ask that it be pronounced thus.

Further, because my parties asked that the witnesses be punished who were presented by the contrary party and who gave false testimony in this case, and this has not been done.

For these reasons and for each one of them, I ask and entreat Your Majesty that you command that the said sentence be revoked and nullified and that my parties be declared free and quit of what is asked and demanded by the contrary party. For this and in whatever is necessary, I implore your royal authority, and I request justice and the costs.

LICENTIATE DELGADILLO [*rubric*]

Gregorio de Saldaña, in the name of the Licentiates Matienzo and Delgadillo, expresses grievances against the sentence which they gave against his parties concerning the matter of Huejotzingo.

xii de henero dxxxii. Traslado.

Asy presentado los dichos señores dixeron que lo oyan e que mandavan y mandaron dar traslado a la otra parte.

Despues de lo suso en xxii dias del dicho mes de henero e del dicho año ante los dichos señores presydente e oydores e en presençia de mi el dicho escriuano pareçio presente el dicho Gonçalo de Herrera en el dicho nonbre e presento el escripto syguiente.

[66]   MUY PODEROSOS SEÑORES

Gonçalo de Herrera en nonbre del Marques del Valle dize que por otras petiçiones ha suplicado a vuestra Magestad no Reçibiese la apelaçion ynterpuesta por parte de los liçençiados Matienço e Delgadillo de la sentençia quel muy Reberendo presidente e oydores dieron sobre lo que ubieron E llevaron del pueblo de Vexoçingo, sin que primero E ante todas cosas depositen e paguen la cantidad en que fueron condenados conforme a derecho e leyes e prematicas de vuestros Reynos pues por la probision presentada por el dicho liçençiados Delgadillo para que no depositen o paguen, escluie cohechos e baraterias e cosas mal llevadas E manda espresamente que en aquello paguen ante todas cosas E pido justiçia y sobre este articulo concluyo.
[*rubrica del Licenciado Altamirano*]

[66v] Gonçalo de Herrera en nonbre del Marques sobre lo de Vaxoçingo contra los liçençiados Matienço e Delgadillo ha se de ler.

xxii de enero dxxxii. A la otra parte que para la primera concluya.

E asy presentado los dichos señores dixeron que mandaban y mandaron dar treslado a la otra parte e que para la primera avdiençia concluya.

Despues de lo suso dicho en xxiii dias del dicho mes de henero e del dicho año ante los dichos señores presydente e oydores e por ante mi el dicho escriuano pareçio presente el dicho Gregorio de Saldaña en el dicho nonbre e presento el escripto syguiente.

[67]   MUY PODEROSOS SEÑORES

Gregorio de Saldaña en nonbre de los liçençiados Matienço e Delgadillo en el pleyto que trata con el Marques del Valle sobre los yntereses de [*Guaxoçingo— between lines; Cuyoacan—canceled*] Rispondiendo a vna petiçion presentada por la parte contraria en que pide que mis partes paguen o depositen la condenaçion, digo que vuestra Magestad no deve mandar hazer cosa alguna de lo pedido por la

January 12, [1]532. Transcript.

When it was thus presented, the said lords said that they heard it and that they commanded that a transcript be given to the other party.

After the abovesaid, on the 22d day of the said month of January of the said year, before the said president and oidores and in the presence of me the said clerk, the said Gonzalo de Herrera appeared present in the said name and presented the following brief.

VERY POWERFUL LORDS

Gonzalo de Herrera, in the name of the Marqués del Valle, says that by other petitions he has entreated Your Majesty not to receive the appeal interposed by the party of the Licentiates Matienzo and Delgadillo from the sentence which the very reverend president and the oidores issued concerning what they had and took from the town of Huejotzingo, unless first and foremost they deposit and pay the amount to which they were condemned, according to the justice, laws, and sanctions of your realms, for according to the writ presented by the said Licentiate Delgadillo so that they should not deposit or pay it, the writ excludes bribery and frauds and ill-gotten goods, and it commands expressly that in such a matter they should pay before everything. And I ask for justice; and on this article I conclude.

    [*Rubric of Licentiate Altamirano*]

Gonzalo de Herrera, in the name of the Marqués, over the matter of Huejotzingo against the Licentiates Matienzo and Delgadillo. It must be read.

January 22, [1]532. To the other party—that he conclude for the first.

When it was thus presented, the said lords said that they commanded that a transcript be given to the other party and that he conclude for the first session.

After the abovesaid, on the 23rd day of the said month of January of the said year, before the said lords president and oidores and in the presence of me the said clerk, the said Gregorio de Saldaña appeared present in the said name and presented the following brief.

VERY POWERFUL LORDS

I, Gregorio de Saldaña, in the name of the Licentiates Matienzo and Delgadillo in the lawsuit which he [*sic*] is conducting with the Marqués del Valle over the interests of Huejotzingo, responding to a petition presented by the contrary party in which he asks that my parties should pay or deposit the amount of their condemnation, say that Your Majesty must not command anything at all to be done of what the

parte contraria porque demas de no ser pedido por parte mis partes no son a ello obligados porque sy alguna leña el dicho pueblo les dio fue porque vuestra Magestad les mando que se syrviesen de la dicha leña y agua y yerva de los yndios desta tierra y de aquello hizieron Relaçion a vuestra Magestad, y como de pueblo de vuestra Magestad lo Resçibirian y no como cosa que pertenesçia ni pertenesçe al dicho Marques ni a ello tenia ni tiene derecho, y no es cohecho ni barateria como la parte contraria menos bien dize, y pues mi parte tiene apelado de la sentençia que en el dicho pleyto se dio y tiene presentada carta y provision de vuestra Magestad para que le sean otorgadas las apelaçiones, por tanto a vuestra Magestad pido y suplico no mande hazer lo pedido por la parte contraria pues mis partes no son a ello obligados y para ello vuestro Real ofiçio ynploro e pido justiçia.

EL LIÇENÇIADO DELGADILLO [*rubrica*]

[*67v*] Saldaña en nonbre de los liçençiados Matienço e Delgadillo en el pleyto con el Marques del Valle sobre los yntereses de Cuyoacan [*sic*] Responde a lo alegado por el dicho Marques sobre el deposyto que pide que hagan de la condenaçion que les fue hecha.

xxiii de enero dxxxii. Al acuerdo.

E asy presentado los dichos señores dixeron que mandaban que se llebase al acuerdo.

E despues de lo suso dicho en xxiii dias del dicho mes de henero e del dicho año ante los dichos señores presydente e oydores e por ante mi el dicho escriuano pareçio el dicho Gregorio de Saldaña en el dicho nonbre e presento el escripto siguiente.

[*68*]   MUY PODEROSOS SEÑORES

Gregorio de Saldaña en nonbre de los liçençiados Matienço e Delgadillo en el pleyto que tratan con el Marques del Valle sobre los tributos de Guaxoçingo Respondiendo a vna petiçion presentada por la parte contraria en que pide que mis partes depositen la condenaçion en que fueron condenados digo que vuestra Magestad no deve mandar hazer cosa alguna de lo pedido e demandado por la parte contraria porque demas de no ser pedido por parte ni en tiempo ni en forma mis partes no son a ello obligados porque tienen apelado de la dicha sentençia y tienen provision de vuestra Magestad para que les sean otorgadas las dichas apelaçiones, y la cantidad en que estan condenados no la huvieron ni llevaron ellos salvo vuestra Magestad y vuestros ofiçiales en vuestro Real nonbre como consta por el proçeso, y no es cohecho ni barateria como la parte contraria menos bien dize syno acreçentar vuestro Real

contrary party asks because besides the fact that it is not requested by the party, my parties are not obligated to it, because if the said town gave them some wood, it was because Your Majesty commanded that they should make use of the said wood, water, and fodder of the Indians of this land. And they made a report of this to Your Majesty, and they would have received it as from a town of Your Majesty and not as a thing that belongs or belonged to the said Marqués, nor did he nor does he have a right to it. And it is not bribery or fraud, as the contrary party says less well. And since my party has appealed from the sentence which was given in the said suit, and has presented a letter and writ of Your Majesty to the effect that the appeals should be granted to him, therefore I ask and entreat Your Majesty that you should not command the execution of what is requested by the contrary party, since my parties are not obligated to it. And for this I implore your royal authority, and I ask for justice.

Licentiate Delgadillo [*rubric*]

Saldaña in the name of the Licentiates Matienzo and Delgadillo in the lawsuit with the Marqués del Valle over the interests of Coyoacán [*sic*], responds to what is alleged by the said Marqués concerning the deposit which he asks that they make of the amount of the condemnation which was made against them.

January 23, [1]532. To the court.

And when it was thus presented, the said lords said that they commanded that it should be brought before the court.

And after the abovesaid on the 23d day of the said month of January of the same year, before the said lords president and oidores and in the presence of me the said clerk, the said Gregorio de Saldaña appeared in the said name and presented the following brief.

Very powerful lords

I, Gregorio de Saldaña, in the name of the Licentiates Matienzo and Delgadillo in the lawsuit which they are conducting with the Marqués del Valle over the tributes of Huejotzingo, responding to a petition presented by the contrary party in which he asks that my parties deposit the amount to which they were condemned, say that Your Majesty must not command the execution of anything requested and demanded by the contrary party because, besides not being requested by a party, nor on time, nor in proper form, my parties are not obligated to it because they have appealed from the said sentence, and they have a writ from Your Majesty to the effect that they should be granted the said appeals. And in regard to the amount for which they are condemned, they did not have or take it but rather Your Majesty took it and your officials in your royal name, as is clear from the trial; and it is not bribery or fraud, as the contrary party says less well, but it was to increase your royal patrimony, as they

patrimonio como lo acreçentaron porque pido E suplico a vuestra Magestad mande pronunçiar e declarar mis partes no ser obligados a pagar ni hazer el dicho deposito pedido por la parte contraria y para ello vuestro Real ofiçio ynploro e pido justiçia.

EL LIÇENÇIADO DELGADILLO [rubrica]

[*68v*] Saldaña en nonbre de los liçençiados Matienço E Delgadillo en el pleyto con el Marques del Valle sobre los tributos de Guaxoçingo Responde a lo alegado por el dicho Marques sobre lo del deposito que pide que hagan de la condenaçion que les fue hecha.

xxiii de enero dxxxii. Acuerdo.

E asy presentado los dichos señores dixeron que mandaban y mandaron que se llevase al acuerdo.

Despues de lo suso dicho en xxv dias del dicho mes de henero e del dicho año ante los dichos señores presydente e oydores e por ante mi el dicho escriuano pareçio el dicho Gonçalo de Herrera en el dicho nonbre e presento el escripto syguiente.

[*9 de abril 1532. A prueva con termino de xx dias y que se hordene la sentençia conforme a la hordenança en faz de Peña e Herrera—canceled.*]

[69]   MUY PODEROSOS SEÑORES

Gonçalo de Herrera en nonbre del Marques del Valle en el pleito que trato en grado de apelaçion contra los liçençiados Juan Ortiz de Matienço e Diego Delgadillo sobre los [*de—canceled*] yntereses de Vexoçingo, Respondiendo al escripto de agrabios por su parte presentado, digo que sin enbargo de lo por ellos dicho e alegado la sentençia de vuestro presidente e oydores se ha de confirmar e Reformar en mejor asy por estar mi parte aRimado a la dicha apelaçion en tiempo e en forma como por lo que se sigue.

Lo vno porque de los avtos del proçeso se justifica la sentençia porque esta claro quel juez que ynjustamente y con dolo y henemistad despoja comete fuerça notoria por Razon de la qual es obligado a todos los daños costas e yntereses a quel dicho mi parte le hizieron por dondel dicho despojo fue ynjusto y violento, y en estimarse e moderarse los dichos yntereses en los dichos tres mill pesos de oro de lo que corre el dicho mi parte fue agrabiado porque atento la calidad de los pueblos e los tributos ser creçidos y las grangerias del dicho mi parte que de los dichos pueblos avia e tenia hera mucha mas cantidad que los dichos tres mill pesos de oro porque sacaban en cada vn año mill e quinientas cabeças de puercos que valian mill e quinientos pesos y daban diez mill fanegas de mahiz e daban Ropa e oro e hazian en las obras del dicho mi parte que todo montaria e valdria justamente en cada vn año seis mill pesos de oro.

did increase it; therefore I ask and beseech Your Majesty to command that it be declared and pronounced that my parties are not obligated to pay or make the said deposit requested by the contrary party; and for this I implore your royal authority and I ask for justice.

LICENTIATE DELGADILLO [*rubric*]

Saldaña, in the name of the licentiates Matienzo and Delgadillo in the lawsuit which he is conducting with the Marqués del Valle over the tributes of Huejotzingo, responds to the allegation made by the said Marqués concerning the matter of the deposit which he asks that they make of the amount to which they were condemned.

January 23, [1]532. Court.

And when it had been thus presented, the said lords said that they commanded that it be taken before the court.

After the abovesaid, on the 25th day of the said month of January of the said year, before the said lords president and oidores and in the presence of me the said clerk, the said Gonzalo de Herrera appeared in the said name and presented the following brief.

VERY POWERFUL LORDS

I, Gonzalo de Herrera, in the name of the Marqués del Valle in the lawsuit which I am conducting in the state of appeal against the Licentiates Juan Ortiz de Matienzo and Diego Delgadillo over the interests of Huejotzingo, responding to the brief of grievances presented by their party, I say that in spite of what is said and alleged by them, the sentence of your president and oidores must be confirmed and improved, both because my party has joined the said appeal in the proper time and form and because of what follows.

First, because from the acts of the trial the sentence is justified, because it is clear that the judge who unjustly and with deceit and enmity despoils anyone commits notorious violence, by reason of which he is obligated to all of the damages, costs, and interests, which is what they did to my said party, and therefore the deprivation was unjust and violent; and in estimating and computing the said interests as the said three thousand pesos of the kind of gold that is current, my said party was injured, because, considering the quality of the towns and the fact that the tributes were great and the profits that my said party had and held from the said towns, the amount was much greater than the said three thousand pesos of gold, because every year they produced fifteen hundred head of pigs which were worth fifteen hundred pesos, and they gave ten thousand fanegas of maize and cloth and gold, and they labored on the works of my party, all of which would be worth and would justly mount up each year to six thousand pesos of gold.

Lo otro digo que no haze al caso dezir que el dicho mi parte sin cavsa tomo los pueblos que heran e son de vuestra Magestad porquel los pudo Repartir como capitan general en nonbre de vuestra Magestad para que los conquistadores e el se pudiesen sostener mayormente en tierra de nuevo Reduçida e de ynfieles puesta devajo del dominio de vuestra Magestad donde lo mueble y Raiz el semejante capitan puede Repartir en Remuneraçion de los gastos e trabajos que se paso en la dicha conquista, mayormente quel no Repartio ni dio propiedad alguna salvo el usofruto de los pueblos para el dicho sustestamiento de sus personas e vidas e avn para que la tierra se pudiese mejor conserbar como se ha conserbado e sostenido y nuestra fe catolica aumentado [*s—canceled*] y esto solamente el dicho [*69v*] mi parte lo conçederia en nonbre de vuestra Magestad e por su voluntad como es publico e notorio, quanto mas que vuestra Magestad tiene aprobado e confirmado los depositos y encomiendas quel dicho mi parte hizo en su persona como pareçe por las çedulas e sobreçedulas que vuestra Magestad le dio con que los dichos liçençiados por el dicho mi parte fueron Requeridos questan puestas en este proçeso las quales con el dicho dolo e mala voluntad no quixeron cumplir, mas antes yendo e biniendo contra ellos despues que les fueron presentados hizieron el dicho despojo al dicho mi parte.

Lo otro digo que menos haze al caso dezir que vuestra Magestad llevo los tributos de los dichos pueblos y que por esto es obligado a los Restituir e seguir la cavsa en vuestro Real nonbre, como cosa que de fecho dizen que se aplico, porque segund derecho el juez que [*de fecho — canceled*] ordinario que de hecho proçede a violento despojo avnque aplique la cosa a la camara de vuestra Magestad o a otro lugar comun es obligado al ynterese e danos en el sindicado como dicho tengo en tanto que ningund Recurso le queda al juez contra la parte en cuio fabor hizo el dicho despojo y los derechos que dizen que quando de fecho se aplica alguna cosa a [*vuestra — canceled*] la camara de vuestra Magestad o a otro lugar comun que el que lo aplica es libre de la dicha Restituçion e ques obligado la vuestra camara o el lugar adonde se aplica a lo Restituir, aquello habla e sentiende en el ofiçial que por el comun esta helexido para cobrar los tributos pechos o derechos que a la tal comunidad perteneçen y no habla en juez ordinario que tiene conoçimiento de cavsas e como la ley en este caso contingens penam no se ha destender ni entender salvo en el mismo caso que habla y asi queda Respondido e satisfecho a lo de contrario se dize porque pido e suplico [*la v — canceled*] a vuestra Magestad confirme en todo la dicha sentençia y haziendo en el caso lo que de justiçia se deve hazer la Reforme en mejor condenando a los dichos liçençiados e a qualquier dellos en los dichos seis mill pesos de oro e pues co[*n*]sta del dolo e despojo viholento de los dichos liçençiados [*me — canceled*] defiera en juramento yn liten del dicho mi parte los yntereses perdidos que perdia e dexo de aver en el tiempo questubo despojado de los dichos pueblos [*70*] pues probada la fuerça como esta contra los dichos liçençiados las perdidas e menoscabos

Further, I say that it does not affect the case to say that my said party, without cause, took the towns that did and do belong to Your Majesty, because he could parcel them out as captain general in the name of Your Majesty, so that the conquerors and he might support themselves, especially in a land of infidels recently subjugated and placed under the dominion of Your Majesty, where such a captain can portion out the movable and immovable goods in remuneration for the expenses and labors which they underwent in the said conquest; especially since he did not parcel out or give any ownership but only the usufruct of the towns for the said support of their persons and lives and even in order that the land might be better conserved, as it has been conserved and sustained, and our Catholic faith has been increased, and my said party would grant this only in the name of Your Majesty and by your will, as is public and well known, all the more so since Your Majesty has approved and confirmed the allotments and encomiendas which my said party made for himself, as is apparent from the decrees and covering letters which Your Majesty gave him, with which the said licentiates were presented as a demand by my party, and they are placed in these proceedings; but with the said deceit and ill will the licentiates did not wish to fulfill them; instead, going and coming against them after they were presented, they deprived my party in the way that has been stated.

Further, I say that it affects the case even less to say that Your Majesty took the tributes from the said towns and that for his reason you are obligated to make restitution of them and to follow the case in your royal name as a matter which they say was adjudicated *de facto,* because according to law, the judge ordinary who proceeds *de facto* to a violent despoilment, even though he adjudicates the thing to the exchequer of Your Majesty or to some other fund of the community, is obligated to the interest and damages in the judgment, as I have said, in such a way that no recourse remains to the judge against the party in whose favor he made the said despoilment. And regarding the laws which state that when something is *de facto* adjudicated to the exchequer of Your Majesty or some other fund of the community, he who adjudicates it is free from the said restitution, and your exchequer or the fund to which it was adjudicated is obligated to make the restitution. This is speaking of and is to be understood of the official who is chosen by the community, in order to collect the tributes, duties, and rights which pertain to that community and it is not speaking of the judge ordinary who is involved in hearing cases; and the law in this case *contingens poenam [concerning a penalty]* must not be extended nor understood except in the very case which is expressed. And this is an answer and response to what is said to the contrary. Therefore I ask and entreat Your Majesty to confirm the said sentence entirely and, doing in the case what must be done according to justice, to reform it for the better, condemning the said licentiates and each one of them to the said six thousand pesos of gold, and, since there is clear evidence of the said licentiates' deceit and violent despoilment, to defer to my said party's oath *in litem [concerning the contention]* regarding the interests that he lost and that he failed to receive during the time that he was deprived of the said towns, because when the violence is proven as it is against the said licentiates, the losses and damages

se pruevan e han de co[n]star por el juramento del dicho mi parte sobre todo lo qual pido cumplimiento de justiçia e negando lo prejudiçial concluyo, e pido ser Reçibido a la prueva conforme a la hordenança, e pido justiçia.

EL LIÇENÇIADO TELLEZ [*rubrica*]

[*70v*] Gonçalo de Herrera en nonbre del Marques del Valle contra los liçençiados Matienço e Delgadillo dize de vien sentençiado e Responde a los agrabios por las otras partes presentado[*s*] e concluye e pide ser Reçibido a prueva conforme a la hordenança en los yntereses de Vexoçingo.

xxv de henero dxxxi[i]. Prueba con termino de xx dias.

Asy presentado los dichos señores dixeron que Resçibian e Resçibieron anbas las dichas partes a prueba con termino de xx dias primeros siguientes para lo qual asy hacer dieron e pronunçiaron la sentençia syguiente.

[*71*] En el plito ques entre partes de la vna abtor demandante don Hernando Cortes [*Marques del Valle — torn*] e sus procuradores en su nonbre e de la otra rreo defendientes los liçençiados Juan Ortiz de Matienço e Diego Delgadillo sobre [*los ynte—torn*]reses del pueblo de Vaxoçingo e su sujeto que pende en este rreal abdiençia en grado de apelaçion para Castilla:

Fallamos que devemos Reçibir e Reçibimos a la parte de los dichos liçençiados a prueba de lo por su parte en este plito dicho e alegado e no provado en la primera ynstançia para que l[*o —torn*] pruebe por escripturas o por confisyon de parte e no en otra manera e de lo nuevamente a nos por su parte dicho e alegado para que lo prueve por la via de prueba que de derecho aya lugar e a la otra parte a prueba de lo contrario sy quisyere salvo jure ynpertinençium et non admitendorum para la qual prueva hazer e la traer e presentar ante nos les damos e asynamos plaso o termino de veynte dias primeros syguientes e el mismo plaso e termino damos e asynamos para ver presentar jurar e conosçer los testigos que la vna parte presentare contra la otra e la otra contra la otra sy quisyere e mandamos a la parte de los dichos liçençiados que prueve todo aquello que ante nos se ofreçio a provar o tanta parte dello que baste para fundar su yntençion so pena de d[*ie — torn*]s pesos de oro para los estrados Reales desta abdiençia sy no lo probare e aperçibimos a las dichas partes que sy de la sentençia que los señores del Consejo Real de las Yndias dieren en el dicho grado apelaren alguna de las dichas partes suplicare ante ellos e se ofreçiere a probar que para la tal prueba ni para juramento de calunia ni confisyon de parte ni presentaçion de escripturas no le sera dado ni senalado mas termino de çinquenta dias desde el dia que le fuere senalado el dicho

are proven and they must be evident through the oath of my said party. Concerning all of this, I ask for the fulfillment of justice, and denying what is prejudicial, I conclude, and I ask to be received to proof in accordance with the ordinance, and I ask for justice.

LICENTIATE TELLEZ [*rubric*]

Gonzalo de Herrera, in the name of the Marqués del Valle versus the Licentiates Matienzo and Delgadillo, makes a statement of "well sentenced" and responds to the grievances presented by the other parties and concludes and asks to be received to proof in accordance with the ordinance in regard to the interests of Huejotzingo.

January 25, [1]531 [sic—1532]. Proof—with a limit of 20 days.

When it was thus presented, the said lords said that they received both of the said parties to proof with a limit of the first twenty days immediately following, and so that it might be done thus, they gave and pronounced the following sentence.

In the lawsuit which is between the parties of, on the one hand, the plaintiff the Marqués del Valle and his attorneys in his name and, on the other hand, the defendants the Licentiates Juan Ortiz de Matienzo and Diego Delgadillo concerning the interests of the town of Huejotzingo and its subject area, which is pending in this royal audiencia in the state of appeal to Castile:

We find that we must receive and we do receive the party of the said licentiates to the proof of what has been stated and alleged on their part in this suit and not proven in the first instance so that they may prove it by documents or by the confession of the other party and not in any other way, and so that they may prove what has newly been stated and alleged to us by their party by whatever method of proof is allowed in the law, and we receive the other party to the proof of the contrary if he wishes *salvo jure impertinentium et non admittendorum* [*observing the law regarding impertinent and inadmissable matters*], and in order to make this proof and to bring it and present it before us, we give and assign them the limit or term of the next immediate twenty days, and we give and assign the same limit and term to see the presentation, swearing, and acknowledgment of the witnesses which the first party may present against the second or the second against the first if he wishes, and we command the party of the said licentiates that they prove everything that they offered to prove before us or at least such a part of it as may be adequate to establish their intention, under penalty of ten pesos of gold for the royal courtrooms of this audiencia if they do not prove it, and we warn the said parties that if from the sentence which the lords of the Royal Council of the Indies may give in the said state of appeal either of the said parties should wish to appeal before them and should offer to give proof, for the said proof and for the oath of slander and the confession of the other party and the presentation of documents, there will not be given to or assigned him more time than fifty days from the day on which the said limit shall

termino e por esta nuestra sentençia jusgando asy lo pronusçiamos e mandamos en estos escriptos e por ellos.

> Episcopus Sancti Dominici [*rubrica*]
> El liçençiado Salmeron [*rubrica*]
> Licentiatus Maldonado [*rubrica*]
> El liçençiado Ceynos [*rubrica*]

Dada e pronunçiada fuesta dicha sentençia por los dichos señores presydente e oydores en veynte e çinco dias del dicho mes de henero e del dicho año, en haz de los procuradores de las dichas partes.

[*71v*] Despues de lo suso dicho en xxvii dias del dicho mes de hebrero e del dicho año ante los dichos señores presydente e oydores pareçio presente el dicho Gonzalo de Herrera en el dicho nonbre e presento el escripto syguiente.

[*72*]   Muy poderosos señores

Gonçalo de Herrera en nonbre del Marques del Valle en el pleito que trato en grado de apelaçion contra los liçençiados Matienço e Delgadillo sobre los yntereses del pueblo e probinçia de Vaxoçingo de que a mi parte ynjustamente despojaron en questan condenados los dichos liçençiados digo quel termino de la prueva con que vuestra Magestad nos Reçibio es pasado pido publicaçion, suplico a vuestra Magestad la mande hazer e pido justiçia y en lo neçesario el Real ofiçio de vuestra Magestad ynploro.
             [*rubrica*]

[*72v*] Gonçalo de Herrera en nonbre del Marques contra los liçençiados sobre la sentençia en questan condenados de los yntereses de Vaxoçingo dize que el termino con que fueron Reçibidos a la prueva en el dicho grado es pasado, pide publicaçion.

27 de hebrero dxxxii. Traslado a la otra parte e que a la primera diga, en haz de Saldaña.

Asy presentado los dichos señores dixeron que mandaban dar traslado a la otra parte e que a la primera avdiençia venga Respondiendo lo qual paso en haz de Saldaña procurador de los dichos liçençiados.

Despues de lo suso dicho en primero dya del dicho mes de março e del dicho año ante los dichos señores presydente e oydores pareçio el dicho Gonzalo de HeRera e presento el escripto syguiente.

have been set for him. And in and through these writings we command and pronounce it by this our sentence, judging it to be thus.

> BISHOP OF SANTO DOMINGO [*rubric*]
> LICENTIATE SALMERÓN [*rubric*]
> LICENTIATE MALDONADO [*rubric*]
> LICENTIATE CEYNOS [*rubric*]

This said sentence was given and pronounced by the said lords president and oidores on the twenty-fifth day of the said month of January of the said year, in the face of the attorneys of the said parties.

After the abovesaid, on the 27th day of the said month of February of the said year, before the said lords president and oidores, the said Gonzalo de Herrera appeared present in the said name and presented the following brief.

VERY POWERFUL LORDS

I, Gonzalo de Herrera, in the name of the Marqués del Valle in the lawsuit which I am conducting in the state of appeal against the Licentiates Matienzo and Delgadillo concerning the interest of the town and province of Huejotzingo of which they unjustly deprived my party, for which the said licentiates have been condemned, say that the time limit for the proof with which Your Majesty received us has passed; I ask for publication; I entreat Your Majesty to command that it be made; and I ask for justice, and insofar as necessary, I implore the royal authority of Your Majesty.
> [*rubric*]

Gonzalo de Herrera, in the name of the Marqués versus the licentiates concerning the sentence in which they are condemned for the interests of Huejotzingo, says that the time limit with which they were received to proof in the said state is passed; he asks for publication.

February 27, [1]532. Transcript to the other party, and that he speak at the first—in the face of Saldaña.

When it had been thus presented, the said lords said that they commanded that a transcript be given to the other party and that at the first session he come and answer; this took place in the face of Saldaña, attorney for the said licentiates.

After the abovesaid, on the first day of the said month of March of the said year, before the said lords president and oidores, the said Gonzalo de Herrera appeared and presented the following brief.

[*73 blank; 73v*]   Muy poderosos señores

Gonçalo de Herrera en nonbre del Marques del Valle en el plito con los liçençiados Matienço e Delgadillo sobre la condenaçion de los yntereses de Baxeçingo digo que yo he pedido publicaçion e las otras partes no an dicho contra ella pido a vuestra Magestad la mande hazer.

Gonçalo de Herrera en nonbre del Marques del Valle en el plito que trato con los liçençiados Matienço e Delgadillo sobre los yntereses de Baxaçingo digo que yo he pedido publicaçion e las otras partes no an dicho contra ella pido a vuestra Magestad la mande hazer.

Primero de março dxxxii. A la otra parte que para la primera diga en haz de Saldaña.

Asy presentado los dichos señores dixeron que mandaban dar traslado a la otra parte e que para la primera avdiençia venga diziendo porque no se deba hacer lo qual paso en haz de Saldaña procurador de los dichos liçençiados.

[*74*]   Despues de lo suso dicho en iii dias del dicho mes de março e del dicho año ante los dichos señores pareçio presente el dicho Gonçalo de Herrera e presento el escripto syguiente.

Muy poderosos señores

Gonçalo de Herrera en nonbre del Marques del Valle en el pleyto que trata con los liçençiados Matienço e Delgadillo sobre los yntereses de Baxaçingo en grado de apelaçion digo quel dicho mi parte probo bien y conplidamente su yntençion e por tal vuestra Magestad la a de pronunçiar e concluyo definitivamente e pido a vuestra Magestad aya el pleyto por concluso.

[*74v*]   Gonçalo de Herrera en nonbre del Marques del Valle en el pleyto con los liçençiados Matienço e Delgadillo sobre los yntereses de Baxaçingo en grado de apelaçion digo quel dicho mi parte probo bien e conplidamente su yntencion e concluyo definitivamente e pido a vuestra Magestad aya el pleyto por concluso.

iii de março 1532. Por concluso para la primera abdiençia en haz de Saldaña.

Asy presentado los dichos señores dixeron que lo avian e obieron por concluso para la primera avdiençia lo qual paso en haz de Saldaña procurador de los dichos liçençiados.

VERY POWERFUL LORDS

I, Gonzalo de Herrera, in the name of the Marqués del Valle in the suit with the Licentiates Matienzo and Delgadillo concerning the condemnation for the interests of Huejotzingo, say that I have asked for the publication, and the other parties have not made a statement against it; I ask that Your Majesty command it to be done.

Gonzalo de Herrera, in the name of the Marqués del Valle in the suit which I am conducting against the Licentiates Matienzo and Delgadillo concerning the interests of Huejotzingo; I say that I have asked for publication and the other parties have not made a statement against it; I ask that Your Majesty command it to be done. [*This repetitive passage appears in the document.*]

March 1, [1]532. To the other party—that he speak at the first—in the face of Saldaña.

When it had been thus presented, the said lords said that they commanded that a transcript be given to the other party and that for the first session he should come and say why it should not be done; this took place in the face of Saldaña, attorney of the said licentiates.

After the abovesaid, on the 3d day of the said month of March of the said year, before the said lords, the said Gonzalo de Herrera appeared present and presented the following brief.

VERY POWERFUL LORDS

I, Gonzalo de Herrera, in the name of the Marqués del Valle in the suit that he is conducting with the Licentiates Matienzo and Delgadillo concerning the interests of Huejotzingo in the state of appeal, say that my said party proved his intention well and completely and Your Majesty must pronounce it as such, and I conclude definitively; and I ask that Your Majesty consider the suit as concluded.

Gonzalo de Herrera, in the name of the Marqués del Valle in the suit with the Licentiates Matienzo and Delgadillo concerning the interests of Huejotzingo in the state of appeal: I say that my said party proved his intention well and completely, and I conclude definitively, and I ask Your Majesty to consider the suit as concluded.

March 3, 1532. As concluded—for the first session—in the face of Saldaña.

When it had been thus presented, the said lords said that they considered it as concluded for the first session; this took place in the face of Saldaña, attorney of the said licentiates.

Despues de lo suso dicho en viii° dias del dicho mes de abrill e del dicho año
ante los dichos señores presydente e oydores e por ante mi el dicho escriuano
pareçio presente el dicho Gonçalo de Herrera e presento el escripto syguiente.

[75]   Muy poderosos señores

Gonçalo de Herrera en nonbre del Marques del Valle en el pleito que trato en
grado de apelaçion con los liçençiados Juan Ortiz de Matienço e Diego Delgadillo
sobre los yntereses del pueblo de Vaxoçingo, digo que en el dicho grado la dicha
cavsa esta conclusa y los dichos liçençiados no han sacado el proçeso de la dicha
cavsa pido a vuestra Magestad les mande que la saquen y enbien en el primer
nabio como son obligados so pena de deserçion.

Otrosi a vuestra Magestad pido que los mande çitar a los dichos liçençiados
para que vayan o enbien a oyr sentençia en la dicha cavsa al vuestro Real Consejo
de las Yndias e para todos los avtos que alla se vbieren de hazer hasta sentençia
difinitiba e tasaçion de costas e carta executoria deste dicho pleito e cavsa, e que
en la dicha çitaçion se pongan las palabras que por vuestra Magestad esta mandado
que se pongan en las dichas çitaçiones por las hordenanças desta Real avdiençia e
pido justiçia e en lo neçesario el Real ofiçio de vuestra Magestad ynploro.
                              [rubrica]

[At the foot of 75 there is some mathematical figuring which has no indicated
relationship with the text.]

[75v]   Gonçalo de Herrera en nonbre del Marques del Valle contra los liçençiados
Matienço e Delgadillo en grado de apelaçion sobre los yntereses de Vexoçingo en
que estan condenados, dize que por su parte esta la dicha cavsa conclusa e las
partes contrarias no han querido concluir avnque les fue mandado pide que se
aya por conclusa e que mande a los dichos liçençiados que saquen el proçeso e lo
enbien como son obligados e que sean çitados conforme a la dicha hordenança.

viii° de abril 1532 [2—canceled] Que si asy es per concluso e que las partes sygan
la cabsa conforme a la hordenança e so la pena della, e que se çitan en forma
conforme a la hordenança en haz de Peña.

Asy presentado en la manera que dicha es los dichos señores lo ovieron por
presentado e dixeron que sy la [dicha — canceled] parte del dicho Marques ha
concluydo e la parte contraria no quiere concluyr que lo abian e ovieron el dicho
plito por concluso e que mandaban que las dichas partes sygan la cabsa [conforme
— canceled] e sean çitados conforme a la[s — canceled] hordenança que sobre
este caso ay y so la pena della. Lo qual paso en haz en Peña procurador de los
dichos liçençiados.

[76] E despues de lo suso dicho en la dicha çibdad treçe dias del mes de abril
año del naçimiento de nuestro Salvador Ihu Xpo de mill e quinientos e treynta

After the abovesaid, on the 8th day of the said month of April of the said year, before the said lords president and oidores and in the presence of me the said clerk, the said Gonzalo de Herrera appeared present and presented the following brief.

VERY POWERFUL LORDS

Gonzalo de Herrera, in the name of the Marqués del Valle in the suit which I am conducting in the state of appeal with the Licentiates Juan Ortiz de Matienzo and Diego Delgadillo concerning the interests of the town of Huejotzingo, I say that in the said state the said case is concluded, and the said licentiates have not copied the proceedings of the said case; I petition Your Majesty to command that they copy it and send it on the first boat, as they are obliged to do under the penalty of abandonment of the suit.

Further I ask Your Majesty that you command the said licentiates to be cited to go or send someone to your Royal Council of the Indies to hear sentence in the said case and for all of the judicial acts that must be made there up to the definitive sentence and the assessment of the costs and the executory letter of this said suit and case, and that in the said citation those words be placed which Your Majesty commands to be placed in the said citations by the ordinances of this royal audiencia; and I ask for justice, and insofar as necessary, I implore that royal authority of Your Majesty.
    [rubric]

Gonzalo de Herrera, in the name of the Marqués del Valle versus the Licentiates Matienzo and Delgadillo in the state of appeal concerning the interests of Huejotzingo for which they are condemned, says that the said case is concluded by his party and the contrary parties have not wished to conclude, although they were commanded to do so; he asks that it be considered as concluded and that you command the said licentiates to copy the trial records and to send it, as they are obliged, and that they be cited in accordance with the said ordinance.

April 8, 1532. That if it is so, as concluded, and that the parties follow the case in conformity with the ordinance and under the penalty of it, and that they be formally cited in accordance with the ordinance, in the face of Peña.

When it had been thus presented in the manner which is stated, the said lords accepted it as presented and said that if the party of the said Marqués has concluded and the contrary party does not wish to conclude, they considered the said suit as concluded and that they commanded that the said parties follow the case and that they be cited in accordance with the ordinance concerning this case and under the penalty of it. This took place in the face of Peña, attorney of the said licentiates.

And after the abovesaid, in the said city on the thirteenth day of the month of April in the year of the birth of Our Savior Jesus Christ one thousand five hundred

e dos años los muy Reberendo e magnificos señores don Sebastian Ramirez obispo
de Santo Domingo e los liçençiados Juan de Salmeron e Alonso Maldonado e
Francisco de Ceynos e Vasco de Quiroga presidente e oydores de la dicha Real
avidençia en presençia de mi Alonso Lucas escriuano dixeron que mandavan e
mandaron a los dichos liçençiados Juan Ortiz de Matienço e Diego Delgadillo
que en el primer nabio que desta Nueva España se partiere para los Reynos de
Castilla enbie[n] el dicho proçeso en publica forma e que llegado el dicho nabio
a los dichos Reynos de Castilla a qualquier puerto dentro de quarenta dias
primeros siguientes presenten este dicho proçeso en el Consejo Real de las Yndias
todo lo qual hagan e cumplan so pena de deserçion por qualquier cosa de las
suso dichas que no hizieren e cumplieren e que los çitaban e çitaron para que
vayan o enbien su procurador ynistruto vien ynformado con su poder bastante
en seguimiento de la dicha cavsa a oyr sentençia difinitiba en ella la qual en su
ausençia e Reveldia no pareçiendo se dara e pronunçiara e se haran todos los avtos
e meritos deste proçeso hasta la difinitiba del e tasaçion de costas si las y vbieren,
la qual sentençia e avtos e notificaçiones que asi se hizieren en su avsençia e
Rebeldia se abran por firmes [*e — between lines*] bastantes como si en sus personas
se les hiziesen e les señalavan e señalaron para ello los estrados del dicho Consejo
Real e que se siga e fenesca el dicho pleyto con la persona que pareçiere en nonbre
del dicho Marques lo qual dixeron que mandavan e mandaron conforme a las
hordenanças de su Magestad desta Real abdiençia e mandaron notificar lo suso
dicho a los dichos liçençiados.

E despues de lo suso dicho en este dicho dia mes e año suso dicho yo Françisco
Maldonado escriuano de sus Magestades notifique la dicha çitaçion e mando de
los dichos señores presidente e oydores al liçençiado Juan Ortiz de Matienço oydor
que fue en esta Real abdiençia el qual dixo quel esta ocupado e detenido en su
casa por mandado de los senores presidente E oydores e que no sabe destos
proçesos cosa alguna [*76v*] por quanto estan en poder del liçençiado Delgadillo,
el qual asymismo esta detenido en las ataraçanas que se le notifiquen al dicho
liçençiado los avtos arriba conthenidos e que a la Repuesta quel diere se Remite
e que el Respondera lo que a su derecho e del dicho liçençiado convenga como
persona que en ello esta ystruto e questo dava [*e dio — between lines*] por su
Repuesta, a lo qual fue testigo Rodrigo de Sabçedo.

Françisco Maldonado escriuano de sus Magestades [*rubrica*]

E despues de lo suso dicho en este dicho dia e mes e año suso dicho yo el dicho
Françisco Maldonado escriuano de sus Magestades notifique la çitaçion e mando
de los dichos señores presidente e oydores de suso contenida al liçençiado Delgadillo
oydor que fue en esta Real avdiençia el qual dixo que dandole Alonso Lucas
escriuano de [*su Magestad — canceled*] camara e de la dicha Real abdiençia este
dicho proçeso que el esta presto de lo enbiar e se presentar con el en seguimiento
de la cavsa en el Consejo Real de las Yndias segund e como le es mandado e que

and thirty-two, the Very Reverend and Excellent Lord Don Sebastián Ramírez, bishop of Santo Domingo, and the Excellent Lords Licentiates Juan de Salmerón, Alonso Maldonado, Francisco de Ceynos, and Vasco de Quiroga, president and oidores of the said royal audiencia, in the presence of me Alonso Lucas, clerk, said that they commanded the said Licentiates Juan Ortiz de Matienzo and Diego Delgadillo that on the first ship that leaves this New Spain for the realms of Castile, they should send the said trial record in public form, and that after the said ship has arrived at any port whatsoever of the said realms of Castile, within the forty days immediately following, they should present this said trial record in the Royal Council of the Indies; all of this they shall do and fulfill under penalty of abandonment of the suit for not doing or fulfilling any of the abovesaid things. And the said lords cited them that they should go or send their attorney, well informed and advised, with their adequate power of attorney, for the continuation of the said case to hear the definitive sentence in it. If they do not appear, in their absence and default it will be given and pronounced, and all the acts and evaluations of this case will be made, up to the definitive sentence and the assessment of the costs, if there are such costs; and the sentence, acts, and notifications which shall have been made thus in their absence and default, shall be considered as firm and adequate, as though they had been made to them personally. And for all of this the said lords indicated the courtrooms of the said Royal Council and commanded that they pursue and complete the said suit with the person who shall appear in the name of the said Marqués. They said that they commanded all of this in accordance with the ordinances of His Majesty for this royal audiencia, and they command that the said licentiates be notified of the abovesaid.

And after the abovesaid, on this said day, month, and year mentioned above, I, Francisco Maldonado, notary of Their Majesties, notified the Licentiate Juan Ortiz de Matienzo, former oidor of this royal audiencia, of the said citation and command of the said lords president and oidores. He said that he is occupied and detained in his house by the command of the lords president and oidores and that he does not know anything at all about these proceedings, inasmuch as they are in the hands of the Licentiate Delgadillo, who is also detained in the arsenal, and that the said licentiate should be notified of the judicial acts mentioned above, and that he defers to the answer which he may give, and that he will answer what is most becoming for his rights and for that of the said licentiate, as a person who is informed in the matter. And he gave this as his answer. Witness to this was: Rodrigo de Saucedo.

FRANCISCO MALDONADO, *notary of Their Majesties [rubric]*

And after the abovesaid, on this said day, month, and year mentioned above, I, the said Francisco Maldonado, notary of Their Majesties, notified Licentiate Delgadillo, former oidor of this royal audiencia, of the citation and command of the said lords president and oidores as contained above. He said that as soon as Alonso Lucas, clerk of the court and of the said royal audiencia, gives him the said trial record, he is ready to send it and to present himself with it for the continuation of the case in the Royal Council of the Indies, just as he is commanded, and that he protests that until

protesta que hasta que se le de no le corra termino ni pare perjuizio a su derecho porque asy este proçeso como otros muchos que trata los ha pedido al dicho secretario e no se han podido sacar hasta agora e questo dava por su Repuesta a lo qual fueron testigos Lope de Samaniego alcaide de las ataraçanas e Juan de la Peña estantes en la dicha çibdad.

FRANÇISCO MALDONADO ESCRIUANO DE SUS MAGESTADES [*rubrica*]

En lo de Guaxoçingo.

Çitaçion de Vexoçingo

[*77 blank; 77v*]   E despues de lo suso dicho en veynte e ocho dias del dicho mes de mayo e del dicho año ante los suso dichos señores presydente e oydores e en presençia de mi el dicho escriuano pareçio presente el dicho Gonçalo de Herrera en el dicho nonbre e presento el escripto siguiente.

[*78*]   MUY PODEROSOS SEÑORES

Gonçalo de Herrera en nonbre del Marques del Valle, digo que mi parte trato pleyto en esta Real avdiençia contra los liçençiados Matienço e Delgadillo el qual fue concluso en grado de apelaçion sobre los yntereses del pueblo de Vexoçingo en que los dichos liçençiados fueron condenados en tres mill e tantos pesos de oro, e al tiempo que la dicha cavsa se concluyo vuestra Magestad mando que las partes contrarias fuesen çitados conforme a la hordenança desta Real avdiençia para que enbiasen en seguimiento de la dicha apelaçion el dicho proçeso e cavsa al vuestro Real Consejo de las Yndias y los dichos liçençiados ni han sacado este dicho proçeso ni han hecho las diligençias que de derecho heran obligados para lo aver enbiado, por donde la [*apelaçion — between lines; sentençia — canceled*] quedo disierta e [*la sentençia — between lines*] pasada en cosa juzgada, de la qual hago presentaçion e de los avtos del dicho proçeso, pido a vuestra Magestad que pronunçiandola por tal me mande dar mandamiento hesecutorio contra las personas E bienes de los dichos liçençiados, e juro a Dios e a esta cruz en anima de mi parte que los pesos de oro en ella contenidos le son devidos e que dellos no le ha sido pagado cosa alguna e pido justiçia y en lo neçesario el Real ofiçio de vuestra Magestad ynploro.

[*78v*]   Gonçalo de Herrera en nonbre del Marques del Valle contra los liçençiados Matienço e Delgadillo pide por desierta la condenaçion de lo de Vaxoçingo, lease.

28 de mayo 1532. Traslado e que con lo que dixere se traya en los estrados.

E presentado el dicho escripto en la manera que dicha es los dichos señores

it is given to him, the allotted time should not run nor should it cause any damage to his right, because he has asked the said secretary both for this trial record and for many others that he is conducting, and it has not been possible for them to be copied up to now. And he gave this as his answer. Witnesses to it were Lope de Samaniego, warden of the said arsenal, and Juan de la Peña, sojourners in the said city.

FRANCISCO MALDONADO, *notary of Their Majesties* [*rubric*]

Concerning the matter of Huejotzingo.

Citation regarding Huejotzingo.

And after the abovesaid, on the twenty-eighth day of the said month of May of the said year, before the abovesaid lords president and oidores and in the presence of me the said clerk, the said Gonzalo de Herrera appeared present in the said name and presented the following brief.

VERY POWERFUL LORDS

I, Gonzalo de Herrera, in the name of the Marqués del Valle, say that my party conducted a suit in this royal audiencia against the Licentiates Matienzo and Delgadillo, which was concluded in the state of appeal, concerning the interests of the town of Huejotzingo, and in it the said licentiates were condemned to pay three thousand and some pesos of gold. And at the time when the said case was concluded, Your Majesty commanded that the contrary parties should be cited in accordance with the ordinance of this royal audiencia so that for the continuation of the appeal they should send the record of the said trial and case to your Royal Council of the Indies. But the said licentiates have neither had a copy made of the said trial nor have they made the efforts to which they were obliged by law in order to have it sent, wherefore the appeal was left abandoned and the sentence has become a settled matter. I make presentation of it and of the acts of the said trial, and I ask Your Majesty that, pronouncing it to be as I have said, you command that I be given an executory mandate against the persons and goods of the said licentiates. And I swear to God and to this cross, on the soul of my party, that the pesos of gold mentioned in it are due to him and that nothing of them has been paid to him. And I ask for justice and insofar as necessary, I implore the royal authority of Your Majesty.

Gonzalo de Herrera, in the name of the Marqués del Valle versus the Licentiates Matienzo and Delgadillo, asks that the condemnation in the matter of Huejotzingo be considered as abandoned. Let it be read.

May 28, 1532. Transcript, and with what he says, let it be brought—in the court-rooms.

And when the said brief had been presented in the manner that is stated, the said

presydente e oydores dixeron que mandavan e mandaron dar traslado a la otra parte e que para la primera avdiençia Responda, e que con lo que dixere o no se trayan los avtos lo qual se notifico en los estrados desta Real avdiençia.

E despues de lo suso dicho en treynta e vn dias del dicho mes de mayo e del dicho año ante los dichos señores presydente e oydores e en presençia de mi el dicho escriuano pareçio presente Gregorio de Saldaña en nonbre de los dichos liçençiados e presento el escripto siguiente.

[79]   MUY PODEROSOS SEÑORES

Gregorio de Saldaña en nonbre de los liçençiados Matienço e Delgadillo Respondiendo a vna petiçion presentada por parte del Marques del Valle en que pide se aya por desierta el apelaçion que mis partes ynterpusieron de la sentençia que contra ellos se dio en favor del dicho Marques sobre los yntereses del pueblo de Guaxoçingo, diziendo que no enbiaron el proçeso en el navio de Pinto, digo que lo pedido por la parte contraria no a lugar de se hazer porque no es pedido por parte ni en tiempo ni en forma y porque a mis partes no les a sido mandado que enbiasen el dicho proçeso en el dicho navio y caso que les fuera mandado que niego Alonso Lucas escriuano desta Real abdiençia no les a dado ni les dio el dicho proçeso en tiempo para que lo pudieran enbiar por aver como ay muchos proçesos que sacar no enbargante que por mis partes le a sido pedido e Requerido le diesen el dicho proçeso segund paresçe por estos Requerimientos que presento en quanto por mis partes haze y no en mas; quanto mas que la hordenança desta Real abdiençia que manda que los proçesos conclusos en grado de apelaçion se enben en los primeros navios no se entiende ni deve entender syno solamente en los procysos hordinarios que penden en esta Real abdiençia y no en las cabsas de comision cometidas por vuestra Magestad al muy Reverendo presidente e oydores della como son estos pleytos y cabsas de Residençia; porque pido e suplico a vuestra Magestad pronunçie no aver lugar lo pedido por la parte contraria por lo qual vuestro Real ofiçio ynploro e pido justiçia.

                         EL LIÇENÇIADO DELGADILLO [*rubrica*]

[79v] [*Gregorio de Saldaña en n*]onbre d[*e los liçençiados*] Matienço e Delgadillo Responde a lo pedido por el Marques del Valle sobre la deserçion del proçeso de Guaxoçingo que dize que no enbiaron a España como heran obligados y presenta çiertos testimonios.

31 de mayo 1532. Que se lleven con todos los abtos al acuerdo.

lords president and oidores said that they commanded that a transcript be given to the other party and that he respond for the first session, and with what he does or does not say let the records of the proceedings be brought. This was made public in the courtrooms of this royal audiencia.

And after the abovesaid, on the thirty-first day of the said month of May of the said year, before the said lords president and oidores and in the presence of me the said clerk, Gregoria de Saldaña appeared present in the name of the said licentiates and presented the following brief.

VERY POWERFUL LORDS

I, Gregorio de Saldaña, in the name of the Licentiates Matienzo and Delgadillo, responding to a petition presented by the party of the Marqués del Valle in which he asks for a decree of abandonment of the appeal which my parties interposed to the sentence which was given against them in favor of the said Marqués over the interests of the town of Huejotzingo, stating that my parties did not send the trial record in Pinto's ship, I say that it is not allowable to do what is asked by the contrary party, because it is not requested by a party, nor on time, nor in proper form and because my parties have not been commanded to send the said trial record in the said ship; and in case they were so commanded, which I deny, Alonso Lucas, the clerk of this royal audiencia, did not give nor has he given them the said trial record on time so that they could have sent it, since there are many records to be copied, in spite of the fact that my parties asked and demanded of him that he should give them [*literally: that they should give him*] the said record, as is apparent from these letters of demand, which I present insofar as they may help my party and no further; all the more so, because the ordinance of this royal audiencia which commands that trials concluded in the state of appeal should be sent on the first ships, is not understood nor should it be understood except solely regarding the ordinary trials which are pending before this royal audiencia and not in cases of commission, committed by Your Majesty to the very reverend president and the oidores of it, as are these suits and cases of the residencia. Therefore I petition and beseech Your Majesty to pronounce that what is asked by the contrary party is not allowable. For this I implore your royal authority, and I ask for justice.

LICENTIATE DELGADILLO [*rubric*]

Gregorio de Saldaña, in the name of the Licentiates Matienzo and Delgadillo, responds to the petition of the Marqués del Valle concerning the abandonment of the lawsuit regarding Huejotzingo, which says that they did not send it to Spain as they were obliged, and he presents certain notarized records.

May 31, 1532. That they be brought before the court with all the acts.

E presentado el dicho escripto en la manera que dicha e[*s*] los dichos señores dixeron que mandavan e mandaron que se llevan con todos los avtos al acuer[*do*] para que en el se vea e provea lo que sea justiçia.

Montan las costas deste proceso tasada[*s — canceled*] cada cosa por estenso conforme al aranzel y echo monton: doss mill e quarenta e quatro maravedis de buena moneda. [*rubrica*]

And the said brief having been presented in the manner which is stated, the said lords said that they commanded that they be taken before the court with all of the acts of the case, so that there it might be seen and a decision made which would be just.

The costs of this trial, everything being assessed in detail in accordance with the set fee and added together, amount to two thousand and forty-four maravedís of good coin. [*rubric*]

Confirmation of the Grant of the Marquesado del Valle, 1560

[*cover*]   Confirmacion que su Magestad hiço al Yllustrisimo señor don Martin Cortes Marques del Va[*lle*] de las xxii villas y lugares que tiene en la Nueua Spaña sin limit[*a*]cion de vasallos con que quede para su Magestad la villa e puerto de Teguantepec.
A 16 de Diziembre de 1560 años.

[*The following is canceled*] porque vos mandamos a todos y a cada vno de vos que luego que esta nuestra carta.

[*rubrica*] 16 de Marzo de 1769 [*in a later hand*]

[*There is an unrelated totaling of pesos and reales at the foot.*]

[*1*] Don Phillippe Por la gracia de Dios Rey de Castilla de Leon de Aragon de las dos Secilias d[e] Hierussalem de Nauarra de Granada de Toledo de Valencia de Gallizia de Mallorcas de Seuilla de Cerdeña de Cordoua de Corcega de Murcia de Jaen de los Algarues de Algezira de Gibraltar de las yslas de Canaria de las Yndias yslas y tierra firme del Mar Oceano, conde de Barcelona, Señor de Bizcaya y de Molina duque de Athenas y de Neopatria conde de Russellon y de Cerdania marques de Oristan y de Gociano archiduque de Abstria duque de Borgonia y de Brabante y de Milan conde de Flandes y de Tirol etcet.
POR quanto el Emperador y Rey mi señor de gloriosa memoria acatando los notables y señalados seruicios que don Hernando Cortes Marques del VALLE hizo a la corona Real de estos Reynos en aver descubierto ganado conquistado y poblado la Nueua España E sus prouincias y auer las puesto debaxo de su yugo y señorio Real le hizo merced gracia y donacion de ciertas villas y lugares en la dicha Nueua España hasta en numero de veynte y tres mill vassallos con sus tierras y aldeas y terminos y jurisdicion ceuil [*1v*] y criminal alta y baxa mero misto ymperio y Rentas y oficios y pechos y derechos y montes y prados y pastos y aguas corrientes estantes y manantes y otras cosas segun mas largamente se contiene en la merced que dello le hizo, su thenor de la qual es este que se sigue.
DON CARLOS Por la gracia de Dios Rey de Romanos E Emperador semper augusto, doña Juana su madre y el mismo Don Carlos por La misma gracia Reyes de Castilla de Leon de Aragon de las dos Secilias de Hierussalem de Nauarra de Granada de Toledo de Valencia de Gallizia de Mallorcas e Seuilla de Cerdeña de Cordoua de Corcega de Murcia de Jaen de los Algarbes de Algezira de Gibraltar de las yslas de Canaria de las Yndias yslas y tierra firme del Mar Oceano condes de Barcelona, Señores de Bizcaya y de Molina duques de Athenas y de Neopatria

Confirmation which His Majesty made to the Most Illustrious Lord Don Martín Cortés, Marqués del Valle, of the 22 towns and places which he has in New Spain, without the limitation of vassals, provided that the town and port of Tehuantepec is left for His Majesty.

On December 16, 1560.

[*rubric*] March 16, 1769. [*In a later hand*]

Don Felipe, by the grace of God, King of Castile, of León, of Aragon, of the two Sicilies, of Jerusalem, of Navarre, of Granada, of Toledo, of Valencia, of Galicia of the Majorcas, of Seville, of Sardinia, of Córdoba, of Corsica, of Murcia, of Jaén, of the Algarve, of Algeciras, of Gibraltar, of the Canary Islands, of the Indies, islands and mainland of the Ocean Sea; Count of Barcelona, Lord of Biscay and of Molina, Duke of Athens and Neopatria, Count of Roussillon and of Cerdagne, Marquess of Oristano and Gociano, Archduke of Austria, Duke of Burgundy, of Brabant, and of Milan, Count of Flanders and of Tirol, etc.

The Emperor and King my lord, of glorious memory, giving recognition to the notable and outstanding services which Don Hernando Cortés, Marqués del Valle, performed for the royal crown of these realms in having discovered, won, conquered, and colonized New Spain and its provinces and in having placed them under his yoke and royal dominion, made to him a grant, favor, and gift of certain towns and places in the said New Spain to a total of twenty-three thousand vassals with their lands, hamlets, and territories, with higher and lower civil and criminal jurisdiction, simple mixed dominion and incomes and offices, taxes and fees, forests, meadows, and pastures, running, standing, and outflowing waters, and other things, as is contained more at length in the grant that he made of it, the tenor of which is as follows.

Don Carlos, by the grace of God, King of the Romans and ever august Emperor; Doña Juana, his mother, and the same Don Carlos, by the same grace, Kings of Castile, of León, of Aragon, of the two Sicilies, of Jerusalem, of Navarre, of Granada, of Toledo, of Valencia, of Galicia, of the Majorcas, of Seville, of Sardinia, of Córdoba, of Corsica, of Murcia, of Jaén, of the Algarve, of Algeciras, of Gibraltar, of the Canary Islands, of the Indies, islands and mainland of the Ocean Sea; Counts of Barcelona, Lords of Biscay and of Molina, Dukes of Athens and of Neopatria, Counts

condes de Russellon y de Cerdania Archiduques de Abstria duques de Borgonia y
de Brabante Condes de Flandes y de Tirol etcet. POR quanto vos Don Hernando
Cortes nuestro gouernador y capitan general de la Nueua España por nos seruir
el año passado de mill y quinientos y diez y ocho años con nuestra licencia fuystes
desde la ysla Fernandina llamada Cuba con vna armada a descubrir La NVEVA
SPAÑA de que teniades noticia E con la gracia de Nuestro Señor y con buena
yndustria de vuestra persona descubristes la dicha Nueua España en que se
yncluyen muchas prouincias y tierras, y las pacificastes y posistes todo debaxo de
nuestro señorio y corona Real y assy lo estan agora. Lo qual somos ciertos que
ha sido con muchos y grandes trabajos y peligros de vuestra persona. E NOS [2]
auemos tenido y tenemos de vos muy bien seruidos en ello. E acatando los grandes
prouechos que de vuestros seruicios han Redundado ansi para el seruicio de Nuestro
Señor y aumento de su sancta fee catholica que en las dichas tierras estauan syn
conoscimiento ni fee se ha plantado, como el acrescentamiento que dello ha
rredundado a nuestra corona rreal de estos Reynos y los trabajos que en ellos aveys
passado y la fidelidad y obidiencia con que siempre nos aveys seruido como bueno
y fiel seruidor y vassallo nuestro de que somos ciertos y certificados, E Porque a
los Reyes es justa y loable cosa hazer mercedes y honrrar a aquellos que bien y
lealmente los siruen porque todos se esfuercen a hazer lo mismo, y porque es Razon
que de lo susso dicho quede perpetua memoria y que los dichos vuestros seruicios
sean satisfechos y otros tomen enxemplo de nos seruir bien y fielmente, Y acatando
que a los Reyes y principes es propia cosa onrrar y sublimar y hazer gracias y
mercedes a sus subditos y naturales, especialmente a aquellos que bien y lealmente
los siruen y aman su seruicio, POR la presente vos hazemos merced gracia y
donacion pura y perfecta y no Reuocable que es dicha entre biuos para agora y
para siempre jamas de las villas y pueblos de Cuynacan, Atlaca Huye, Matalcingo,
Toluca, Calimaya, Quanauaca, Guastepeque, Acapixtla, Yautepeque, Tepuzclan,
Guaxaca, Cuynlapa, Etlan, Tenquila Hacoa, Teq[ua]ntepeque, Xalapa, Vtlatepeque,
Atroye[ ]m, Equetasta, Tustla, Tepeca, Yzcalpan, que son en la dicha Nueua Spaña
hasta en numero de veynte y tres mill vassallos con sus tierras y aldeas y terminos
y vassallos y jurisdicion ceuil y criminal alta y baxa mero misto ymperio y Rentas
y oficios y pechos y derechos y montes y prados y pastos y aguas corrientes estantes
[2v]y manantes y con todas las otras cosas que nos touieremos y lleuaremos y nos
pertenesciere y de que podamos y deuamos gozar y lleuar en las tierras que para
nuestra corona Real se señalaren en la dicha Nueua España y con todo lo otro
al señorio de las dichas villas y pueblos de susso declaradas perteneciente en
qualquier manera para que todo ello sea vuestro y de vuestros herederos y
subcessores y de aquel o aquellos que de vos y dellos oviere titulo o causa y Razon,
y para que lo podays y puedan vender y dar y donar y trocar y cambiar y
enagenar y hazer dello y en ello todo lo que quissieredes y por bien touieredes
como de cosa vuestra propria libre y quita y desembargada avida por justo y

of Roussillon and of Cerdagne, Archdukes of Austria, Dukes of Burgundy and of Brabant, Counts of Flanders and of Tirol, etc.

You, Don Hernando Cortés, our governor and captain general of the New Spain, in order to serve us, went with our permission in the year one thousand five hundred and eighteen from the Fernandine Island named Cuba, with an armada to discover the New Spain, of which you had knowledge, and with the grace of Our Lord and the good industry of your person, you discovered the said New Spain, in which are included many provinces and lands, and you pacified them and placed it all under our dominion and royal crown, and thus they are at the present. We are certain that this has been with many and great labors and dangers to your person, and we have considered and do consider ourselves as well served by you in this matter. And acknowledging the great benefits which have resulted from your services both for the service of Our Lord and the increase of his holy Catholic faith (for in those said lands they were without knowledge or faith and it has been planted) and for the increase which has resulted from it for our royal crown of these realms, and recognizing the labors which you have undergone in them and the fidelity and obedience with which you have always served us as our good and faithful servant and vassal, of which we are certain and assured, and because it is a just and laudable thing for kings to show favors and to honor those who serve them well and loyally so that everyone may be encouraged to do the same, and because it is right that there should remain a perpetual memorial of the abovesaid and that your said services should be rewarded and that others should take an example of serving us well and faithfully, and recognizing that it is a proper thing for kings and princes to honor and exalt and to grant favors and rewards to their subjects and natives, especially to those who serve them well and faithfully and love their service, by the present letter we make you the grant, favor, and donation. pure and perfect and irrevocable, *inter vivos*, as it is said, for now and forever more, of the towns and peoples of Coyoacán, Atlacahualoya, Matalcingo, Toluca, Calimaya, Cuernavaca, Oaxtepec, Acapistla [*or Yeca pixtla*], Yautepec, Tepoztlán, Oaxaca, Cuilapa, Etla-Tenquila, Hacoa [*or Bacoa*], Tehuantepec, Jalapa, Utlatepec, Atroyatlan and Cotaxtla, Tuxtla, Tepeca, and Izcalpan, which are in the said New Spain, up to a total of twenty-three thousand vassals with their lands, villages, territories, and vassals, with higher and lower civil and criminal jurisdiction, simple mixed dominion, and incomes and offices, taxes and fees, forests, meadows, and pastures, running, standing, and outflowing waters, and all the other things which we might have and take for ourselves and might pertain to us and which we could and should enjoy and take in the lands which are set aside for our royal crown in the said New Spain and with everything else pertaining to the dominion of the said towns listed above in any manner whatsoever, so that all of it may belong to you and your heirs and successors or to the person or persons who have title or cause and reason from you or them. And we give it to you in such a way that you and they can sell, give, and donate it, trade, exchange, and alienate it, and do with it and in it everything that you wish and consider good, as a thing of your own, free, quit, and unencumbered, possessed by a just and right title, although we

derecho titulo, Reteniendo como Retenemos en nos y para nos y para los Reyes
que despues de nos Reynaren en estos nuestros Reynos la soberania de nuestra
justicia Real, E que las appelaciones que de vos o de vuestro alcalde mayor que en
las dichas villas y pueblos oviere vaya ante nos y ante los de nuestro consejo y
oydores de las nuestras audiencias y chancill[er]ias E que nos hagamos y mande-
mos hazer justicia en ellas cada vez que nos fuere pedida y vieremos que compla
a nuestro seruicio de la mandar hazer, E que no podades vos ni vuestros herederos
y subcesores hazer ni hedificar de nueuo fortalezas algunas en los dichos pueblos
y sus tierras y terminos sin nuestra licencia y Special mandado Y Retenemos ansy
mismo para nos y para los Reyes que despues de nos vinieren los mineros y
encerramientos de oro y plata y de otros qualesquier metales y las salinas que
oviere en las dychas tierras y que corra alli nuestra moneda y de los Reyes que
despues de nos Reynaren, E todas las otras cossas que andan con el señorio Real
y no se pueden ni deuen del separar ni apartar, y con que obedezcays y acogays
en las dichas villas y pueblos a nos y a los Reyes que despues de nos sucedieren
[3] en estos dichos nuestros Reynos cada vez que alli llegaremos de noche o de
dia en lo alto y baxo ayrados o pagados con pocos o con muchos, E que hagades
dende guerra y paz cada y quando vos lo mandaremos o embiaremos a mandar,
Y vos damos poder complido para que por vuestra propria autoridad podays
entrar y prehender y continuar la posesion de los dichos pueblos en quanto toca
a los dichos veynte y tres mill vassallos con los que en ellos oviere y terminos y
jurisdiciones y Rentas y pechos y otras cosas que a nos nos pertenesciere y de que
podamos y deuamos gozar en las dichas tierras que para nos fueren señaladas
segun dicho es, y lo aver y lleuar para vos y para los dichos vuestros herederos y
subcessores como dicho es, con las limitaciones y cebciones y condisciones de susso
declaradas, Y con tanto que si ovieredes de henagenar los dichos veynte y tres mill
vassallos no sea con yglesia ni monasterio ni con persona de orden ni de Religion
ni de fuera de estos dichos nuestros Reynos y Señorios Syn nuestra licencia y
Spresso mandado ni los podays vender a otras personas sin Requerir a nos y a los
Reyes que despues de nos vinieren, Para que sy lo quissieremos tanto por tanto lo
podamos Hazer, E que a los que en qualquier manera ovieren los dichos veynte
y tres mill vassallos y lugares pasen las exebciones y limitaciones susso dichas y
no en otra manera, E por la pressente desde oy dia de la fecha desta nuestra carta
en adelante para siempre jamas vos apoderamos en los dichos pueblos hasta en el
dicho numero de los dichos veynte y tres mill vassallos con sus aldeas y vasallos
jurisdicion y Rentas pechos y derechos terminos y cosas susso dichas segun y de la
manera que dicha es, y vos damos la posession señorio y propriedad de todo ello
assi y segun que a nos pertenesce para vos y para vuestros herederos y sub[3v]cessores
con las limitaciones y cessiones susso contenidas y vos constituymos por verdadero
señor de todo ello, E por esta dicha nuestra carta o su traslado signado de

retain in and for ourselves and for the kings who may reign after us in these our kingdoms the sovereignty of our royal justice. And we retain the right that the appeals that are made from you or from your alcalde mayor in the said towns shall go before us and before the members of our council and the oidores of our audiencias and chanceries and that we may carry out justice and command that it be carried out in them whenever it is asked of us and when we see that it befits our service to command it to be done and that neither you nor your heirs may build or rebuild any fortresses in the said towns and their lands and territories without our permission and special command.

And likewise we retain for ourselves and for the kings who may come after us the mines and veins of gold and silver and any other metals whatsoever and the salt pits that may exist in the said lands. And we retain the right that our coinage and that of the kings who may reign after us shall be used there, and all of the other things that go with royal dominion and cannot or should not be separated or parted from it, and on condition that in the said towns you obey and receive us and the kings who succeed us in these our said realms whenever we come there, whether by night or by day, in elevation or in humiliation, wrathful or peaceful, with few or with many. And from there you shall make war and peace whenever we shall command or shall send you a command.

And we give you complete power that on your own authority you can enter, seize, and continue the possession of the said towns insofar as it is related to the said twenty-three thousand vassals, with those who are in them, and the territories, jurisdictions, incomes, taxes, and other things which may pertain to us and which we could and should enjoy in the said lands which might be set aside for us, as has been said. And we give you power to have and take it for yourself and for your said heirs and successors, as has been said, with the limitations, exceptions, and conditions declared above, and with the condition that if you shall have to alienate the possession of the said twenty-three thousand vassals, it shall not be to a church or monastery nor to a member of a religious order nor to anyone from outside these our said realms and dominions, without our permission and express command. And you cannot sell them to other persons without first notifying us or the kings who may come after us, so that if we want it we can make the purchase for an equal amount. And to those who may come to possess the said twenty-three thousand vassals and places in any way whatsoever, the abovesaid exceptions and limitations shall also pass, and not in any other way.

And by the present letter, from today, the date of this our letter, and in the future forevermore, we place you in authority over the said towns, up to the said number of the said twenty-three thousand vassals with their villages and vassals, jurisdiction and income, taxes and fees, territories and things mentioned above, according to and in the manner which has been stated. And we give you the possession, dominion, and ownership of all of it, just as it pertains to us, for you and for your heirs and successors with the limitations and concessions contained above and we constitute you as the true lord of all of it.

escriuano publico mandamos a los concejos justicia y Regidores caualleros escuderos oficiales y homes buenos de los dichos pueblos y sus tierras que luego que con ella fueren Requeridos sin apelacion ni dilacion alguna vos ayan y Resciban y tengan por señor y poseedor de las dichas villas y pueblos y cosas susso dichas, y vos apoderen en todo ello a vuestra voluntad y presten la obidiencia y rreuerencia que como a señor dellas vos es deuida y vos deuen dar y prestar y vos den y entreguen las varas de la justicia ceuil y criminal de las dichas villas y pueblos desuso declaradas, y vssen con vos y con los que vuestro poder ovieren en los ofiçios de justicia y jurisdycion dellas, y vos acudan y rrespondan con las Rentas y pechos y derechos y cosas susso dichas de que como dicho es en las tierras y pueblos que para nuestra corona Real fuere señalado en la dicha tierra nos pertenesciere y de que podamos y deuamos gozar y no a otro alguno. Y mandamos al Yllustrissimo Principe Don Philippe nuestro muy charo y muy amado hijo y nieto y a los ynfantes perlados duques marqueses condes maestres de las ordenes rricos omes y a los del nuestro consejo y oydores de las nuestras audiencias alcaldes y alguaziles de la nuestra cassa y corte y chancillerias y a los priores comendadores y subcomendadores alcaydes de los castillos y casas fuertes y llanas, y a todos los concejos justicia y Regidores caualleros y escuderos officiales y omes buenos de todas las cibdades y villas y lugares de estos dichos nuestros Reynos y señorios y de la dicha Nueua Spaña Yndias yslas y tierra firme del Mar Oceano asy a los que agora son como a los que seran de aqui adelante y a cada vno y qual[4]quier dellos que vos cumplan y guarden y hagan guardar y cumplir esta dicha merced y donacion que nos assi vos hazemos en todo y por todo segun que en ella se contiene y contra el thenor y forma della vos no vayan ni passen ni a los dichos vuestros herederos y subcessores en tiempo alguno ni por alguna manera, lo qual todo queremos y mandamos que ansi se haga y cumpla no embargante qualesquier leyes y ordenamientos prematicas senciones de estos dichos nuestros Reynos y señorios que en contrario de esto sean y ser puedan con las quales y con cada vna dellas de nuestro proprio motu y cierta sciencia y poderio Real absoluto aviendolas aqui por ynsertas y yncorporadas dispensamos y las abrogamos y derogamos quanto a esto toca y atañe quedando en su fuerça y vigor para en las otras cosas adelante.

E POR quanto nos avemos mandado hazer y se han hecho ciertas ordenanças cerca del buen tratamiento de los naturales de la dicha tierra mandamos que seays obligado A las guardar con los dichos veynte y tres mill vassallos de que ansy vos hazemos merced so las penas en ellas contenidas, Su thenor de Las quales dichas ordenanças es este que se sigue:

DON CARLOS Por la gracia de Dios Rey de Romanos E Emperador semper augusto, doña Juana su madre y el mismo Don Carlos por la misma gracia Reyes de Castilla de Leon de Aragon de las dos Secilias de Jherusalem de Nauarra de Granada de Toledo de Valencia de Gallizia de Mallorcas de Seuilla de Cordeña de

And by this our letter or by a copy of it signed by a notary public, we command the councils, justice and aldermen, knights, squires, tradesmen, and good men of the said towns and lands that as soon as they are notified with this letter, without any appeal or delay, they shall accept and receive and hold you as lord and possessor of the said towns and things mentioned above and shall place you in authority over all of it at your will and shall offer you the obedience and reverence which is due to you as the lord over these things and which they must give and show to you. And they shall give and deliver to you the rods of civil and criminal justice of the said towns named above, and they shall use them by your authority and that of the men who may have your power in the offices of justice and jurisdiction over those towns. And they shall come and respond to you with the incomes, taxes, and fees and with the things mentioned above which, as has been said, would belong to us in the lands and towns which would be set aside for our royal crown and would belong to us in the said land and which we could and should enjoy, and not to any other person.

And we command the Most Illustrious Prince Don Felipe, our very dear and very beloved son and descendant, and the infantes, prelates, dukes, marquesses, counts, masters of the orders, grandees, and the members of our council and oidores of our audiencias, alcaldes and constables of our house, court, and chanceries, and the priors, knight-commanders and sub-commanders, wardens of the castles and of houses with moats and of country houses, and all of the councils, justice, and aldermen, knights and squires, tradesmen and good men of all of the cities, towns, and places of these our said realms and dominions and of the said New Spain, Indies, islands and mainland of the Ocean Sea, both those who are at the present and those who will be henceforth, and to each and every one of them, that they observe and fulfill for you and see to it that this said grant and donation is observed and fulfilled, which we thus make to you, in every way, according as it is contained in this letter; and they shall not go against the tenor and form of it with you or with your said heirs and successors at any time or in any way. We wish and command that it shall be done and fulfilled in this way, notwithstanding any laws and edicts or pragmatic sanctions of these our said realms and dominions which are or can be contrary to it; and from each and every one of them, of our own impulse and with certain knowledge and absolute royal power, as though they were here inserted and incorporated, we dispense, abrogate, and derogate them insofar as it regards and appertains to this, retaining their force and vigor for other matters in the future.

And whereas we have commanded that certain ordinances be drawn up concerning the good treatment of the natives of the said land, and they have been drawn up, we command that you be obligated to observe them with regard to the said twenty-three thousand vassals which we thus grant you. The tenor of the said ordinances is as follows.

Don Carlos, by the grace of God, King of the Romans and ever august Emperor; Doña Juana, his mother, and the same Don Carlos, by the same grace, Kings of Castile, of León, of Aragon, of the two Sicilies, of Jerusalem, of Navarre, of Granada, of Toledo, of Valencia, of Galicia, of the Majorcas, of Seville, of Sardinia, of

Cordoua de Corcega de Murcia de Jaen de los Algarues de Algezira de Gibraltar de
las yslas de Canaria de las Yndias yslas y tierra firme del Mar Oceano condes [4v] de
Barcelona señores de Vizcaya y de Molina duques de Athenas y de Neopatria condes
de Ruysellon y de Cerdania archiduques de Abstria duques de Borgoña y de Brabante
condes de Flandes y de Tyrol etcet.

A VOS el nuestro pressidente y oydores de la nuestra audiencia y chancilleria
Real de la Nueua Spaña que Resside en la cibdad de Mexico, E a vos los Reue-
rendos In XPO padre fray Julian Garces obispo de Tuxcaltecle, y fray Juan de
Cumarraga electo obispo de Mexico, E a vos los debotos padres prior y guardian
de los monasterios de Sancto Domingo e Sanct Francisco de la dicha cibdad de
Mexico, Salud e gracia bien sabeys lo que por nuestras prouissiones vos esta mandado cerca de la ynformacion que aveys de aver de los yndios naturales de essa
tierra de las personas que los tienen encomendados E otras cosas cerca de su buen
tratamiento. Agora sabed que nos somos ynformados que de las personas a quien
estan encomendados y rrepartidos los dichos yndios y de otras muchas personas
spañoles que en essa tierra Ressiden, han Rescibido y de cada dia rresciben muchos
malos tratamientos Especialmente en las cossas que de yusso seran declaradas, lo
qual demas de ser en tanto desseruicio de Dios Nuestro Señor y tan cargosso a
nuestra Real conciencia y contrario a nuestra rreligion xpiana porque todo es estoruo
para la conuersion de los dichos yndios a nuestra sancta fee catholyca que es nuestro
principal desseo y yntencion y lo que todos somos obligados a procurar viene dello
mucho ynconuiniente para la poblacion y perpetuydad de la dicha tierra, porque a
causa de los excessiuos trauajos y bexaciones que les han hecho y hazen han muerto
muchos que lo vno y lo otro como veys es en tan grande daño y en tan desseruicio
de Nuestro Señor y daño [5] de nuestra corona rreal, E visto en el nuestro Consejo
de las Yndias, por la confiança que de vuestras personas tenemos, fue acordado que
vos Lo deuiamos mandar cometer y hazer sobre ello LAS ORDENANÇAS
Siguientes.

PRIMERAmente, porque somos ynformados que muchos de los dichos Spañoles
diziendo que faltan bestias para lleuar sus mantenimientos y prouissiones y otras
cossas para seruicio de sus personas y casas y tratos y de otra manera de vnos lugares
a otros toman de los yndios que hallan y las mas vezes por fuerça y contra su voluntad
sin se los pagar los cargan y hazen que lleuen acuestas todo lo que los dychos Spañoles
quieren, E assi mismo los Spañoles que tienen yndios encomendados Les hazen lleuar
cargas para mantenimiento de los esclauos que traen en las minas largas jornadas De
cuya causa y por el mucho trauajo que dello Resciben los dichos yndios se mueren
y otros huyen y se van y ausentan y dexan sus assientos y lugares, POR ENDE mandamos y defendemos firmemente que agora y de aqui adelante ningun Spañol de
ninguna calidad y condicion que sea no sea osado de cargar ni cargue yndio alguno
para que lleue alguna cosa acuestas de ningun pueblo a otro ni por ningun camino
ni en otra manera publica ni secretamente contra la voluntad de los tales yndios ni
de su grado sin paga ni con ella sin que lo lleuen em bestias como quissieren, Pero

Córdoba, of Corsica, of Murcia, of Jaén, of the Algarve, of Algeciras, of Gibraltar, of the Canary Islands, of the Indies, islands and mainland of the Ocean Sea; Counts of Barcelona, Lords of Biscay and of Molina, Dukes of Athens and Neopatria, Counts of Roussillon and of Cerdagne, Archdukes of Austria, Dukes of Burgundy and of Brabant, Counts of Flanders and of Tirol, etc.

To you our president and oidores of our audiencia and royal chancery of the New Spain which resides in the city of Mexico, and to you the Reverend in Christ Father Fray Julián Garcés, Bishop of Tlaxcala, and Fray Juan de Zumárraga, bishop-elect of Mexico, and to you the devoted fathers, prior, and guardian, of the friaries of Saint Dominic and Saint Francis of the said city of Mexico, health and grace. You know well what has been commanded to you by our decrees regarding the information which you must gather concerning the Indian natives of that land, concerning the persons who have them in encomiendas, and other matters concerning their good treatment. Now you must know that we have been informed that from the persons to whom the said Indians are entrusted and parceled out and from many other Spanish people who reside in that land, they have received and do daily receive many mistreatments, especially in the matters which will be detailed below. Besides being such a disservice to God Our Lord and so burdensome to our royal conscience and contrary to our Christian religion, because it is all an obstacle to the conversion of the said Indians to our holy Catholic faith, which is our principal desire and intention and that after which we are all obliged to strive, there results from it much difficulty for the colonization and perpetuation of the said land, because, by reason of the excessive labors and vexations that have been and are imposed on them, many have died; and both the one and the other, as you see, are very harmful and a disservice to Our Lord and harmful to our royal crown. This having been considered in our Council of the Indies, because of the confidence that we have in your persons, it was agreed that we should command that it be committed to you and that the following ordinances be issued concerning it.

First, we are informed that many of the said Spaniards, saying that they lack beasts to take their supplies and provisions and other things for the service of their persons and houses and businesses and for other purposes from one place to another, take some of the Indians whom they find and, most frequently by force and against their will without paying them, they place burdens on them and make them carry on their backs everything that the said Spaniards wish. And likewise the Spaniards who have Indians in encomienda make them carry burdens for the support of the slaves whom they have in the mines at great distances. For this reason and because of the great amount of work which they receive from it, the said Indians die, and others flee and go away and absent themselves and leave their settlements and places.

Therefore we command firmly and prohibitively that, as of now and from this time forward, no Spaniard, of whatever rank or condition he may be, shall dare to load any Indian so that he will carry anything on his back from one town to another by any road or in any manner, publicly or secretly, against the will of such Indians or by their free will, without pay or with it, except that they may carry it on beasts as they

permitimos que los yndios que al presente estan encomendados a los dichos Spañoles el tributo o seruycio que son obligados a les dar se los puedan lleuar hasta el lugar donde la persona Ressydiere [5v] no passando veynte leguas de su pueblo, y sy les mandaren que los lleuen a las minas y a otras partes do a el no rressidiere no se haga sin su voluntad de los yndios y pagandoselo primeramente no passando en esto las dichas veynte leguas, y porque nuestra yntincion es de Releuar los dychos yndios y no dalles de nueuo trauajos E ympussiciones y a este propossito se ordena esto, VOS mandamos que si vieredes que la priuusion [sic—*provision*] de las dichas veynte leguas es contra derecho y fuera de Razon proueereys y moderareys con justicia como vieredes que couiene al descargo de nuestras conciencias, So pena que qual- quier persona que contra el thenor de esta dicha ordenança fuere o passare por la primera vez pague por cada yndio que asy cargare cient pesos de oro, y por la segunda trezientos, y por la tercera aya perdido y pierda sus bienes, Las quales penas sean applicadas, la tercia parte para el juez que lo sentenciare, y la otra tercia parte para el acusador, y la otra tercia parte para la nuestra camara, y mas que le sean quitados los yndios que tuuiere encomendados.

OTRO SY Porque somos ynformados, que muchas de las dichas personas tienen por grangeria de hazer bastimentos en los pueblos que assi tienen encomendados y lleuallos a vender a las minas y otras partes lo qual lleuan los dichos yndios acuestas de que Reciben mucho trabajo, POR ENDE mandamos y defendemos que ninguna persona pueda lleuar ni lleue con los dichos yndios a las minas ni a otra parte alguna bastimentos ni otras cosas a lo vender, So pena que qualquier persona que contra el thenor desta dicha ordenança fuere o pa[6]sare por la primera vez pague por cada yndio que assi cargare cient pesos de oro, y por la segunda vez trezientos, y por la tercera aya perdido y pierda sus bienes, las quales penas sean applicadas la tercia parte para el juez que lo sentenciare, y la otra tercia parte para el acussador y la otra tercia parte para la nuestra camara, y mas que le sean quitados los yndios que tuuiere encomendados.

ASIMISMO Somos ynformados que muchas personas de los que tienen pueblos de yndios encomendados lleuan y tienen en sus casas mugeres de los dichos pueblos para hazer pan a los esclauos que andan en las minas y para seruicio de sus casas y asi los traen Como a esclauos y hazen estar sin sus maridos y hijos fuere de los dichos pueblos de lo cual se sigue mucho daño, POR ende ordenamos y mandamos que ninguna persona pueda tener ni tenga muger de los dichos pueblos que touieren encomendados para hazer pan a los esclauos que touieren en las minas ni para seruicio de sus casas ni para otra cosa alguna sino que libremente las dexen estar y Ressidir en sus casas con Sus maridos y hijos y avnque digan que las tienen de su voluntad y se lo paguen, so pena que por cada vez que se hallare que tiene qual- quier o qualesquier yndias en sus casas contra el thenor desta ordenança yncurra en pena cient pesos de oro para la nuestra camara y fisco por cada vna.

may wish. But we permit that the Indians who at present are entrusted to the said Spaniards can carry to them the tribute or service which they are obligated to give them to the place where the person resides, not going beyond twenty leagues from their town. And if they command them to take them to the mines or to other places where that person does not reside, it shall not be done except at the will of the Indians and with prior payment, not going beyond the said twenty leagues in this.

And because it is our intention to relieve the said Indians and not to give them renewed labors and impositions, and for this purpose this ordinance was made, we command you that if you see that the decision regarding the said twenty leagues is contrary to right and reason, you shall decide and determine with justice whatever you may see is best for the discharge of our consciences. We command this under the penalty that whatever person shall go or act against the tenor of this said ordinance, for the first time he shall pay a hundred pesos of gold for each Indian whom he shall have thus burdened; and for the second time, three hundred; and for the third time, he shall suffer the loss of his goods. These fines shall be applied as follows: one third for the judge who passes sentence; one third for the accuser; and the other third for our exchequer. And, moreover, the Indians whom he may have in encomienda shall be taken from him.

Furthermore, we are informed that many of the said persons make a business of raising foodstuffs in the towns which they have in encomienda and of taking them to the mines and other places to sell them. And the said Indians carry them on their backs, from which they undergo much labor. Therefore, we command prohibitively that no person can use the said Indians to take provisions or anything else to the mines or any other place to sell it, under the penalty that whatever person goes or acts against the tenor of this said ordinance, for the first time he shall pay a hundred gold pesos for each Indian whom he shall have thus burdened; and for the second time, three hundred; and for the third time he shall suffer the loss of his goods. These penalties shall be applied as follows: one third for the judge who passes sentence; one third for the accuser; and the other third for our exchequer. And, moreover, the Indians whom he may have in encomienda shall be taken from him.

Likewise, we are informed that many of the persons who have towns of Indians in encomienda take and keep in their houses women from the said towns to make bread for the slaves who are in the mines and for the service of their houses, and thus they treat them as slaves and they cause them to be separated from their husbands and children away from the said towns, from which much harm follows. Therefore, we ordain and command that no one can or may have a woman from the said towns which he has in encomienda to make bread for the slaves whom he may have in the mines nor for the service of his houses nor for any other thing, but they shall freely let them be and reside in their houses with their husbands and children, even though they may say that they have them there by their own will and they pay them, under the penalty that for each time that it is found that he has any Indian women in his houses against the tenor of this ordinance, he shall incur the penalty of one hundred pesos of gold for our exchequer and treasury for each woman.

OTROSY Somos ynformados que como quiera que los que asi tienen encomendados los dichos yndios por les estar defendido no los [6v] hechen a las minas sino a los que son sus esclauos, pero vsan con ellos de otra cautela en que son muy mas fatigados y trabajados que es que los hazen ayudar a los dichos esclauos a descopetar y hechar madres de Rios y otros edificios, Por ende ordenamos y mandamos que ningunos yndios que estouieren encomendados a qualquier ni qualesquier personas puedan ayudar ni ayuden a los esclauos que anduuieren en las minas a descopetar ni hechar madres de Rios ni arroyos ni otro ningun hedifficio que se ouiere de hazer en las minas a este proposito del sacar del oro, saluo que lo hagan los dichos esclauos que andouieren en las dichas minas, so pena de cinquenta pesos de oro para la nuestra camara por cada vez que se le prouare que ouiere hechado y tenido en las dichas minas qualquier yndio para trabajar en qualquier de las cosas susso dichas.

YTEN SOMOS ynformados que las personas que tienen esclauos y quadrillas en las dichas minas no quieren sacar dellas a los dichos esclauos ni ocupallos en otras cossas y haziendas y hazen que los dichos yndios que asi tienen encomendados hagan las casas en que moran y esten los dichos esclauos y gente que anda en las dichas quadrillas en lo qual los dichos yndios son muy trabajados y fatigados, POR ende ordenamos y mandamos y defendemos que ninguna persona pueda hazer ni haga las casas en que ouiere de estar y morar los dichos esclauos y gente que andouieren en las minas con los dichos yndios que assi les estan encomendados, y que quando se ouieren de mudar las quadrillas de vnas minas a otras no puedan lleuar ni lleuen con los yndios que asi touieren encomendados las herramientas y bateas, saluo que las lleuen los dichos esclauos, So pena que por cada [7] yndio que ocupare en el hazer de las dichas casas caya y yncurra en dozientos pessos de oro Repartidos y applicados EN LA FORMA susso dicha:

Y PORQVE Somos ynformados que muchas pessonas desde los puertos de mar lleuan a la cibdad de Mexico y a otros partes desa Nueua Spaña bastymentos y otras cosas con los dichos yndios En mucho daño y agrauio dellos, Mandamos que ningunas personas puedan lleuar ni lleuen de los dichos pueblos a ningun pueblo de christianos ni a otra parte alguna los dichos bastimentos ni otra cosa de carga que ellos ayan de traer, Pero permitymos que los yndios que de su voluntad se quissieren alquilar en los dichos puertos para descargar las naos solamente y lleuar carga de la nao a tierra con que no passe de media legua lo pueda hazer, So pena que pague por cada vez que lo contrario hiziere cient pesos de oro Repartidos en la manera que de suso se contiene.

OTROSY Mandamos que ningunas personas que touieren yndios encomendados no puedan hazer ni hagan con ellos casas para vender saluo aquellas en que ouieren de biuir, E que sy aquellas vendieren no puedan hazer ni hagan otras con los dichos yndios avnque las quieran para su morar, So pena que qualquier persona que contra el thenor de esta ordenança hiziere casas con los dichos yndios que touiere encomendados para biuir o bender pierda las cassas que hiziere y sean applicadas para nuesta camara y fisco, y mas yncurra en pena de cient pesos PARA LA Dicha nuestra CAMARA.

Furthermore, we are informed that although, because it is forbidden to those who have the Indians in encomienda to cast them into the mines but they should use their slaves for this, they employ another device with them by which they are subjected to much greater fatigue and labor, and that is that they make them help the said slaves dig out and lay canals from the rivers and build other structures. Therefore we command and ordain that no Indians who have been entrusted to any person whatsoever can or may help the slaves who are in the mines to dig out or lay canals from rivers or arroyos or build any other structure which must be built in the mines for this purpose of taking out gold, but the slaves who are in the mines must do this, under the penalty of fifty pesos of gold for our exchequer for each time that it is proven against any person that he has put or kept in the said mines any Indian whatsoever to work on any of the abovesaid things.

Further, we are informed that the persons who have slaves and slave gangs in the said mines do not want to take the said slaves out of those mines nor to occupy them in other things and enterprises, and they see to it that the said Indians whom they have in encomienda build the houses in which the slaves and men who are in the said gangs live and reside. And in this the Indians suffer great labor and fatigue. Therefore we ordain and command as a prohibition that no one can or may build the houses in which the said slaves and men who are in the mines are to live, with the help of the Indians who are thus entrusted to him; and when it is necessary to move the gangs from one mine to another, they cannot nor shall they use the Indians whom they have in encomienda to carry the tools and troughs, but the said slaves shall carry them, under the penalty that for each Indian whom anyone puts to work in building the said houses he shall become liable to two hundred pesos of gold, to be divided in the form stated above.

And we are informed that many persons from the seaports take provisions and other things to the city of Mexico and other parts of that New Spain with the help of the said Indians, causing them much harm and injury. We command that no one can or shall take from the said towns to any other town of Christians nor to any other place the said provisions or any other kind of freight which they must carry, but we permit that the Indians who of their own free will may wish to hire themselves out in the ports solely to unload the ships and to take the cargo from the ship to the shore may do so, provided it is not more than half a league. We command this under the penalty that he who does the contrary shall pay one hundred pesos of gold, to be divided in the manner which is contained above.

Furthermore, we command that no one who has Indians in encomienda can or shall use them to build houses for sale, but only the houses in which he is to live, and if he sells those houses he cannot nor shall he use the said Indians to build others, even though he wants them for his dwellings, under the penalty that whoever, against the tenor of this ordinance, shall have used the said Indians whom he has in encomienda to build houses for living or for sale, shall lose the houses that he has built and they shall be applied for our exchequer and treasury, and moreover he shall be subject to the penalty of a hundred pesos for our said exchequer.

ASIMISMO, Somos ynformados que en el hazer guerra a los yndios y en el toma-llos [7v] por esclauos en la dicha Nueua España se hazen munchos males y daños porque toman por esclauos A los que no lo son en lo qual Dios Nuestro Señor es muy deseruido y la tierra y naturales della Reciben mucho daño, para rremedio de lo qual avemos mandado despachar y esta dada vna nuestra prouission fecha en Toledo a veynte dias del mes de nouiembre de este pressente año, la qual vos man-damos embiar con estas nuestras ordenanças y vos encargamos y mandamos que hagays que se guarde y compla y execute so las penas en ella CONTENIDAS.

OTROSI Somos ynformados que cerca del herrar de los esclauos que se toman en las guerras se hazen muchos males, cerca de lo qual avemos mandado despachar otra nuestra prouission fecha en Toledo el dicho dia del dicho año la qual vos man-damos ansy mismo embiar con estas nuestras ordenanças, POR ende vos mandamos que hagays que se guarde y cumpla y execute como en ella se contiene So las penas EN ELLA CONTENIDAS.

E PORQVE Somos ynformados que las personas que tienen encomendados pueblos de yndios piden y apremian a los dichos yndios a que les den tributo de oro no siendo obligados a ello y sobre ello les prenden y atormentan y amenazan y ponen otros temores hasta que se lo dan de que viene mucho daño a la tierra y es causa de la despoblacion de los dychos pueblos, porque los yndios para aver el oro que les piden venden por esclauos los hijos y paryentes para tener contentos a los que los tyenen [8] encomendados se van y huyen dellos, por ende mandamos y defendemos que entre tanto que en esto y en las otras cosas tocantes a los dichos yndios se da orden, nin-guna persona pida ni tome de los dichos yndios que touieren encomendados oro alguno mas de aquello que ellos de su voluntad sin premia alguna les quissieren dar ni otra cosa alguna saluo aquellas tan solamente que en el lugar donde ellos moran oviere, y esto sea en aquella cantidad que son obligados y no mas, So pena que lo que de otra manera tomaren o pidieren lo pagaran con el quatro tanto para la nuestra camara, y demas de tornar a los dichos yndios lo que contra el tenor de esta Ordenança dellos RESCIVIEREN.

E PORQVE Somos ynformados que al tiempo que los dichos yndios hazen sus simenteras y labranças los christianos españoles que los tienen encomendados y en administracion, y otras personas los ocupan y embaraçan en sus proprias haziendas y grangerias, por manera que ellos dexan de sembrar y hazer las dichas sus labranças y sementeras, de que viene mucho daño a los dichos yndios y Spañoles, porque de aquello Redunda faltalles los mantenimientos y prouissiones y biuir en mucha necessi-dad, Por ende por la pressente vos encargamos y mandamos que proueays como en los tiempos de las simenteras sean mas Releuados y se les de lugar para que las hagan como mas buenamente se pudiere hazer.

OTROSI PORque somos certifficados que las dychas personas que tienen esclauos y yndios en las minas no mirando el seruicio de Dios Nuestro [8v] Señor ni la conuersion dellos a nuestra sancta fee catolica que es nuestro principal desseo

Likewise, we are informed that in making war on the Indians and in taking them as slaves in the said New Spain, many evils and injuries are done because they take as slaves those who are not such, and God is very badly served in this and the land and its natives receive much harm. As a remedy for this we commanded that a decree of ours be dispatched, and it was issued, dated in Toledo on the twentieth day of the month of November of this present year. We command that it be sent to you with these our ordinances, and we charge and command you that you shall have it observed, fulfilled, and executed, under the penalties contained in it.

Furthermore, we are informed that concerning the branding of the slaves that are taken in the wars, many evils are committed. Concerning this we have commanded that another decree of ours be dispatched, dated in Toledo on the said day of the said year, and we command that it likewise be sent with these our ordinances. Therefore we command you that you shall have it observed, fulfilled, and executed as it is expressed in it, under the penalties contained in it.

And we are informed that the persons who have towns of Indians in encomienda, ask and compel the said Indians to give them tribute of gold, even though they are not obligated to it, and concerning this matter they apprehend, torture, and threaten them and cause them other fears until they give it to them. From this there results much harm to the land and it is the cause for the depopulation of the said towns, because in order to obtain the gold which they ask for, they sell their children and relatives as slaves in order to satisfy their encomenderos, and they go away and flee from them. Therefore, we command as a prohibition that until such a time as order is established in this and other matters referring to the said Indians, no one shall ask nor take any gold from the said Indians whom he has in encomienda except that which they may wish to give them of their free will and without any compulsion, and he shall not take anything else except only those things which are available in the place where they dwell, and this shall be in that amount to which they are obligated and no more. We command this under the penalty that whatever they may take or ask in any other way, they shall pay four times as much for our exchequer, besides returning to the said Indians what they have received from them against the tenor of this ordinance.

And we are informed that at the time when the said Indians do their planting and fieldwork, the Spanish Christians who have them entrusted to their administration, and other people, occupy and impede them with work on their own properties and enterprises, so that they neglect to do their planting and to make their fields and seedplots, and from this there comes much harm to both the Indians and Spaniards because the result of it is that they lack provisions and their source of livelihood and they live in great need. Therefore by the present letter we charge and command that you see to it, in the best way possible, that at planting time they be relieved of work to a greater extent and that they be given an opportunity to plant their fields.

Further, we have been notified that the said persons who have slaves and Indians in the mines, not considering the service of God Our Lord nor their conversion to our holy Catholic faith, which is our principal desire and intention, neglect them without

y yntencion los dexan sin les dar ni poner personas en los tales pueblos y estancias que les digan missa y ynstruyan y ynformen en las cosas de la fee, E por falta desto no uienen tan presto en conoscimiento della como conuernia y vernian si desto se touiesse el cuydado y Recaudo necessario y es en gran cargo de conciencia de las tales personas cuyos son, POR ENDE mandamos que agora y de aqui adelante qualesquier personas que touieren yndios libres o esclauos en las minas que sean obligados de tener y tengan personas Religiosas o ecclesiasticas de buena vida y exemplo que los dotrinen y enseñen en cosas de nuestra sancta fee catholica, y que a lo menos todos los domingos y fiestas principales del año los hagan juntar para ello y les hagan oyr missa, E que sy asy no lo hiziere el perlado o protector de los dichos yndios a costa de las tales personas pongan quien lo haga, Sobre lo qual les encargamos LAS CONCIENCIAS.

Y PORQVE la yntencion de los mas Spañoles que han passado y passan a esa tierra no es de assentar y permanecer en ella Saluo de la desfrutar y Robar a los naturales della lo que tienen, y a causa de hallar entre ellos de comer se andan vagamundos holgazanes de vnos pueblos a otros tomando de los yndios todo lo que han menester y lo que los yndios tienen para su sustentacion y sobre ello les hazen muchas fuerças y agrauios E ansi mismo lo hazen los otros Spañoles que van y vienen a las minas, y desde la cibdad de Mexico a los puertos de la Vera Cruz y Medellin por los pueblos donde passan de que se siguen muchos males E ynconuinientes en la tierra y es causa de la despoblacion della, POR ENDE por esta ordenança [9] Mandamos y defendemos que no se consienta que aya en la dicha tierra los dichos bagamundos, E que los que no touieren haziendas o encomiendas de yndios con que se sustentar o no estuuieren con amos los echen della, So pena de cient açotes, E asi mismo defendemos que ninguna ni alguna persona por los pueblos y estancias donde passaren asy yendo desde la dicha cibdad de Mexico a los dichos puertos o a las minas o de vnos pueblos a otros en qualquier manera no pidan ni demanden a los dichos yndios ni a ninguno dellos ningunos mantenimientos prouissiones ni otras cosas algunas de las que ellos touieren sino fuere dandoselo ellos de su voluntad y pagandoles por ello lo que justamente valiere, So pena que qualquier cosa que de otra manera tomaren a los dichos yndios se la paguen con el doblo y demas que la paguen con el quatro tanto, la mitad para la nuestra camara, y de las otras dos partes, la vna para el acusador que lo acusare, y la otra el JVEZ QVE LO SENTENCIARE.

Y PORQVE Somos ynformados y por experiencia ha parescido que sacando los yndios de sus pueblos tierras y naturalezas para otras yslas e tierras so color que son esclauos y por otra causas y colores que los xpianos Spañoles buscan los mas dellos se mueren E no solo Rescibe daño la tierra en salir estos della y morirse por no estar en su naturaleza, Pero tambien se dexan morir y toman otros Resabios malos y enemistad y desamor con los christianos porque les lleuan de

providing or placing persons in those towns and estancias who may say Mass for them and instruct them and inform them regarding the matters of the faith. And because of this lack, they do not come so quickly to the knowledge of it as is becoming or as quickly as they could come if the necessary care and provision were taken for this; and this is a great burden on the consciences of those to whom they belong. Therefore, we command that as of now and from this time forward, any person whatsoever who has free Indians or slaves in the mines shall be obligated to have and shall have religious or ecclesiastical persons of good life and example who may indoctrinate them and teach them in the matters of our holy Catholic faith, and at least on all Sundays and principal feasts of the year, they shall have them brought together for this and to hear Mass. And if they do not do this, the prelate or protector of the said Indians shall put someone there who will do it, at the cost of those persons, and concerning this we burden their consciences.

And the intention of most of the Spaniards who have gone and are going across to that land is not to settle down and remain in it but to reap its fruits and to rob its natives of what they have, and because they find something to eat among them, they wander about as vagabonds and idlers from one town to another, taking from the Indians everything that they need and everything that the Indians have for their support, and because of this they inflict on them much violence and injury. And likewise the other Spaniards who go to and from the mines and from the city of Mexico to the ports of Vera Cruz and Medellín, do the same thing in the towns through which they pass. From this many evils and unbecoming things result in the land, and it is the cause of its depopulation. Therefore, we command prohibitively that it shall not be allowed that the said vagabonds shall be in the said land, and that those who do not have properties or encomiendas of Indians with which to support themselves or are not with employers shall be cast out of it, under the penalty of one hundred lashes. And likewise we forbid anyone who passes through the towns and farms, whether going from the said city of Mexico to the said ports or to the mines or from one town to another in any manner whatsoever, to ask or demand of the said Indians or of any one of them any provisions or support or anything else that they may have unless the Indians give it to them of their own free will and the travelers pay them its just value, under the penalty that for anything that they may take in any other manner, they shall pay twice its value to the said Indians and, besides this, they shall pay four times its value, half for our exchequer, and of the other two parts, one for the person who makes the accusation and the other for the judge who passes the sentence.

And we have been informed, and it has become apparent by experience, that when the Indians are taken from their towns, land, and native surroundings to other islands and lands under the pretext that they are slaves or for other causes and excuses which the Christian Spaniards figure out, most of them die; and not only does the land receive harm from the fact that they leave it and die because of not being in their native environment, but also they are allowed to die and others are left with a bad taste and enmity and disaffection for the Christians, because they take

su compañia y conuersacion de sus mugeres y hijos y hermanos y deudos y vezinos, y creen que lo mismo haran dellos otro dia, y es en mucho desseruicio de Dios y daño de la dicha tierra y yndios della y en su diminuycion, Por ende ordenamos [9v] E Mandamos que agora ni de aqui adelante ninguna ni algunas personas no sean osados de sacar ni saquen de la dicha Nueua Spaña para estos nuestros Reynos ni para las yslas ni tierra firme ni otra parte alguna ningunos yndios naturales della no embargante que digan y aleguen y muestren que son sus esclauos, So pena que por cada yndio que ansi sacaren paguen para nuestra camara y fisco cient pesos de buen oro, y demas sea obligado a lo boluer a su costa a la dicha tierra y pueblo DE DONDE ASSI LO SACARE.

Y PORQVE podra ser que algunas personas no mirando nuestro seruicio ni el bien ni conseruacion de los dichos yndios desseando que no se guarden estas ordenanças por sus ynteresses particulares supplicasen dellas o de alguna dellas y desta causa oviessen algun estoruo dilacion o suspension en el cumplimiento y execucion della, Mandamos que las guardeys y cumplays y executeys y hagays guardar y cumplir y executar en todo y por todo Segun que en ellas y en cada vna dellas se contiene, sin embargo de qualquier appelacion o supplicacion que por la dicha tierra y vezinos particulares DELLA FVERE YNTERpuesta.

PORQVE vos mandamos que veades las dychas ordenanças que de susso se contienen y las hagays luego pregonar publicamente por las plaças y mercados y otros lugares acostumbrados de la dicha cibdad de Tenuxtitan Mexico por manera que venga a noticia de todos, y ninguno dellos pueda pretender ynorancia [*10*] Y si despues de hecho el dicho pregon alguna o algunas personas fueren o passaren contra lo contenido en las dichas ordenanças o alguna cossa dellas executays en ellos y en sus bienes las penas en ellas contenidas sin embargo de qualquier appelacion o supplicacion que cerca de ello fuere ynterpuesta, porque nuestra merced y voluntad es que se guarden y executen ynviolablemente, Sobre lo qual vos encargamos las conciencias y descargamos con vosotros las nuestras: por la confiança que de vuestras personas tenemos. Dada en la cibdad de Toledo a quatro dias del mes de diziembre año del nascimiento de Nuestro Saluador Jesu Xpo de mill y quinientos y veynte y ocho años. Yo el Rey [*In margin: El R Emperador A 4 de Diziembre 1528 años*]. Yo Francisco de los Couos secretario de sus cesarea y catholicas Magestades la fize escreuir por su mandado. F. Garcia episcopus oxomenssis. El doctor Beltran. El licenciado de la Corte. Registrada, Juan de Samano. Vrbina por chanciller.

LAS quales dichas ordenanças que de suso van yncorporadas y cada vna dellas VOS mandamos que guardeys y cumplays en todo y por todo segun que en ellas y en cada vna dellas se contiene, so las penas en ellas contenidas como dicho es, y los vnos ni los otros no fagades ni fagan ende al por alguna manera so pena de la nuestra merced y de cient mill marauedis para la nuestra camara a cada vno de vos que lo contrario hiziere, So la qual dicha pena mandamos a qualquier

them from the company and companionship of their wives, children, brothers, relatives, and neighbors, and they believe that they will do the same thing with them on another day. And this does great disservice to God and harm to the land and to its Indians and contributes to their decline. Therefore, we ordain and command now and for the future that no person or persons shall dare to take nor shall they take from the said New Spain for these realms of ours, nor for the islands or mainland or any other place, any Indian natives of it, notwithstanding that they may say and allege and show that they are their slaves, under penalty that for every Indian whom they thus take out they shall pay a hundred pesos of good gold for our exchequer and treasury, and moreover, he shall be obliged at his own cost to return him [*Spanish: lo*] to the said land and town from which he took him [*Spanish: lo*].

And it is possible that some people, not considering our service nor the well-being and conservation of the said Indians, wishing that these ordinances not be observed because of their particular interests, may appeal from them or from any one of them, and for this reason there might be some delay, obstacle, or suspension in their fulfillment and execution. Therefore, we command that you observe, fulfill, and execute them and see to it that they are observed, fulfilled, and executed in their entirety, just as it is contained in them and in each one of them, notwithstanding any appeal of any kind whatsoever that may be interposed by the said land or by individual freeholders of it.

Therefore, we command that you regard the said ordinances which are contained above and that you see to it that they are immediately proclaimed publicly in the plazas, markets, and other customary places of the said city of Tenochtitlan Mexico, in such a way that they may come to the knowledge of all and that no one may pretend ignorance of them. And if after the said proclamation has been made, any person or persons shall go against what is contained in the said ordinances or against any point of them, you shall execute upon them and their goods the penalties expressed in them, notwithstanding any appeal whatsoever which may be interposed concerning it, because our desire and will is that they be observed and executed inviolably. Concerning this we lay a burden on your consciences and unburden our own through you because of the confidence that we have in your persons. Given in the city of Toledo on the fourth day of the month of December of the year of Our Savior Jesus Christ one thousand five hundred and twenty-eight. I the King. [*In the margin: The King and Emperor. December 4, 1528.*] I, Francisco de los Cobos, secretary of His Imperial and Their Catholic Majesties, had it written by his command. Fr. García, Bishop of Osma. Doctor Beltrán. Licentiate De la Corte. Registered, Juan de Sámano. Urbina, pro-chancellor.

These said ordinances which are incorporated above, and every one of them, we command that you observe and fulfill in every respect as is contained in them and in each one of them, under the penalties contained in them, as has been said. And no one among you shall go contrary to it in any manner, under the penalty of the loss of our favor and of a hundred thousand maravedís for our exchequer against every one of you who does the contrary. Under the same penalty we command every notary

escriuano publico que para esto fuere llamado que vos emplaze que parescades
ante nos en la nuestra corte doquier que nos seamos desde el dia que vos emplazare
hasta seys meses primeros siguientes a dar Razon porque asy no lo deueys hazer
y cumplir porque nos sepamos en como se cumple nuestro mandado. DADA en
Barcelona a seys dias [*10v*] del mes de julio año del nascimiento de Nuestro
Saluador Jesu Xpo de mill e quinientos y veynte y nueue años. Yo el Rey. Yo
Francisco de los Couos secretario de sus cessarea[*s—added*] y catholicas Magestades
la fize escreuir por su mandado. Fr[*co — added*] G. Eps oxomensis. El doctor
Beltran el licenciado de la Corte. Registrada, Francisco de Briuiesca chanciller,
EL LICENCIADO XIMENEZ [*In margin: A seis de Julio de mil quinientos veinte
y nueve*]

DESPVES de lo qual su Magestad ymperial por sus cartas y prouissiones mando
que se contassen al dicho don Hernando Cortes Marques del Valle los veynte
y tres mill vassallos comprenhendidos en la merced que le auia hecho y dio la
orden que se auia de tener en el contar dellos, E mando que acabados de contar se
entregassen al dicho Marques con Su jurisdicion de la forma y manera contenida
en la dicha merced, E que todos los otros pueblos que touiesse para en quenta
de la dicha merced Se pusiessen en su Real corona y se cobrassen las Rentas y
tributos dellas para su Magestad ymperial y por virtud de lo ansy proueydo y
mandado, Don Antonio de Mendoça visoRey que fue de la dicha Nueua Spaña
començo a contar los veynte y tres mill vassallos, y sobre la manera del contar
dellos y como se entendian en aquellas partes los vassallos, y sobre que el dicho
Marques pretendia no ser necessaria la dicha quenta, y que la merced que le avia
sido hecha por su Magestad ymperial comprehendia todas las villas y lugares en
ella nombrados sin limitacion ni Restricion de numero de vassallos, y nuestro
procurador fiscal que el dicho Marques no avia de aver mas de hasta numero
de los dichos veynte y tres mill vaslallos conforme a la dicha merced, porque la
prouission della dezia que se le hazia merced de los dichos veynte y dos lugares
hasta en numero [*11*] de los dichos veynte y tres mill vassallos, porque aunque en
sido limitada hasta en cantidad de los dichos veynte y tres mill vassallos, Se trato
la dicha merced se contenia que se le davan veynte y dos villas o lugares avia
pleyto ante nos en el nuestro Consejo de las Yndias y por ambas las dychas partes
fueron cerca dello dichas y alegadas muchas Razones y Rescibidos a prueua y
hecha publicacion, y conclusso el negocio se dio sentencia por los del dicho nuestro
consejo, Su thenor de la qual ES ESTE QVE SE SIGVE.

EN EL PLEYTO que es y se ha tratado entre don Hernando Cortes Marques
del Valle ya difunto, E Alonso de Sanct Juan su procurador en su nombre y
como señor de la ynstancia, E DON Martin Cortes su hijo Marques que agora
es de VALLE, E don Pedro de Arellano Conde de Aguilar su curador y Alonso
de Sanct Juan su procurador actor de la vna parte, y el fiscal de su Magestad
de la otra sobre las causas y Razones en el processo Contenidas:

FALLAMOS que deuemos declarar y declaramos que la donacion y merced que

public who may be called for this purpose that he shall summon you to appear before us in our court, wherever we may be within the first six months immediately following the day on which he shall have summoned you, to give reason why you should not do and fulfill it thus, so that we may know in what way our command is fulfilled. Given in Barcelona on the sixth day of the month of July of the year of the birth of Our Savior Jesus Christ one thousand five hundred and twenty nine. I the King. I, Francisco de los Cobos, secretary of His Imperial and Their Catholic Majesties, had it written by their command. Fr. García, Bishop of Osma. Doctor Beltrán. Licentiate De la Corte. Registered, Francisco de Briviesca, Chancellor, Licentiate Ximénez. [*In the margin: On July sixth, one thousand five hundred and twenty-nine.*]

After this His Imperial Majesty commanded by his letters and decrees that the twenty-three thousand vassals comprehended in the grant that he had made him should be counted for the said Don Hernando Cortés, Marqués del Valle, and he set up the order that was to be followed in counting them. And he commanded that when the counting had been completed, they should be delivered over to the said Marqués with the jurisdiction over them, in the form and manner expressed in the said grant, and that all of the other towns that he might have to be counted for the said grant should be placed under the royal crown, and the incomes and tribute from them should be collected for His Imperial Majesty. And by virtue of what was thus determined and commanded, Don Antonio de Mendoza, former viceroy of the said New Spain, began to count the twenty-three thousand vassals. And a lawsuit was conducted before us in our Council of the Indies concerning the manner of counting them and what was meant by vassals in those regions and concerning the fact that the said Marqués maintained that the counting was not necessary and that the grant that had been made to him by His Imperial Majesty comprehended all of the towns and places named in it without limitation or restriction of the number of vassals, and our prosecuting attorney maintained that he was not to have more than the number of twenty-three thousand vassals in conformity with the said grant because the decree said that he was made a grant of the said twenty-two places up to a total of the said twenty-three thousand vassals, because even though in the said grant it was expressed that twenty-two towns or places were given to him, it had been limited to the amount of the said twenty-three thousand vassals. And many reasons were stated and alleged concerning it by both of the said parties. And after they were allowed to present evidence, and the publication was made, and the business was concluded, a sentence was passed by the members of our said council, the tenor of which is as follows.

In the lawsuit which is and has been conducted between Don Hernando Cortés, Marqués del Valle, now deceased, and Alonso de San Juan, his attorney in his name and master of the instance, and Don Martín Cortés, his son, present Marqués del Valle, and Don Pedro de Arellano, count of Aguilar, his guardian, and Alonso de San Juan, his attorney, plaintiffs, on the one hand, and the prosecutor of His Majesty, on the other hand, concerning the causes and reason expressed in the proceedings:

We find that we must declare and we do declare that the donation and grant

su Magestad hizo al dicho Marques del Valle fue de veynte y tres mill vassallos en las villas pueblos aldeas o subjectos terminos y jurisdicion en la carta de la dicha donacion contenidos y no de todas las villas y pueblos aldeas o subjectos terminos y jurisdiction contenidos en la dicha donacion en lo que excedieren del dicho numero, E que anssy mismo en la quenta de los dichos vassallos entren y se quenten los vezinos de los subjectos o aldeas como los de los otros pueblos principales, E con que assi mismo cada casa y fumo se quente por vn vezino y vassallo segun y de la manera que se quentan [*11v*] en Castilla el vezino y vassallo y conforme a estas declaraciones mandamos que se haga y proceda en la dicha quenta de vassallos, y en quanto a esto confirmamos el auto por nos dado a cinco dias del mes de octubre de mill y quinientos y quarenta años de que por parte del dicho Marques fue supplicado sin embargo de las Razones por parte del dicho Marques dichas y alegadas, y hecha la dicha quenta como dicho es, todo lo que paresciere exceder del dicho numero de lo que el Marques tiene y possee condenamos al dicho Marques y al dicho procurador en su nombre a que dentro de veynte dias como fuere rrequerido con la carta executoria desta nuestra sentencia lo torne buelua y rrestituya a su Magestad con los frutos y rrentas que la parte de los dichos pueblos que assy excediere del dicho numero vuieren Rentado, desde el dia que el dicho Marques don Hernando se obligo de hazerlo assy y comforme a la dicha obligacion pressentada en este processo, la qual mandamos que vaya ynserta en la carta executoria desta nuestra sentencia, y en todo lo demas pedido y demandado por las dychas partes se lo deuemos denegar y denegamos, E no hazemos condenacion de costas, y por esta nuestra sentencia diffinitiua anssy lo pronunciamos y mandamos. El Marques. El licenciado Gregorio Lopez. Licenciado Tello de Sandoual. El doctor Riuadeneyra. El licenciado Viruiesca. [*In margin: hasta aqui*]. Y al pie de la dicha sentencia esta escripto de letra del dicho doctor Riuadeneyra lo siguiente, Ha de firmar el señor DOCTOR HERNAN PEREZ.

DE LA QVAL dicha sentencia fue supplicado por parte de vos don Martin Cortes Marques del Valle hijo y heredero que quedastes en la casa y mayoradgo del dicho Marques don Hernando Cortes vuestro padre [*12*] y estando anssi suplicado de la dicha sentencia, por vuestra parte nos fue pedido y supplicado que acatando los muchos grandes y leales seruicios que el dicho Marques vuestro padre avia hecho a la corona rreal destros rreynos, y a lo que vos nos aviades seruido en las jornadas que aviamos hecho a los nuestros estados de Flandes y Ynglaterra, y en la guerra contra francesses quando fue presso el condestable de Francia y ganada San Quintin, E otras tierras del Rey de Francia, y a lo mucho que aviades gastado en nuestro seruicio, E teniendo consideracion que hera poca la Renta que de lo que el dicho fiscal pretendia podia Resultar a nuestro patrimonio rreal y que a vos os seria gran daño y diminucion de vuestro estado y autoridad os hiziesse merced de confirmaros la dicha merced que se avia hecho al dicho Marques don Hernando Cortes vuestro padre de las dichas veynte y dos villas y lugares declaradas en ella con sus vassallos y jurisdicion y rrentas

which His Majesty made to the said Marqués del Valle was of twenty-three thousand vassals in the towns, villages and subject territories and jurisdiction expressed in the letter of the said donation and not of all of the towns, villages or subject territories and jurisdiction expressed in the said donation insofar as they may exceed the said number; and likewise in the counting of the said vassals, the citizens of the subject towns or villages shall be entered into the account, the same as those of the principal towns, also with the condition that every house and hearth be counted as a citizen and vassal in the same way that the citizen and vassal are counted in Castile. And we command that they act and proceed in the said counting of vassals in conformity with these declarations, and in regard to this we confirm the judicial decree handed down by us on the fifth day of the month of October of the year one thousand five hundred and forty from which the party of the said Marqués appealed, notwithstanding the reasons stated and alleged by the party of the said Marqués. And when the said reckoning is completed as has been said, we condemn the said Marqués and the said attorney in his name that within twenty days of receipt of a summons with the executory letter of this our sentence, he shall return, give back, and restitute to His Majesty everything that shall appear to be in excess of the said number of that which the said Marqués holds and possesses, together with the fruits and incomes which may have been paid by that part of the said towns which exceeds the said number from the day on which the said Marqués Don Hernando obligated himself to do it in this way and in conformity with the said obligation presented in these proceedings, which we command to be inserted in the executory letter of this our sentence. And in regard to everything else requested and demanded by the said parties, we must deny it and we do deny it. And we do not make a condemnation of the costs. And thus we pronounce and command this as our definitive sentence. The Marqués. Licentiate Gregorio López. Licentiate Tello de Sandoval. Doctor Rivadeneyra. Licentiate Briviesca. And at the foot of the said sentence, in the hand of the said Doctor Rivadeneyra, the following is written: The Lord Doctor Hernán Pérez must sign.

From the said sentence an appeal was made on the part of you, Don Martín Cortés, Marqués del Valle, son and heir who have remained in the house and entail of the said Marqués Don Hernando Cortés, your father. And the appeal having thus been made from the said sentence, on your part we were asked and entreated that we should give recognition to the many great and loyal services which the said Marqués, your father, had done for the royal crown of these realms, and of how you had served us in the journeys which we have made to our states of Flanders and England and in the war against the French when the lord high constable of France was captured and when Saint-Quentin and other lands of the King of France were conquered, and of the great amount that you have spent in our service, and that taking into account that the income which could result for our royal patrimony from what the prosecutor claimed would be slight but that for you it would be a great harm and reduction of your estate and authority, we should do you the favor of confirming you in the said grant which had been made to the said Marqués Don Hernando Cortés, your father, of the said twenty-two towns and places expressed in it, with their vassals and

como en la dicha merced se contenia sin que el dicho nuestro fiscal os traxesse en pleyto ni os demandasse parte de las dichas villas ni lugares ni vassallos dellas ni se tratasse de rrestringuir ni diminuyr la dicha merced so color del dicho quento de vassallos ni de averse hecho mincion en ella de los dichos veynt y tres mill vassallos, pues las mercedes Reales y hechas por tan señalados seruicios se auian de amplear y estender y no rrestringuir o como la mi merced fuesse, E yo acatando lo suso dicho, E teniendo pressentes los buenos grandes señalados y leales seruicios que el dicho Marques don Hernando Cortes hizo a la corona Real destos Reynos y el gran prouecho que de sus seruicios Redundo, anssi para el seruicio de Dios Nuestro Señor y avmento de su sancta fee catholica en aquellas partes Como a nos y a nuestra rreal corona y a lo que vos el dicho don Martin Cortes nos aveys [12v] seruido, y auiendoseme consultado por los del dycho nuestro Consejo de las Yndias he tenido por bien de hazer merced A VOS el dicho don Martin Cortes MARQVES del VALLE de os Aprouar y confirmar la merced de las dychas veynte y dos villas y lugares con sus aldeas y jurisdicion y derechos que anssy la Magestad del Emperador mi señor hizo en la dicha Nueua Spaña al dicho Marques don Hernando Cortes vuestro padre sin limitacion ni Restrycion de numero de vassallos, CON TANTO que el puerto de Teguantepeque con sus subjetos, que es puerto en la Mar del Sur quede para nos y para la corona rreal de estos Reynos con su jurisdicion ceuil y criminal y Rentas y prouechos que en el oviere, quedando a vos el dicho Marques, las estancias de ganados que en ello touieredes, y mandando os nos pagar en otra parte la rrenta que Se averiguare que teneys en el dicho puerto de Teguantepeque y sus subjetos, POR ENDE por la pressente Aprouamos y confirmamos a vos el dicho Don Martin Cortes Marques del Valle y a vuestros herederos y subcessores en vuestra cassa y mayoradgo la dicha merced susso yncorporada que ansi fue hecha por su Magestad ymperial al dicho don Hernando Cortes vuestro padre libre y plenariamente sin ninguna Lymitacion ni Restricion de vassallos como sy en ella no se oviera hecho mincion de numero de vassallos, y si necessario es os hazemos de nueuo la dicha merced, Y Mandamos que vos y ellos perpetuamente ayays y tengays las villas y lugares en la dicha merced contenidas con sus tierras y aldeas, y con todos los vassallos que en ellas oviere sin limitacion ni Restricion de numero dellos, y con los terminos [13] y jurisdicion ceuil y criminal alta y baxa mero misto ymperio como fue concedido por la dicha merced al dicho Marques don Hernando Cortes vuestro padre, y con todas las Rentas y oficios y pechos y derechos y montes y prados y pastos y aguas corrientes estantes y manantes, y con todas las otras cossas que nos touieremos y lleuaremos y nos pertenesciere o de que podamos o deuamos gozar y lleuar en las tierras que nos tenemos y estan en nuestra corona Real en la dicha Nueua España, y con todo lo otro al señorio de las dichas villas y pueblos declarados en la dycha merced y que fue concedido al dicho DON Hernando Cortes vuestro padre, y Siendo

jurisdiction and incomes, as was contained in the said grant, without allowing that our said prosecutor should draw you into a lawsuit nor demand of you part of the said towns, places, or their vassals nor that any attempt should be made to restrict or lessen the said grant under the guise of the said count of vassals or of the mention having been made in it of the said twenty-three thousand vassals, for the royal grants made for such outstanding services are to be amplified and extended and not restricted; or that I should do what my desire might be.

And I have acknowledged the abovesaid and have kept in mind the good, great, outstanding, and loyal services which the said Marqués Don Hernando Cortés did for the royal crown of these realms and the great profit which resulted from his services, both for the service of God Our Lord and the increase of His holy Catholic faith in those parts, as well as for us and our royal crown, and also what you, the said Don Martín Cortés, have done for us in our service. And when I was consulted by the members of our said Royal Council of the Indians, I thought it well to grant to you, the said Don Martín Cortés, Marqués del Valle, the favor of approving and confirming the grant of the said seventy-two towns and places, with their villages and jurisdiction and rights, which His Majesty, the Emperor, my lord, made to the said Marqués Don Hernando Cortés, your father, in the said New Spain, without limitation or restriction of the number of vassals, with the condition that the port of Tehuantepec with its subject towns, which is a port on the South Sea, shall remain for us and for the royal crown of these realms, with its civil and criminal jurisdiction and incomes and profits which may come from it, leaving to you, the said Marqués, the ranches of livestock which you may have in it, and commanding that we pay you in another place the income which it may be determined that you have in the said port of Tehuantepec and its subject towns.

Therefore by the present letter we approve and confirm to you, the said Don Martín Cortés, Marqués del Valle, and to your successors and heirs in your house and entail the said grant incorporated above, which was thus made by His Imperial Majesty to the said Don Hernando Cortés, your father, freely and completely, without any limitation or restriction of vassals, as though no mention had been made of vassals in it; and if it is necessary we make the said grant to you anew.

And we command that you and they shall have and hold perpetually the said towns and places expressed in the said grant, with their lands and villages and all of the vassals who are in them, without limitation or restriction of their number, and with the boundaries and higher and lower civil and criminal jurisdiction, simple mixed dominion, as was conceded by the said grant to the said Marqués Don Hernando Cortés, your father, and with all of the incomes and offices, taxes and fees, forests, meadows and pastures, and running, standing, and outflowing waters, and with all the other things which we might have and take and which would pertain to us or which we might and should enjoy and take in the lands which we hold and which are under our royal crown in the said New Spain, and with everything else which was granted to the said Don Hernando Cortés, your father, pertaining to the dominion of the said towns expressed in the said grant. And if it is necessary, we

necessario vos apoderamos en todo ello ansi en posesion como en propriedad plenariamente y sin diminuycion alguna, ECEPTO la villa y puerto de Teguantepeque con
sus subjetos, porque esta con el dicho puerto y sus subjetos La diuidimos y apartamos
de la dicha merced y la encorporamos en nuestra Real corona para que sea nuestra
y de la corona de Castilla perpetuamente, Con el señorio Renta y vassallaje y
jurisdicion ceuil y criminal E con todo lo demas a ello pertenesciente, Sin que a vos
el dicho Marques ni a vuestros herederos ni subcessores os quede en ello cossa alguna,
sino fuere las estancias de ganados que al pressente teneys en ello, QVE estas queremos
que os queden para vos y para vuestros subcesores para os aprouechar dellas como
quissieredes y por bien touieredes. LA QVAL dicha merced y confirmacion hazemos
no embargante qualesquier çedulas y prouissiones que se ayan dado para contar los
dichos vassallos y poner en la corona Real los que excediessen del dicho numero o
de otro qualquiera, y los autos hechos sobre la quenta y numero dellos, y los pleytos
que cerca [*13v*] de lo susso dicho aya avido y aya entre vos y el dicho nuestro fiscal y
la sentencia que assi fue dada por los el dicho nuestro consejo que de susso va
yncorporada y otros qualesquier porueymientos que cerca de lo a ello tocante se ayan
hecho LO QVAL todo y los processos de los dychos pleytos damos por ningunos y
los casamos y anullamos como sy nunca se ovieran hecho, ni passado, ni la dicha
sentencia se ovyera dado, Y MANDAMOS al pressydente y oydores de la nuestra
audiencia Real de la dicha Nueua Spaña que luego que con esta nuestra carta fueren
Requeridos hagan averiguar la Renta sin la jurisdicion que vos el dicho Marques
teneys en la dicha villa y puerto de Teguantepeque y sus subjetos anssy en dinero y
maiz como en otras cossas que sea de el señorio y vassallaje dello, Syendo para ello
citada la parte de nuestro procurador fiscal y la de vos el dicho Marques, Y ANSY
averiguado La Renta de Maiz y otras cossas que hallaren que verdaderamente teneys
os la consignen y señalen en algun pueblo nuestro que este en comarca de otras
haziendas de vos, el dicho Marques, PARA QVE en el tal pueblo ayays y tengays la
dicha Renta perpetuamente sin que en el tengays otra entrada ni salida mas de la
dicha rrenta que siendo os senalada por el dicho nuestro pressydente y oydores, NOS
por la pressente OS la señalamos, PARA QVE la ayays y tengays vos y los dichos
vuestros herederos y subcessores en la dicha vuestra cassa y mayoradgo perpetuamente
como dicho es, Y LA rrenta de dinero que se aueriguare tener en la dicha villa y
puerto de Teguantepeque y sus subjetos os la consignen en los nuestros officiales de
la dicha Nueua Spaña, A LOS [*14*] QVALES MANDAMOS ansi a los que agora
son Como a los que Seran de aqui adelante y a otros qualesquyer personas que por
nos y en nuestro nombre touieren cargo de nuestra hazienda en la dycha Nueua Spaña
que paguen a vos el dycho Marques y a los dichos vuestros herederos y subcessores en
vuestra cassa y mayoradgo en cada vn año perpetuamente lo que ansy os fuere
consignado por el dicho nuestro pressydente y oydores, Y ENCARGAMOS al

place you in authority over all of it, both in the possession and in the ownership, completely and without any diminution, excepting the town and port of Tehuantepec with its subject towns, because we divide and separate this town with the said port and its subject towns from the said grant, and we incorporate it into our royal crown so that it may belong to us and to the crown of Castile perpetually, with the dominion, income, vassalage, civil and criminal jurisdiction, and everything else pertaining to it, without there remaining for you, the said Marqués, nor for your heirs or successors anything at all in it, except the ranches of livestock which you have in it at present. And it is our will that they should remain there for you and your successors so that you may make use of them as you may wish and consider good.

We make this said grant and confirmation notwithstanding any decrees and writs whatsoever which may have been given for the counting of the said vassals and for placing those who exceeded the said number or any other number under the royal crown, and notwithstanding the judicial acts carried out regarding the reckoning and number of them, and the lawsuits which have been and are being conducted regarding the abovesaid between you and our said prosecutor, and the sentence that was thus given by the members of our said council, which is incorporated above, and any other writs whatsoever which may have been issued concerning matters pertaining to it. All of this and the proceedings of the said lawsuits we declare to be null, and we repeal and annul them as though they had never taken place or been done and as though the said sentence had never been given.

And we command the president and oidores of our royal audiencia of the said New Spain that as soon as it is demanded of them through this our letter, they shall see to the verification of the income without jurisdiction which you, the said Marqués, have in the said town and port of Tehuantepec and its subject towns both in money and maize and in other things which pertain to the dominion and vassalage of it, and for this there shall be cited the party of our prosecuting attorney and the party of you, the said Marqués. And when they have thus verified the income from maize and other things which they find that you truly have, they shall assign and set it aside for you in some town of ours which is in the neighborhood of other properties belonging to you, the said Marqués, so that in that town you shall have and hold the said income perpetually without having any other access to the town besides the said income. And when it is set aside for you by our said president and oidores, we set it aside for you by the present letter, so that you and your said heirs and successors in your said house and entail shall have and hold it perpetually, as has been said. And concerning the income in money which it may be verified that you have in the said town and port of Tehuantepec and its subject towns, they shall assign it to be paid to you by our treasury officials of the said New Spain. And we command them, both those who have the office now and those who will have it in the future, and any other persons whatsoever who for us and in our name may have charge of our exchequer in the said New Spain, that they shall pay to you, the said Marqués, and to your said heirs and successors in your house and entail every year perpetually what shall thus have been assigned to you by our said president and oidores.

Illustrissimo Principe DON CARLOS nuestro muy charo y muy amado Hijo E a las ynfantas nuestras muy charas y muy amadas hermanas, Y A LOS perlados Duques Marqueses Condes Ricos omes Maestres de las ordenes pryores comendadores y sub-comendadores, Y MANDAMOS a los alcaydes de Los Castillos y Cassas Fuertes y llanas, y a los de el nuestro Consejo pressydentes E oydores de las nuestras audyencias Alcaldes alguaziles de la nuestra casa y corte y chancillerias, y a todos los concejos Corregidores assistente Gouernadores Alcaldes Alguaziles Merinos Preuostes E otras justicias y juezes Qualesquier De todas las Cibdades Villas y lugares de estos nuestros Reynos y Señorios y de las Nuestras Yndias yslas y tierra firme del Mar Oceano y a cada vno dellos en sus lugares y jurisdiciones que guarden y hagan guardar esta dicha nuestra carta de Merced y confirmacion, E contra [*14v*] el thenor y forma della no vayan ni passen ni consientan yr ni pasar en tiempo alguno ni por alguna manera. Dada en la cibdad de Toledo a diez y seis dias del mes de diziembre de mill y quinientos y sesenta años.

YO EL REY

Yo Francisco de Erasso seçretario de su Magestad Real la fize screuir por su mandado. [*rubrica*]

Registrada, OCHOA DE LUYANDO [*rubrica*]

Chanciller, MARTIN DE RAMOYN [*rubrica*]

LICENCIADO DON JUAN SARMIENTO [*rubrica*]

EL DOCTOR VAZQUEZ [*rubrica*]

EL LICENCIADO CASTRO [*rubrica*]

EL LICENCIADO VALDERRAMA [*rubrica*]

EL LICENCIADO DON GOMEZ ZAPATA [*rubrica*]

Dupplicada

Vuestra Magestad aprueua y confirma a don Martin Cortes Marques del Valle la merced que se hizo al Marques don Hernando Cortes su padre de XXii villas y lugares en la Nueua Spaña en que vuiese XXiiiU vasallos, y de nueuo le haze merced de las dichas villas y lugares sin limitacion ni ni [*sic*] Restricion de vasallos, no embargante qualquier pleto que sobre ello aya avido y sentencia y otros autos que se ayan dado, con que quede para vuestra Magestad la villa y puerto de Teguantepeque con sus sujectos sin que al dicho Marques le quede en ello mas de solo las estancias de ganados que alli tuuiere, y dandosele en otra parte la Renta que se averiguare que tiene en la dicha villa y puerto.

And we charge the Most Illustrious Prince Don Carlos, our very dear and very beloved son, and the infantas, our very dear and beloved sisters, and the prelates, dukes, marquesses, counts, grandees, masters of the orders, priors, knight-commanders and sub-commanders, and we command the wardens of the castles and of the houses with moats and of the country houses, and the members of our council, presidents and oidores of our audiencias, alcaldes, constables of our house and court and chanceries, and all the councils, corregidores, assistant governors, alcaldes, constables, judges of the sheepwalks, provosts and whatsoever other judges and justices of all the cities, towns, and places of these our realms and dominions and of our Indies, islands, and mainland of the Ocean Sea and to each one of them in their places and jurisdictions, that they shall observe and see to the observance of this our letter of favor and confirmation. And against the tenor and form of it they shall not go nor act, nor consent that anyone go nor act at any time or in any manner. Give in the city of Toledo on the sixteenth day of the month of December of the year one thousand five hundred and sixty.

I THE KING

I, Francisco de Eraso, secretary of His Royal Majesty, had it written by his command. [*rubric*]

Registered, OCHOA DE LUYANDO [*rubric*]

Chancellor, MARTÍN DE RAMOYN [*rubric*]

> LICENTIATE DON JUAN SARMIENTO [*rubric*]
>
> DOCTOR VÁZQUEZ [*rubric*]
>
> LICENTIATE CASTRO [*rubric*]
>
> LICENTIATE VALDERRAMA [*rubric*]
>
> LICENTIATE DON GÓMEZ ZAPATA [*rubric*]
>
> Duplicate

Your Majesty approves and confirms to Don Martín Cortés, Marqués del Valle, the grant that was made to the Marqués Don Hernando Cortés, his father, of 22 towns and places in New Spain in which there would be 23,000 vassals, and anew you make him the grant of the said towns and places without limitation or restriction of vassals, in spite of any lawsuit which may have been carried on concerning it and any sentence or other judicial acts which may have been given, on condition that the town and port of Tehuantepec with its subject towns be set aside for Your Majesty, without the said Marqués retaining any right in it except only the ranches of livestock which he has there, and giving him in another place the income which it is verified that he has in the said town and port.

([*15*] En la ciudad de Mexico veinte e vn dias del mes de henero de mill e quinientos e sesenta e tress años estando en acuerdo el muy Yllustre señor visorrei president e oydores de la avdiencia Real desta Nueba España en presençia de mi Antonio de Turcios escribano mayor della, fue presentada este previlegio e merced de su Magestad por el Yllustre señor don Martin Cortes Marques del Valle e pidio el Cumplimiento del y por los dichos senores presidente E oydores vista la obedescieron con toda Reberençia E acatamiento debido e que se hara y Cumplira lo que su Magestad manda.

ANTONIO DE TURCIOS [*rubrica*]

[*On a paper sheet following the parchment cover*] Se remitio a Madrid testimonio de este priuilijio con fecha de 11 Septiembre del año de 1731.

In the city of Mexico on the twenty-first day of the month of January of the year one thousand five hundred and sixty-three, the Very Illustrious Lord Viceroy, president, and oidores of the royal audiencia of this New Spain being in session, in the presence of me, Antonio de Turcios, its major scribe, this privilege and grant of His Majesty was presented by the Illustrious Lord Don Martín Cortés, Marqués del Valle, and he requested the fulfillment of it. When it had been seen by the said lords president and oidores, they showed obedience to it with all due reverence and respect and said that what His Majesty commands will be done and fulfilled.

ANTONIO DE TURCIOS [*rubric*]

A notarized copy of this privilege was sent to Madrid with the date of September 11 of the year 1731. [*Note on manuscript in a later hand*]

Questionnaires from the Trial of the
Second Marqués del Valle
for Conspiracy, 1566

[186] Probança del fiscal contra el Marques del Valle.

Por las preguntas siguientes sean preguntados los testigos que por la parte del liçençiado Contreras fiscal desta Real Avdiençia en nonbre del fisco e de la rreal justiçia son o seran presentados en el pleyto que trata contra el Marques del Valle sobre el crimen lese magestatis conçitaçion y alçamiento.

i Primeramente si consosçen A las partes y al dicho [*do*]n Martin Corthes Marques del Valle y a don Martin y a don Luis Cortes sus hermanos y a don Luis de Velasco y a Diego Arias de Sotelo y a Baltasar y Pedro de Aguilar y al liçençiado Xpoval de Ayala de Espinoza y a don Baltasar y don Pedro de Quesada y a Agustin de Villanueva y Alonso de Servantes su hermano y si conosçieron A Alonso Davila Alvarado y Gil Gonçales Davila su hermano difuntos.

ii Yten si saben vieron o an oydo dezir que el dicho Marquez comunicava y tratava muchas vezes secretamente con el dicho Alonso Davila y Gil Gonçales su hermano y con los dichos don Martin y don Luis Cortes sus hermanos Ansi en su casa como en casa de Alonso Davila de noche y a oras sospechosas y muchas y diversas vezes y en otras partes.

iii Yten si saben que En la comunicaçion que entre los suso dichos se tratava y juntas que se hazian hera que el dicho Marquez se Alçase contra la obidiençia de su Magestad y Rey don Felipe nuestro señor y se hiziese Rey desta tierra, tomandola para si dando trasças de la forma que se avia de hazer y de que manera Avian de matar Al presidente e oydores y las demas personas que quiziesen bolver por el partido de su Magestad.

iiii° Yten si saben que tratando el dicho Marques de lo suso dicho dezia que hera mejor matar a los oydores vna noche en sus casas y por los Açoteas porque seria Ansi mas seguro que de otra manera.

v Yten si saben que el dicho Marquez publico que Abia vna çedula de su Magestad para que no susçediesen los nietos de los encomenderos sino que se acabase la susçeçion En la segunda vida y Ansi lo [*de*][*186v*]claro A muchas personas y encomenderos Diziendo que no convenia que se pasase por tal cosa y que el Rey les quitava sus haziendas y Ansi mesmo que a el le Avian noteficado Vna çitatoria por donde El fiscal del consejo le ponia demanda de su Estado o de la mayor parte del ynçitando A los dichos encomenderos y A otras muchas personas para Atraellos A su voluntad y que Estuviesen odiosos al seruiçio de su Magestad todo para hefetuar El dicho

Inquiry of the prosecutor against the Marqués del Valle

By the following questions let the witnesses be interrogated who are or shall be presented on the part of the Licentiate Contreras, prosecutor of this royal audiencia, in the name of the exchequer and royal justice in the suit which he is conducting against the Marqués del Valle concerning the crime of *laesae majestatis* [treason], incitement, and rebellion.

1. First, whether they know the parties and the said Don Martín Cortés, Marqués del Valle, and Don Martín and Don Luis Cortés, his brothers, and Don Luis de Velasco and Diego Arias de Sotelo and Baltasar and Pedro de Aguilar and Licentiate Cristóbal de Ayala de Espinosa and Don Baltasar and Don Pedro de Quesada and Agustín de Villanueva and Alonso de Cervantes, his brother, and whether they knew Alonso de Ávila Alvarado and Gil González de Ávila, his brother, both deceased.

2. Further, whether they know, saw, or have heard it said that the said Marqués often communicated and treated secretly with the said Alonso de Ávila and Gil González, his brother, and with the said Don Martín and Don Luis Cortés, his brothers, in his own house as well as in the house of Alonso de Ávila, at night and at suspicious hours and at many and various times and in other places.

3. Further, whether they know that in the communication which took place between the abovesaid and in the meetings which they held, the intent was that the said Marqués should rebel against the obedience of His Majesty and King Don Felipe our lord and that he should make himself king of this land, taking it for himself, and they gave indications of the way in which it was to be done and of how they were to kill the president and oidores and the other persons who might wish to turn back to the party of His Majesty.

4. Further, whether they know that while the said Marqués was discussing the abovesaid, he asserted that it would be better to kill the oidores on one night in their houses and through the roofs because it would be safer thus than any other way.

5. Further, whether they know that the said Marqués disclosed that there was a decree from His Majesty to the effect that the grandchildren of encomenderos would not inherit the encomiendas but that the inheritance would stop with the second life, and he declared this to many people and encomenderos, saying that it was not right that such a thing should happen and that the King was taking their properties from them, and he likewise stated that they had notified him of a summons by which the prosecutor of the Council [*of the Indies*] had placed a demand upon his estate or the greater part of it, and in this way he stirred up the said encomenderos and many other persons in order to attract them to his will and lead them to be discontent with

Alçamiento y Rebelion y tenellos muy propiçios y a su voluntad quando los oviese menester.

vi Yten si saben que el dicho Marquez con voluntad que tenia y A tenido de se alçar con la dicha Nueva España tratava del derecho que tenia su Magestad en esta tierra con personas Ansi letrados o no letrados Espeçialmente con don Alonso Chico de Molina, dean desta sancta yglesia de Mexico, y un fray Luis Cali de la horden de señor San Francisco, tratando con Ellos y tomando paresçeres questa tierra con mas titulo y Justiçia pertenesçia A su padre don Hernando Cortes que no A la Real Magestad y Rey don Felipe nuestro señor.

vii Yten si saben que Estando Alonso Davila En el pueblo de Guatlitlan en el [*Al—written over*] tiempo que se le notefico Al dicho Marquez El Enplazamiento aRiba dicho El dicho Marquez le Escrivio que viniese luego A esta çibdad porque Ansi convenia y que Avia Ruines nuevas de España para Atraer A su opinion Al dicho Alonso Davila lo qual visto por el dicho Alonso Davila vino A esta çibdad con toda presteza y fue a la posada del dicho Marques Adonde trataron deste negoçio y alçamiento ynstigandole El dicho Marques diziendo que su Magestad procurava de le quitar su hazienda por donde el dicho Alonso Davila quedo prendado del dicho Marquez para hefetuar el dicho negoçio y alçamiento.

viii° Yten si saben que para el mesmo hefecto y para Atraer a los Animos de los encomenderos y los demas el dicho Marques publico vna carta que le escriuio de España Diego Fferrer su soliçitador Diziendo que su Magestad y los de su consejo avian [*187*] Proveydo que no Avia lugar de se hazer lo que se pedia por parthe desta çibdad y Nueva España serca de la perpetuidad desta tierra y encomiendas, lo qual ansi mesmo propuso en el cabildo desta çibdad por terçeras personas todo A fin de yndinar los vecinos A quien tocava contra el seruiçio de su Magestad y para los Atraer A su voluntad y proposito digan lo que saben.

ix Yten si saben que el dicho Marques para hefetuar El dicho alçamiento vna noche Entre otras muchas noches que fue en casa del dicho Alonso Davila secretamente se metio En una Recamara y hablo con el liçençiado Espinoza para dar horden En el dicho Alçamiento y como se avia de hefetuar Adonde hablaron muy largo En el dicho Rebelion y lo mesmo En otras muchas partes y muchas vezes.

x Yten si saben que Ansi mesmo El dicho Marques hablo sobre lo suso dicho con Pedro de Aguilar en su propia casa sobre el dicho Alçamiento y Rebelion y que lo tuviese secreto y no lo descubriese A persona alguna, y despues viniendo A notiçia del Avdiençia rreal persuadio Al dicho Pedro de Aguilar que delante de vno[*s—canceled*] de los oydores con Juramento negase lo que Avia oydo visto y sabido de todo El dicho alçamiento y que no se pudiese provar con [*por—written over*] el dicho Pedro de Aguilar.

xi Yten si saben que el dicho Marques con muchos Ruegos promesas y otros

the service of His Majesty, all this in order to bring about the said rebellion and uprising and to have them very sympathetic and subject to his will when he might need them.

6. Further, whether they know that the said Marqués, with the determination that he had of rebelling with the said New Spain, discussed the right that His Majesty had in this land with both learned and unlearned people, especially with Don Alonso Chico de Molina, dean of this holy church of Mexico, and a certain Fray Luis Cali [*i.e.,* *Cal*] of the Order of the Lord Saint Francis, discussing with them and getting their opinions that this land belonged to his father Don Hernando Cortés with greater right and justice than to the royal Majesty and King Don Felipe, our lord.

7. Further, whether they know that because Alonso de Ávila was in the town of Cuautitlan at the time that the said Marqués was notified of the summons mentioned above, the said Marqués wrote to him that he should come immediately to this city because it was for the best and because there was terrible news from Spain, in order to attract the said Alonso de Ávila to his opinion, and when the said Alonso de Ávila saw it, he came to this city with all haste and went to the residence of the said Marqués where they discussed this business and uprising, and the said Marqués stirred him up, saying that His Majesty was trying to take away his properties from him, and as a result the said Alonso de Ávila remained pledged to the said Marqués for the purpose of carrying out the said business and uprising.

8. Further, whether they know that for the same end and in order to attract the wills of the encomenderos and of the others, the said Marqués made public a letter which his agent Diego Ferrer wrote him from Spain in which he reported that His Majesty and the members of his council had determined that it was not allowable to do what was asked on the part of this city and New Spain concerning the perpetuity of this land and the encomiendas, and he likewise presented this in the cabildo of this city through third persons, all for the purpose of arousing the freeholders whom it would affect against the service of His Majesty and to attract them to his will and design; let them say what they know.

9. Further, whether they know that the said Marqués, in order to bring about the said uprising, one night among the many others when he was secretly in the house of the said Alonso de Ávila, withdrew into a private room and talked with Licentiate Espinosa in order to establish order in the said uprising as to the way that it should be carried out, and there they spoke at great length regarding the said rebellion, and they did the same in many other places and at many other times.

10. Further, whether they know that the said Marqués likewise spoke concerning the abovesaid with Pedro de Aguilar in his own house, concerning the said uprising and rebellion, and asked that he keep it secret and not reveal it to anyone, and later, when it came to the notice of the royal audiencia, he persuaded the said Pedro de Aguilar that in the presence of one of the oidores he should deny on oath what he had heard, seen, and known concerning all of the said uprising and that it should be impossible to prove anything with the said Pedro de Aguilar.

11. Further, whether they know that the said Marqués, with many entreaties, prom-

ofresçimientos persuadia al dicho Pedro de Aguilar que como buen soldado en su tienpo favoresçiese en el dicho negoçio y tuviese mucho secreto porque el dicho Marquez se lo satisfaria muy bien y ansi el dia que prendieron Al dicho Marques tenia determinado de le dar cavallos y dineros y otras cosas para que se fuese desta çibdad y que negase que no Avia tratado con El dicho Marquez ni otra persona El dicho Rebelion y alçamiento.

xii Yten si saben que abiendose tratado del dicho negoçio y Rebelion entre el dicho Marquez del Valle y el dicho Alonso Davila [*187v*] vn dia de fiesta se hizo Regozijo en casa del dicho Marques ya noche y el dicho Alonso de Avila hera el que prençipalmente hazia la dicha fiesta y para el dicho hefecto vino de sus Pueblos de Guatitlan con mucha comida y otras cosas de Regozijo Aconpañado de mucha Jente Española y com [*sic*] maxcaras disfrasçadas como yndios haziendo mucho Regozijo, dando muchos sucheles con letras y motetes Em [*sic*] metro Ansi al dicho Marques como A la Marqueza su muger poniendo A manera de guirnalda en la cabeça vna corona y A el dicho Marques se le dio Vn suchil con vna letra que dezia no temas la cayda, pues Es para mayor subida E toda la fiesta Endereçandose A que el dicho Marques Avia de ser Rey desta tierra, lo qual El dicho Marques Admitio con grande contento sabiendo Al fin En que lo suso dicho se Enderesçava, y otros muchos motetes y coplas y rromançes dirigidos Al proposito del dicho Alçamiento que pido que los dichos motetes se muestren A los dichos testigos.

xiii Yten si saben que diziendo el dicho Pedro de Aguilar Al dicho Marquez que se queria yr desta tierra por quitarse desto enbaraços E porque no se prosçediese contra el si se supiese del dicho Alçamiento y que el Abia jurado lo que su señoria le avia mandado le dixo El dicho Marques que no tuviese pena y que ya que se fuese seria mejor venir a cosa hecha, dando A entender questaria hefetuado El dicho Rebelion.

xiiii° Yten si saben que el dicho Alonso de Abila Abiendo tratado del dicho Rebelion con el dicho Marquez se quexava El dicho Alonso Davila que El dicho Marquez le avia metido en el dicho negoçio y biendo que no tenia ya Remedio porque sabia que por la Real Avdiençia se hazia Ynformaçion dezia que Dios se lo demandase Al dicho Marques que tanto mal le avia hecho y que el quieto y pasifico Estaba y muy contento y que si le prendiesen sobre Este negoçio que el abia de declarar todo lo que Avia pasado con el dicho Marques y como el les abia metido En ello A el y a don Luis Cortes y al dean por donde se tiene Entendido y tienen por çierto los testigos que el dicho Marquez fue el prençipal promoveedor de Este negoçio y el que conçito todos los demas para que se hefetuase El dicho alçamiento y Rebelion.

[*188*]**xv** Yten si saben que tratando el dicho Pedro de Aguilar con el dicho Marques

ises, and other offerings, persuaded the said Pedro de Aguilar that as a good soldier in his time he should favor the said business and keep it very secret because the said Marqués would be very well satisfied at this, and thus on the day that they arrested the said Marqués, he had determined to give him horses and money and other things so that he should leave this city and that he should deny that he had dealt with the said Marqués or anyone else concerning the said rebellion and uprising.

12. Further, whether they know that after the said business of rebellion had been discussed between the said Marqués del Valle and the said Alonso de Ávila, on a day of fiesta there was a party in the house of the said Marqués after nightfall, and the said Alonso de Ávila was the one who principally organized the said fiesta and for that purpose he came from his towns of Cuautitlan with much food and other things for merrymaking, accompanied by many Spanish people; and masquerading as Indians making great merriment, they gave many flower garlands [*sucheles, perhaps from xochitl, Nahuatl for flower*] with inscriptions and mottoes in verse both to the said Marqués and to the Marquesa his wife, placing a kind of garland on her head as a crown, and to the Marqués was given a garland [*suchil*] with an inscription that said, "Do not fear the fall, since it is for a greater rise," and the whole fiesta was dedicated to the fact that the said Marqués was to be the king of this land, and the said Marqués allowed it with great satisfaction, knowing the purpose to which the abovesaid was dedicated; and there were many other mottoes and couplets and ballads directed to the purpose of the said uprising, and I ask that the said mottoes be shown to the said witnesses.

13. Further, whether they know that when the said Pedro de Aguilar told the said Marqués that he wanted to leave this land in order to free himself from these troubles and so that they would not take action against him if the said uprising became known and that he had sworn what his lordship had commanded him, the said Marqués told him that he should not worry and that he should go away now; it would be better to come when the matter was done, giving him to understand that the said rebellion would be carried out.

14. Further, whether they know that the said Alonso de Ávila, having discussed the said rebellion with the said Marqués, complained that the said Marqués had involved him in the said business, and seeing that there was no longer any remedy because he knew that the royal audiencia was making an investigation, he said that God would demand it of the said Marqués that he had done him so much ill and that he was quiet and peaceful and very content and that if they should arrest him for this business, he would reveal everything that had happened with the said Marqués and how he had involved him and Don Luis Cortés and the dean in it, from which it is understood and the witnesses hold as certain that the said Marqués was the principal promoter of this business and that he incited all of the others so that the said uprising and rebellion should be carried out.

15. Further, whether they know that when the said Pedro de Aguilar was dealing with the said Marqués and told him how he had confessed to a friar of the Order of Saint Dominic and that the friar had not wanted to absolve him because what he

E diziendole como se avia confesado con un Religioso de la Horden de Sancto Domingo e que no lo Avia querido Asolver siendo fingido lo que dezia porque ya se sabia En alguna manera lo que se trataba del dicho Alçamiento y Rebelion y el dicho Marques no supiese que Avia salido del dicho Pedro de Aguilar le Respondio El dicho Marquez que porque lo abia descubierto y dicho al dicho fraile que tanbien El se avia confesado y le avian Absuelto A el y a los demas y entonçes Respondio El dicho Pedro de Aguilar pues si vuestra señoria hallo quien le Asolviese A mi no quizieron Asolverme sin que lo dixese A los oydores, y el dicho Marques le Replico, mira el pobrezillo como tenia buenas ganas, se aRonjo con el fraile declarandole en su confision lo que thenia en su pecho y el fraile lo publico.

xvi Yten si saben que teniendo sospecha El dicho Marquez que el dicho Pedro de Aguilar Avia descubierto El trato suso dicho le dixo que mayor traiçion hera descubrir A los Amigos que del se avian fiado que si se hiziera y efetuara El dicho Rebelion y alçamiento que se Avia tratado y tratava contra su Magestad.

xvii Yten si saben que sabiendo El dicho Marquez El dicho Rebelion y alçamiento de que se tratava, procurava que A su salvo se hiziese y que hecho le hiziesen Rey, por manera que el dicho Marquez lo sabia queria E ynçitava y tenia proposito E gran voluntad que el dicho Rebellion y alçamiento se hefetuase y que se tuviese Entendido que otros lo hazian y no el.

xviii° Yten si saben que con el mesmo disinio y determinaçion que El dicho Marquez tenia para hefetuar El dicho Alçamiento y Rebelion desimulava con el negoçio, diziendo a algunos frailes e A otras Personas que se tratava de algunas niñerias generalmente E que no Abia de que hazer cavdal dellas por Entretener El negoçio y que si en alguna manera viniese a notiçia de los oydores que solamente tuviesen creydo lo que el dicho Marques dezia por tenellos Engañados y desvelados para que despues mas A su salbo se hefetuase.

xix Yten si saben que tratando El dicho Balthasar de Aguilar E Agustin de Villanueva con el dicho Marquez que se hazia ynformaçion por [*188v*] Esta Real Abdiençia sobre el dicho Alçamiento e Rebellion Respondio el dicho Marques no creais que se haga ynformaçion porque no se puede saber cossa ninguna y si la hizieren o prendieren alguno se hefetuara El negoçio E por Estas Açoteas con gran façilidad llamare personas que maten los oydores.

xx Yten si saben que el dicho Marquez Estando En España y pasando por el Reyno de Françia trato con el Rey de Françia que enbiase soldados A la punta de Santa

said was made up, since in some way what was being discussed about the said uprising and rebellion was already known, and the said Marqués should not know that it had come from the said Pedro de Aguilar, the said Marqués asked him why he had revealed and told it to the said friar, saying that he had also confessed and that they had absolved him and the others; and then the said Pedro de Aguilar replied, "Well, if your lordship found someone who would absolve him, they did not want to absolve me unless I told it to the oidores," and the said Marqués answered him, "Look at the poor little man, how he had good intentions, he let himself go with the friar, revealing to him in his confession what he had in his heart and the friar made it public."

16. Further, whether they know that when the said Marqués became suspicious that the said Pedro de Aguilar had revealed the discussions mentioned above, he told him that it was a greater treason to expose one's friends who had trusted in him than if he had carried out the said rebellion and uprising which had been and was being considered against His Majesty.

17. Further, whether they know that even though the said Marqués knew of the said rebellion and uprising which was being discussed, he made every effort that it should be carried out without harm to him and that after it was completed they would make him king; so that the said Marqués knew of it, wanted it, incited it, and had the strong intention and will that the said rebellion and uprising should be carried out, but it was understood that others would do it and not he.

18. Further, whether they know that with the same design and determination which the said Marqués had to carry out the said uprising and rebellion, he dissembled with regard to the business, saying to some friars and other people that it was generally a matter of some childish ideas and there was no reason to make anything big out of them, in order to keep the matter going, and so that if it came to the knowledge of the oidores in any way, they would only have believed the statements which the said Marqués made in order to keep them deceived and off guard, so that later it might be carried off with less danger to himself.

19. Further, whether they know that while the said Baltasar de Aguilar and Agustín de Villanueva were discussing with the said Marqués the fact that an investigation was being made by this royal audiencia concerning the said uprising and rebellion, the said Marqués replied: "Don't believe that an investigation is being made, because it is not possible that anything is known, and if they do it or arrest anyone, the business will be carried out, and with great ease I will summon across these roofs people to kill the oidores."

20. Further, whether they know that while the said Marqués was in Spain and passed through the Kingdom of France, he discussed with the King of France that he should send soldiers to the Punta de Santa Elena and that from there they might carry on

Elena y que desde alli podrian tener comerçio y trato con Esta Nueva España A donde el dicho Marquez pensava de yr de proximo.

xxi   Yten si saben que Atento lo conthenido en las preguntas Antes desta quando en esta tierra se supo que Pero Melendes de Baldes Avia hecho castigo En los franceses questaban En la dicha punta de Santa Elena E tenido vitoria y tomado los navios y hecho otras muchas cosas en serviçio de su Magestad E se avia Apoderado En todo Ello y en el dicho puerto y puertos El dicho Marques se yntristeçio mucho dello no pudiendo desimular El desgusto que avia Resçebido tanto que lo notaron y sintieron los de su casa e fuera della por donde se tiene Entendido la Aliança y Amistad que tenia con el dicho Rey de Françia para que le diese favor E Ayuda En el Alçamiento desta tierra.

xxii   Yten si saben que el dicho Marques para hefetuar El dicho alçamiento y Rebelion tuvo tratos En Guathemala y se escrevia con muchas personas y jente de aquella tierra y particulares y encomenderos y tuvo cartas que quando En esta tieRa se hiziese el dicho Alçamiento Alla harian lo mesmo y le corresponderian con la hubidiençia y vasallaje como A Rey y Señor y dellos tuvo cartas E Avisos digan lo que saben.

xxiii   Yten si saben que Aviendo tratado El dicho Marques con las demas personas ARiba conthenidas el dicho Alçamiento theniendo notiçia que por Esta Real Abdiençia se tratava de hazer Ynformaçion y castigo confiado de su persona dixo que si alguna cosa se avia de tratar Avia de ser [*189*] contra el con todo Rigor y no contra otras Personas y que Asi le paresçia que se avia de hazer theniendo Entendido que contra el no se determinara la dicha Avdiençia y que no se Prosçediese contra los demas porque se encubriese El dicho Alçamiento y Rebelion y engañar A los señores presidente E oydores de la dicha avdiençia.

xxiiii°   Yten si saben que siendo partiçipe el dicho Diego Arias de Sotelo en el dicho Rebelion juntamente con el dicho Marquez El dia que se fue desta çibdad A la provinçia de Mechuacan a çiertos Pueblos de yndios E haziendas que alla tiene fue A la posada del dicho Marques A despedirse del y Abrasçandole El dicho Marques le dixo vaya v. m. señor Diego Arias nora buena que quando se oviere de hefetuar Aquel negoçio os dare Aviso dirigendo las dichas palabras A El dicho Alçamiento y Rebelion.

xxv   Yten si saben que demas de los contenidos ARiba con quien se Juntava el dicho Marques para hefetuar El dicho Rebelion lo comunicava con un Bernaldino Maldonado soldado de los del Peru que byvia en casa de Bernaldino Pacheco de Bocanegra vezino E Regidor de Mexico E con otros que se dezian los Pisarros que Ansimesmo Avian venido del Peru, personas Escandalosas delinquentes E Aparejadas para El dicho Rebelion.

commerce and trade with this New Spain where the said Marqués was thinking of going very soon.

21. Further, whether they know that, considering the content of the questions preceding this one, when it was known in this land that Pero Meléndez de Valdez [*Pedro Menéndez de Ávilés*] had inflicted punishment on the French who were on the said Punta de Santa Elena, and had gained a victory and taken the ships and done many other things in the service of His Majesty and had gained control of all of it and of the said port and ports, the said Marqués was very much saddened over it and was not able to hide the grief that he received from it, so much so that people inside and outside of his household noted and felt it, whence is understood the alliance and friendship which he had with the King of France so that he might give him favor and aid in the uprising in this land.

22. Further, whether they know that in order to bring about the said uprising and rebellion the said Marqués had dealings with Guatemala and carried on correspondence with many people of that land, both private individuals and encomenderos, and he received letters to the effect that when he carried out the said uprising in this land, they would do the same there, and they corresponded with him with the obedience and servitude as to a king and lord, and he received letters and reports from them; let them say what they know.

23. Further, whether they know that after the said Marqués had discussed the said uprising with the other persons mentioned above and when it had come to his attention that this royal audiencia was discussing the question of instituting an investigation and inflicting punishment, trusting in his own person, he said that if anything was to be treated, it should be against himself, with all rigor, and not against other people, and that it seemed to him that it should be done in this way, since he took it for granted that the said audiencia would not make a decision against him and that no action would be taken against the others because the said uprising and rebellion would be concealed and the lords president and oidores of the said audiencia would be deceived.

24. Further, whether they know that the said Diego Arias de Sotelo being a participant in the said rebellion together with the said Marqués, on the day that he left this city for the Province of Michoacán for certain towns of Indians and properties that he has there, he went to the residence of the said Marqués to tell him good-by, and when he embraced him, the said Marqués told him, "Go, my lord Diego Arias, it is well. When it is time to carry out that business, I will let you know," and he was directing his words to the said uprising and rebellion.

25. Further, whether they know that besides those mentioned above with whom the said Marqués was associated in order to carry out the said rebellion, he communicated it to a certain Bernaldino Maldonado, one of those soldiers from Peru who lived in the house of Bernaldino Pacheco de Bocanegra, freeholder and regidor of Mexico, and to others who were called the Pizarros, who had also come from Peru, scandalous and offensive persons, who were ready for the said rebellion.

xxvi Yten si saben que tratandose vn dia en casa de Francisco de Merida Regidor desta çibdad sobre la çitatoria que noteficaron Al dicho Marques dixo que no yria A España sobre el dicho negoçio y que Antes se dexaria hazer pedaços que yr Alla con yntinçion de adquirir Esta tierra para si y con voluntad del dicho Alçamiento y Rebelion.

xxvii Yten si saben que Estando vn dia el dicho Marques en casa de doña Ynes de Perea y asimesmo Ribadeneyra dixo El dicho Marques Juro A Diole que me huelgo que de una parte nos Rodeen françeses y por otra los soldados de la China y Estonçes dixo Ribadeneira, señor Abiendo tantas yslas para cada vno de los que fueren Avra la suya y se podra llamar Rey Entonçes Respondio el dicho Marquez, cada bno [*189v*] se ymagina rrey por donde dava A Entender querello El ser por donde se colixe su Animo y asi creen los testigos y tienen por çierto que de la Abundançia que tenia En el coraçon lo manifestava con la boca con el deseo de ser Rey y alçarse con esta tierra, Digan lo que saben.

xxviii° Yten si saben etc. que tratandose del dicho Alçamiento y Rebelion Entre el dicho Marquez y Alonso de Avila le dixo El dicho Marquez Al Alonso Davila que jente teneis para hefetuar Este negoçio Respondio El Alonso Davila que mucha Jente tenia A lo qual rreplico El dicho Marquez pues si Asi es yd y matad A los oydores que yo Aqui Estoy declarando muy bastantemente su prençipal yntento para se Alçar con Esta tierra digan lo que saben.

xxix Yten si saben etc. que estando malo don Pedro de Arellano ya difunto devdo muy sercano del dicho Marquez yendolo a ver por Razon de su enfermedad le dixo que se levantase y que se entenderia en la cofradia de San Ypolito y rrespondiendo El dicho don Pedro A que proposito trataua de Aquella cofradia el dicho Marquez le dixo que no hera Aquella la cofradia sino otra de que se trataua que hera de çierta Jente para el dicho Rebelion y alçamiento y asi el dicho Marques hablaua por figuras y si fiadamente.

xxx Yten si saben que con el deseo que el dicho Marquez tenia de se alçar con esta tierra con quien prençipalmente trataua del negoçio sobre la Justiçia della hera con frai Luis Cali fraile de la horden de señor San Francisco y fue vna noche por miedo que no fuese sentido A vn poblesuelo sujeto de la çiudad de Tezquco A donde trato del dicho negoçio.

xxxi Yten si saben que el dicho fraile dezia Al dicho Marquez y a los demas de la dicha liga y confederaçion que Abia De publicar por los pulpitos y predicarlo Estando hefetuado El dicho Rebelion questa tierra justamente pertenesçia al dicho Marques del Valle y que su padre la Abia ganado lo qual El dicho fraile comonico con el licenciado Espinoza de Ayala y con otras personas digan lo que saben.

[*190*] **xxxii** Yten si saben etc. que el dicho Marques del Valle procuraua y a

26. Further, whether they know that one day in the house of Francisco de Mérida, regidor of this city, when they were discussing the summons that they had served on the said Marqués, he said that he would not go to Spain concerning the said business and that he would rather let himself be cut to pieces than go there, and he did this with the intention of acquiring this land for himself and with the intention of carrying out the said uprising and rebellion.

27. Further, whether they know that one day when the said Marqués was in the house of Doña Inez de Perea, and likewise Rivadeneyra, the said Marqués said, "I swear to you by God that I am happy that on the one side we may be surrounded by the French and on the other by the soldiers of China," and then Rivadeneyra said, "Sir, since there are so many islands, for each one of those who went, each will have his own and can be called king," and then the said Marqués answered, "Everyone imagines himself king," whence he gave it to be understood that he wished to be such himself, and from this his intention is gathered, and thus the witnesses believe and hold for certain that his mouth manifested it from the abundance that he had in his heart, with the desire to be king and to rise up with this land; let them say what they know.

28. Further, whether they know etc., that when the said Marqués and Alonso de Ávila were discussing this said uprising and rebellion, the said Marqués asked Alonso de Ávila, "What men do you have in order to carry out this business," and Alonso de Ávila answered that he had many men, to which the said Marqués answered, "Well, if that is so, go and kill the oidores; I am here," revealing very adequately that his principal intention was to rise up with this land; let them say what they know.

29. Further, whether they know etc., that while Don Pedro de Arellano, a very close relative of the said Marqués, now deceased, was ill and the Marqués went to see him because of his illness, the Marqués told him that he should get up and should look into the matter of the Confraternity of Saint Hippolytus and when the said Don Pedro asked why he was talking about that confraternity, the said Marqués told him that that was not the confraternity that he was talking about but rather another, which was made up of certain people for the said rebellion and uprising, and the said Marqués spoke thus through figures and, indeed, trustingly.

30. Further, whether they know that in the desire that the said Marqués had of rising up with this land, the person with whom he principally discussed the justice of the affair was Fray Luis Cal of the Order of the Lord Saint Francis, and for fear of being seen, he went one night to a village, subject to the city of Texcoco, where he discussed the said affair.

31. Further, whether they know that the said friar told the said Marqués and the others of the said league and confederation that when the said rebellion had been carried out, he should publish and preach from the pulpits that this land justly belonged to the said Marqués del Valle and that his father had won it, and the said friar communicated this to the said Licentiate Espinosa de Ayala and to other persons; let them say what they know.

32. Further, whether they know etc., that the said Marqués del Valle, with the desire

procurado con deseo de ser Rey de husar de las serimonias Reales Ansi En querer hazer Estandartes rreales para los traer como Rey y señor y Asimesmo traer o tener vn sello grande y procuro Asimesmo quando salia fuera desta çibdad o quando caminava de traer vna lança Alta y derecha A manera de guion Digan los testigos lo que desto saben.

xxxiii Yten si saben que el dicho Marques pretendia que todos los desta çibdad lo Aconpañasen Asi los que no heran de su casa ni llevauan salarios ni gajes como si fueran sus criados diziendo que sino lo hazian los Avia de castigar y afrentar donde pretendia la superioridad y señorio desta tierra tanto que mucha Jente se escandalizo dello hasta los del cabildo desta çibdad.

xxxiiii° Yten si saben etc. que con el yntento que tenia de ser senor desta tierra tenia en poco las justiçias della y siendo obligado de las honrrar y fauoresçer no lo hazia Antes las ynjuriava y afrentaua y asi susçedio que siendo alcalde hordinario Jullian de Salazar veçino desta çibdad porque vna noche le quito las Armas A bnos criados suyos el dicho Marques junto A la plaça desta çibdad fue A dondo Estaua el dicho Jullian de Salazar y le dixo palabras muy Afrentosas siendo como es honbre honrrado comedido y muy paçifico sin dar ocasion alguna al dicho Marquez para ser ynjuriado y por fuerça le hizo boluer las Armas A los dichos sus criados haziendo Grandes Amenazas al dicho alcalde yendo El dicho Marquez Armado y con mucha gente que le Aconpañaba.

xxxv Yten si saben que el dicho Marques en las juntas y trasças que hazia dezia que se Avia de ayudar del rrey de Françia y de Yngalaterra y enbiar sus enbaxadores y tener comerçio y contrataçion con los dichos rreynos porque con lo que trajesen dellos y de otros Estaria bien bastesçida esta tieRa y de lo que Esta produzia y la China y desta manera no tendria nesçeçidad de lo que se traxese de España.

[*190v*] **xxxvi** Yten Si saben que el dicho Marquez Juntamente con los demas sus consortes dezia y publicava que hecho El dicho Alçamiento y apoderado en este rreyno para mas siguridad del ynbiaria A su Santidad su enbaxador con gran suma de dinero y vn gran presente para que le confirmase El rreino y le hiziese la Ynvistidura del y se la diese.

xxxvii Yten si saben que Baltasar de Aguilar A sido muy grande Amigo del dicho Marques y le dio vn cavallo Rozillo muy presçiado que valia dos mill pesos y el dicho Marquez le Enbio seteçientos y Asi mesmo el dicho Baltasar de Aguilar tenia cuydado que los cauallos del dicho Marques Estuviesen bien tratados E ynpuestos como honbre que sabia bien conosçer como se Avian de tratar cavallos lo qual no hiziera el dicho Balthasar de Aguilar sino hera por la Estrecha Amistad que tenia con el dicho Marquez y asi El dicho Marquez le tenia En mucho y lo preferia a otros muchos Amigos que entrauan en su casa Ansi en el Asiento de su mesa quando comia como En otras cosas donde se conosçia la honrra que le hazia.

to be king, has endeavored to use the royal ceremonies, both in wanting to make royal standards in order to bear them as a king and lord and also in carrying or keeping a great seal, and also when he went outside of this city or when he traveled, he managed to have a lance carried, raised and straight out, after the manner of a royal standard; let the witnesses say what they know about this.

33. Further, whether they know that the said Marqués had pretensions that everyone in this city should accompany him, even those who were not members of his household nor received salaries or wages, as though they were his servants, saying that unless they did it, he would punish and insult them, and in this he made pretensions to the superiority and lordship of this land, so much so that many people were shocked at it, even the members of the cabildo of this city.

34. Further, whether they know etc., that with the intention that he had of being the lord of this land, he showed little respect for its justices and, although he was obliged to honor and favor them, he did not do it, but rather he injured and insulted them; and thus it happened that one night because Julián de Salazar, alcalde ordinario and freeholder of this city, took away the arms from some servants of his, the said Marqués, who was near the plaza of this city, went to where the said Julián de Salazar was and spoke very insulting words to him, even though he is an honorable man, gentle and very peaceful, without giving any occasion at all to the said Marqués for such an insult; and by force the Marqués made him give the arms back to his said servants, making great threats to the said alcalde; and the said Marqués and many of the people who accompanied him were armed.

35. Further, whether they know that in the meetings and plans that the said Marqués made, he said that he would need the assistance of the Kings of France and England and would have to send his ambassadors and maintain commerce and trade with the said realms because with what they would bring from them and other kingdoms and with what this land and China would produce, this land would be well supplied, and in this way it would not need what was brought from Spain.

36. Further, whether they know that the said Marqués, together with his other partners, said and made public that once the said uprising was completed and they had gained power in this kingdom, for greater security he would send an ambassador to His Holiness with a great amount of money and a large present so that he would confirm him in the kingdom and make the investiture of it for him and give him the investiture.

37. Further, whether they know that Baltasar de Aguilar has been a very good friend of the said Marqués and that he gave him a very prized roan horse which was worth two thousand pesos and the said Marqués sent him seven hundred pesos; and likewise the said Baltasar de Aguilar saw to it that the horses of the said Marqués were well treated and stabled, as a man who knew well about the care of horses; and the said Baltasar de Aguilar would not have done this if it had not been for the close friendship which he had with the said Marqués, and the said Marqués valued him very highly and preferred him to many other friends who entered his house, both in his seating at the table when he ate there and in other things; and from this is known the honor which he showed him.

xxxviii° Yten si saben que el mesmo dia que se prendio El dicho Marques el dicho Baltasar de Aguilar Andava En vn cauallo del dicho Marques continuando la Amistad Antigua por manera que entre le dicho Marques y el dicho Baltasar de Aguilar no Avia odio ni henemistad liviana ni capital.

xxxix Yten si saben que Asimesmo tenia el dicho Marquez grande Amistad con Agustin de Villanueva y Alonso de Servantes su hermano los quales Entravan muchas vezes en casa del dicho Marques y lo Aconpañavan y tenian grande Amistad sin Aver lo contrario ni otro Rincor ni odio A lo menos que fuese capital ni hazer cavdal para fundar Enemistad.

xl Yten si saben que Asimesmo El dicho Baltasar de Aguilar no solamente con el dicho Marquez pero con sus hermanos thenia muy Estrecha amistad En tanto que si algun de[*191*]Vdo Suyo dezia mal del dicho Marquez se lo Reprehendia y los Atraia A su seruiçio.

xli Yten si saben que continuando o continuandose la dicha Amistad Entre el dicho Marquez del Valle y sus hermanos con el dicho Baltasar de Aguilar y Agustin de Villanueva En çierta fiesta y torneos que se hazian y estaua hordenada de hazer El dicho Agustin de Villanueva manthenia juntamente con don Martin Cortes hermano del dicho Marques El dicho torneo y el dicho Baltasar de Aguilar hera conpañero del dicho Marques En la quadrilla que el sacaba sin thener odio ni Enemistad los vnos con los otros ni los otros con los otros sino mucho bien y tratandose con mucha Afiçion Asi En obras como En palabras, digan los testigos lo que saben.

xlii Yten si saben que todo lo suso dicho Es publico y notorio y es publica boz y fama.

EL LIÇENÇIADO CONTRERAS Y GUEBARA [*rubrica*]

[*191v*] Ynterrogatorio del fiscal contra el Marques del Valle.

En xviii° de setiembre 1566. A la contraria parte. Por presentado y se Exsaminen Por antel secretario Sancho Lopez. [*rubrica de Sancho Lopez*]

En la çiudad de Mexico A diez y ocho dias del mes de setiembre de mill y quinientos y sesenta y seis años ante los señores presidente y oydores del audiencia Real de la Nueva España se leyo el ynteRogatorio de suso contenido presentado por el liçençiado Contreras y Guevara fiscal de su Magestad y por los dichos señores visto lo oveiron por presentado y mandaron que los testigos que por virtud del se ovieren de presentar los examine el secretario Sancho Lopez.

SANCHO LOPEZ DE AGURTO [*rubrica*]

38. Further, whether they know that on the same day when the said Marqués was arrested, the said Baltasar de Aguilar was riding on a horse of the said Marqués, continuing their long-standing friendship, so that between the said Marqués and the said Baltasar de Aguilar there was no hatred or enmity, either slight or mortal.

39. Further, whether they know that the said Marqués also had a great friendship with Agustín de Villanueva and Alonso de Cervantes, his brother, and they frequently entered the house of the said Marqués and accompanied them and had a great friendship with him, without anything of the contrary nor any rancor or hatred, at least not any that would be mortal or sufficient to form a basis for enmity.

40. Further, whether they know that the said Baltasar de Aguilar had a very close friendship not only with the said Marqués but also with his brothers, to such a degree that if any of his relatives said anything bad about the said Marqués, he would reprove him for it, and he attracted them to his service.

41. Further, whether they know that, continuing the said friendship of the said Marqués del Valle and his brothers with the said Baltasar de Aguilar and Agustín de Villanueva, in a certain fiesta and tournaments which were organized and carried out, the said Agustín de Villanueva entered the said tournament with Don Martín Cortés, brother of the said Marqués, and the said Baltasar de Aguilar was the companion of the said Marqués in the foursome with which he came out, without any of them having any enmity for the others but rather much good will, treating one another with great affection both in words and deeds; let the witnesses say what they know.

42. Further, whether they know that all of the abovesaid is public and well known and is a matter of public report and opinion.

LICENTIATE CONTRERAS Y GUEVARA [*rubic*]

Questionnaire of the prosecutor against the Marques del Valle

On September 18, 1566. To the contrary party. As presented and that they be examined in the presence of the secretary Sancho López. [*rubric of Sancho López*]

In the city of Mexico of the eighteenth day of the month of September of the year one thousand five hundred and sixty-six, before the lords president and oidores of the royal audiencia of the New Spain, the questionnaire contained above and presented by Licentiate Contreras y Guevara, prosecutor of His Majesty, was read, and when it was seen by the said lords, they accepted it as presented and commanded that the secretary Sancho López examine the witnesses who would be presented in virtue of it.

SANCHO LÓPEZ DE AGURTO [*rubric*]

[*192*] Segundo ynteRogatorio.

Muy poderoso señor

El liçençiado Çespedes De Cardenas vuestro fiscal en el pleito que trato con el Marques don Martin Cortes, digo que despues quel suso dicho paso a estas partes de Yndias para efeto de alçarse con esta tierra y señorio della negando a vuestra Real persona la obidiençia y fidilidad que como leal vasallo le deue para mejor lo efetuar procuro átribuyrse a si mesmo muchas preminençias de las que a vuestra Real persona pertenesçen e que los vasallos E criados se las guardasen y le tratasen como si el en efeto fuera señor vniversal desta tierra y acatandose de muy poderoso y pretendiendo por miedos ser obedeçido y haziendo cosas que solos los Reyes y señores acostunbran hacer en sus propios Reinos y tierras de lo qual se vee y entiende tener el suso dicho fabricado lo que agora tantas vezes trato y comunico y efetuara si no ubiera sido preso y para que lo suso dicho conste a vuestra Alteza suplico mande los testigos que presentare se exsaminen por estas preguntas [*a*]ñedidas.

1   Primeramente si sauen y ansi es publico quel dicho Marques despues que bino a esta çibdad de Mexico de los rreinos de Castilla todas las vezes que salia de su casa llebaua un paje a cauallo con una lança alta enarbolada y metido el quento della en una funda de cuero que yba colgando del arçon delantero y en lo neto una como bolsa de terçiopelo que pareçia hir coxida o çerrada y della pendia unas borlas de seda por la dicha lança que propiamente paresçia guion rreal y el dicho paxe llevaba vna çelada de haeçero en la cabeça y de esta manera el dicho Marques andaua por esta çibdad e yba a las casas Reales y entraba en ellas e caminaua y ansi salio a rreçibir al liçençiado Balderrama besitador al tiempo que en esta çibdad entro y porque el virrei don Luys de Belasco le enbio a mandar que hiziese quitar el dicho guion pues el llevaba el de su Magestad el dicho Marques se altero y se puso en terminos de desacatarse con el dicho birrei si el dicho liçençiado Balderrama no lo apaçiguara y rremediara digan etc.

2   Yten si saben quel dicho Marques dixo y publico que todos los vecinos desta çibdad de qualquier calidad le avian de bolver aconpanar topandole en las calles e hirse con el y a los que no lo hiziesen les habia de hazer dar de palos y afrentallos y matallos y para este efeto hizo tomar a sus [*s—canceled*] pajes espadas y traxo trasi criados suyos con palos en baxo de la capa e tubo nesçesidad para evitar este ynconviniente la çibdad y rregidores de juntarse en cavildo en dia estraordinario e tratar del rremedio dello y ansi fueron al vesitador a dalle quenta y el susodicho lo efetuara sino le fueran a la mano.

[*En distinta letra*] Va enmendado, sus y testado vna s [*rubrica*]

Second Questionnaire

VERY POWERFUL LORDS

I, Licentiate Céspedes de Cárdenas, your prosecutor in the suit which I am conducting with the Marqués Don Martín Cortés, say that after the abovesaid Marqués came to these regions of the Indies for the purpose of rebelling with this land and its overlordship, denying to your royal person the obedience and fidelity which he owes you as a loyal vassal, in order the better to carry it off, he attempted to attribute to himself many preeminences of the kind that pertain to your royal person, and he endeavored that his vassals and servants should observe them and treat him as though he were in effect the universal lord of this land, being esteemed as a very powerful person, trying to enforce obedience by fear, and doing other things which only the kings and lords are accustomed to do in their own realms and lands. From this it is seen and understood that the abovesaid Marqués had devised what he then discussed and communicated so many times, and he would have put it into effect if he had not been arrested. And so that the abovesaid may be clearly evident, I beseech Your Highness to command that the witnesses whom I may present be examined by these added questions.

1. First, whether they know, and it is thus public, that the said Marqués, after he came to this city of Mexico from the realms of Castile, every time that he left his house took along a page on horseback with a tall lance raised and with the butt end of it placed in a leather sheath which was hanging from the saddlebow and on the bare part of it there was a kind of purse of velvet which seemed to be gathered or closed, and from it hung some silk tassels along the lance, which appeared to be properly a royal standard, and the said page wore a steel helmet on his head; and in this manner the said Marqués went through this city and went to the government buildings and entered them and traveled, and thus he went out to receive the inspector, Licentiate Valderrama, at the time when he entered this city; and, because the Viceroy Don Luis de Velasco sent him a command that he should remove the said standard in consideration of the fact that the Viceroy was carrying the standard of His Majesty, the said Marqués was upset and was on the verge of treating the said Viceroy with disrepect if the said Licentiate Valderrama had not quieted him and remedied the situation; let them say, etc.

2. Further, whether they know that the said Marqués said and announced that all of the freeholders of this city, of whatever rank, would have to turn around and accompany him and go along with him when they met him in the street and that as to those who would not do it, he would have them beaten and insulted and killed; and for this reason he had his pages take swords, and behind him he brought his servants with clubs beneath their capes; and in order to avoid this problem it was necessary for the regidores of the city to meet in council on a special day and to discuss a solution of it; and so they went to the inspector to give him a report, and the abovesaid would have been put into effect if they had not been at hand.

[*In a different hand*] It is corrected "sus," and an "s" is marked out. [*rubric*]

[*192v*] **3** Yten si saben y ansi es publico quel dicho Marques hizo hazer un sello de plata del tamaño del de su Magestad y en el sus armas y esculpido un coronel y sin ser lo se yntitulaba de duque en un letrero que alRededor del dicho escudo se puso el qual hazia para sellar y despachar con sus negocios y lo hiziera si Ortuño de Ybarra fator no se le tomara al tiempo que lo llevaua a quyntar y el virrery que a la sazon hera no se le mandara detener e su Magestad por su Real çedula mando que no vsase del.

4 Yten si sauen quel dicho Marques hizo e junto gente de ynfanteria en esta çibdad de Mexico y con vanderas tendidas y la gente puesta en horden de guerra salio desta çibdad a rreçibir a la Marquesa su muger que pasaua de un pueblo a otro a vna legua desta çiudad de Mexico.

5 Yten si saben e ansi es publico quel dicho Marques e su muger en esta çibdad quando yuan a misa Ansi a la yglesia mayor como a los monesterios se hazian llevar sitial con sus doseles de terçiopelo y almohadas de lo mesmo segun lo acostumbravan las personas Reales e sus visorreyes digan.

6 Yten si saben que porque una noche Julian de Salazar Alcalde hordinario quito vnas espadas a vnos criados suyos el dicho Marques se armo e con muchos criados salio de su casa en busca del dicho alcalde que andaua rrondando y le maltrato de palabras y le dixo que en esta çibdad no conoçian al Marques del Valle e quan poderoso hera quel les haria algun dia quen sus camas le soñasen y ansi le hizo que les bolviese las armas a los dichos sus criados maltratando al dicho alcalde digan lo que zerca desto paso.

7 Yten si saben que para baptizar su hijo el dicho Marques hizo hazer desde la puerta de su casa hasta la yglesia mayor vn tablado mas alto que vn honbre de manera que para subir el el era por escalones e por otros tales deçendian en la yglesia e por el dicho tablado llevaron al hijo del dicho Marques a batizar a la dicha yglesia y estaua todo çercado de vanderas y estandartes de sus armas y de sus pueblos desde su casa hasta la yglesia mayor.

8 Yten si saben que quando la Marquesa su muger entro en esta çibdad dio horden e procuro que la Real avdiençia y el arçobispo e yglesia e çibdad la saliesen a rreçibir como en efeto salieron media legua desta çibdad y la aconpañaron y entraron con ella digan.

9 Yten si saben que al tiempo que los desta Real avdiençia ynbiaron a llamar al dicho Marques para le prender como le prendieron en las casas Reales estaba con el el liçençiado [*rubrica*] [*193*] Espinosa de Ayala testigo de la sumaria ynformaçion y estavan a la dicha ora tratando de cosas del dicho alçamiento y dando horden como se avian de hazer los estandartes e banderas para el dicho efeto.

10 Yten si saben quel dicho Marques publico por esta çibdad que tenia vna carta

3. Further, whether they know, and it is thus public, that the said Marqués had a silver seal made of the same size as that of His Majesty, with his arms and a crown engraved on it, and in the inscription which was placed around the said coat of arms he entitled himself duke although he was not such, and he made it in order to seal and send with his affairs; and he would have done so if Ortuño de Ibarra, the factor, had not taken it from him when he took it to pay the duty on it and if the Viceroy at that time had not commanded that it be kept back from him and His Majesty by his royal decree commanded that he should not use it.

4. Further, whether they know that the said Marqués organized a band of foot soldiers in this city of Mexico and, with unfurled banners and the men placed in the formation of war, he went out of this city to receive his wife, the Marquesa, who was passing from one town to another about a league from this city of Mexico.

5. Further, whether they know, and it is thus public, that when the said Marqués and his wife went to Mass in this city, whether in the cathedral or in the friaries, they had a seat of honor brought with its canopies of velvet and cushions of the same material, in the same way that royal persons and their Viceroys are accustomed to do; let them say.

6. Further, whether they know that because Julián de Salazar, the alcalde ordinario, took away their swords from some of his servants one night, the said Marqués armed himself and left his house with many of his servants in search of the said alcalde who was making his rounds, and he mistreated him with words and told him that in this city they did not know the Marqués del Valle and how powerful he was and that someday he would make them dream of him in their beds; and thus he made him give back their weapons to his said servants, abusing the said alcalde; let them say what happened concerning this.

7. Further, whether they know that for the baptism of his son the said Marqués had a scaffold built from the door of his house to the cathedral, higher than a man, so that one had to go up on it by stairs and to descend by others in the church, and along the said structure they carried the son of the said Marqués to the said church to be baptized, and it [*or he?*] was completely surrounded with banners and standards of his coat of arms and of his towns from his house to the cathedral.

8. Further, whether they know that when the Marquesa, his wife, entered this city, he gave an order and saw to it that the royal audiencia and the archbishop and the cabildos of the cathedral and city should go out to receive her, as in reality they did go out for half a league from this city and accompanied her and entered with her; let them say.

9. Further, whether they know that at the time that the members of this royal audiencia summoned the said Marqués in order to imprison him, as they did imprison him in the government houses, Licentiate Espinosa de Ayala, a witness in the summary investigation, was with him and at that said time they were discussing matters of the said uprising and determining how the standards and banners should be made for that purpose.

10. Further, whether they know that the said Marqués made known throughout this

de corte en que le avisauan que su Magestad no queria perpetuar esta tierra en los conquistadores e sus hijos y deçendientes y la mostro a muchas personas y la enbio al cavildo e ayuntamiento desta çibdad para efeto de yndignar a los suso dichos y quel dicho alçamiento se efetuase.

Otrosi a vuestra alteza suplico mande tomar su confision al dicho Marques y preguntalle las cosas suso dichas.

Otrosi a vuestra Alteza suplico mande se ponga en este proçeso vn treslado de la Real çedula de su Magestad que vino sobre el dicho sello y ansimesmo vn treslado del proçeso que se hizo quando el dicho Marques quito las armas al dicho Julian de Salazar alcalde de lo qual todo hago presentaçion e para ello el liçençiado Çespedes de Cardenas.

En la çibdad de Mexico a veinte e nueve dias del mes de novienbre de mill e quinientos y sesenta e seys años ante los señores presidente e oydores del avdiençia Real de la Nueba España se leyo la peticion destrotra parte contenida e por los dichos señores vista mandaron que se ponga en el proçeso Joan SeRano escriuano.

Corregido con el original questa en el Rollo de peticiones.

GORDIAN CASASANO [rublica]

[Interrogatorio del Marques del Valle]

[226]   MUY PODEROSO SEÑOR

A los testigos que son o fueren Presentados Por parte De don Martin Cortes Marques del Valle en el pleyto que contra el trata el licenciado Contreras vuestro fiscal sobre lo de que le tiene acusado pido y suplico a vuestra Alteza se les Hagan las preguntas siguientes y Por ellas se esaminen.

Primeramente si conocen Al dicho Marques y al dicho fiscal y al licenciado Balderrama Del consejo rreal de su Magestad E Visitador general que fue desta Nueua España y a don Luis de Velasco y Agustin de Villanueua y a Baltasar de Aguilar y Alonso de Ceruantes y El licenciado Espinosa y a Pedro de Aguilar y a don Baltasar de Quesada y a don Pedro de Quesada Denunciadores y Personas que En esta causa dieron memorias contra el dicho Marques y otras personas y si conocen Al factor Hortuño de Ybarra y a Jhoan de Samano alguazil mayor Desta ciudad y a don Sancho Sanchez de Muñon maestre escuela de la yglesia catredal della y a Francisco de Morales rrelator que fue En esta rreal avdiencia y si conoçieron al Virrey don Luis de Velasco y si tienen noticia de la causa y rrazon sobre que a sido y es este pleyto digan lo que saben.

city that he had a letter from the court in which they informed him that His Majesty did not wish to perpetuate this land in the conquerors and their children and descendants [*i.e. to make the encomiendas perpetually inheritable*], and he showed it to many people and sent it to the cabildo and municipal government of this city, for the purpose of angering the abovesaid people and so that the said uprising would be carried out.

Moreover, I entreat Your Highness that you command that a confession be taken from the said Marqués and that he be asked the abovesaid things.

Moreover, I entreat Your Majesty that you command that there be placed in this trial record a copy of the royal decree of His Majesty which came concerning the said seal and likewise a copy of the suit which was conducted when the said Marqués took away the arms from the said alcalde Julián de Salazar, and I make presentation of all of it for this purpose. Licentiate Céspedes de Cárdenas.

In the city of Mexico on the twenty-ninth day of the month of November of the year one thousand five hundred and sixty-six, before the lords president and oidores of the royal audiencia of New Spain, the petition of this other party was read as incorporated above, and when it had been seen by the said lords, they commanded that it be placed in the proceedings. Juan Serrano, notary.

Corrected with the original, which is in the roll of petitions.

GORDIÁN CASASANO [*rubric*]

Questionnaire of the Marqués del Valle

VERY POWERFUL LORD

I ask and entreat Your Highness that the witnesses who are or may be presented by the party of Don Martín Cortés, Marqués del Valle, in the suit which the Licentiate Contreras, your prosecutor, is conducting against him concerning the matter about which he has accused him, be asked the following questions and be examined according to them.

First, if they know the said Marqués and the said prosecutor and Licentiate Valderrama of the Royal Council of His Majesty and former Inspector General of this New Spain and Don Luis de Velasco and Agustín de Villanueva and Baltasar de Aguilar and Alonso de Cervantes and Licentiate Espinosa and Pedro de Aguilar and Don Baltasar de Quesada and Don Pedro de Quesada, denouncers and persons who gave statements in this case against the said Marqués and other persons, and if they know the Factor Ortuño de Ibarra and Juan de Sámano, alguacil mayor of this city, and Don Sancho Sánchez de Muñón, maestrescuela [*high-ranking member of the chapter of canons*] of the cathedral church of the city, and Francisco de Morales, formerly relator in this royal audiencia, and whether they knew the Viceroy Don Luis de Velasco and whether they have knowledge of the cause and reason concerning which this suit has been and is being conducted; let them say what they know.

Si saben etc. cren Vieron oyeron dezir que quando Al dicho Marques por prouision de su Magestad se notifico la demanda que en el rreal Consejo de Yndias por El fiscal se le auia puesto mostro muy buen senblante sin apasionarse y dio a Entender que estaua muy confiado De que su Magestad y los del dicho su Real Consejo Entendida y sabida la Verdad de su justiçia le harian merced y se la guardarian y que se sabria la rrelaçion siniestra quel dicho Visorrey contra el aVia hecho En que parecio aVer fundado El dicho fiscal su demanda y que En qualquier suçeso quel pleyto tubiese y aVnque quedase con sola la capa y la espada aVia de seruir a su Magestad y morir por su seruicio En quanto se ofreçiese digan lo que saben.

Si saben etc. que AViendo se dicho y publicado en esta ciudad Averse despachado Vna rreal cedula açerca de ynpedir la tercera sucesion en las [*226v*] encomiendas de yndios muchas Personas sintieron dello gran pena y se ynquietaron y desasosegaron En general Diziendo palabras de descontento y sentimiento y El dicho Marques procuro por todas las Vias posibles de les amansar y quietar dandoles A Entender que la rreal persona les haria toda merced ynformado de la Verdad y que los señores oydores desta rreal aVdiencia y los del cabildo escribirian E ynformarian de lo que conViniese y no contento con esto el dicho Marques dio quenta dello al dicho señor licenciado Balderrama Visitador y le rrogo muy mucho que hablase todos los Vezinos que pudiese animandolos y poniendoles grande esperança de que su Magestad lo rremediaria y que ydo El a los rreynos de Castilla lo procuraria y asi hablo El dicho señor Visitador a muchas personas y se quietaron Digan lo que saben.

Si saben etc. que Assimismo El dicho Marques Procuro que los del dicho cabildo y personas que tenian pueblos de yndios En Encomienda Enbiasen a los dichos rreynos Vn procurador con poderes bastantes que por todos hablase y procurase con su Magestad y los de su rreal consejo El bien desta tierra y Vezinos españoles della y soliçito a muchas personas que para Ello se hubiese de hazer a su Magestad ayudasen de sus haziendas y trato con las Dichas personas que nombrasen y Elijiesen a don Martin Cortes su hermano y El dicho Marques prometio de su parte que ayudaria de su hazienda digan lo que saben.

Si saben etc. que demas de lo que dicho es En la pregunta Antes desta El dicho Marques scriuio a Francisco de Eraso secretario del dicho rreal consejo y del Estado dandole rrason del dicho general descontento y de otras cossas que conVenian al rreal seruiçio para que por su parte hablase con la rreal persona de su Magestad boluiendo por los desta tierra y que les hiziese merced digan lo que saben.

Si saben etc. que con lo que dicho es en las Preguntas Antes desta El dicho general descontento se aplaco y çeso y como despues algunas personas en particular

If they know, etc., believe, saw, or heard it said that when the said Marqués was notified by a writ of His Majesty of the demand which the prosecutor had placed against him in the Council of the Indies, he showed a very good mien, without becoming disturbed; and he gave it to be understood that he was very confident that when His Majesty and the members of his Royal Council had understood and known the truth of his just rights, they would show him favor and maintain it toward him and that they would recognize the vicious report which the said viceroy had made against him, upon which the said fiscal appeared to have founded his demand, and that no matter what the outcome of the suit might be and even though he was left with only his cape and sword, he would have to serve His Majesty and die for his service insofar as that might present itself; let them say what they know.

If they know, etc., that after it had been said and made public in this city that a royal decree had been dispatched concerning the matter of preventing the third inheritance of the encomiendas of Indians, many people were very afflicted and disquieted and upset over it in general, speaking words of discontent and resentment, and the said Marqués tried by all means possible to calm and quiet them, giving them to understand that the royal person would show them every favor once he had been informed of the truth and that the lords oidores of this royal audiencia and the members of the cabildo should write to him and inform him of what would be most fitting; and not content with this, the said Marqués gave an account of it to the said Lord Inspector Licentiate Valderrama and begged him very strongly that he should speak with as many of the freeholders as possible, encouraging them and giving them great hope that His Majesty would remedy it and that when he had returned to the realms of Castile he should try to bring it about; and so the lord inspector spoke to many people and they calmed down; let them say what they know.

If they know, etc., that likewise the said Marqués brought it about that the members of the cabildo and persons who had towns of Indians in encomienda should send an attorney to the said realms with adequate powers of attorney, who might speak for them all and intervene with His Majesty and the members of his Royal Council concerning the welfare of this land and of its Spanish freeholders; and he solicited from many people that they should help His Majesty with their properties for what would have to be done regarding this, and he discussed with the said persons that they should name and choose Don Martín Cortés, his brother; and the said Marqués promised that for his part he would help from his income; let them say what they know.

If they know, etc., that besides what was stated in the question preceding this one, the said Marqués wrote to Francisco de Eraso, secretary of the said Royal Council and of the State, giving him a report of the said general discontent and of other things which were becoming for the royal service, so that for his part he might speak with the royal person of His Majesty, taking the part of the people of this land and requesting that His Majesty favor them; let them say what they know.

If they know, etc., that as a result of what has been said in the questions preceding this one, the said general discontent was calmed and ceased; and, since some individ-

mostraron ynquietud y El dicho Marques lo supo y tubo noticia dello procuro
que lo supiesen los dichos señores Visitador E oydores y para los aVisar pareciendole
que por su calidad no lestaria bien yr lo a dezir llamo al padre fray Miguel De
AlVarado Vicario general de la orden [227] De señor San Agustin y le auiso De
todo Ello y con su aViso El dicho fray Miguel de Alvarado lo fue a dezir y dixo
a los dichos señores visitador E oydores y la persona En quien mas se sentia en
el dicho tiempo la dicha ynquietud Era El dicho Baltasar de Aguilar Digan lo
que saben.

vii Si saben etc. que Asimismo El dicho Marques quando Pasaba lo que dicho
es En las preguntas antes desta y conoçia de algunas otras personas algun descontento
De lo que se aVia dicho de la dicha çedula que dezian proybir la terçera suçesion
les procuraua y Procuro quietar y sosegar poniendoles buenas esperanças de las
merçedes que la Real persona haria a todos los que En estas partes le aVian
serbido y serbian y pareciendole que las palabras que las dichas personas dezian
y sentimiento que mostrauan Era de poca sustançia trato con fray Diego de
Olarte prouinçial de la orden del bienauenturado San Francisco Hombre de muy
santa bida y largo curso y espiriençia y que a que rreside En esta Nueua España
mas de quarenta años lo que devia hazer y El dicho fray Diego de Olarte le
aconsejo que bastaua aplacar segun esta dicho a las dichas personas y Enbiar
a dezir a los dichos Visitador E oydores lo que dixo Al dicho fray Miguel De
Aluarado con el propio fray Miguel y con El dicho prouinçial Digan lo que saben.

viii° Si saben etc. que Por ser El dicho fray Diego De Olarte de la calidad y
Vida En la pregunta antes desta rreferido los Virreyes y gouernadores que an
sido En esta Nueua España [*le — canceled*] comunicaban con el las cosas muy
arduas y del gouierno Della y por espiriencia de lo que sucedio En los consejos
que les daua se conoçio aVer Acertado en lo que con su pareçer hazian y
hordenaVan digan lo que saben.

ix Si saben etc. que antes quel dicho señor Visitador licenciado Balderrama se
partiese desta çiudad para yrse a los rreynos de Castilla se dixo al dicho Marques
que en el pueblo de Tezcuco se abia dicho quel dia que en cassa del dicho Hortuño
de Ybarra se hazia y hizo la fiesta de la tornaboda del dicho Alonso de Cerbantes
y la hija de don Diego de Guebara En vn torneo los que torneasen se alçarian
con la tierra y quel dicho Baltasar de Aguilar seria maestre de campo y En
sabiendolo El dicho Marques [227v] Dio dello Luego notiçia Al dicho señor
Visitador E hizo que los Propios que al dicho Marques se la auian dado se la
diesen al dicho señor Visitador y asi se la Dieron y por diVulgarse y Publicarse
lo que dicho es çeso de hazerse El dicho torneo Digan lo que saben.

x Si saben etc. que Por El mes de Hebrero Pasado deste año de sesenta y seis
El dicho Marques Determino de yrse desta ciudad a la Villa de Tuluca de su

ual persons later gave evidence of disquiet and the said Marqués knew of it, he saw to it that the said lords inspector and oidores should know of it; and in order to inform them of it, since it seemed to him that because of his rank it would not be good for him to go to speak of it, he called Father Fray Miguel de Alvarado, Vicar General of the Order of the Lord Saint Augustine, and informed him of all of it; and as a result of his warning the said Fray Miguel de Alvarado went to speak of it, and he told the said lords inspector and oidores; and the person in whom the said disquiet was most evident during the said time was the said Baltasar de Aguilar; let them say what they know.

7. If they know, etc., that likewise, when that which has been stated in the preceding questions happened, and the said Marqués knew from some other persons something of the discontent concerning what had been said about the said decree which they said would prohibit the third inheritance, he tried to quiet and pacify them, giving them good expectations of the favors which the royal person would show to all those who had served and would serve him in these parts; and, since it seemed to him that the words which the said persons spoke and the feeling which they expressed were of little consequence, he discussed what he should do with Fray Diego de Olarte, Provincial of the Order of the Blessed Saint Francis, a man of very holy life and of great age and experience, who has lived in this New Spain for more than forty years; and the said Fray Diego de Olarte advised him that it was enough to calm the said people, as has been said, and to notify the said inspector and oidores of what he had said to the said Fray Miguel de Alvarado by way of the same Fray Miguel and the said provincial; let them say what they know.

8. If they know, etc., that because the said Fray Diego de Olarte is a man of the character and life expressed in the question preceding this one, the viceroys and governors who have served in this New Spain conferred with him regarding the most difficult matters regarding its government; and from the experience of what has happened as a result of the counsels which he gave them, it is known that they have struck the mark in what they have done or ordained with his advice; let them say what they know.

9. If they know, etc., that before the said Lord Inspector Licentiate Valderrama left this city in order to go to realms of Castile, the said Marqués was told that it had been said in the town of Texcoco that on the day when they celebrated the day after the wedding of the said Alonso de Cervantes and the daughter of Don Diego de Guevara in the house of the said Ortuño de Ibarra, those who were riding in a tournament would rebel with the land and that the said Baltasar de Aguilar would be the maestre de campo; and when the said Marqués knew of it, he immediately gave notice of it to the said lord inspector, and he saw to it that the communications which had been given to the said Marqués should be given to the said lord inspector, and they were given to him; and because what has been said was divulged and made public, the said tournament was not held; let them say what they know.

10. If they know, etc., that during the month of February past of this this year of sixty-six, the said Marqués determined to leave this city for the town of Toluca in his

Estado y para Ello mando adereçar la cassa de la dicha villa y Enbio muncha parte de su rrecamara y la demas Estaua ya liada y cargada para Enbiar y El dicho Marques y la Marquesa su muger aparejados Para yrse digan lo que saben.

xi Si saben etc. que sabiendo El dicho señor Visitador licenciado Balderrama como El dicho Marques Estaua De partida Para su marquesado como se contiene En la pregunta antes desta y que se auia de yr En partiendose El dicho señor Visitador Desta tierra El dicho señor Visitador con los demas señores oydores Desta rreal avdiençia le rrogaron con mucha importunaçion que no se fuese y se Estubiese quedo En esta dicha ciudad Para Estar mas presto en lo que se ofreciese al rreal seruicio y El dicho Marques lo obedeçio y huVo por bien E hizo tornar las dichas azemilas Digan lo que saben.

xii Si saben etc. que Assimismo El dicho Marques pretendio quel dicho señor licenciado Balderrama no se fuese desta dicha ciudad y Nueua España ni dexase Esta tierra Hasta que Viniese a Ella El Visorrey que se espera porque yendose antes las personas que hubiesen tenido algun mal yntento no se declarasen mas y se Viniesen a desVergonçar y causar algun escandalo y alboroto y esta diligençia con El dicho señor Visitador hizo El dicho Marques muchas Vezes por si y por otras personas Digan lo que saben.

xiii Si saben etc. que En Vn nabio que partio desta Nueua España seis meses poco mas o menos antes que la dicha flota y En la misma flota el dicho Marques Enbio poder bastante a Diego Ferrer su ayo que fue que rreside En corte de su Magestad para tratar con la rreal persona de que le hiziese merced de le dar En los rreynos de Castilla en trueque de su marquesado la rrenta y Vasallos que le pareciese aVnque fuese la mitad menos Digan lo que saben.

[228] **xiiii°** Si saben que Assimismo En la Dicha flota Enbio El dicho Marques a los dichos rreynos de Castilla treynta mill castellanos Poco mas o menos sin otros mas de Veynte e cinco mill que pago aca a personas a quien deVia y al parte del dote de doña Jhoana Cortes su hermana Digan lo que saben.

xv Si saben etc. que partido El dicho señor Visitador Desta dicha ciudad El dicho Marques le scriuio dandole rrelacion y notiçia De palabras que algunas personas aVian dicho De ynquietud y desasosiego y la carta le alcanço En la ciudad De los Angeles y de alli le rrespondio El dicho señor Visitador con otra letra y carta que le enbio Digan lo que saben.

xvi Si saben etc. que quando Algunas Perssonas En esta dicha ciudad con El dicho Marques trataban de que otras andauan alteradas y desasosegadas y que se temian De algun alboroto El dicho Marques se les mostraua y mostro muy leal y seruidor De su Magestad y les dezia quel Rey Era su gallo y que En su seruicio aVra de morir Animando y Exortando a los demas aquiesen lo mesmo digan lo que saben.

xvii Si saben etc. que Despues quel dicho Marques del Valle don Martin Cortes

estate, and for this purpose he commanded that his house in the said town be set in order and he sent a great part of his household furniture there and the rest was already tied up and loaded in order to send it, and the said Marqués and his wife the Marquesa were ready to leave; let them say what they know.

11. If they know etc. that when the said Lord Inspector Licentiate Valderrama knew that the said Marqués was on the point of leaving for his marquisate, as is mentioned in the question preceding this one, and that he had to go, when the said lord inspector was leaving this land, he, with the other lords oidores of this royal audiencia, begged him with great insistence that he should not leave but that he should stay in this said city in order to be more at hand for whatever might arise for the royal service; and the said Marqués obeyed and accepted it as good and had the said pack animals brought back; let them say what they know.

12. If they know, etc., that likewise the said Marqués sought to keep the said Licentiate Valderrama from leaving this said city and New Spain and from departing from this said land until the Viceroy who was expected should arrive, because if he should leave beforehand, the persons who might have had some bad intention would no longer be exposed and they might come to act shamelessly and to cause some scandal or public disturbance; and the said Marqués made these said efforts with the said lord inspector many times both of himself and through other persons; let them say what they know.

13. If they know, etc., that in a ship which left this New Spain six months, more or less, before the said fleet, and in the fleet itself, the said Marqués sent an adequate power of attorney to Diego Ferrer, his former tutor, who resides in the court of His Majesty, in order that he might deal with the royal person that he should do him the favor of giving him in the realms of Castile the income and vassals which would seem good to him in exchange for his marquisate, even though it were a half less; let them say what they know.

14. If they know that likewise in the same fleet the said Marqués sent to the said realms of Castile thirty thousand castellanos, more or less, besides another twenty-five thousand which he paid here to people to whom he owed them and to the account of the dowry of his sister Doña Juana Cortés; let them say what they know.

15. If they know, etc., that after the said lord inspector had left this city, the said Marqués wrote to him, giving him a report and information concerning the words of disquiet and discontent that some people had spoken, and the letter caught up with him in the City of the Angels [*Puebla*], and from there the said lord inspector answered with another letter which he sent to him; let them say what they know.

16. If they know, etc., that when some people in this city discussed with the said Marqués the fact that others were going around disturbed and dissatisfied and that they were afraid of some public disturbance, the said Marqués showed himself as a very loyal servant of His Majesty and told them that the King was his leader and that he would die in his service, animating and exhorting the others that they should agree to the same thing; let them say what they know.

17. If they know, etc., that after the said Marqués del Valle, Don Martín Cortés,

Vino de los dichos rreynos de Castilla A Esta çiudad De Mexico y Nueua España
de ordinario En ella a tenido y tubo y tiene muchos Emulos y Enemigos y se a
conoçido y sabido del aVer procurado pocos o ningunos amigos y hordinariamente
Entre muchas personas se a murmurado y murmuraua del poco cuydado que tenia
en procurar amistades y se lo tenian y tubieron a mal porque En ello se Hazia
y hizo malquisto con los mal [*sic — mas*] de la tierra digan lo que saben.

xviii°   Si saben etc. que la noche En quel Dicho Alonso DaVila Aluarado En casa
del dicho Marques hizo con otras personas En abitos de yndios la fiesta En que se
hallo El dicho señor Visitador fue dicho al dicho señor Visitador que la dicha fiesta
se hazia para causar algun motin y alboroto y El dicho señor Visitador lo dixo al
dicho Marques El qual se armo y hizo que se armasen sus hermanos y çiertos criados
del dicho Marques y otras personas y todos Estubieron aconpañando el dicho señor
Visitador hasta que se acauo la çena y rregozijo y se fue a su posada sin aVer abido
senal ni muestra de do se pudiese colejir lo que asi se dezia aVerse dicho al dicho
señor visitador digan lo que saben.

[*228v*]**xix**   Si saben etc. que todo El tiempo quel dicho señor Visitador Balderrama
Residio En esta ciudad De Mexico y Nueua España huso de su juridicion y entendia
En los negocios de gouernacion y justicia que le pareçia y se hallaua todas las Vezes
que queria en los rreales acuerdos y presidia y presidio en ellos Despues de la muerte
del dicho Visorrey don Luis de Velasco digan lo que saben.

xx   Si saben etc. que Pocos dias despues quel dicho Marques Vino de los rreynos
de Castilla antes De Entrar En esta dicha ciudad lescriuio Gonçalo Çerezo alguazil
mayor desta corte Vna carta Por la qual En efeto le persuadia que ganase muchas
Voluntades y que ganandolas haria todo lo que quiesiese En esta tierra y le acudirian
y que no lo haziendo seria solo y Estaria malquisto, El dicho Marques le rrespondio
scriuiendole quel no Venia a ganar Voluntades sino A seruir al rrey Y a sus ministros
y otras palabras En que daua A Entender Estar muy libre y apartado de todo genero
de querer ganar ni grangear Voluntades digan todo lo que saben que En la Vna y
otra carta se contenia.

xxi   Si saben etc. que dende que asi El dicho Marques bino A Esta tierra de los
rreynos de Castilla que puede aVer quatro años poco mas o menos sienpre Y a la
contina se a tratado muy llanamente y con muy poco acompañamiento no teniendo
mas criados de los mas necesarios a su seruiçio y cassa y ordinariamente Estubo desa-
perçibido de armas y tanto que a abido y ay muchos Vezinos particulares desta ciudad
que tienen y an tenido muchas mas armas y nunca menos criados ni armas tubo
que de vn año A Esta parte digan lo que saben.

xxii   Si saben etc. quel dicho Marques ydo El dicho señor Visitador muy de ordinario Visitaua y aconpañaua a los dichos señores oydores adVertiendoles de muchas
cossas que Entendia conVenir al rreal seruicio espeçialmente les hablo sobre la
paçificaçion de los yndios chichimecas que an andado y andauan Alterados y ofrecio

came from the realms of Castile to this city of Mexico and New Spain, ordinarily he has had and has in it many rivals and enemies, and it has been known of him that he has gained few or no friends; and ordinarily there has been muttering among many people about the little care that he has shown to gain friendships, and they held it against him because in this he made himself hated by most of the people in the land; let them say what they know.

18. If they know, etc., that on the night when the said Alonso de Ávila Alvarado and other persons in Indian costumes held the fiesta in the house of the said Marqués at which the said lord inspector was present, the said lord inspector was told that the said fiesta was being held in order to cause some kind of riot and public disturbance, and the said lord inspector told the said Marqués about it; and the latter armed himself and saw to it that his brothers and certain of his servants and other persons were armed and they all accompanied the said lord inspector until the supper and merriment were finished; and he went to his residence without there being any sign or evidence from which one might gather what it was said the inspector had been told; let them say what they know.

19. If they know, etc., that during the whole time that the said Lord Inspector Valderrama resided in this city of Mexico and New Spain, he exercised his jurisdiction and looked into whatever matters of justice and government seemed best to him; and whenever he wished he was present in the assemblies of royal government, and he presided over them after the death of the said Viceroy Don Luis de Velasco; let them say what they know.

20. If they know, etc., that a few days after the said Marqués came from the realms of Castile, before he entered this city, Gonzalo Cerezo, the alguacil mayor of this court, wrote him a letter in which in effect he encouraged him that he should win many wills and that, having won them, he might do whatever he wished in this land and they would support him, and that if he did not do it, he would be alone and would be hated; and the said Marqués answered him in writing that he was not coming to win wills but to serve the King and his ministers and other words in which he gave him to understand that he was very free and separate from any desire to gain or win wills; let them say everything that they know was contained in the one and the other letter.

21. If they know, etc., that from the time that the said Marqués thus came to this land from the realms of Castile, which was possibly four years ago, a little more or less, he has always lived very plainly and with a very small retinue, not keeping more servants than the most necessary for his service and his house, and ordinarily he was unprovided with arms, so much so that there have been and are many private freeholders of this city who have and have had many more arms; and he has never had fewer servants or arms than for the past year; let them say what they know.

22. If they know, etc., that the said Marqués, after the departure of the said lord inspector, very regularly visited and accompanied the said lords oidores, bringing to their attention many things that he knew would be good for the royal service, and he spoke to them especially about the pacification of Chichimeca Indians who were and

su persona y hazienda para El rremedio dello y lo comunico con otras muchas
personas honrradas desta çiudad pidiendoles su pareçer como honbres de esperiencia
a fin de aVisar con El mejor a los dicho señores oydores digan lo que saben.

[*229*] **xxiii** Si saben etc. que Asimismo ydo El dicho señor Visitador El dicho
Marques hablo algunas Vezes al capitan Jhoan de Çespedes Preguntandole si tenia
buen rrecaudo y guarda En lo de la muniçion de artilleria y armas El qual dixo
ser muy poco lo que los dichos señores oydores le mandauan librar para Ello y
llebo consigo al dicho capitan a cassa de los dichos señores oydores y trato con
ellos que le proueiesen de todo lo necesario para El dicho buen rrecaudo y asi se
lo prometieron de hazer digan lo que saben.

xxiiii° Si saben etc. quel dicho Virrey don Luis de Velasco Por muchas bias descu-
brio, mostro y dio a entender tener segun En efeto tenia y tubo grande odio y mala
Voluntad al dicho Marques y a todas sus cossas i sintio mucho El calor quel dicho
Marques daua al dicho señor Visitador, En especial la diligençia que puso El dicho
Marques En que los pueblos De yndios asi de la rreal cabeça como del dicho su marquesado se bisitasen y tasasen los tributos En lo que buenamente pudiesen dar segun
se tasaron y creçieron de lo qual peso mucho al dicho Visorrey y a muchos rreligiosos
a quien El dicho birrey pretendia y pretendio contentar En ello y En lo demas que
los dichos rreligiosos querian Digan lo que saben y declaren En particular lo que
bieron hazer y dezir al dicho birrey contra El dicho Marques.

xxv Si saben etc. que Assimismo El dicho Virrey continuando El odio y mala
Voluntad que asi tenia al dicho Marques escriuio contra el asi a su Magestad como
a otras personas de su rreal cassa y corte muchas cartas con siniestra rrelaçion digan
lo que saben.

xxvi Si saben etc. que antes quel dicho Virrey muriese y despues de muerto El
dicho don Luis de Velasco su hijo asimismo mostro tener gran odio y Enemistad
al dicho Marques y a sus cossas diziendo contra el muchas palabras de yndinaçion
y amenaçandole de que le aVia de hazer todo El mal y daño que pudiese y dixo y
publico quel dicho Marques le aVia hecho tasar su yndios y que le quitasen la mayor
parte de lo que tributauan y que se aVia de vengar del En mas que valian los pueblos
cien Vezes.

[*229v*] **xxvii** Si saben etc. que Podra AVer Año y medio poco mas o menos que
los dichos Alonso de Çerbantes y Baltasar de Aguilar y Juan Juarez y otros sus
deVdos tubieron pendencia y quistion de cuchilladas con Bernaldino de Bocanegra
Vezinos todos desta dicha ciudad y con don Hernando de Cordoua su hermano y
al [*sic—el*] dicho Marques por tener a los dichos Bernaldino de Bocanegra y don
Hernando por amigos y allegados a su cassa acudio a los Visitar y bisito y no a los
dichos Alonso de Ceruantes y Baltar [*sic*] de Aguilar de lo qual los dichos Baltasar
de Aguilar y Alonso de Çeruantes y Agustin de Villanueua hermano del dicho Alonso
de Cerbantes y todos sus Devdos mostraron gran sentimiento quexandose del dicho

have been very unsettled; and he offered his person and property to solve the problem, and he made it known to many honorable people of this city, asking them their opinions as men of experience in order to be able to give better advice to the said lords oidores; let them say what they know.

23. If they know, etc., that likewise after the departure of the said lord inspector, the said Marqués spoke several times with Captain Juan de Céspedes, asking him whether he had a good security and safeguard on the stores of artillery and arms, and he said that what the said lords oidores commanded him to be issued for that was very little; and he took the said captain with him to the house of the said lords oidores and he discussed with them that they should provide him everything necessary for the said safeguarding, and they promised to do it; let them say what they know.

24. If they know, etc., that the said Viceroy Don Luis de Velasco showed, revealed, and made known in many ways that he had, as he really did have, a great hatred and ill will for the said Marqués and for all of his affairs; and he deeply resented the warmth of the reception which the said Marqués gave to the said lord inspector and especially the diligence which the said Marqués showed in seeing to it that the Indian towns of both the Royal Crown and of his said marquisate should be visited and the tributes assessed on what they could well give, as they were assessed and increased, which greatly saddened the said Viceroy and many friars whom the said Viceroy always tried to satisfy in this matter and in the other things that the friars wanted; let them say what they know and let them explain in particular what they saw the said Viceroy do and say against the said Marqués.

25. If they know, etc., that likewise the said Viceroy, continuing to show the hatred and ill will which he thus held for the said Marqués, wrote against him many letters, both to His Majesty and to other persons of his royal household and court, with vicious reports; let them say what they know.

26. If they know, etc., that before the said Viceroy died and after his death, the said Don Luis de Velasco, his son, likewise showed that he had a great hatred and enmity for the said Marqués and his affairs, speaking against him many words of indignation and threatening him that he would do him all the ill and harm that he could; and he said and made known that the said Marqués had caused his Indians to be assessed and that they would take from him the greater part of what they were giving as tribute and that he would take vengeance for it a hundred times more than the towns were worth.

27. If they know, etc., that possibly a year and a half ago, a little more or less, the said Alonso de Cervantes and Baltasar de Aguilar and Juan Juárez and other relatives of theirs had a dispute and quarrel in which they came to blows with Bernaldino de Bocanegra, all freeholders of this said city, and with Don Hernando de Córdoba his brother; and because the said Marqués considered the said Bernaldino de Bocanegra and Don Hernando as friends and supporters of his house, he went to visit them, and he visited them and not the said Baltasar de Aguilar and Alonso de Cervantes; and because of this the said Baltasar de Aguilar and Alonso de Cervantes and Agustín de Villanueva, brother of the said Alonso de Cervantes, and all of their

Marques y Amenazandole de que le harian quanto mal y daño Pudiesen y dezian y dixeron contra el palabras de muy gran menosprecio digan los testigos lo que saben.

xxviii°   Si saben etc. que demas del sentimiento que los dichos Agustin De Villanueua, Alonso de Cerbantes y Baltasar de Aguilar y los demas sus devdos mostraron al dicho Marques por lo que dicho es En la pregunta antes desta luego se desbiaron del y dexaron de acompañarle y de Entrar En las cassas de su morada como antes lo solian hazer digan lo que saben.

xxix   Si saben etc. quel dicho don Luis de Velasco Por ser los dichos Agustin de Villanueua, Alonso de Çerbantes y Baltasar de Aguilar sobrinos de doña Beatriz de Andrada muger de don Francisco de Velasco su tio y hermano del dicho Virrey a tenido y tiene Estrecha amistad con ellos y pasada la dicha quistion y pendencia y lo que acerca dello dicho es En las demas preguntas antes desta les ofrecio su persona y quanto tubiese asi contra los dichos Bocanegras, como contra El dicho Marques Digan lo que saben.

xxx   Si saben etc. que Podra aVer nuebe meses poco mas o menos quel dicho Marques pretendio hazer En esta rreal avdiencia Vna ynformaçion contra El dicho Virrey tocando En cossas de su onor lo qual Venido a notiçia del dicho don Luis su hijo rreclamo y contradixo lo susodicho y torno a conçebir por Ello nueuo odio y pasion contra El dicho Marques digan lo que saben.

xxxi   Si saben etc. que los dichos Don Luis de Velasco, Agustin de Villanueua, Alonso de Cerbantes y Baltasar de Aguilar y otros sus deVdos dende al dicha pendençia y quistion an andado muy juntos y aliados murmurando y detratando del dicho Marques digan lo que saben.

[230] **xxxii**   Si saben etc. que Por El mes De mayo del Año Proximo Pasado de sesenta y çinco los dichos Agustin de Villanueua y Baltasar de Aguilar con la Enemistad y odio que tenian al dicho Marques trataron De Encontrarse con el y no quitarle las gorras ni hazerle comedimiento alguno para desabrirle y ocasionarle y asi lo hizieron y pusieron por obra muchas Vezes con otros DeVdos suyos andando para El dicho Efeto de ordinario En quadrillas y muy apercebidos y armados y aVnquel dicho Marques los bia y notaua sus malas entrañas y descomedimientos no hazia caudal dello digan lo que saben.

xxxiii   Si saben etc. que sabido Por El dicho Marques que los Dichos Agustin de Villanueua y Baltasar de Aguilar y los demas sus devdos dezian hazer lo que dicho es En la pregunta antes desta por ofender al dicho Marques y darle ocasion a que se desabriese y desmandase contra Ellos, El dicho Marques yndinado y ocasionado por Ello mando que çiertos criados suyos andubiesen con el aperçebidos y que En Encontrando al dicho Agustin de Villanueua y Baltasar de Aguilar y biendo que no le hazian comedimiento alguno los afrentasen y maltratasen lo qual supieron los

relatives showed great resentment, complaining about the said Marqués and threatening him that they would do him all the ill and harm that they could, and they spoke words of very great contempt against him; let the witnesses say what they know.

28. If they know, etc., that besides the resentment which the said Agustín de Villanueva, Alonso de Cervantes, and Baltasar de Aguilar and the rest of their relations showed toward the said Marqués because of what has been said in the question preceding this one, they then turned aside from him and ceased to accompany him and to enter into his dwelling houses as they had customarily done previously; let them say what they know.

29. If they know, etc., that the said Don Luis de Velasco, because the said Agustín de Villanueva, Alonso de Cervantes, and Baltasar de Aguilar are nephews of Doña Beatriz de Andrada, wife of Don Francisco de Velasco, his uncle and brother of the said Viceroy, has had and has a close friendship with them; and after the said quarrel and fight and what has been said about it in the other questions preceding this one, he offered them his person and whatever he might possess both against the said Bocanegras and against the said Marqués; let them say what they know.

30. If they know, etc., that possibly nine months ago, a little more or less, the said Marqués attempted to make in this royal audiencia a judicial inquiry against the said Viceroy, related to matters of his honor; and when it came to the knowledge of the said Don Luis his son, he opposed and contradicted the abovesaid, and because of it he again conceived new hatred and passion against the said Marqués; let them say what they know.

31. If they know, etc., that the said Don Luis de Velasco, Agustín de Villanueva, Alonso de Cervantes, and Baltasar de Aguilar and other relatives of theirs, since the time of the said dispute and fight, have gone about very much united and allied, defaming and murmuring against the said Marqués; let them say what they know.

32. If they know, etc., that during the month of May of last year, sixty-five, the said Agustín de Villanueva and Baltasar de Aguilar, as a result of the hatred and enmity which they held for the said Marqués, went out of their way to meet him and not take off their caps to him nor show him any respect in order to harass him and stir him up; and they did it and put it into effect many times with other relatives of theirs, going about ordinarily in gangs for this purpose, very well prepared and armed; and although the said Marqués saw them and noted their bad dispositions and incivilities, he did not make a great thing out of it; let them say what they know.

33. If they know, etc., that when the said Marqués came to know that the said Agustín de Villanueva and Baltasar de Aguilar and the rest of their relatives said that they were going to do what was said in the question preceding this one in order to offend the said Marqués and give him an occasion to harass them and take immoderate action against them, the said Marqués, angered and irritated by that, commanded that certain of his servants should go around prepared with him, and that when they should meet the said Agustín de Villanueva and Baltasar de Aguilar and should see that they did not make any sign of respect, they should insult and mistreat them; and

dichos Agustin de Villanueua y Baltasar de Aguilar y bino a su noticia digan lo que saben.

xxxiiii° Si saben etc. que sabiendo los dichos Agustin de Villanueua y Baltasar de Aguilar lo que se contiene En la pregunta antes desta con los demas sus deVdos se juntaron En cassa del dicho Hortuño de Ybarra y con ellos El dicho Juan de Samano y En otras partes y trataron jurando y confederandose para matar o afrentar malamente al dicho Marques diziendo contra el palabras de mucha ynjuria y menosprecio y se armaron muchas Vezes y andubieron juntos y en quadrilla para ponerlo En Execucion digan lo que saben.

xxxv Si saben etc. que sabido Por El Reverendisimo Arçobispo desta ciudad y El alcayde Albornoz y otros Vezinos honrrados della lo que dicho es En las preguntas antes desta de las ocasiones que los dichos Agustin de Villanueua y Baltasar de Aguilar y algunos de sus devdos daban al dicho Marques y lo quel dicho Marques tenia acordado de hazer contra Ellos fueron a hablar y hablaron al dicho Marques y trataron con el de que çesase su enojo y les rrespondio que pretendia castigar a los dichos sus Emulos y Enemigos por los descomedimientos y ocasiones que le avian hecho y no porque le aconpañasen y asi quedo sin dar rresulucion en el casso.

[*230v*] **xxxvi** Si saben etc. que AVnque los dichos Agustin de Villanueua y Baltasar de Aguilar y los dichos sus devdos pasado lo que dicho es En la pregunta antes desta encontrando al dicho Marques no le quitauan las gorras ni le hablauan ni aconpañauan ni Entrauan En su cassa Ecepto El dicho Baltasar de Aguilar que algunas y muy pocas Vezes yva a Ellas y hablaua con El dicho Marques digan lo que saben.

xxxvii Si saben etc. que quando segun Esta dicho En la pregunta antes desta El dicho Baltasar de Aguilar yba a cassa del dicho Marques Era y fue cautelosamente y con yntento de asegurarle y tener ocasion so color de amistad fingida de le poder perjudicar y asi En saliendo de cassa del dicho Marques y algunas Vezes de aVer comido con el a la mesa daua quenta dello al dicho Agustin de Villanueua y a otros sus devdos diziendoles que Venia de cassa de aquel vellaco del Marques y El y Ellos murmurauan largo y con mucha pasion del dicho Marques y de su casa y hermanos y criados y El dicho Baltasar de Aguilar rreferia lo que dezia aver pasado En particular con El dicho Marques y tratadose a su mesa y en su presençia digan lo que saben.

xxxviii° Si saben etc. que despues de la pendencia y quistion que los dichos Bocanegras tubieron con los dichos Jhoan Juarez y Alonso de Çerbantes y Baltasar de Aguilar y los demas El dicho Baltasar de Aguilar dixo a los dichos sus devdos que le dexasen a El con El dicho Marques y Ellos se lo hubiesen con los demas y que

the said Agustín de Villanueva and Baltasar de Aguilar knew of this and it came to their attention; let them say what they know.

34. If they know, etc., that when the said Agustín de Villanueva and Baltasar de Aguilar knew of what is contained in the question preceding this one, together with their other relatives they met in the house of the said Ortuño de Ibarra, and the said Juan de Sámano with them, and also in other places, and they held discussions, swearing and forming alliances to kill or vilely insult the said Marqués, speaking against him very insulting and contemptuous words; and they frequently armed themselves and went about together in a gang in order to put it into execution; let them say what they know.

35. If they know, etc., that when the Most Reverend Archbishop of this city and the alcaide Albornoz and other honorable freeholders of it came to know of what was described in the questions preceding this one concerning the occasions for anger that the said Agustín de Villanueva and Baltasar de Aguilar and some of their relatives were giving to the said Marqués and what the said Marqués had agreed to do against them, they went to speak and spoke to the said Marqués, and they tried to get him to give up his anger; and he answered them that he was trying to punish his said rivals and enemies for the disrespect and occasions for disturbance that they had afforded him and not so that they would accompany him; and thus it remained, without any solution being given to the case.

36. If they know, etc., that in spite of the occurrence of what has been said in the question preceding this one, when the said Agustín de Villanueva and Baltasar de Aguilar and their said relatives met the said Marqués, they did not take their caps off to him nor speak to him nor accompany him nor enter his house, except the said Baltasar de Aguilar, who went to his house some very few times and spoke with the said Marqués; let them say what they know.

37. If they know, etc., that when, as has been said in the preceding question, the said Baltasar de Aguilar went to the house of the said Marqués, he did so craftily and with the intention of reassuring him and to have an occasion to harm him under the guise of pretended friendship; and thus when he left the house of the said Marqués, sometimes after having eaten with him at the table, he gave an account of it to the said Agustín de Villanueva and other relatives of his, telling them that he came from the house of that knave of a Marqués; and he and they grumbled at length and with great passion about the said Marqués and about his household and brothers and servants; and the said Baltasar de Aguilar reported what he said had happened in particular with the said Marqués and what they had discussed at his table and in his presence; let them say what they know.

38. If they know, etc., that after the quarrel and dispute which the said Bocanegras had with the said Juan Juárez and Alonso de Cervantes and Baltasar de Aguilar and the others, the said Baltasar de Aguilar said to his said relatives that they should let him take care of the said Marqués and that they should take care of the others and that he swore to God that, with the horse that he had, he obligated himself to turn

juraua a Dios que con El cauallo que tenia se obligaua de poner la barrigaEnçima de la cabeça o cara del dicho Marques digan lo que saben.

xxxix   Si saben etc. que asimesmo El dicho Baltasar de Aguilar quando como dicho es entraua En cassa del dicho Marques y comia con el algunas Vezes a la mesa pasada la dicha pendençia salido Vn dia de la dicha cassa dixo muchas palabras feas contra El dicho Marques y Entre otras que juraua a Dios que En medio de la plaça aVia de arremeter a El y comersele a bocados y de ordinario antes y despues de la dicha pendencia Entrando y dexando de Entrar En cassa del dicho Marques dezia contra El palabras de mucha desVerguença y alebosia y de muy mal xpiano y desagradecido digan lo que saben.

xl   Si saben etc. quel dicho Baltasar de Aguilar desde que los testigos le conocen [*231*] sienPre y a la continua Le an bisto ser A sido y es honbre cauteloso E muy doblado y de muy poca fee y Verdad y alevoso contra sus amigos y devdos y que se a preçiado y preçia dello y En esta rreputaçion y de muy mal xpiano y desagrade-çido Digan lo que saben.

xli   Si saben etc. quel dicho Baltasar de Aguilar Demas de ser de la suerte y con-dicion que en la pregunta antes desta se rrefiere El dicho Marques lo tenia y tubo en la misma opinion y rreputacion y asi lo dezia y dixo a muchas personas y que se rrecataua del por tenerle por muy mal hombre y de muy mala lengua digan lo que saben.

xlii   Si saben etc. quel dicho Baltasar De Aguilar En muchas pendençias y quis-tiones que a tenido En esta ciudad siempre a acometido a las personas con quien a rreñido a traiçion y con Ventaja y armas Enhastadas Vsando con ellos de alevosia y esto es notorio a muchas personas digan lo que saben.

xliii   Si saben etc. que muchos dias antes de la dicha pendencia El dicho Baltasar de Aguilar trato de querer Vender o dar al dicho Marques Vn cauallo rrosillo y pasada la dicha pendencia hablo a Diego Rodriguez Horozco para que hablase al dicho Marques que todaVia tomase El dicho cauallo y El dicho Marques dixo al dicho Diego Rodriguez que porque no pensase el dicho Baltasar de Aguilar que por ocasion de la dicha quistion dexaua de tomar El dicho cauallo y pagarsele que se lo Enbiase y se lo Enbio y por El le hizo dar y pagar seteçientos pesos de oro y Veynte pesos mas que se dieron al moço que le traxo digan todo lo que çerca desto saben.

xliiii°   Si saben etc. que mostrando El dicho Baltasar de Aguilar El odio y capital Enemistad que tenia con El dicho Marques antes que diese las memorias En esta causa por las carnes toliendas proximas pasadas dixo ante muchas personas que Pues El dicho Marques no le aVia dado mas de setecientos pesos por su cauallo Valiendo mas que auia de hazer que le costase toda su hazienda digan lo que saben.

the Marqués upside down [*or: to place the horse's belly on top of the Marqués' head or face*]; let them say what they know.

39. If they know, etc., that likewise when the said Baltasar de Aguilar entered the house of the said Marqués, as has been said, and sometimes ate with him at table, one day after the said fight when he left the said house, he said many ugly words against the said Marqués; and among other things he said that he swore to God that he would attack him in the middle of the plaza and eat him up by the mouthful; and ordinarily both before and after the said fight, whether he entered the house of the said Marqués or abstained from entering it, he spoke against him many shameless and traitorous words, words of a very bad Christian and an ingrate; let them say what they know.

40. If they know, etc., that for as long as the witnesses have known the said Baltasar de Aguilar, always and continuously he has been and is, and they have seen that he is, a wary man and very two faced, a man of little credibility and truth, treacherous toward his friends and relatives, and he has and does pride himself in it and in such a reputation and in that of a very bad Christian and an ingrate; let them say what they know.

41. If they know, etc., that besides the fact that the said Baltasar is a man of the type and character described in the preceding question, the said Marqués held that same opinion and estimation of him and he said as much to many people and told them that he was careful about him because he considered him as a very bad man with a very bad tongue; let them say what they know.

42. If they know, etc., that in the many quarrels and fights that the said Baltasar de Aguilar has had in this city, he has always attacked the people with whom he has argued treacherously and with an advantage and with his weapons raised, using trickery with them, and this is well known to many people; let them say what they know.

43. If they know, etc., that many days before the said fight the said Baltasar de Aguilar discussed wanting to sell or give to the said Marqués a roan horse, and after the said fight he asked Diego Rodriguez Orozco to tell the said Marqués that he might still take the said horse; and the said Marqués told the said Diego Rodríguez that the said horse should be sent, so that the said Baltasar de Aguilar would not think that because of the said fight he had declined to take it and pay him for it; and it was sent, and he saw to it that he was paid seven hundred pesos of gold for it and twenty pesos more which were given to the boy who brought it; let them tell everything that they know about this.

44. If they know, etc., that during the most recent carnival [*carnes toliendas*], the said Baltasar de Aguilar, showing the hatred and capital enmity that he held for the said Marqués before he made his statement in this case, said in the presence of many persons that, since the said Marqués had not given him more than seven hundred pesos for his horse, even though it was worth more, he would see to it that it cost him all of his wealth; let them say what they know.

xlv Si saben etc. que los dichos [*sic*] Agustin de Villanueua dende El dia de la dicha quistion y pendençia no Entro En cassa del dicho Marques hasta la noche del Sabado Santo que fue a hablarle juntamente con el dicho Baltasar de Aguilar y los testigos creen y tienen por cierto lo que de suso Esta contra Ellos articulado que Entraron con cautela pare [*sic—para*] le poder mejor perjudicar y dañar digan lo que saben.

[*231v*] **xlvi** Si saben etc. que quando Asi los dichos Baltasar de Aguilar y Agustin de Villanueua segun se contiene En la pregunta antes desta Entraron En cassa del dicho Marques a hablarle En sabiendo El dicho Marques que Entrauan se rrecato dellos y dixo a don Martin Cortes su hermano que no saliese de alli de donde Estaua porque se temia no le Viniesen a hazer los suso dichos algun mal por tenerlos por Enemigos y aver tanto tiempo quel dicho Agustin de Villanueua no Entraba En su casa y Venia a tales oras y asi estubo rrecatado El dicho don Martin digan lo que saben.

xlvii Si saben etc. que Estando El dicho Marques El Miercoles Santo de la quaresma proxima pasada rrecojido en el monesterio de Santiago desta ciudad y aViendose El propio dia confesado fue de noche a le hablar El dicho Baltasar de Aguilar y le dixo quel dicho Agustin de Villanueua le aVia dicho que se hazia contra El dicho Marques ynformaçion y quel dicho Agustin de Villanueua lo sabia del dicho don Luis de Velasco y Entro a dezirle lo que dicho es en el coro de la yglesia y Entro y salio del sin hazer oracion ni acatamiento alguno a Dios ni a su templo y El dicho Marques le dixo que no creya que los señores oydores hiziesen ynformaçion contra el porque no avia de que y que creya quera ynvençion del dicho don Luis de Velasco y que hablase al dicho Agustin de Villanueua para que hiziese quel dicho don Luis se lo dixese delante de testigos E ydo El dicho Baltasar de Aguilar luego yncontinente dixo El dicho Marques lo que con el avia pasado a Bernaldino de Bocanegra y a fray Luis Cal rreligioso digan lo que saben.

xlviii° Si saben etc. que asimismo ydo El dicho Baltasar de Aguilar del dicho monesterio El dicho Marques dixo a los dichos fray Luis Cal y Bernaldino de Bocanegra que tenia miedo no hubiese venido El dicho Baltasar de Aguilar con alguna trayçion por la rruin opinion En que le tenia y que devia Venir por espia para hazerle algun tiro El y sus devdos pareçiendoles que hallarian oportunidad En Verle rrecojido y sin criados en el campo y apartado desta çiudad en el dicho monesterio y pidio las llaues al guardian de la dicha cassa para tenerlas en su poder y se le dieron y las tubo y puso rrecaudo en las puertas para que no se dexase Entrar persona alguna.

xlix Si saben etc. que luego como paso lo dicho En la pregunta antes desta en la mesma ora El dicho Marques salio y con el El dicho Bernaldino de Bocanegra y

45. If they know, etc., that from the day of the said quarrel and fight, the said Agustín de Villanueva did not enter the house of the said Marqués until the night of Holy Saturday, when he went to talk to him together with the said Baltasar de Aguilar; and the witnesses believe and hold for certain what has been said against them in the preceding articles, namely, that they entered with cunning in order to do him greater damage and harm; let them say what they know.

46. If they know, etc., that when, as has been expressed in the preceding question, the said Baltasar de Aguilar and Agustín de Villanueva entered the house of the said Marqués to talk to him, as soon as the said Marqués knew that they were entering, he was on his guard with them; and he told Don Martín Cortés, his brother who was there, that he should not leave because he was afraid that they were coming to do him some harm, since he considered them as enemies and it had been such a long time since the said Agustín de Villanueva had come into his house and he came at such an hour, and so the said Don Martín was on his guard; let them say what they know.

47. If they know, etc., that on the Wednesday of Holy Week of the past Lent, while the said Marqués was in retreat in the friary of Santiago of this city and had made his confession that very day, the said Baltasar de Aguilar went to speak to him at night and told him that the said Agustín de Villanueva had told him that an investigation was being made against the said Marqués and that the said Agustín de Villanueva knew of it from the said Don Luis de Velasco; and when he came into the choir of the church to tell him what has been said above, he entered and left without saying a prayer or making any sign of reverence to God or His temple; and the said Marqués told him that he did not believe that the lords oidores would make an investigation against him because there was no reason for it and that he believed that it was an invention of the said Don Luis de Velasco and that he should tell the said Agustín de Villanueva that he should have the said Don Luis tell it to him before witnesses; and as soon as the said Baltasar de Aguilar had left, the said Marqués immediately spoke of what had happened with him to Bernaldino de Bocanegra and Fray Luis Cal, a religious; let them say what they know.

48. If they know, etc., that likewise after the said Baltasar de Aguilar had left the said monastery, the said Marqués told the said Fray Luis Cal and Bernaldino de Bocanegra that he was fearful lest the said Baltasar de Aguilar had come with some kind of treachery, because of the vile opinion that he had of him, and that he must have come as a spy in order to make some strike against him and his relatives, when it seemed to them that they would find an oportunity when they saw him withdrawn and without servants, in the countryside and separated from this city in the said friary; and he requested the keys from the guardian [*religious superior*] of the said house so as to have them in his possession, and they were given to him, and he took them and placed a guard on the doors so that no one should be allowed to enter.

49. If they know, etc., that immediately after the incident that is described in the question preceding this one, within the same hour the said Marqués went out, and

anbos a dos y Vinieron a dar noticia de lo que aVia pasado con El dicho Baltasar de Aguilar [232] A los señores oydores Desta Real avdiençia y Viniendo le pareçio El dicho Marques que seria mejor saber primero si en casa del dicho Baltasar de Aguilar y los demas sus devdos avia algun rremor o bulliçio de armas o junta de gente y asi lo hizo yendo por las mas casas que de los suso dichos supieron y despues y despues [sic] El dicho Bernaldino de Vocanegra por rruego del dicho Marques fue a la Eredad del dicho Baltasar de Aguilar a saber lo mismo y Visto que no avia señal de alboroto se fue El dicho Marques a sus cassas y Visito a la Marquesa su muger y dio quenta dello al dicho don Martin su hermano y se boluio la misma noche al dicho monesterio digan lo que saben.

L Si saben etc. que Pasado lo que dicho es en la pregunta antes desta Vn dia de los de Pascua Florida luego siguiente El dicho Marques fue a cassa del señor doctor Villalobos a le visitar y [le—*between lines*] dyo quenta de lo quel dicho Baltasar de Aguilar con el avia pasado en el dicho monesterio la dicha noche del dicho Miercoles Santo y lo que despues el mesmo Baltasar de Aguilar y El dicho Agustin de Villanueua El dicho Sabado Santo En la noche aVian benido a dezirle en las casas de su morada Digan lo que saben.

Li Si saben etc. que los dichos Agustin de Villanueua y Baltasar de Aguilar son nietos de Leonel de Cerbantes Vezino que fue desta ciudad ya difunto El qual el Marques don Hernando Cortes padre del dicho Marques don Martin Cortes tubo preso muchos dias y le quiso cortar la cabeça por Esçesos y delitos que avia fecho y despues El dicho Marques don Hernando Cortes en la rresidençia que se le tomo de capitan general y gouernador que fue destas partes tacho al dicho Leonel de Cerbantes de Enemigo capital y le puso otros defetos y tachas digan todo lo que cerca desto supieren En particular.

Lii Si saben etc. quel dicho licenciado Espinosa es natural de la villa de Carrion de los Condes de los rreynos de Castilla donde Era natural El dicho Visorrey don Luis de Velasco y es El dicho don Luis de Velasco su hijo y En la dicha villa an bibido sus antecesores de cuya causa Entre los dichos licenciado Espinosa y don Luis de Velasco avido y ay de muchos años a esta parte estrecha amistad y conversacion y la misma hubo Entre El dicho Virrey y El dicho licenciado Espinosa digan lo que saben.

[232v] **Liii** Si saben etc. que los dichos Jhoan de Samano y maestre Escuela An sido y son yntimos amigos de los dichos don Luis de Velasco y Agustin de Villanueua con los quales an tenido y tienen Estrecha conversacion y muy hordinaria y los dichos don Luis de Velasco y Agustin de Villanueua an tenido y tienen por confesor al dicho maestreescula [sic] digan lo que saben.

Liiii° Si saben etc. [que — *blotted*] los dichos maestreescuela y Juan de Samano En esta dicha ciudad de[mas — *blotted*] de dos años a esta [par — *blotted*]te an sido y son Emulos y Enemigos capitales Del dicho Ma[rques y — *blotted*] de sus

the said Bernaldino de Bocanegra with him, both together, and they came to give notice of what had happened with the said Baltasar de Aguilar to the lords oidores of this royal audiencia; and when they had come, it seemed to the said Marqués that it would be better to find out first whether in the house of the said Baltasar de Aguilar and the rest of his relatives there was some sound of voices or rattle of arms or gathering of people; and he did that, going by most of the houses that they knew belonged to the abovesaid, and later the said Bernaldino de Bocanegra, at the request of the said Marqués, went to the country estate of the said Baltasar de Aguilar to find out the same thing; and seeing that there was no sign of disturbance, the said Marqués went to his own house and visited the Marquesa his wife and gave an account of it to the said Don Martín his brother and returned that said night to the said friary; let them say what they know.

50. If they know, etc., that after the occurrence that is described in the preceding question, one day during the Easter Week immediately following, the said Marqués went to the house of the Lord Doctor Villalobos to visit him, and he gave him an account of what had happened between him and the said Baltasar de Aguilar in the said friary on the said night of the said Wednesday of Holy Week and what the said Baltasar de Aguilar and the said Agustín de Villanueva had come to tell him later in his dwelling house during the night of the said Holy Saturday; let them say what they know.

51. If they know, etc., that the said Agustín de Villanueva and Baltasar de Aguilar are grandsons of Leonel de Cervantes, formerly a freeholder of this city, now deceased, whom the Marqués Don Hernando Cortés, father of the said Marqués Don Martín Cortés, held prisoner for many days and wanted to cut off his head because of the excesses and crimes that he had committed; and later in the residencia which was taken of the said Marqués Don Hernando Cortés as former captain general and governor of these parts, he challenged the testimony of the said Leonel de Cervantes as a capital enemy and he brought out other defects and challenges against him; let them tell everything that they know about this in detail.

52. If they know, etc., that the said Licentiate Espinosa is a native of the town of Carrión de los Condes in the realms of Castile, of which the said Viceroy Don Luis de Velasco was a native and the said Don Luis de Velasco his son is a native, and their ancestors have lived in the said town; and for this reason between the said Licentiate Espinosa and Don Luis de Velasco there has been for many years past and still is a close friendship and interchange, and the same was true between the said Viceroy and the said Licentiate Espinosa; let them say what they know.

53. If they know, etc., that the said Juan de Sámano and the maestrescuela have been and are intimate friends of the said Don Luis de Velasco and Agustín de Villanueva with whom they have had and do have a close and familiar interchange; and the said Don Luis de Velasco and Agustín de Villanueva have had and do have the said maestrescuela as their confessor; let them say what they know.

54. If they know, etc., that the said maestrescuela and Juan de Sámano for more than the past two years have been and are rivals and mortal enemies of the said

h[*ermanos — blotted*] y por tales notoriamente an Estado y Estan conocidos digan lo que saben.

Lv   Si saben etc. que Pocos dias Antes que fuese El dicho Marques detenido en las casas rreales donde Esta dixo El dicho Juan de Samano En presencia de algunas personas que juraua a Dios que pensaua con la Enemistad del dicho Marques adelantar la casa de su padre vn buen pedaço digan lo que saben.

Lvi   Si saben etc. que abia tres meses Poco mas o menos questando El dicho maestreescuela de la santa yglesia desta dicha ciudad En la plaça publica della con otras personas diziendo Juan de Villagomez que Porquel dicho Marques no procuraria amistad de los dichos don Luis de Velasco y Juan de Samano y de los demas sus aliados rrespondiendo El dean que que se le daua El Marques dellos dixo El dicho maestreescuela no se le da nada pues de aqui a poco lo Vereis digan lo que saben.

Lvii   Si saben etc. que ser los dichos Don Luis de Velasco Agustin de Villanueua y Baltasar de Aguilar, Alonso de Çervantes, Juan de Samano y maestreescuela Emulos y enemigos capitales del dicho Marques y de sus hermanos a sido y es En esta dicha ciudad publico y notorio y dello aVido y ay publica boz y fama digan lo que saben.

Lviii°   Si saben etc. que quando En esta dicha ciudad segun arriba Esta articulado se dixo y publico aver çedula que Proybia la terçera suçesion En los yndios de Encomienda vna de las personas que mas sentimiento mostraron fue El dicho Juan de Samano diziendo que juraua a Dios que no era cossa de çufrir y que sobre defender su Encomienda de yndios moriria y que dexaria maldiçion [*233*] A sus hijos si asi no lo hiziesen lo qual dezia con gran coraje y enpuñandose en su espada digan lo que saben.

Lix   Si saben etc. que Antes quel dicho licenciado Espinosa y Pedro de Aguilar y don Baltasar y los demas denunciadores diesen sus memorias y denunçiaçiones En esta causa muchas y diVersas Vezes se juntaron con ellos de noche y dia En cassa del dicho licenciado y En otras partes los dichos Juan de Samano y maestreescuela y se hallaron presentes al escreuir y ordenar las dichas memorias y se a dicho y publicado En esta dicha ciudad y se tiene por cossa cierta que Ellos las ordenauan o muy gran parte dellas digan lo que saben.

Lx   Si saben etc. que despues que Al dicho fiscal por Esta rreal avdiençia Se le mando dar y dio la boz para que acusase al dicho Marques los dichos licenciado Espinosa y Pedro de Aguilar, Agustin de Villanueua, Baltasar de Aguilar don Pedro y don Baltasar de Quesada y maestreescuela y Juan de Samano y Francisco de Morales muy de ordinario an ydo y fueron a hablar al dicho fiscal a las cassas de su morada Ençerrandose con el y hallandose presentes a lo que se ordenaua y Respondia En esta causa y algunos dellos lleuauan por escripto memorias de lo que se abia de alegar y todos soliçitauan y procurauan En esta dicha causa contra El dicho Marques ynçitandose y dandose avisos vnos a otros, los testigos

Marqués and his brothers in this city, and as such they have been and are very well known; let them say what they know.

55. If they know, etc., that a few days before the said Marqués was detained in the government buildings where he is now, the said Juan de Sámano said in the presence of some people that he swore to God that with the enmity of the said Marqués, he would improve the fortunes of his father's house a good bit; let them say what they know.

56. If they know, etc., that three months ago, a little more or less, the said maestre-scuela of the holy church of this said city was in the public plaza of it with other people, and Juan de Villagómez asked why the said Marqués did not try to gain the friendship of the said Don Luis de Velasco and Juan de Sámano and the rest of their allies; and when the dean asked what concern they were to the said Marqués, the said maestrescuela said, "Nothing is of any concern to him, as you will see in a little while from now"; let them say what they know.

57. If they know, etc., that the fact that the said Don Luis de Velasco, Agustín de Villanueva, Baltasar de Aguilar, Alonso de Cervantes, Juan de Sámano, and the maestrescuela are rivals and mortal enemies of the said Marqués and of his brothers, has been and is public and well known in this city, and there is public knowledge and discussion of it; let them say what they know.

58. If they know, etc., that when, as has been detailed above, it was stated and published in this city that there was a decree which prohibited the third inheritance of the Indians in encomienda, one of the people who showed the most resentment was the said Juan de Sámano, who said that he swore to God that it was not a matter to be borne and that concerning the matter of defending his encomienda of Indians he would die and that he would leave a curse to his children if they did not do it thus; and he said this with great mettle, grasping the handle of his sword in his hand; let them say what they know.

59. If they know, etc., that before the said Licentiate Espinosa and Pedro de Aguilar and the other denouncers gave their memorials and denunciations in this case, the said Juan de Sámano and the maestrescuela met with them on many different occasions by night and by day in the house of the said licentiate and in other places and they were present when the said memorials were written and set in order; and it has been said in this said city and it is accepted as a certain fact that they set them in order, or at least a very great part of them; let them say what they know.

60. If they know, etc., that after the said prosecutor was commanded by this royal audiencia to be given and was actually given the authority that he should accuse the said Marqués, the said Licentiate Espinosa and Pedro de Aguilar, Agustín de Villa-nueva, Baltasar de Aguilar, Don Pedro and Don Baltasar de Quesada, the maestres-cuela, Juan de Sámano, and Francisco de Morales very regularly went and have gone to speak to the said prosecutor in his dwelling house, closeting themselves with him and being present at what was ordered and answered in this case; and some of them carried written memorials of what was to be alleged, and they all solicited and pleaded in this case against the said Marqués, inciting and giving advice to one

declaren particularmente todo lo que oyeron, Entendieron y supieron en rrazon dello digan lo que saben.

Lxi Si saben etc. que Assimismo Los En la pregunta antes desta contenidos despues del detenimiento del dicho Marques por muchas Vias an procurado ynquirir y buscar personas que testificasen contra el ynçitandolas para que le perjudicasen y procurasen saber dellos cosas en daño del dicho Marques digan lo que saben.

Lxii Si saben etc. que no solos los susudichos An hecho y hizieron lo que se contiene En las dos preguntas antes desta pero ordinariamente todos los dias an acudido y cuden a cassa de los señores oydores desta Real avdiencia a los hablar de dia y de noche mostrandose no solo denunçiadores pero partes que pretendian su propio ynterese y Vengança y con [233v] Palabras procurauan yndiñar A los dichos señores oydores contra El dicho Marques y sus hermanos digan lo que saben.

Lxiii Si saben etc. que los dichos licenciado Espinosa y Pedro de Aguilar, Agustin de Villanueua y Baltasar de Aguilar y los demas denunçiadores despues que dieron las dichas memorias y denunciaciones an dicho publicado que pretenden por lo que En ellas dixeron y afirmaron que su Magestad les haga merçedes digan lo que saben.

Lxiiii Si saben etc. que demas de lo arriba articulado çerca de ser los dichos denunçiadores y Juan de Samano y maestreescuela y Francisco de Morales soliçitadores En esta causa con El dicho fiscal y los señores oydores desta rreal avdiencia de que le ayan sido y sean es publica boz y fama En toda Esta dicha ciudad y dello a aVido y ay notoriedad digan lo que saben.

Lxv Si saben etc. que algunos meses Antes quel dicho Marques fuese como Esta detenido por Esta causa Vn dia Vino a las casas de su morada El dicho fray Miguel de Aluarado y le dixo aver sabido que los señores oydores desta rreal aVdiençia hazian ynformaçion contra El dicho Alonso DaVila y quel dicho Alonso Davila Estaua muy desabrido dello diziendo hallarse El ynocente y sin culpa y luego El propio dia El dicho Marques fue a hablar y hablo al dicho señor dotor Villalobos y le dio quenta dello y de como El dicho rreligioso le declaro que la persona que aviso a El y al dicho Alonso Dauila Era El dicho Pedro de Aguilar y El dicho señor dotor Villalobos rrespondio que llamaria al dicho Alonso Davila y le hablaria que bien sabia de donde tenia origen aquellas cossas y quel mesmo tomaria El dicho al Pedro de Aguilar digan lo que saben.

Lxvi Si saben etc. que teniendo El dicho Marques notiçia quel dicho don Luis de Velasco dezia que se hazian ynformaciones contra el y que En ello le disfamaua y que Hortuño de Ybarra aVia dado al dicho Pedro de Aguilar cantidad de dineros porque dixese su dicho contra el dicho Marques se quexo de anbos a dos al dicho señor dotor Villalobos y al señor dotor Horozco oydores y les rrogo que lo mandasen rremediar y castigar y al dicho señor dotor Villalobos [234] Pidio

another; let the witnesses tell in detail everything they heard, understood, and knew in relation to it; let them say what they know.

61. If they know that likewise since the detainment of the said Marqués, those mentioned in the preceding question have tried in many ways to search out and seek persons who would testify against him, inciting them that they should prejudice his cause and they should try to know from them matters which would be harmful to the said Marqués; let them say what they know.

62. If they know, etc., that not only have the abovesaid done what is contained in the two preceding questions, but also regularly every day they have hastened and do hasten to the house of the lords oidores of this royal audiencia to speak to them by day and by night, showing themselves not only as denouncers but as parties who were supporting their own interests and vengeance; and with their words they have tried to arouse the said lords oidores against the said Marqués and his brothers; let them say what they know.

63. If they know, etc., that after the said Licentiate Espinosa, Pedro de Aguilar, Agustín de Villanueva, Baltasar de Aguilar, and the other denouncers gave the said memorials and denunciations, they have said and made public that they aspire that because of what they have said and affirmed in them, His Majesty will grant them favors; let them say what they know.

64. If they know, etc., that besides what has been detailed above concerning the fact that the said denouncers and Juan de Sámano, the maestrescuela, and Francisco de Morales are solicitors in this case, together with the said prosecutor and the lords oidores of this royal audiencia, there is public report and knowledge that they have been and are such to him, and there has been and is widespread knowledge concerning this, and it is a matter of public report in this whole city; let them say what they know.

65. If they know that several months before the said Marqués was detained for this case, as he is now, one day the said Fray Miguel de Alvarado came to his dwelling house and told him that he had learned that the lords oidores of this royal audiencia were making an investigation against the said Alonso de Ávila and that the said Alonso de Ávila was very upset about it, saying that he was innocent and without fault; and then on the same day the said Marqués went to speak and did speak with the said Lord Doctor Villalobos and gave him an account of it and of how the said friar had made known to him that the person who made it known to him and the said Alonso de Ávila was the said Pedro de Aguilar; and the said Lord Doctor Villalobos answered that he would summon the said Alonso de Ávila and would speak to him, that he knew well where those matters originated and that he would also take a statement from Pedro de Aguilar; let them say what they know.

66. If they know, etc., that when the said Marqués had word that the said Don Luis de Velasco said that investigations were being made against him and that in it he defamed him and that Ortuño de Ibarra had given to the said Pedro de Aguilar a quantity of money so that he would make his statement against the said Marqués, he complained about both of them to the said Lord Doctor Villalobos and to the Lord

que mandase llamar Al dicho Pedro de Aguilar y le hiziese que declarase con juramento lo que con El dicho Hortuño de Ybarra avia pasado tocante al dicho Marques y esto hizo con gran soliçitud muchas Vezes asi con el dicho señor dotor Villalobos como con el secretario Cassasano ante quien aVia de pasar digan lo que saben.

Lxvii   Si saben etc. que Pocos dias Antes quel dicho Pedro de Aguilar diese su primera memoria y denunciacion En esta causa fue llamado por El señor dotor Çaynos oydor que agora preside En esta Real audiencia y traydo antel y preguntandole El dicho señor dotor si sabia algo açerca de algun alçamiento o otra cossa que se quisiese Hazer En esta ciudad y Nueua España contra el rreal seruicio, rrespondio que no sabia cossa alguna y asi lo dexo y despidio El dicho señor dotor Çaynos de si digan lo que saben.

Lxviii°   Si saben etc. que Para benir El dicho Baltasar de Aguilar a dar la memoria y denunciacion que En esta causa dio Despues destar sabido y publicado ante los señores oydores desta Real audiencia lo que se dezia del alçamiento fue conpelido, forçado y apremiado y puestole muchos temores por doña Beatriz de Andrada su tia muger del dicho don Francisco de Velasco y por otras personas Y asi lo dixo y manifesto El dicho Baltasar de Aguilar y lo a dicho El dicho don Luis de Velasco digan lo que saben.

Lxix   Si saben etc. que Prosiguiendo los dichos Baltasar de Aguilar y Agustin de Villanueua la Enemistad capital que asi conçibieron y tenian contra El dicho Marques llego a tanto su desVerguença y atrebimiento que Podra aver ____ ____ [*lacuna marked in text*] poco mas o menos que Vn dia dixeron a Vn esclauo negro del dicho Agustin de Villanueua que se dize Molinilla que si seria hombre para dar de palos a los señores oydores y diziendo El dicho negro que si, le tornaron a dezir que no querian que los diese sino al arçobispo y al dicho Marques y afirmandose El dicho negro En que tanbien lo haria le dixeron que no lo aVia de dar sino al Marques y Entonces le mandaron que truxese vn palo y que sino pudiese darle con el al dicho Marques se lo arrojase y asi andubo con el dicho palo muchos dias con los dichos Agustin de Villanueua y Baltasar de Aguilar Digan y declaren En particular todo lo que acerca de lo que dicho es supieron y Entendieron.

[*234v*] **Lxx**   Si saben etc. que Demas y aliende de lo que En las demas Preguntas Esta articulado de la Enemistad que los dichos Agustin de Villanueua y Alonso de Çerbantes y Baltasar de Aguilar y Juan de Samano y don Luis de Velasco y El maestreescuela tenian y tienen al dicho Marques an dicho y publicado contra el otras muchas palabras y hecho obras en que claramente an dado a Entender ser le Enemigos capitales y que le deseaban y abian de procurar En quanto En si fuese todo El mal y daño que pudiesen los testigos declaren En particular lo que asi les bieron E oyeron dezir contra El dicho Marques y sobre todo declaren lo que saben.

Doctor Orozco, oidores, and he begged them that they should command that it be remedied and punished; and he petitioned the said Lord Doctor Villalobos that he should command that the said Pedro de Aguilar be summoned and should have him state under oath what had happened between him and the said Ortuño de Ibarra concerning the said Marqués; and he did this many times with great solicitude both with the said Lord Doctor Villalobos and with the Secretary Casasano before whom it would have to take place; let them say what they know.

67. If they know, etc., that a few days before the said Pedro de Aguilar gave his first memorial and denunciation in this case, he was summoned by the said Lord Doctor Ceynos, now presiding oidor in this royal audiencia; and when he was brought before him, the said lord doctor asked him if he knew anything about some uprising or other matter that anyone might want to carry out in this city and New Spain, and he answered that he did not know anything at all; and the said Lord Doctor Ceynos left it at that and dismissed it; let them say what they know.

68. If they know, etc., that in order to get the said Baltasar de Aguilar to come to give the memorial and denunciation which he gave in this case, after what was said about the uprising was known and published before the lords oidores of this royal audiencia, he was compelled, forced, and urged and subjected to many fears by Doña Beatriz de Andrada, his aunt, the wife of the said Don Francisco de Velasco, and by other persons; and the said Baltasar de Aguilar stated and declared this, and the said Don Luis de Velasco has said it; let them say what they know.

69. If they know, etc., that as the said Baltasar de Aguilar and Agustín de Villanueva pursued the mortal enmity that they had conceived and held against the said Marqués, their insolence and boldness reached such a level that one day, possibly [lacuna in text] ago, a little more or less, they asked a Negro slave of the said Agustín de Villanueva, named Molinilla, whether he would be man enough to cane the lords oidores; and when the said Negro said yes, they changed it and said that they did not want him to cane them but rather the archbishop and the said Marqués; and when the said Negro affirmed that he would also do that, they told him that he should not do it except to the Marqués; and then they commanded him that he should carry a stick and that if he could not cane the said Marqués with it, he should throw it at him; and thus for many days he went about with the said stick with the said Agustín de Villanueva and Baltasar de Aguilar; let them state and explain in detail everything that they knew or understood about what has been said.

70. If they know, etc., that besides what has been detailed in the other questions about the enmity which the said Agustín de Villanueva, Alonso de Cervantes, Baltasar de Aguilar, Juan de Sámano, Don Luis de Velasco, and the maestrescuela did and do hold for the said Marqués, they have said and made public against him many other words and have done deeds in which they have clearly given it to be understood that they are his mortal enemies and that they desired for him and would endeavor, as far as it was possible, to do him harm; let the witnesses explain in detail what they have thus seen and heard them say against the said Marqués, and concerning everything, let them declare what they know.

Lxxi Si saben etc. que Asimismo los dichos Agustin de Villanueua y Alonso de Çerbantes, Baltasar de Aguilar, Juan de Samano, maestreescuela y don Luis de Velasco an sido y son tan façiles de yndinarse que por muy libianas ocasiones an concebido y conçiben con todos los que los an Enojado y Enojan aborrecimiento grande y Enemistad mortal y se an preciado y precian dello, digan lo que saben.

Lxxii Si saben etc. que despues quel dicho Marques fue detenido En las casas Reales donde agora Esta dixo El dicho Baltasar de Aguilar a algunas personas que juraua a Dios que si sabia que alguna persona murmuraua del que luego que lo supiese abra de yr a dezir a los señores oydores que Era traydor para que quitasen la cabeça digan lo que saben.

Lxxiii Si saben etc. quel dezir quel aVerse dicho En esta çiudad por algunas personas quel dicho Marques supiese o tubiese noticia del alçamiento que se dezia o fuese culpado En el, procedio de los Emulos y Enemigos del dicho Marques En las demas preguntas rreferidos y toda la otra gente desta rrepublica Vniversalmente an dicho y dizen y tienen Entendido Estar El dicho Marques ynocente y sin culpa alguna y aVerle sido ynpuesto y leuantado falsamente y dello es publica boz y fama En esta ciudad y Nueua España.

Lxxiiii° Si saben etc. que Podra aVer dos años y medio poco mas o menos que con liçençia desta rreal aVdiencia los conquistadores y pobladores se juntaron En cassa del dicho Marques y nombraron personas que En nombre de todos hiziesen ynstruçion y memoria y diesen poderes a quien les pareçiese que rresidiese En corte de su Magestad [235] Y tratase lo que conViniese A Esta tierra y las nombradas Enbiaron su ynstrucion y Poderes a Diego Ferrer ayo que fue del dicho Marques rresidente En la dicha corte digan lo que saben.

Lxxv Si saben etc. quel dicho Diego Ferrer Despues de aVer scripto que rrecibio los dichos poderes E ynstrucion y que haria todo lo que se le Encargaua torno a escreuir al dicho Marques aver dado peticion En el rreal consejo açerca de la perpetuydad de las Encomiendas de yndios y que se le rrespondio no aVer lugar por El presente digan lo que saben.

Lxxvi Si saben etc. que teniendo noticia algunos Regidores Del cabildo desta ciudad de lo contenido En la pregunta antes desta binieron a hablar al dicho Marques y le rrogaron que les diese El capitulo de la carta del dicho Diego Ferrer que tocaua a lo que dicho es diziendo quererlo para que con mas breuedad se Elijiese procurador que En nombre del dicho cabildo fuese a la dicha corte y con mucha ynportunacion se le hubo de dar digan lo que saben.

Lxxvii Si saben etc. que Podra aver vn año poco mas o menos quel dicho Marques trato con algunos de los rregidores Del dicho cabildo que se hiziese vna cofradia

71. If they know, etc., that likewise the said Agustín de Villanueva, Alonso de Cervantes, Baltasar de Aguilar, Juan de Sámano, the maestrescuela, and Don Luis de Velasco have been and are so quick to anger that for very slight motives they have conceived and do conceive a great abhorrence and mortal enmity for all of those who have angered and do anger them; and they have boasted and do boast of this; let them say what they know.

72. If they know, etc., that after the said Marqués was detained in the government buildings where he is at the present, the said Baltasar de Aguilar told some people that he swore to God that if he knew of anyone murmuring about it, as soon as he knew of it he would go to tell the lords oidores that he was a traitor, so that they would cut off his head; let them say what they know.

73. If they know, etc., that the fact that it is said and has been said by some people in this city that the said Marqués knew or had knowledge concerning the uprising, as it was called, or that he was involved in it, proceeded from the rivals and enemies of the said Marqués who are named in the other questions; and that all of the other people of this community universally have said and say and take it for granted that the said Marqués is innocent and without any fault and that [*the charges have*] been falsely imputed and brought against him; and concerning this there is public report and knowledge in this city and New Spain.

74. If they know that possibly two and a half years ago, a little more or less, with the permission of this royal audiencia, the conquerors and colonists met in the house of the said Marqués and named persons who in the name of them all would compose an instruction and memorial and would issue powers of attorney to the person who would seem best to them who would reside in the court of His Majesty and would treat of the matters which would be best for this land; and the named persons sent their instruction and powers of attorney to Diego Ferrer, former tutor of the said Marqués, who is resident in the said court; let them say what they know.

75. If they know, etc., that after the said Diego Ferrer wrote that he had received the said powers of attorney and the instruction and that he would do everything that he was commissioned to do, he wrote again to the said Marqués that he had presented a petition in the Royal Council concerning the perpetuity of the encomiendas of Indians and that he had been given the answer that for the present it was not allowable; let them say what they know.

76. If they know, etc., that when what has been said in the preceding question came to the knowledge of some of the regidores of the council of this city, they came to speak to the said Marqués, and they begged him to give them the paragraph of the letter of the said Diego Ferrer which concerned what has been said, saying that they wanted it so that as soon as possible a representative might be chosen who would go to the said court in the name of the said city council, and because of their great insistence he had to give it to them; let them say what they know.

77. If they know, etc., that possibly a year ago, a little more or less, the said Marqués discussed with some of the regidores of the said city council that a confraternity

En jonor y rreverencia del señor San Ypolito y se fundase en la yglesia del dicho santo y lo que se hizo y trato açerca dello se puso y asento en el libro del dicho cabildo y las capitulaciones hechas por El dicho Marques dio a don Luis de Castilla que las lleuo al dicho cabildo digan lo que saben.

Lxxviii° Si saben etc. que Para çierta fiesta De Vn torneo que don Martin Cortes hermano del dicho Marques tenia acordado de hazer para El dia que la Marquesa saliese a missa del parto que tubo abia tres meses poco mas o menos El dicho Marques mando hazer Vnos gallardetes de tafetan Encarnado y blanco y negro para poner en vn castillo los quales corto Hontiveros sastre y los hizo pintar Tufino bordador En cuya cassa y poder Estan los testigos declaren la hechura de los dichos gallardetes y lo que En ellos se pinto y obro y sobre todo digan lo que saben.

Lxxix Si saben etc. que despues quel dicho Marques Vino a Esta ciudad de Mexico y Nueua España muchas y diVersas Vezes an ydo los alguaziles a Executar y cumplir los mandamientos Executorios y de otra condicion a las cassas de la morada del dicho Marques Estando El En ellas y Executandolos en su [235v] Presençia Sin quel dicho Marques lo Estorbase ni mostrase pena ni a los dichos alguaziles les dixese palabra mala antes les mostraba buen rrostro y animaua para que no lo dexasen de hazer asi siempre que se les mandase digan lo que saben.

Lxxx° Si saben etc. que Podia AVer quinze meses Poco mas o menos que Julian de Salazar siendo alcalde hordinario quito las espadas a ciertos criados del dicho Marques y los trato mal de palabra sin darle Ellos ocasion y avnquel dicho Marques le Enbio a Rogar que les boluiese las armas y Se le dixo de su parte no solo no se las quiso boluer pero dixo palabras descomedidas y En menospreçio del dicho Marques digan lo que saben.

Lxxx°i Si saben etc. que Vn domingo que Doña Ynes De Perea biuda En las cassas de su morada desta dicha ciudad conbido a comer a sus hijos y yernos y otra parentela Estando alli Xpoual Doñate El viejo gouernador que fue de Xalisco y Jhoan Velasquez de Salazar y Hernando de Ribadeneyra y otras personas y El dicho Marques que alli Estaua no dixo las palabras que don Baltasar de Quesada del rrefiere En su primera denunciacion y memoria que Pido se muestren a los testigos y se les lean las palabras della tocantes a lo que la dicha noche y En la dicha cassa dixo El dicho don Baltasar aver hablado y tratado El dicho Marques y sobre todo declaren lo que paso y si el dicho Marques dixera las dichas palabras rreferidas por El dicho don Baltasar los testigos las oyeran y Entendieran y no pudiera ser menos por aVerse hallado presentes todo El tiempo quel dicho Marques El dicho dia Estubo en la dicha cassa lo qual fue y paso despues de aVer benido la nueua de como Miguel Lopez de Legazpi avia llegado a las yslas del poniente y quedaua

should be formed in honor and reverence to the Lord Saint Hippolytus and that it should be established in the church of the said saint; and all that was done and discussed concerning it was placed and set down in the book of the said city council; and the articles which were composed by the said Marqués he gave to Don Luis de Castilla who took them to the said city council; let them say what they know.

78. If they know, etc., that for a certain fiesta and tournament which Don Martín Cortés, brother of the said Marqués, had agreed to give for the day on which the Marquesa would go out to Mass after giving birth, which she did three months ago, a little more or less, the said Marqués commanded that some pennants be made of white, black, and flesh-colored taffeta to be placed on a castle; and Ontiveros, the tailor, cut them and Tufino, the embroiderer, had them painted, and they are now in the latter's house and possession; let the witnesses declare the workmanship of the said pennants and what was painted and worked on them, and concerning it all let them say what they know.

79. If they know, etc., that on many and various occasions since the said Marqués came to this city of Mexico and New Spain, the constables have gone to execute and fulfill executory commands and those of other kinds in the dwelling houses of the said Marqués while he was in them; and they executed them in his presence, and he did not become disturbed nor show any distress nor did he speak a bad word to the said constables; rather, he showed them a good face and encouraged them that they should not leave off doing always thus what was commanded them; let them say what they know.

80. If they know, etc., that possibly fifteen months ago, a little more or less, Julián de Salazar, who was alcalde ordinario, took away the swords from certain servants of the said Marqués and mistreated them by word, without their having given him any occasion for it; and although the said Marqués sent to ask him to return their arms to them and he was told this in the name of the Marqués, he not only did not wish to return them, but he spoke disrespectful and contemptuous words of the said Marqués; let them say what they know.

81. If they know, etc., that one Sunday when the widow Doña Inez de Perea invited her sons and sons-in-law and other relatives to eat in her dwelling house in this city, and Cristóbal de Oñate the Elder, former governor of Jalisco, Juan Velázquez de Salazar, Hernando de Rivadeneyra, and other people were there, the said Marqués, who was also there, did not speak the words which Don Baltasar de Quesada reports of him in his first denunciation and memorial; and I ask that they be shown to the witnesses and that the words be read to them concerning what the said Don Baltasar stated that the said Marqués had spoken of and discussed on the said night and in the said house, and above all let them declare what happened; and if the said Marqués had spoken the said words as reported by the said Don Baltasar, the witnesses would have heard and understood them, and it could not be otherwise because they were present all of the time on the said day while the said Marqués was in the said house; this took place after the news had arrived that Miguel López de Legazpi had reached

poblado en la ysla de Çibu digan lo que saben.

Lxxx°ii   Si saben etc. que sabido En esta ciudad como Pero Melendez Auia desbaratado los françeses questauan poblados En la punta De Santa Elena El dicho Marques se holgo y Regozijo mucho aVnquestaua Enfermo jugo a las cañas En compañia del señor doctor Horozco oydor desta Real avdiencia en el juego que se hizo por la dicha nueua digan lo que saben.

[236] **Lxxx°iii**   Si saben etc. que Despues quel dicho Marques Esta y Reside En Esta ciudad de Mexico y Nueua España En los mandamientos y prouisiones que a dado Para los ministros de la justicia de su Estado De hordinario a dicho y dize lo primero que los dichos ministros auian de guardar Era El seruicio de Dios y del rrey y despues El suyo digan lo que saben.

Lxxx°iiii°   Si saben etc. quel dicho fray Luis Cal guardian Del monesterio de la dicha ciudad de Tezcuco demas de ser español cauallero hijodalgo notorio en la orden del glorioso San Francisco a sido y es persona muy prencipal y de quien se a hecho y haze mucha quenta E muy gran teologo y predicador E de muy buen Exemplo Vida y doctrina digan lo que saben.

Lxxx°v   Si saben etc. que dende que los testigos conoçen al dicho Marques o a lo menos dende que segun dicho es Vino a Esta Nueua España sienpre y a la continua le an visto ser y a sido y es muy seruidor de su Magestad y afiçionado a su rreal seruicio digan lo que saben.

Lxxx°vi   Si saben etc. que Asimismo El dicho Marques A sido y es buen xpiano temeroso de Dios y de su conciencia digan lo que saben.

Lxxx°vii   Si saben etc. que Por lo que dicho es En las preguntas Deste ynterrogatorio los testigos creen y tienen por cierto quel dicho Marques En lo tocante al dicho alçamiento que se dezia aVerse querido yntentar y hazer no tendria ni tubo culpa alguna los testigos declaren por [lo — *canceled*] que lo tienen y creen ser ansi y sobre todo digan lo que saben.

Lxxx°viii°   Si saben etc. que todo lo suso dicho A sido y es Publico y notorio En esta dicha çiudad y Nueua España y En las otras partes y lugares donde dello se a tenido y tiene noticia digan lo que saben.

          EL MARQUES [*rubrica*]
          EL LICENCIADO MARCOS DAVALOS [*rubrica*]
          EL LICENCIADO SEDEÑO [*rubrica*]
          EL BACHILLER FRANCISCO DE ARRIAZO [*rubrica*]

En la ciudad de Mexico diez y seis dias del mes de setiembre de mill y quinientos y sesenta y seis años ante los senores presidente e oydores del audiencia Real de la Nueua España fue presentado el ynterrogatorio de don Martin Cortes Marques del

the islands of the west [*Philippines*] and was settled on the Island of Cebu; let them say what they know.

82. If they know, etc., that when it was known in this city how Pedro Menéndez had defeated the French who had settled in the Punta de Santa Elena, the said Marqués was very happy and made merry; and even though he was sick, he jousted with cane spears in the company of the Lord Doctor Orozco, oidor of this royal audiencia, in the games which were organized because of the said news; let them say what they know.

83. If they know, etc., that since the said Marqués has been and resides in this city of Mexico and New Spain, in the commands and writs that he has given for the ministers of justice of his estate, ordinarily he has said and does say that the first thing that the said ministers would have to observe would be the service of God and of the King and afterwards his own service; let them say what they know.

84. If they know, etc., that the said Fray Luis Cal, guardian of the friary of the said city of Texcoco, besides being a Spanish knight and well-known hidalgo in the order of the glorious Saint Francis, has been and is a very outstanding person and one in whom much stock is and has been placed, and a very great theologian and preacher, and a person of very good example, life, and teaching; let them say what they know.

85. If they know, etc., that since witnesses have known the said Marqués, or at least since, as has been said, he came to this New Spain, they have always and constantly seen him to be, and he has been and is, a great servant of His Majesty and devoted to his royal service; let them say what they know.

86. If they know, etc., that likewise the said Marqués has been and is a good Christian, fearful of God and of his conscience; let them say what they know.

87. If they know, etc., that because of what has been said in the questions of this questionnaire, the witnesses believe and hold as certain that, in regard to the said uprising which, it was said, the said Marqués wanted to attempt and carry out, he would not nor did he have any fault; let the witnesses explain why they hold and believe that it is so, and concerning everything let them say what they know.

88. If they know, etc., that all the abovesaid has been and is public and well known in this said city and New Spain and in the other parts and places where they have had and do have knowledge of it; let them say what they know.

The Marqués [*rubric*]
Licentiate Marcos Dávalos [*rubric*]
Licentiate Sedeño [*rubric*]
Bachelor Francisco de Arriazo [*rubric*]

In the city of Mexico on the sixteenth day of the month of September of the year one thousand five hundred and sixty-six, before the lords president and oidores of the royal audiencia of the New Spain, the questionnaire of Don Martín Cortés, Marqués

Valle de suso contenido e por los dichos señores visto lo ovieron por presentado en quanto es pertinente y mandaron que por el se examinen los testigos ante el señor doctor Horozco oydor desta Real audiencia y por presencia de Sebastian Vazquez y Juan de Horozco Receptores desta Real audiencia cada vno por si.

SANCHO LOPEZ DE AGURTO [*rubrica*]

del Valle, contained above, was presented; and when it had been seen by the said lords, they accepted it as presented insofar as pertinent, and they commanded that the witnesses be examined according to it before the Lord Doctor Orozco, oidor of this royal audiencia, and in the presence of Sebastián Vázquez and Juan de Orozco, secretaries of this royal audiencia, each one by himself.

SANCHO LÓPEZ DE AGURTO [*rubric*]

Glossary

Agua y cordeles	Water and ropes with which prisoners were tortured, usually while they were on a rack.
Alcaide	Warden.
Alcalde	Local judge.
Alcalde mayor	Spanish official in charge of a district.
Alcalde ordinaric	Municipal judicial official.
Alguacil	Constable.
Audiencia	High court and governing body of an extensive area in Spanish America.
Ayuntamiento	Municipal government.
Beneficiado	One who holds a benefice or church preferment.
Cabildo	Municipal or town council.
Calpisque	Overseer or administrative official.
Carga	Load.
Castellano	Unit of coinage.
China	Country of China or any portion of the Far East, particularly the Philippine Islands.
Criado	Servant; in the 16th century could be a member of the household.
Dean	Dean of a cathedral chapter.
Encomendero	One who holds Indians in his charge in encomienda.
Encomienda	The right to tribute from the Indians of a specified town or district; in theory it also entailed responsibility for their Christianization and protection.
Estancia	Subordinate Indian community; farm.
Familiar	Minor official of the Inquisition.
Fanega	Unit of dry measurement, about 1.5 bushel.
Fiscal	Government attorney or prosecutor.
Juez comisario	Judge appointed to investigate and impose justice in a particular situation.
Juez de provincia	Judge of a province.
Ladina,-o	Spanish-speaking or adapted to Spanish society (used of a person of non-Spanish background).

Licenciado	Licentiate; holder of a university degree intermediate between a baccalaureate and a doctorate.
Macegual	Indian commoner or laborer.
Maestre de campo	Military officer of rank comparable to a colonel.
Maestrescuela	Dignitary in a cathedral chapter who formerly had the duty of teaching ecclesiastical sciences.
Maravedi	Small unit of coinage.
Marquesado	Marquisate, usually applied in the Harkness Mexican manuscripts to the Marquesado del Valle de Oaxaca.
Mayordomo	Majordomo; custodian.
Obraje	Workshop, usually for the weaving of woolen cloth.
Oidor	Judge of an audiencia.
Oro de minas	High grade of gold.
Privilegio	Special grant or concession, usually for some special service or achievement.
Probanza	Proof or evidence, usually of special services performed.
Procurador	Attorney, usually acting in behalf of another person.
Provisión	A legal instrument conferring a benefice.
Real	Unit of coinage.
Receptor	Secretary or person authorized to take testimony.
Regidor	Alderman, member of a cabildo.
Relator	An official who summarized court proceedings, correspondence, etc.
Residencia	Judicial review made at the end of an official's term of office.
Sobre cédula	Cedula that confirms and includes another cedula.
Tepuzque	Gold mixed with copper.
Vara	Unit of measurement, about 33 inches; also a rod of justice.
Villa	Town which enjoys peculiar privileges by charter.
Visitador	Inspector.

Bibliography

Clemence, Stella R.   Deed of emancipation of a Negro woman slave, dated Mexico, September 14, 1585. Hispanic American historical review, v. 10, Feb. 1930: 51–57.   F1410.H66, v. 10

Cline, Howard F.   Hernando Cortés and the Aztec Indians in Spain. *In*   U.S. *Library of Congress*. Quarterly journal, v. 26, Apr. 1969: 70–90.
Z881.U49A3, v. 26

Fernández del Castillo, Francisco.   Algunos documentos del archivo del Marquesado del Valle (Hospital de Jesus). *In* Sociedad mexicana de geografía y estadistica. Boletin, t. 43, enero/abr. 1931: 17–40.

Friede, Juan.   The coat of arms of Hernando Cortés. *In*   U.S. *Library of Congress*. Quarterly journal, v. 26, Apr. 1969: 64–69.   Z881. U49A3, v. 26

Goldberg, Rita.   Nuevos datos sobre Don Martín Cortés, II Marqués del Valle de Oaxaca. *In*   Mexico. *Archivo General de la Nación*. Boletin, 2. ser., v. 9, enero/jul. 1968: 324–366.   F1203.M563, 2. ser., v. 9

Gonzalez Obregón, Luis.   Los precursores de la independencia mexicana en el siglo XVI. Paris, Mexico, V^{da} de C. Bouret, 1906. 388 p.   Micro 15831 F

Greenleaf, Richard E.   The Mexican Inquisition of the sixteenth century. Albuquerque, University of New Mexico Press [1969] 242 p.   BX1740.M6G73

———— Zumárraga and the Mexican Inquisition, 1536–1543. Washington, Academy of American Franciscan History, 1961 [°1962] 155 p. (Academy of American Franciscan History. Monograph series, v. 4)   BX4705.Z8G7 1962

Orozco y Berra, Manuel.   Noticia histórica de la conjuración del Marqués del Valle, años de 1565–1568. Formada en vista de nuevos documentos originales, e seguida de un estracto de los mismos documentos. Mexico, Tip. de R. Rafael, 1853. 72, 502 p.   Micro 22412 F

Riley, G. Micheal.   Fernando Cortés and the Cuernavaca encomiendas, 1522–1547. The Americas, a quarterly review of Inter-American cultural history, v. 25, July 1968: 3–24.   E11.A4, v. 25

Spain. *Archivo General de Indias, Seville.* Indice de documentos de Nueva España existentes en el Archivo de Indias de Sevilla. Mexico [Impr. de la Secretaria de Relaciones Exteriores] 1928–31. 4 v. (Monografias bibliograficas mexicanas, no. 12, 14, 22–23)   CD1859.S3A5 1928

Suárez de Peralta, Juan. La conjuración de Martín Cortés y otros temas. Selección y prólogo de Agustín Yañez. Mexico, Universidad Nacional Autónoma, 1945. xx, 193 p. (Biblioteca del estudiante universitario, 53)   F1231.S87

Toro, Alfonso. Codice del archivo de los Duques de Monteleone y Marqueses del Valle. *In* Mexico (City). *Museo Nacional de arqueología, história y etnografía.* Anales, época 4, no. 20, 1925: 58–64.

Valderrama, Jerónimo. Cartas del licenciado Jerónimo Valderrama y otros documentos sobre su visita al gobierno de Nueva España, 1563–1565. Mexico, J. Porrúa, 1961. 420 p. (Documentos para la história del México colonial, 7)   F1231.V27

Zavala, Silvio. Nuño de Guzmán y la esclavitud de los indios. História mexicana, v. 1, enero/mar. 1952: 410–428.   F1201.H5, v. 1

Index

Note: This index is principally to personal and place names. Certain titles and place names included in the royal grants that have only imperial or dynastic significance have been omitted. For names appearing in the transcribed and translated documents only the page numbers of the translations are given. The original forms appear in the transcriptions on the pages facing the translations.

Names were less standardized in the 16th century than they are today, and many are inconsistently recorded in the manuscripts; this is to some extent reflected in the index. Members of the same family are in certain cases arbitrarily brought together in the index under the common element in their names.

☆U.S. GOVERNMENT PRINTING OFFICE: 1974 O—469–724